IN SEARCH OF VISHWAKARMA

In Search of Vishwakarma

Mapping Indian Craft Histories

edited by

VIJAYA RAMASWAMY

PRIMUS BOOKS

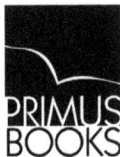

PRIMUS BOOKS
An imprint of Ratna Sagar P. Ltd.
Virat Bhavan
Mukherjee Nagar Commercial Complex
Delhi 110 009

Offices at
CHENNAI LUCKNOW
AGRA AHMEDABAD BENGALURU COIMBATORE
DEHRADUN GUWAHATI HYDERABAD JAIPUR JALANDHAR
KANPUR KOCHI KOLKATA MADURAI MUMBAI
PATNA RANCHI VARANASI

First published 2019

ISBN: 978-93-5290-839-4 (hardback)
ISBN: 978-93-5290-840-0 (POD)

Published by Primus Books

Lasertypeset by Sai Graphic Design
Arakashan Road, Paharganj, New Delhi 110 055

Contents

NORTHERN PERSPECTIVES ON THE VISHWAKARMA

SOUTHERN PERSPECTIVES ON THE VISHWAKARMA

Preface

> The Indian Craftsman conceives of his art, not as the accumulated skill of ages but as originating in the divine skill of Viswakarma and revealed by him....
>
> —ANANDA K. COOMARASWAMY, *The Indian Craftsman*

It is only in the last four decades that the mapping of everyday lives and histories has become a significant work domain for the Indian academia. Although remarkable strides have been made towards looking at the peasant society in Indian history, other areas still remain a virgin terrain. Research works focusing exclusively on the history of crafts and artisanal communities are few and far between. Ananda Kentish Coomaraswamy, the Sri Lankan scholar, set in motion the process of mapping the history of Indian crafts with his monograph, *The Indian Craftsman,* published way back in 1909 and in his collection of essays titled *The Dance of Siva*, which was published in 1918. Kamaladevi Chattopadhyaya's and Pupul Jayakar's writings on Indian craftspersons were pioneering works in the difficult task of penning the history of crafts and craftsmen. Kamaladevi wrote her *Glory of Indian Handicrafts* in 1976, while Jayakar's *The Earthen Drum*—which focussed exclusively on rural crafts—followed in 1980. Meera Mukherjee's writings in the context of Bengal are also well known. Her first major book on crafts, *Metal Craftsmen in India* was published in 1978, while the better known work, *In Search of Viswakarma*, was published in 1994.

Following in their footsteps, younger scholars began to study the early histories of the Vishwakarma community in different regions. Jan Brouwer's book *The Makers of the World: Caste, Craft and Mind of South Indian Artisans,* published in 1995, was one such effort, although this was written from the perspective of a sociologist. In 1986, Pupul Jayakar commissioned me to do a monograph on *Weaver Folk Traditions* for the Handloom and Handicrafts Board. This manuscript, which lay with the Crafts Museum for many years, finally saw the light of day when it was published under the title *The Song of the Loom* in 2013. This edited volume, which draws on the work done by scholars working with vernacular material, is a further step in mapping craft histories.

The present volume seeks to bring together histories of crafts from the precolonial period to the early years of colonial rule in India, written from regional perspectives. Although one could think of the inclusion of the works of a few scholars from outside India who have worked on the history of crafts, the aim was to bring together scholars from various regional centres, who have mastery over inscriptional and literary sources available in their region/subregion. Therefore, the presence of metropolitan scholars will be less marked in a volume of the present sort, which seeks to understand subaltern histories through the voice of scholars situated within their regions/subregions, and who are best equipped to study craft histories from multifarious perspectives using different linguistic tools.

New Delhi VIJAYA RAMASWAMY

Acknowledgements

I am grateful to the many members of the Vishwakarma community who have made this book possible—the craftsmen of Nachiyar Koil, Swamimalai, Madurai, and Arumbavur (Tiruchirapalli), who readily gave their time and experiences, making my personal as well as academic journey of three decades into the history of the Vishwakarma community, a memorable one.

My thanks to the Nehru Memorial Museum & Library which, under its former director Mahesh Rangarajan, enabled me to bring together historians from various regions and subregions to speak on artisanal histories. This conference, held in October 2014, on mapping Indian craft histories, was the starting point of the present collection, which grew out of the core essays presented at this seminar.

I am also exceedingly grateful to Jawaharlal Nehru University's University Grants Commission (UGC) programme called Universities with Potential for Excellence Phase II (UPE-II), which, under Makarand Paranjape's project on 'Cultural Crossroads', enabled me, as one of the project investigators, to undertake a field trip to Kerala and Tamil Nadu between 2015 and 2017 to study the Vishwakarma.

I am also a partner investigator in a collaborative project led by Kirin Narayan and Ken George from the Australian National University, Canberra, under the Discovery International Award given by Australian Research Council, which has, as its theme 'Building India: Religion, Craft and Infrastructure in Contemporary Asia'. This three year project commenced in 2017. I am grateful to Ken, Kirin, and Mahesh Sharma for sharing ideas on the Vishwakarma in the past one year. I am particularly grateful to Kirin for contributing an essay to this volume. Her valuable piece was, in fact, the last essay to find a place in the volume.

Recently, I had the opportunity to deliver the keynote address at a conference related exclusively to crafts at the University of Jaffna, Sri Lanka. The theme was 'Tradition/Transformation: Craft, Practice and Discourse' held between 9 and 12 of May 2018. I also had the opportunity to visit a number of craft villages including the bronze centre at Tirunelveli (in Jaffna district), where the craftsmen are known as Kammalar, just as in Tamil Nadu. They say that they are migrants from the Tanjavur and Tirunelveli (in Tamil Nadu) regions and produce crafts in bronze and wood, following the designs used by the Tamil craftsmen.

One of the purposes of putting together a volume of this sort is that it should be seen as academic activism in the push towards the revival of crafts and the survival of craftsmen. I am, therefore, extremely grateful to Jaya Jaitly for incorporating her experience of working with craftsmen into this volume.

I extend my warm gratitude to my fellow travellers on the path of mapping Indian craft history, who have made this volume possible by contributing their invaluable findings pertaining to their own regions and their period of specialization. My very special thanks to Professor R.N. Misra for writing a piece exclusively for this anthology, and also for giving me his gracious permission to reproduce one of the sections from his monograph *Ancient Artists and Art Activity*, published by the Indian Institute of Advanced Study, Shimla, in 1975.

Finally, my loving thanks to my husband Krish for finding the time to correct and critique what I write.

New Delhi VIJAYA RAMASWAMY

Cosmic World of Medieval Craftsmen

An Introduction

VIJAYA RAMASWAMY

> Vishwakarma, Lord of the arts, master of a thousand crafts, carpenter of the gods and builder of their palaces divine, fashioner of every jewel, first of craftsmen by whose art men live, and whom, a great and deathless God, they continuously worship.
>
> —*Mahabharata*, 1: 2592

> The Indian craftsman conceives of his art, not as the accumulated skill of ages, but as originating in the divine skill of Vishwakarma and revealed by him. Beauty, rhythm, proportion, ideas have an absolute existence on an ideal plane, where all who seek may find. The reality of things exists in the mind, not in the detail of their appearance to the eye. Their inward inspiration, upon which the Indian artist is taught to rely, appearing like the still small voice of God, that God was conceived of as Vishwakarma. He may be thought of as that part of divinity which is conditioned by a special relation to artistic expression or in another way, as the sum total of consciousness, the group soul of individual craftsmen of all times and places.
>
> —ANANDA K. COOMARASWAMY, *The Indian Craftsman*

In the world view of the traditional Indian craftsman, crafts and worship had a symbiotic relationship. In pre-historic India, there were exquisite bell metal objects, characterized by their high content of tin. These crafted objects were not different from objects of aesthetic beauty. Beautiful objects were not just produced for their own sake. Everything had value and utility. Moreover, since a person is innately creative and cannot mechanically produce anything, what was produced carried the maker's aesthetic tastes and world view.

It would therefore be a truism to state that in a craft-based society, a definition that would be true of many pre-industrial traditional societies, all crafted objects were an extension of the personality of the crafts persons. Kamaladevi Chattopadhyaya, who was instrumental in salvaging Indian crafts from the twin onslaughts of colonialism and consumerism, defined this symbiotic relationship between the craftsman, the process of crafting, and the resultant product: 'craftsmanship grew from the village community, its joys and burdens, the change of seasons, the memories filled with song and verse, legends, myths and local romances, from the core and substance of their daily existence . . . they wove a rough and forceful art'.[1]

The present collection of essays rewind forwards, zigzagging through centuries, to locate the Vishwakarma in space and time with the constant awareness that the present is embedded in the past and the past gets reworked into the present as myth, oral/community history, or as signifiers of caste issues and social justice. Although none of the essays in the present anthology specifically deal with the curious twists and turns that issues of caste, economic parity, and social justice bring about in the case of the Vishwakarma, these concerns exist as a subtext in quite a few of these essays, especially in my piece 'Casting the Vishwakarma in Peninsular India', and also in the essays by Jan Brouwer and Kirin Narayan. To raise just one thought-provoking question—why is it that 'Brahminization', 'Sanskritization', and upward social mobility, which dominated Vishwakarma caste politics till 1947, when India attained independence, gave way to a trend towards downward mobility by the Vishwakarma craftsmen, including the goldsmiths and the carpenters, claiming 'Reservation' as 'Other Backward Castes' (OBC)? In present times, the different groups of the Vishwakarma have aligned with diverse political parties in their quest for 'Reservation'. Perhaps some answers may be sought for this curious turn of events in the history of the Vishwakarma community and the socio-economic vicissitudes that craft persons have been through.

The craft persons, collectively referred to as Vishwakarma today, constituted a unique craft/artisanal collective that cut through caste and class lines, having as its constituents the humble blacksmith and carpenter as well as the affluent *sthapati*, who was the mason-cum-architect, and the *pon kollar* or goldsmith. The primary identity of crafts persons stemmed from their community, rather than their caste identity. The majority of medieval inscriptions emphasize that an artisan belonged to the Vishwakarma *kula*, rather than detailing his caste affiliation.

Inscriptional evidence makes it amply clear that despite belonging to different professions and jatis, the craftsmen claimed a collective entity that transcended caste and class to form a larger community of crafts persons.

Jaya Jaitly's perceptive piece, which forms the lead essay in this collection, is aptly about 'In Search of Vishwakarma and His Progeny', in which she situates the hereditary legacy of crafting skills passed on from father to son in their particular profession and the future of these hereditary craftsmen in today's economic scenario of high technology and consumerism-backed industries. Today's tilt towards speed and mechanized efficiency is in striking contrast to a past where excellence came not from speed but from creative leisure, in which objects of our material culture—pots and pans, as well as our spiritual icons in the temples—were crafted individually and artistically.

The collective history of the Vishwakarma, also known as Panchalar or Pancha Kammalar, because they consist of five artisanal communities—goldsmiths (*tattan*), braziers (*kannan*), blacksmiths (*karuman* or *kollan*), carpenters (*tachchan*), and masons (*silpi* or *kal-tachchan*)—can be said to have begun between the fifth and the eighth century, in the great era of temple-building, especially in peninsular India. Craftsmen known by the generic term of 'Vishwakarma', the divine architect of the Gods, played a crucial role in the early medieval economy of India. While the rural landscape continued to dominate the economy, there was, at the same time, the emergence of urban centres, which had as their nucleus the great temples, whose construction went in tandem with the process of state formation in India, beginning with the Gupta Dynasty in northern India around the fifth century CE and the Pallavas in Tondaimandalam around the seventh century CE. The Vishwakarma community was an integral part of this development of temple urbanism while continuing to be a part of the village community in the countryside.

In medieval peninsular India, the Vishwakarma constituted a group of five comunities and were known in the Tamil country as Kammalar, in Karnataka as Panchāḷar, and in Andhra as the Panchananamuvaru. However in many of the medieval inscriptions, they are also collectively referred to as the Rathakarar or the Kammāḷa-Rathakarar. The outstanding example of this particular nomenclature for craftsmen is a twelfth century inscription from Tiruvarur in Nagapattinam (Tanjavur district) which is a lengthy record dealing with the mixed caste status of the community, concluding with decisions by the Brahmin elders on where to locate them in terms of social hierarchy and in terms of their profession(s).[2] Today, they prefer to use the nomenclature 'Vishwakarma'—the divine architect from whom they claim descent. The essays by Jan Brower and myself reflect the myriad ways in which the Vishwakarma have been imaged in history and their own self-imaging of their rituals and social location.

The castes also claimed a Brahminical status and proclaimed themselves to be Vishwabrahmins, as opposed to the brahmins, whom they stigmatized as Go-Brahmins. They held that they belonged to a fifth Veda (*Panchama Veda*) which is superior to the existing four Vedas. In focusing entirely on the Kammāḷar, one also attempts to answer an oft-repeated question—why did the Kammāḷa-Rathakarar consist only of these five categories, i.e. the three types of smiths, the mason-architect, and the carpenter, and no other? The logical answer would be that it was these five groups who were primarily engaged in the temple-building activities that revived under the Cholas in the eighth–ninth century. The construction did not involve the mere erection of shrines, but the building up of an entire temple town complex spread over a vast area, such as the Srirangam temple at Tiruchirapalli. The Kammalar, weavers, and merchants were situated in the various streets located on all four sides of the temple complex.

The term 'Vishwakarma' begins to appear in inscriptions referring to the smiths from the eleventh, and more specifically, from the twelfth century onwards. The precise nomenclature used is 'Vishwakarma kula' or 'Vishwakarma kulaja'. The Chebrolu inscription of 1118 CE, the Nadindla inscription of 1141 CE, and the Tellapur inscription dated 1417 CE state that the smiths and sculptors belonged to the Vishwakarma *kula*.[3]

The socio-economic status of the Vishwakarma as a collective body, as well as the differentiation and stratification that existed among them in pragmatic terms, depended upon the nature of their role, which, in turn, was linked to their physical location. It would be erroneous to treat craftsmen as a monolithic unit despite their banding together as the 'Vishwakarma'. The distinction between an artisan and a craftsman may seem 'fuzzy' because of the shifting nature of their occupations but it is nevertheless important to make this distinction. Unless one is aware of the complex layers that underlay craft development in early medieval India, it is possible that one may impose one's own teleological vision as 'orientalist' 'imperial/colonial', or Marxist historians did, by imaging the medieval craftsman as a static, immobile figure enmeshed within a 'honey-combed' caste structure. It was this colonial construct of 'caste' that was questioned and critiqued by Nicholas B. Dirks.[4] Dirks indicated that notions of caste were extremely fuzzy in the precolonial Indian society. It is of course well known that the term 'casta' has its origin in the Portuguese language and was used by Portugal to characterize their limited understanding of the Indian social structure. *Casta* in both Spanish and Portuguese originally meant simply a population of people or animals possessing common inherited traits. It was the British administrators who 'cast' it within certain hard frames of a honeycombed caste structure and went on to create caste-based census and caste-based armies.

One of the ways of breaking up this discourse on caste-based occupations is to look at the producers of craft objects as distinct from the producers of purely utility commodities. Is the man routinely laying bricks or being employed as a workman in the construction of a dam an artisan or a craftsman? Would the hereditary maker of ploughs in a village have the same position in economy and society as the icon-maker? Inscriptional evidence clearly indicates that they represented two different kinds of economies, both of which existed parallel to each other. While the maker of ploughs would exist in the village community with a certain degree of relative physical immobility, socio-economic security, and comparatively static living standards, the metal craftsman, benefiting from the temple economy and an expanding clientele, would be more mobile and have greater opportunities for improving his income, while also facing a greater number of risks. His risks would primarily arise from the withdrawal of patronage or the decline of temple centres with the fall of dynasties, as happened in the twelfth–thirteenth century, with the decline and fading out of the Chola State. Thus, it can be said that while every craftsman was an artisan, every artisan was not a craftsman, because his relationship to the medieval economy, both in terms of his location and function, differed significantly from that of his urban counterpart. To give an example, even among the goldsmiths, there were two distinct hierarchical categories. At the lower level was the small-time *tattan* or goldsmith essentially catering to a custom-determined market, who worked on a piece-wage and lived at the subsistence level. They can be seen even today in south India, sitting at street corners and eking out a living by repairing chains or ornaments and also piercing ears and noses (a must for women and the girl child among many south Indian communities). At the higher level was the big-time goldsmith referred to in the inscriptions as *perumtattan* (literally, great goldsmith), indicating a master-craftsman employing apprentice goldsmiths, catering to a fairly wide market and forming a part of the urban setup.

Another question that comes to mind when one looks at the plethora of evidence on the Vishwakarma is the precise character of this grouping and whether the relationship between community and caste could be termed a dichotomous one. What is the link between the jati structure or caste system, within which the categories of craftsmen (among others) are said to be located, and the Vishwakarma community, which is obviously cutting across caste lines? For long, beginning with theorists like Max Weber and Karl Marx, caste has been regarded as a major factor for India's economic and technological backwardness. The classic statement by Marx that crafts in the Indian context 'either petrify into castes or ossify into guilds'[5] was taken up by historians like Morris D. Morris to argue for a situation of technological stasis in the craft structure. Marx, commenting on the fineness of the Dacca muslins, in fact concludes on a note of irony by saying, 'It is only the special skill accumulated from generation to generation and transmitted from father to son that gives to the Hindu, as it does to the spider, this proficiency!'[6]

Many of the authors in this anthology, such as I. Lakshmi, Nagendra Rao, and Anna Varghese, have endeavoured to show that the functioning of the Vishwakarma as a community collective, comprising five socially and economically differentiated jatis, thereby cutting through the caste system and rendering it fluid, if not porous, reflects the ground situation, at least in south India's craft history. Many of the essays, especially the two written by R.N. Misra, throw light on a social structure that was much more dynamic and complex than the Orientalist understanding of crafts and caste. The situation was comparatively fuzzy and community solidarity in certain situations may have taken precedence over jati solidarity.

All this is not to say that caste was not an important factor in the Indian society. Caste distinctions certainly continued and craftsmen in the rural setting seem to have been known by their individual jati affiliation, rather than as members of the Vishwakarma *kula*. It is possible to argue that it is in the context of temple-building where these five craft groups worked in such close coordination that the concept of Vishwakarma *kula* seems to have predominated over that of separate caste identities. This can be deduced by the location of the inscriptions referring to the Vishwakarma *kula* in the early medieval times, whether one is looking at the Cholas, the Pandyas, or the Eastern Chalukyas.[7] Having argued for a more open interpretation of craft groups cutting across caste and embracing the wider notion of craft community, one cannot logically push forward this argument to state that the five jatis within the Vishwakarma community were exogamous. No evidence is forthcoming, one way or the other, in this regard. However, working backwards from the Kallidaikurichi inscription of the seventeenth century, which records the legal dissociation of the five jatis, one could presume that the five castes may have been exogamous up to that point.[8] If economic status was a factor, then the Vishwakarma goldsmiths located in the temple town would have much more in common, in terms of forming matrimonial alliances, with the affluent smiths settled there in the town, than with their poor village counterpart. Although one can deduce the fluidity of caste boundaries among these crafts, in the absence of more concrete evidence, it is not possible to determine as to how open the Vishwakarma community was to social and familial interaction among the five disparate jati categories.

Most of the contributors to this volume have relied heavily upon inscriptional evidence to research on the socio-economic dynamics of the Vishwakarma community. The essay by Pushpa Prasad, in fact, uses only epigraphical sources to reconstruct the lives and contributions of the Sultanate builders and craftsmen. Similarly, all the five essays which focus on peninsular India—those by Subbarayalu, Lakshmi, Rao, Anna Varghese, and myself—focus on the plethora of inscriptions available from this region. Inscriptions throw a great deal of light on the Vishwakarma community for the simple reason that these were carved by the engravers or *aasari/achari* who belonged to this community. One of the major debates has centred on the issue of literacy. It has been broadly agreed upon that the brahmins were perhaps the only literate community. The inscriptions engraved by the Vishwakarma craftsmen, cast a new light on this issue. I would strongly invoke the probability that the Vishwakarma craftsmen could have been the only noticeably literate community other than the brahmins. This is because quite a few inscriptions carry eulogies and mythologies relating to the Vishwakarma, which was obviously not patron-commissioned but inserted by the individual engravers themselves.

Paintings are also a valuable source for reconstructing the social life of craftsmen in precolonial as well as colonial times. Syed Nadeem Rezavi is known for his masterly handling of Mughal miniature paintings in reconstructing the lives of craftsmen. In this particular essay, he has, while referring to Mughal miniatures, primarily used major Persian texts written in the Persian court like Abul Fazl's *Ā'in-i-Akbari*, Gulbadan Begum's *Humayun Nama*, and Abu'l Qasim Namakin's *Munsha'āt-i Namakīn*.

It is interesting to note that one of the generic names of the Pancha Kammalar is 'Rathakarar' or the chariot makers, by which name they are referred to in the Chola inscriptions of the eleventh and twelfth centuries. The name reveals the skill of the carpenters in fashioning the ornamental wooden chariots, which were equally important for temple rituals and as a means of transportation of people, especially royalty. However, wood carving today is a craft that has, by and large, moved away from the temple towns into the rural countryside, with a view to tap cheap labour. One does not quite know as to when this shift started taking place. The Vishwakarma carpenters hardly manufacture any chariots or palanquins now. Thus, over centuries, wood carving as a craft has completely changed its focus. Unlike as in pre-modern south India, when the *tachchaachariyan* was equally important in the village community as in the temple complex, the wood carvers of today carve only drawing room screens, ornamental panels, lamp stands, and at times some rare images also meant for display in secular surroundings, but not for ritual purpose. Traditional chariot-making is confined to Avinasi, Avudaiyar in the Coimbatore region and Arantangi in Pudukottai.

Over centuries, there has been no change in the type of wood recommended for fine wood carving. The *Visvakarma Vastu Shastram*, a canonical text on architecture, recommends the use of *tungu vaagai* (botanical name *Albizia lebbeck*), *mavalinga*(?), and *maa*, i.e. mango wood. While both *vaagai* and mango are locally available, *mavalinga* wood (said to be lighter than mango wood) comes from Jayankonda *mandalam*, the *bhel* (botanical name *Aegle marmelos*, also known as Bengal quince) wood which also they use comes from Tiruchirapalli and is bought wholesale from timber merchants. In an interview, Balaraman, the craftsman carving a huge Krishna idol in wood, said that the wood for the image (measuring 84 in. by 24 in., i.e. 7 ft. tall) weighs 80 kg. at the initial stage (interview with craftsman Ramaswamy Asari at Arumbavur, 12 May 1986). After drilling holes in it and shaping the image, its weight would be reduced by about 30 kg., and when the wood dries up, there would be a further weight loss of about 20 kg. So, the final weight of the image was around 30 kg. My own intensive field research in the Tiruchirapalli region, especially in the craft village of Arumbavur during the years 1970–86, have enabled me to track continuity and change in craft activities in Arumbavur from the past to the comparatively recent present. So far as the market for the Arumbavur wood crafts is concerned, the medieval guilds like the 'Ainnurruvar' have been replaced today by rich individual merchants coming from

Karaikkudi or Chettinad, who buy the craft products wholesale from the craftsmen and sell them at exorbitant prices to distant regions, including foreign lands.

Another question in relation to the craft communities is the extent of penetration of the outside world into the traditional preserve of the Vishwakarma craft group. A unique inscription from Varikunta (in Cuddapah district) states that a Boya (tribal hunter community of Andhra region, known today as Valmiki Boya) named Tippana (who was obviously a non-Vishwakarma) built the local temple for a lump sum contract of 20 *rukas*. The inscription is a late one dated 1529 CE, but it points to a certain degree of social flux which was most likely a post-Chola phenomenon.

George Varghese addresses both these key issues of outsider penetration into a traditional area of craft production and changes brought about by growing consumerism. He takes the example of soaring gold prices and its impact on goldsmiths. He argues that gold as an object becomes a critical template caught between the two contrasted concepts of cultural preservation through traditional craft communities and the waves of consumerism and growing demand brought about by a market-driven economy.

Whether one could use the term 'guild' for Vishwakarma artisanal groups, is a question that needs to be addressed. We have repeatedly referred to the five craft groups which, historically, comprised the Vishwakarma community. Whether the craft-caste organization of the goldsmiths or the carpenters could be termed 'guild' is extremely problematic. They had their basis more upon community and kinship ties which cemented their social identity, rather than being based on production structures and commercial patterns seen in medieval economy. The Vijayanagar Empire provides clear evidence of the independence of south Indian craft guilds and the 'benevolent role of the State in promoting crafts and commerce.' The best evidence of this is to be seen in the text *Amuktamalyada* said to have been authored by King Krishnadeva Raya himself.[9] The essay by I. Lakshmi focusses on the community networking of the Panchananamuvaru—the smiths and sculptors of precolonial Andhra. While the presence of guilds in southern India is fuzzy, they had a controlling presence in craft production in northern India, which is one of the facets of medieval crafts which Nadeem Rezavi addresses in the context of the Mughal Empire.

Mythology and folklore is at the substratum of the social life of all traditional communities, and the plethora of myths, legends, and folksongs which enrich our understanding of the Vishwakarma community has been the central focus of the essay by Kirin Narayan and the partial focus of Jan Brouwer's essay. Brouwer in his essay looks briefly at the oral tradition of Kanta Kottai or the magnetic fort which has been dealt by him in detail in his other writings.[10]

This anthology has not made any conscious attempt to gender the study of crafts and craftsmen. One is compelled to use the term 'craftsmen' rather than 'crafts persons' because women were an ancillary, albeit indispensable, part of craft activities, while men were central to it. The names listed in almost all inscriptions seem to be only of those of men. An overarching patriarchal framework can be clearly perceived in early craft structures. Women by and large functioned in an ancillary or subordinate capacity in the work of the smiths. In the craft of the blacksmiths, women are allowed to work the bellows, but are not permitted to forge the iron. In jewellery-making among the goldsmiths and the silversmiths, women are engaged in the tasks of polishing, fine cutting, and embellishing the designs, but not given a primary role in the designing or making of the ornaments. The goldsmith community called 'Bayala Akkasaliga', literally 'itinerant goldsmiths' seems to have trained both men and women in the art of goldsmithy.[11] Again, one does not hear of women sculptors at all, especially in the craft of icon-making. So, one can logically assume that women were marginalized in the whole craft process.

There were, however, two notable exceptions, both from Dharwar, pertaining to the eleventh and twelfth centuries respectively. One from Gadag, inscribed under the image of Uma Mahesvara, mentions that the sculpture was made by Revakabbarasi, the wife of Vavanarasa.[12] The other from Kalkeri states that the image of Suryadeva was made by Saraswati Gandidasi Malloja.[13] In the first case, the female sculptor is essentially defined in terms of her marital relationship, while in the second, only the name of the father is given, which was the usual practice in all inscriptions. The mention of just two women out of nearly eighty inscriptions relating to craftsmen's names shows that exception proves the rule. However, it does seem that women might have sometimes taken to crafts out of economic necessity. Among the Gudigara caste in Karnataka, women are said to have taken over the family profession[14] in the case of death of the male member, and this included goldsmithy—perhaps both the crafting as well as the sale.[15]

The present anthology of essays does not, by and large, really take up the comparative absence of women from the craft-map of pre-modern India. There is, however, one notable exception—the essay by Kirin Narayan, which studies the oral tradition relating to the daughters of Vishwakarma. Narayan's fascinating piece is on the daughters of Vishwakarma, and on an oral tradition that is indigenous to the Gujarat region and rendered unique by its absence in other parts of India. Randal Ma is a twin goddess with two faces—one silver and the other brass/bronze. Hailing from a traditional Sutar family of Gujarat, Kirin's is an emic narrative of the Vishwakarma community.

This anthology should hopefully be of interest not only to academicians, sociologists, folklorists, and craft-historians, but also to the practitioners of culture care, who are keen on keeping alive craft traditions and ensuring a brighter future for the children of Vishwakarma. It is this activism which led to the foundation of the Dilli Haat by Jaya Jaitly way back in 1994, as well as her more recent Dastakari Haat Samiti. I believe a meaningful study of the past of the Vishwakarmas would help to give way to a better present and future for them. The present anthology should therefore be seen as academic activism with culture care as its seminal motif.

Notes

1. Kamaladevi Chattopadhyaya Papers, Nehru Memorial Museum & Library, cited in Reena Nanda, *Kamaladevi Chattopadhyaya: A Biography*, New Delhi: Oxford University Press, 2002, p. 126.
2. *South Indian Inscriptions* (hereafter *SII*), vol. XVII, no. 603. This remarkable inscription is in Sanskrit and has lengthy passages which are quotes from the *Dharmashastras* and the writers of ethico-legal codes like *Yajnavalkya*, in an attempt to determine whether the Rathakara or anuloma or pratiloma castes should be allowed to perform rituals like sacrifices or the wearing of sacred thread. This record has been analysed at length in J.D.M. Derrett, 'Two Inscriptions Concerning the Status of the Kammalas and the Application of Dharmasastra', in *Professor K.A.N. Sastri Felicitation Volume*, ed. S. Ganesan, Madras: Nilakanta Sastri Felicitation Committee, 1971, pp. 34–55.
3. *SII*, vol. VI, no. 117; *SII*, vol. VI, no. 673, etc. Some of these records have been analysed in E. Sivanagi Reddy, 'Shilpins in Early and Medieval Andhra', presented at the Second International Seminar on Mayonic Science and Technology, Kerala, January 1997, p.10.
4. See Nicholas B. Dirks, *Castes of Mind: Colonialism and the Making of Modern India*, Princeton: Princeton University Press, 2001.

5. Karl Marx, *Capital*, vol. I, translated into English from the third German edition by S. Moore and E. Aveling, ed. Fredrich Engels, Moscow: Foreign Languages Publishing House, 1958, pp. 339–40.
6. Ibid., p. 340.
7. *Inscriptions of Andhra Pradesh*, Cuddapah district, vol. II, no. 107. For the details of the inscription, see Reddy, 'Shilpins in Early and Medieval Andhra', p. 7.
8. *Annual Report of Epigraphy* (hereafter *ARE*), 309 and 378 of 1916; Report 1917, para 55.
9. My Presidential address to the Medieval Indian history section at the 64th session of the Indian History Congress, held in Mysore in 2003, titled 'Crafts and Artisans in South Indian History', has dealt with an overview of craft history in peninsular India. It also specially addresses the theme of social status of craftsmen in the Vijayanagar Empire. See *Proceedings of the Indian History Congress* (hereafter *PIHC*), Patna, 2004, pp. 300–36. The Presidential address by S. Settar in this same volume, titled 'Footprints of Artisans in History: Some Reflections on Early Artisans of India', is also a remarkably fine study of tracking artisanal history in Karnataka by looking at the Ashokan inscriptions and edicts; *PIHC*, pp. 1–43.
10. Although multiple oral versions of this community tradition exist, an excellent textual analysis is to be found in Jan Brower, 'The Story of the Magnetic Fort', in *The Makers of the World*, Delhi: Oxford University Press, 1995. Also see Jan Brouwer, 'The Story of the Magnetic Fort', in *Tradition in Structural Anthropology*, eds. A. de Ridder and J.A.J. Karremans, Netherlands: E.J. Brill, 1987. This is not to say that this is the only authentic version since other oral traditions differ from it in significant respects.
11. Jan Brouwer, 'A Matter of Liminalities: A Study of Women and Crafts in South India', *Man in India*, vol. 67, no. I, March 1987, p. 6.
12. *ARE*, 464 of 1961–2.
13. *ARE*, 109 of 1949–50.
14. For an interesting discussion on this theme, see Brower, 'A Matter of Liminalities'.
15. For a brief discussion on women in craft activities, see my Presidential address 'Crafts and Artisans in South Indian History', *PIHC*, pp. 10–11.

Reflections on the Vishwakarma

1

In Search of Vishwakarma and His Progeny

JAYA JAITLY

Professor Ramaswamy has devoted a lot of time to the study of the Vishwakarma community. You find her studies referring to this community, which is often described as a unified grouping of five subgroups—carpenters, blacksmiths, bell metal workers, goldsmiths, and stonemasons—who believe that they are the descendants of Vishwakarma, through his sons. Manu was said to have worked with iron; Maya in wood; Tvashtha in brass, copper, and alloys; Silpi in stone; and Vishvajna was said to be a goldsmith and jeweller. The kammāḷars in south India, who claim to be their descendants, are well versed in the *shilpa shastras,* the art treatises in Sanskrit laying out all the religious and technical processes to be followed in their work in order to achieve perfect results. Forms and formats are rigid and the process of creating an object is considered a part of a spiritual exercise. Till date, the Vishwakarma community worships various forms of this deity (Vishwakarma) and follows the five Vedas: *Rig Veda*, *Yajur Veda*, *Sama Veda*, *Atharva Veda*, and *Pranava Veda*.

Vishwakarma is mentioned repeatedly in the *Rig Veda* 10.81.7, but it would be best to quote from the *Mahabharata*, as used by Ananda K. Coomaraswamy,[1] which is, 'Visvakarma, Lord of the arts, master of a thousand handicrafts, carpenter of the gods and builder of their palaces divine, fashioner of every jewel, first of craftsmen, by whose art men live, and whom, a great and deathless god, they continually worship.' He is said to be the god of all architects, engineers, and craftspeople, the supreme architect of the universe, Brahma in another form. He, thus,

The hesitation I feel when taking up a tough challenge is outweighed by the excitement and intellectual curiosity of being able to explore new ideas to build upon older ones. Therefore, I must thank the Nehru Memorial Museum & Library, and Professor Vijaya Ramaswamy, for offering me this opportunity and especially the honour of speaking at the opening of a fascinating conference.

provides an overarching umbrella, including everyone involved with work and creative expression.

Vishwakarma has always held a place of fascination for me. It began when I saw simple workers from different artisanal professions, shop floors, and construction sites pausing work for a day dedicated to his name, to clean their machines, tools, and instruments and adorn them with flowers. Then they prayed to him, since it was Vishwakarma who enabled them to flourish their skills. It seemed so fundamental an act, imbued with utmost respect for one's own work and a recognition that the blessings of a higher being are needed to successfully execute one's skills at work.

Vishwakarma is obviously a concept that is commonly depicted as an elderly figure sporting a white beard. It is a concept honouring work and the encouragement of creativity and excellence. So we should see Vishwakarma Jayanti, celebrated immediately after Ganesh Chaturthi, as an occasion honouring creativity, skills, and thus, the dignity of labour. This day always seems more important to me than the innumerable holidays accorded to different communities and religions in our secular nation. To stop work for just a day in order to respect the workplace and the materials that enable one to work seems to me a highly sophisticated concept that is only partially matched by the Western concept of Labour Day, which refers essentially to the working class in organized environments. It is also equally important to note that Vishwakarma Day brings together artisans and craftspeople, mechanics and carpenters, and architects and artists from a number of communities to celebrate their patron and guardian. Descendants of the professional artisan castes associated specifically with Vishwakarma, who today may be involved in some wholly unrelated profession, also take pride in celebrating this day.

On the basis of the belief that all gods having different attributes in the Hindu pantheon are ultimately one, and the soul of the 'one' resides in each of us, Vishwakarma too can be appropriated by all artisan groups apart from the original five, and indeed, by anyone involved in creative expression. It is from this position that my study of what Vishwakarma means to craftspeople began. Being an activist in the field, and spending more time in dusty villages and narrow lanes of small and big towns in search of people who uphold India's craft traditions than in libraries and among books, I found that not only is the 'progeny' of Vishwakarma spread far and wide, but that craftspeople do not need to go to temples to seek him. The true manifestation of 'work is worship' is found when one watches crafts persons at work. The silence, the meditative quality of their concentration, the systematic and meaningful application of techniques, and the choice of suitable colours make the final product almost like an offering to a higher being. The earnings from this work are then attributed to this higher being, thereby making traditional knowledge and skills, workmanship, spirituality, income, and livelihood part of an integral whole that constitutes a meaningful creative life. This perspective is wholly and satisfyingly Indian. It is also what has cradled and nurtured our crafts, inclusive of and beyond castes and religions.

We often refer to the 'mapping' of crafts. I began my quest for the reach and spread of Vishwakarma's progeny and products through the literal process of creating maps. It began when I saw a map of the markets of Bangkok, presented in water colour, by an American artist Nancy Chandler in the early 1990s. It struck me that if shopping in such a small country could be presented in this attractive fashion, the multitude of crafts, artworks, and textiles that India offered should be actually mapped to lead people to them. These maps took on a slow and steady momentum of their own. It took fifteen years to cover all the states. Some new states were formed in between, and the map of Telangana now will have to be created, separate from Andhra Pradesh. Political and geographical evolutions reflect the evolution of India's art and crafts over millennia as being an ever-changing phenomenon, responding to the times and needs of the people.

At one level, these maps were meant as shopping guides, with the locations of the manufacture of crafts and sometimes even with some guidance on how to get to a certain village or locality. At another level, the maps had to bring out interesting differences in the processes of manufacture of crafts, depending on local cultures, availability of raw materials and histories. For example, we discovered that in Odisha, women of a certain tribe wore similar blue saris for a festival, while their priestess wore saris specially woven in yellow. Thus, colour becomes spiritually meaningful beyond mere aesthetics.

I wanted these maps to be inexpensive and accessible to young students and travellers who cannot afford coffee-table books that just look beautiful but serve no great purpose. Coincidentally, they came in useful to the United Nations Development Programme (UNDP) and state governments after the supercyclone in Odisha and the Gujarat earthquake. The maps made it easier to locate artisan pockets which needed to be provided with relevant relief for the craftspeople to carry on their traditional vocations. I would like to believe that it was Vishwakarma who was ensuring the continuity of their creativity. Coming around a full circle, these maps were combined with a new, freshly expanded text to create the *Crafts Atlas of India*. It was selected by *Choice*, the premier review journal in USA, which recommends books to colleges and universities all over the country, in which they choose around 600 from over 25,000 publications for their excellence of scholarship and presentation. All the maps were done in different art forms of India by artists from respective states, and every known craft, art, and textile was covered. It was nice to know that knowledge about India's crafts and their practitioners would reach students through our initial and very modest attempt at mapping in an artistic way. The Surveyor General of India's office had to certify all international boundaries of the maps as accurate, so there was some scientific accuracy involved within the art work.

The major caveat that I will add here is that I am fully aware that we could not possibly have discovered all the crafts of India. Besides, some of the crafts that have been recorded may have since disappeared, while several others may have sprung up after the time of documentation and hence remain unrecorded on these maps. But that is the very beauty of the creative craft process of India. It is like a mighty river that forever absorbs new material, throws some away onto its banks, changes course, and meanders as it wishes, depending on the pulls and pressures of the surrounding environment. Sometimes, like the Varuna and Assi rivers that gave Varanasi its name, crafts dry up and become pathetic and sullied representations of their initial selves. At other times, new channels open, providing people with fresh opportunities for expressing their creativity and earning their livelihood. This is their beauty, and discovering them brings constant excitement. Change too is constant, and the search for ever-evolving progenies and legacies of Vishwakarma continues, like a river, for ever.

I have come across cultural histories in unintended and interesting ways. My project 'Akshara, Crafting Indian Scripts' (2012) was inspired by my reaction to the constant lack of self-worth expressed by craftspeople, who considered themselves illiterate despite being excellent in craftsmanship. They felt themselves to be at a disadvantage, not knowing English or not having the knowledge to operate computers. They also believed that if their children went to school, craft skills would no longer remain relevant, and yet there were hardly any honourable 'jobs' available for many of the literate, let alone the semi- or neoliterate.

To persuade them to turn to their linguistic roots, study the scripts of their regional tongues, and apply these through creative calligraphy using their craft skills, we mobilized more than 70 practitioners in 21 different skills, like weaving, embroidery, carving, metalwork, ceramics, folk art, and many other forms, using 15 of the 22 official Indian languages. Out of this exploration came over 150 museum-quality objects that opened up a whole new design vocabulary. But this was not all. When I told them to use their own scripts in the form of alphabets, verses, names, phrases, *shlokas*, songs, and local stories deeply embedded in their local cultures, a wealth of ideas and cultural histories turned up from this freshly tilled soil.

To give you some examples: women in Bihar do simple forms of embroidery, which are being developed into more sophisticated products than mere quilts for a *charpai*. Applique is one of them. I asked them to create wall hangings based on local stories or festivals and embroider the words of songs in their local dialects. They came out with religious songs sung while standing in the water at Chhat Puja and Madhushravani, a festival when a newly married girl returns to her mother's home for the first time, to be seated among flowers. They also brought out a moving old folk song telling of a potter, a farmer, and a boatman, lamenting the fact that Sita's fate would have been very different had she been married into their family, where she would have been tended with love and care, rather than meet the unhappy end after marrying into a royal household. The subtle challenges to existing attitudes of caste, class, and gender, set to verse in gentle tones and accompanied by poignant embroidered images, are as sophisticated as any brought out by the intellectual community.

Likewise, traditional artists in southern India came up with calligraphy in *kalamkari*, offering snippets of a song that described a bride's face adorned with turmeric as yellow as a marigold. In Kashmiri *kani* weaving, we created a shawl in the colours of a pigeon. The weaver found a dead pigeon since he could not capture the colours of a live one on his mobile phone. He took it to the dyer who faithfully created yarn in shades of grey with touches of salmon pink, since the pigeon's legs were of that colour. A new colour palate thus came into being. An old folk song welcoming the monsoon in Gujarat, when it was advisable to eat *karela* to ward off malaria, and a hidden welcome to visitors to a home lovingly carved into a wooden door handle were some of the many forms of communication through craft and calligraphy that came about. Crafts found a new avenue of expression on fresh artefacts and objects of daily use and have since spawned a variety of spin-offs that take inspiration from a single idea of how to apply old skills in a new way within a very Indian, very local, perspective.

A search for traditional names given by handloom weavers to colours of their saris evoked an era of aesthetic sophistication that would far outshine any Parisian fashion palette or marketing phrase. To express the subtle differences in shades within a similar colour, old documents reveal names like *kapur-safed* (camphor white), *makkai* (creamy corn), and *subz-kishmish* (fresh raisins). Old texts describe the colour white further by referring to the colour of white mist, or of steam rising from boiled milk. To neglect, and worse, to ignore such subtle and sophisticated terminology coming from often illiterate weavers and dyers, who honour handwork and creativity, and to do this in the face of the seasonal colour diktats from the fashion world of the West, is to do disservice to our own heritage that Vishwakarma encompasses.

Looking at trends in the publishing world, and in government policy-making for the development of crafts, I spotted a gaping hole that was widening as crafts became more commercialized, imitative, and export-oriented. To be like the Chinese seemed to be the goal. How can we be like them? We are Indian. We have our own identities and cultural histories from which our crafts are created. It came to me that the Vishwakarma's terrain had no institution of national importance to recognize research, document, and add value to crafted objects. Cultural histories and stories add immense economic value to a work of art. Everyone wants the story behind its maker and its making. So I proposed the idea of setting up the Hastkala Akademi on the lines of the Sangeet Natak, Lalit Kala, and Sahitya Akademis, but in a new environment free of unwarranted governmental influence, and bureaucratic deathtraps. Happily, the 2014 budget announced its allocation of Rs.30 crore for this purpose, with the intention of a public-private partnership model where enlightened patrons would fund, but not control, the work of the Akademi.

Every journey into the crafts persons' world is one of discovery and wonder. There must be something that drives these children of Vishwakarma to remain true to their traditions and processes of work, never paying any heed to how harsh, difficult, or tedious they may appear to be. On recent tours to 25 places in India to photo-document different craft, art, and textile forms that expressed the meaning of success, for a Google project for its Art & Culture platform, we found practices motivated by the drive for excellence, marketing opportunities, community demand and support, and love of the people for their own heritage. If anyone visits a tiny village in Chhattisgarh called Ambikapur, in Sarguja district, they will find an indigenous craft form that sprang simply from a woman's desire to express herself in a world where she found herself isolated. Her eyes roamed over the soil she stood on, the water that flowed nearby, the colours made by leaves, and the spices in her kitchen. Putting all these to work, her fingers deftly created toys for her child, then a shelf, or a lamp, and finally a wonderland of birds, animals, gods and mortals, leaves and flowers, and geometric shapes that became a home which was a museum of her skills. It, however, did not stop there. Her work took her across the world and inspired others in the village, who are today creating similar, magical decorations on their walls, windows, and doorways. A new art form, closer to tradition than to modernity, was thus born. In a weaver's home in Bengal or a terracotta artisan's hut in Odisha, there will always be a decorated area at the entrance or in the courtyard, where the tulsi plant grows and the evening lamp is lit in prayer. There are no images of gods or goddesses there, only aura of prayer and the seeking of blessings automatically and wordlessly, are directed towards the god who takes care of artisans. In Bagh, Madhya Pradesh, the printing process comprises sixteen stages, with hard labour involved in soaking metres of cloth, drying them, treating the surface, printing in many stages with carved wooden blocks, drying them again, washing them in a stream of clear water, and then drying them yet again. Similarly, bell metal workers in Kerala follow many elaborate processes to make lamps that adorn temples and ornaments for traditional dancers. These cultures, fostered by the all-pervading spirit of Vishwakarma, keeps Indian heritage and culture alive amidst a fast-changing world of automation and technology. Here again, the person who does this work, will pray to it as a tool he needs to use to earn an honest livelihood.

To end, I would like to quote Ananda K. Coomaraswamy's words on Vishwakarma:

> Beauty, rhythm, proportion, idea have an absolute existence in an ideal plane, where all who seek may find. The reality of things exists in the mind, not in the detail of their appearance to the eye. Their inward inspiration upon which the Indian artist is taught to rely, appearing like the still, small, voice of god, that god was conceived of as Vishvakarma. He may be thought of as that part of divinity which is conditioned by a special relation to artistic expression: or in another way, as the sum total of consciousness, the group soul of the individual craftsmen of all times and places.[2]

Notes

1. Ananda K. Coomaraswamy, *Visvakarma: Examples of Indian Architecture, Sculpture, Painting, Handicraft,* New Delhi: Munshiram Manoharlal Publishers, 1978.
2. Ananda K. Coomaraswamy, 'Religious Ideas in Craftsmanship', in *The Indian Craftsman*, London: Probsthain & Co., 1909.

2

Under the Curse of Gold

Kerala's Gold Boom and the Exit of Vishwakarma Goldsmiths

GEORGE VARGHESE K.

Introduction to Gold's Anthropology in Kerala

We should begin with an experience I had when doing the first phase of my fieldwork on gold in Kerala in the early 2000s. A friend from abroad visited me at that time and he shared an interesting experience with me. In no pub or bar where he went to have a drink could he find a girl or woman drinking. Similarly, when he visited some gold shops to buy Keralian jewellery for his girlfriend, he found those shops thronged by women and hardly any men. When I discussed this experience with a local person, he insightfully observed that when the women of Kerala save some money they go and buy jewellery, while on the other hand, when the men happen to get some extra money they go and spend it in bars. According to him, the gold shops and bars have become exclusive gender havens in Kerala. When I made a tentative investigation of this socio-economic nuance, I found that not only do both gold and alcohol dominate the commodity regime in Kerala, but there is also a rough parity in their annual fiscal turnover. Perhaps it is only in Kerala, as compared to anywhere else in the world, that these commodities are being consumed in high quantities and in a way that is becoming gender-exclusive. A noteworthy incident in this context is that sometime back in Perinthalmanna, a town in Malappuram district, a woman who came to buy a bottle of alcohol in a public vending shop (these shops are nicknamed 'Beverage outlets') was beaten up by the male customers waiting to buy alcohol there, in a spiteful discharge of moral arrogance. The irony was that she had come to buy the bottle for her alcoholic husband, who was convalescing after an accident at home.

The celebration of gold in Kerala has engaged all possible public spaces and means of mass communication, inundating them with lucrative messages. Like a contagion, it is everywhere: in the TV channels, newspapers, magazines, on compound walls, road dividers, traffic islands, over bus stops, police stations, temples, churches, and where not. It seems there is no escape from its hammering ambience wherever one turns to in Kerala. The ad posters and billboards of the gold shops cover the fragile geography of the land like crops. In many of them, until recently, gold and its sheen were something associated only with the female body and its beauty. But things have shifted to a new tack of late. Gold is almost on every body possible and of all ages today. Gold-clad old women smiling with their toothless jaws can be seen in certain billboards, visibly happy with their precious possession. In Neendakara, a fishing harbour near Kollam, the image in the ad of a gold shop (Chunkath Prince Jewellers) is that of a fully ornamented dolphin, which was matched with the surrounding watery environment. In the precinct of the famous Sarkara Devi Temple of Chirayinkeezhu, the ad image of a gold shop (Aisha Jewellers) has in it none other than Sree Narayana Guru, the saint-reformer of Kerala, sitting above a fully gold ornamented danseuse. In this metonymic co-positioning, the saint seemed to be implicitly sponsoring the shop's merchandise. Perhaps the catchiest one was the image on the hoarding of the Sunny Jacob Jewellers at Chinnakkada in Kollam city. In this hoarding, there was Saddam Hussein himself, standing in full military regalia, sponsoring the gold jewellery of the shop. But the Iraqi dictator's image vanished in the aftermath of his death in 2006. The new image that took over his place for some time was that of a camel in the Arabian Desert, fully strapped with golden chains and harness. Interestingly, in another recent shift, the image has been reverted to the archetypal Keralian bride, wearing gold jewellery like an armour plate on her chest.

What becomes noteworthy in the paragraphs so far is that gold passes through a network of connections, ranging from brides, dancers, alcohol, billboards, dolphins, and camels to saint-reformer Sree Narayana Guru and even the dictator Saddam Hussein. This multiplicity of disparate connections definitely becomes puzzling, persuading us to approach gold's regime in Kerala more cautiously. Alcohol and gold are two entirely different objects; dolphins are sea creatures, while camels are desert animals; Sree Narayana Guru was a saint-reformer who lived from the mid-nineteenth to early twentieth century in Kerala; and Saddam Hussein was the dictator of Iraq who met with his end at the displeasure of the USA. This can immediately raise the issue of representation that why should gold and its high volume of trade and consumption not be considered as part of the economic infrastructure, and the variegated images in which it gets represented as part of the ideological superstructure? The question is sensible to an extent, but for the fact that both the production and consumption of gold in Kerala have many more secrets and surprises that cannot be captured with a Marxist or empiricist paradigm. The following parts of this essay do not explore the general scenario of gold in Kerala, but focus on one issue: the deskilling and displacement of traditional Vishwakarma goldsmiths from the scene of gold-jewellery manufacturing in the context of the gold boom in Kerala. The question that can be posed is, why, when people are buying more gold and merchants making more profit, are its traditional makers, the Vishwakarma goldsmiths, being pushed towards poverty and professional extinction? This exploration is made from a specific theoretical perspective that gives added emphasis to the material nature of gold rather than the general socio-economic factors. The findings of this study are based on the ethnographic work done on gold in Kerala in the early twenty-first century, off and on, mostly around Thrissur, in the central part of Kerala. Thrissur is the biggest centre of gold-jewellery manufacturing in Kerala from the 1980s onwards.

According to a survey made among the Malayali gold workers in Thrissur in May–July 2014 (see Fig. 2.1), the numerical position of Vishwakarma goldsmiths is still dominant, but is getting increasingly displaced by gold workers from other castes, religions, and states. Gold-jewellery making, which was the exclusive preserve of the Vishwakarma goldsmiths, the traditional artisan caste of Kerala till the middle of 1980s slowly eroded from their grip under the impact of a variety of forces. Some of the major reasons were the perennial distrust of goldsmiths as tricksters; the advent of the super-sized and ornate gold shops; availability of a flood of gold jewellery in different fashions and designs; gold jewellery entering the 'wholesale manufacturing' sector; mechanization of jewellery-making; and the incoming of gold jewellery from states like Maharashtra, West Bengal, Rajasthan, Tamil Nadu, and so on. This has also made radical shifts in the political identity of the Vishwakarma community. Though many sociological factors are at work in this muddled scenario, the most important one to be reckoned with is the very complexity of the metal gold itself. In other words, gold as a

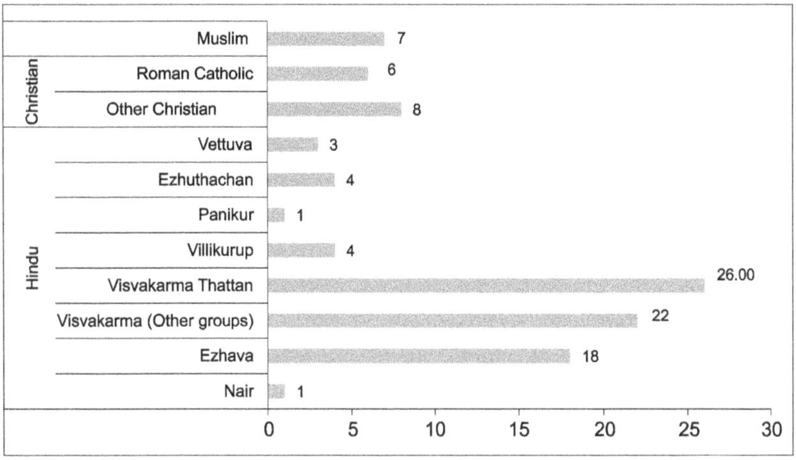

FIG. 2.1: The religious and caste composition of the Malayali gold workers in Thrissur (in per cent)

Source: Updated survey conducted from May to July 2014 at Thrissur, Kerala

material, and its metallurgic complexities over-determine the present predicament of the Vishwakarma goldsmiths to a great extent. This argument definitely demands further theoretical clarification. It is most relevant in this context to look into the noisy wrangle between the 'material school' and the 'material culture school' in the human and social sciences at present.

Engaging Objects Philosophically

The material culture school argues that objects, things, and artefacts have theoretical significance since they are socially and culturally embedded. On the other side, the material school contends that objects and artefacts have significance of their own, not because of their abstract materiality, but because of their concrete composition through specific materials. In this context, Richard Handler highlights the critical difference between materials and material culture. For him, the very idea of the concept of 'material culture' as being different from 'materials' is a contradiction in terms since the former connotes an abstract culture which exists on its own plane, independent from the material things. To be more realistic, there is a cultural dimension to the materials produced by humans and a material dimension to the cultural accomplishments that humans are capable of. For example, a material object like a knife or a pot will have a cultural distinctness as part of the milieu in which it is produced. On the other hand, a cultural representation like a language has a material form too, as waves of sound or as lines on paper language can be visualized as a material individuation. So the concept 'material culture' becomes a misnomer.[1]

'Material culture studies' has evolved as an independent sub-discipline of anthropology and archaeology. Charles Tilley defines it thus: 'The field of material culture studies is one concerned with the relationship between artefacts and social relations irrespective of time and place. It aims to explore systematically the linkage between the constitution of social reality and material-culture production and use.'[2] On the other hand, for Tim Ingold, who is a critic of material culture studies, concepts like 'material culture' and 'materiality' have nothing to do with 'materials' as such, which form the bedrock of these concepts and discourses. The engagements of scholars on material culture 'are not with the tangible stuff of craftsmen and manufacturers but with the abstract ruminations of philosophers and theorists. To understand materiality, it seems, we need to get as far away from materials as possible.'[3] For him, to substitute 'materials and their properties' with 'materiality of objects' is nothing but intellectual distortion.

Ingold problematizes the relationship between materials and materiality in an interesting manner. Drawing from Christopher Gosden, he raises certain pertinent problems. Though we can see stars and their light, we cannot touch either of them. In that case, are they material realities? Similarly, is moon a material reality for all of us, or only to the astronauts who can walk on it? Where do we place a shadow? It is not a material reality like a rock or a tree, but we find it as real as both of them. Again, we stand under the shadow of a tree to cool off from sunlight. Then what about air? Though we do not see it, we breathe, move through, and survive in its transparent medium. Moreover, where can we place smoke and fire?[4]Around five million people live in cave dwellings in the world. We say houses are built, but can we say that the caves are 'built' in the same manner? Hence the material nature of reality has extremely complex ontological and expressional levels, distinctly different from the physicalist and sociological conceptions of the material culture school.

David Pye, a professor of furniture design, articulates a very stimulating argument about the structure and composition of objects and things. For him, the attributes of the material meditate the relation between objects and their makers. He conceptualizes the elementary materials like metals, clay, stones, and so on, as congeries of different 'properties' and 'qualities'. Take for example, a metal like lead. There is a mixture of properties and qualities in it which have different levels of importance to different people working on it. For an ordinary person, the weight or ductility of lead may be the important concern. He or she, for all practical purposes, might not be interested in facts such as its low melting point, low resistivity, impenetrability to X-rays or the toxic properties of lead. But these properties are important for a scientist. On the other hand, for a craftsman working with lead, its melting point, ductility, and malleability become important, not its electrical resistivity or reaction to X-rays. In this context, it is necessary to differentiate between properties and qualities of a material. The properties of materials are objective and measurable. They are important for a scientist. The qualities, on the other hand, are subjective. They are ideas to those who work on them, like craftsmen. Each craftsman or artist has his own idea of stoniness or metallic essence.[5]

Perhaps we need to travel through the philosophical track for a while to capture the complexity of objects and materials. The notion of multiplicity as developed by the philosopher Alain Badiou becomes useful in this context. We do not address the enormous complexity of his philosophical system here, but engage with the select concepts of 'event', 'multiple', and 'void'. For Badiou, there is multiplicity or sets of multiples in everything. Philosophy, truth, and subject are posited within the arbitrary structures of the multiple and these get manifested through what Badiou calls 'events'. Truth lies only in the events. Philosophy does not produce any truth as such. It only locates the conditions of truth, which are events. For Badiou, philosophy in its history is nothing but a 'de-substantialization of truth'.[6] An event is an uncharacteristic occurrence in being, or the surging forth of non-being. It eludes the count-as-one of the multiple, and something that needs to be subtracted from the 'one' for the benefit of the pure multiple. Event is 'that-which-is-not-being-*qua*-being'.[7] But truth lies only in the event that is a subtractive seizure from the 'one'. There is also a paradox here. A truth is at once something new, hence something rare and exceptional, yet touching the very being of that of which it is the truth. In this sense, it is also the most stable and closest to the initial state of things in the ontological sense.[8] The event occurs in situations of multiples. The truth lies in the pure event among them which is an unusual one. It is a 'supplement', or what Badiou calls an 'additional signifier'. Catching of the truth in the event is equivalent to the naming of this additional signifier, which is a complex process. This naming occurs at a point of time after the event and hence every truth is post-evental. In other words, event is not coequal or coextensive with being, and is a 'wandering excess' whose truth lies in a future anterior. The event, when it occurs, is an 'obscure event'. Take for example the Cultural Revolution in China or May 1968 events in Paris or the Iranian Revolution. The meaning of none of them could be fixed at the point when they occurred with their uniqueness. The Cultural Revolution or May 1968 events cannot be explained by canons of orthodox Marxism, or the Iranian Revolution within the framework of the holy Koran. There are some 'excesses' in these pure events, which may be identified and 'named' later.

Now events and their multiple sites do not confine to social situations alone, but spread out to organisms and to non-living materials as well. Events are trans-beings, bordered on the void from which they emerge. Void does not mean nothingness, or its emergence a theological one of *ex nihilo*. Events are fragments of being, which are part of an evental site. This, however, does not mean that they are fragments of the site. There is a peculiar ontological-mathematical logic working here. In this context, Badiou gives the example of a cat. A living organism like a cat is also an evental site for him. By the same logic, even non-living objects are also the same. In the case of the cat, it is constituted by multiple organs and submultiples of those organs. Take the case of the liver in the cat. It is an important organ in the physiological constitution, which in turn is composed of liver cells. The liver is a solid, integrated, organic part of the totality called cat. But the liver is not an evental site, since the vitality of the cat and the vitality of the liver are indistinguishable and have same value. But it is not so in case of the liver cells by which the liver is composed. The cells of the liver and the liver itself have different ontological status as evental sites. The cells are composed of chemical molecules and are not 'organic' in the same sense as the liver is. A chemically determined molecule is not 'alive' in the same sense as the liver may be said to be alive. Even if it is 'objectively' a part of the cat, the aggregate of the molecules is not a vital component in the same sense as the liver. We may say that with the aggregate of the molecules we reach the edge of the cat's vitality. The cat as an aggregate of molecules and as a multiple of vital organs are two expressions of same essence but conceptually separated by a void.[9]

The cat's example as a multiplicity equips us better to understand the composition of materials as discussed by Ingold and Pye. What Badiou explicates through this example is that in any organism or object, there are clusters of amorphous materials, qualities, and properties that are organized in a unique logic, separated by borders and thresholds. Once we analyse these levels of organization, we find them astonishingly dissimilar and even contradictory in certain cases. In the cat's example, we find that though the liver is a component in the overall vital constitution of the organism, it is nonetheless constituted of cells which, in turn, are composed of dead chemicals. So the vital organism of the cat is ultimately constituted of dead materials. But in a reverse logic, the dead materials compose different vital organs like heart, liver, lungs, etc., which in their totality form the organic configuration of the cat. The passage from the cat at the macro level to the dead chemicals at the micro level is made through different types of live organs and tissues. This line that connects the molecular level with the molar level is punctuated with different threshold points which Badiou calls void. So when Pye speaks of the different qualities of lead which become relevant to different people, the totality of these qualities immanent in the metal is organized in a way similar to Badiou's cat. The electrical resistivity of the lead has nothing to do with its weight, or the melting point shares hardly anything with the impenetrability of X-rays. Hence, these qualities and properties are separated by a void. From this, it could be inferred that we do not know yet all the qualities and properties that are immanent in lead. Perhaps a newly discovered laser ray might bring out a different property in lead—a possibility we cannot rule out. So between these unconnected properties in lead there exists a Badiouan void.

Deceits of Gold and Artisans' Uncertainties

So how do these new insights about materials and objects become helpful in analysing the predicament of the Vishwakarma goldsmiths in Thrissur? Let us explore this problem step by step. Kerala is one of the highest gold-consuming states in India with around 20 per cent share in the national trade and consumption. The demand for gold jewellery in India in 2015 was 654.30 tons.[10] From various unofficial sources, it has been calculated that Kerala has used up to an average of 130 to 135 tons of gold per year in the last decade without much fluctuation.[11] It would be interesting to note that USA, the most economically powerful nation in the world, used only 120 tons of gold for jewellery in 2015.[12]

Despite this great volume of gold trade and the high value it procures, the plight of goldsmiths is abysmally pathetic. What we would discuss is the crucial role that the metal gold plays in the marginalization of the Vishwakarma goldsmiths, who till late 1980s completely controlled the jewellery-making scene of Kerala. How does gold as a material become important in their downfall? As we had discussed earlier in the initial paragraphs, gold is not an object or material but a passion or addiction.[13]

Gold's metallurgic, cultural, economic, and historical singularities testify this. These singularities form a multiplicity organized at varying levels and separated by a metaphysical void as we learned from Badiou. Let us turn to it now.

Gold is a scarce metal with astonishingly inconsistent occurrence in human history. At the end of the sixteenth century, which followed the discovery of America, the total gold in the world was only 750 tons; but by the end of the nineteenth century, it swelled up to 10,000 tons.[14] A century later, at the end of twentieth century, the quantity of gold increased astronomically to 150,000 tons, fifteen times more than what was at the end of nineteenth century. It should also be remembered that gold is a metal of high specific gravity (19.32 g./cu. cm.). So the total amount of gold on earth, 150,000 tons at the end of the twentieth century, can be fitted into 60 cu. ft. This is roughly equivalent to the volume of three twelve-room houses and could be transported in a single ocean liner (if only the ship doesn't sink). At the end of 2015, the quantity of gold increased to 186,700 tons, an increase of 37,000 tons within fifteen years from 2000, which shows the enormous demand for gold.[15] Though gold is a heavy metal, it is very soft. Pure 24-carat gold is not very shiny, and is soft like putty. It is the most malleable and ductile of metals as well. According to Brian Kettell, an expert on gold's economics and metallurgy, even in ancient Egypt, a skilful gold-beater could hammer gold bullion to such fineness that it took 250,000 sheets to produce a layer 1 in. thick. Nowadays, a single ounce can be beaten into a thin translucent sheet of 10 sq. m. (108 sq. ft.) area. Its ductility is equally amazing. One ounce of gold can be drawn into a wire 50 mi. long. Again, only one ounce of gold is needed to plate a 1,000 mi. long copper wire. A more telling example should be that the gold thread drawn from a single ton of gold would stretch from earth to moon and back. Malleability and ductility of gold at all temperatures are of a far higher degree than of any other metal.[16]

From the perspective of Badiou and Pye, we find that gold's multiplicity is an aggregate of aesthetic, economic, metallurgic, and cultural properties and qualities ordered in an inconsistent logic. Let us cull the qualities and properties relevant to the goldsmith, and explore how these played a critical role in their systematic degradation throughout history. The most important attribute that affects the goldsmith directly is the metallurgic subtlety of gold. This does not mean that other qualities or properties like value or beauty are not important. Since the goldsmith is a master craftsman, he knows thoroughly about the possibilities of manipulating the metallurgic potentials. Take for example, the malleability of gold. A single ounce can be beaten into a sheet of 108 sq. ft. Hence, gold becomes the cheapest means to coat ornaments made of cheaper metals or gild them and fake them as gold. It is interesting to see that the most economical way to coat other objects is to gild them. But the fake that is created is also of gold itself and not of any other metal like platinum or copper. Hence, gold becomes its own mask ironically. Slavoj Zizek pointed out somewhere that an Argentine dictator escaped the resistance of the people by wearing his own mask. People were agitating in front of his palace wearing his mask as a protest; he caught hold of one of these masks and escaped wearing it. Gold in fact becomes the alter ego of this dictator who masked himself with his own mask. The fakes are made because gold is valuable; on the other hand, gold is the cheapest material for making these fakes also. These two contradictory qualities, of being very costly and very cheap at the same time, exist side by side within gold, separated by an ontological void as Badiou postulates. In Badiou's terms, the malleability of gold is an evental site. The more important point is that the goldsmith has complete control of these metallurgic potentials and it is a matter of ethical choice or fear of punishment that constrains him from exercising them as he pleases. Then how did this metallurgic conundrum push them into a social category of fraudsters and cheats over the course of history?

The goldsmiths (called *thattan* in Malayalam) enjoyed a high status in Kerala in early times. They were attached to temples, palaces, and aristocratic houses. They used to wear sacred threads like brahmins and they made jewellery only for the higher castes. It is noteworthy that the lower castes were forbidden to wear gold ornaments in the early period in Kerala. According to K.S. Vijayan, a senior goldsmith from Olari, Thrissur, the aristocratic Muslim ladies who were forbidden to see any other males could in fact meet their goldsmiths in person. They talked about them with due affection as *ente thattan* or 'my goldsmith'. The goldsmiths were called *desathu thattan*, meaning 'the goldsmith of the land'. Nambi Chadayan, the goldsmith scribe of the first Syrian Christian copperplate,[17] was officially designated by the king as 'the Grand Goldsmith of the Cheraman Country'.[18] According to Vijayan, 'He was a highly trustworthy person, *Visvasthan* [in Malayalam], which derived from the very name of his mythological forefather *Visvajna* himself.' On the other hand, goldsmiths also suffered from universal disparagement as fraudsters. Manu spoke of goldsmiths as 'deceivers in open daylight'.[19] In Kerala, the commonest usage is a play on his name: *thattan thattum* (the goldsmith will compulsively filch). Another one is *Thattan Thottal Patthinettu*, meaning, 'If the goldsmith touches the gold you will get back only eight parts out of ten.' Yet another one is that even if a goldsmith's mother gives him gold to make a *tali* (the *mangalyasutra* of Hindu married women), he will steal from it.[20]

Many of the psychocultural apprehensions of society on the goldsmiths' fraudulent practices are baseless, according to K.V. Ramakrishnan from Viyyur. He asks, 'How could such congenital swindlers thrive all through history in all parts of the world?' The main allegations against goldsmiths are two. The first one is that the goldsmith never delivers the jewellery in time to the customer. Gold ornaments are most important in ceremonies like marriage and in the case of the Hindu marriages, they are conducted on auspicious occasions—called *muhurtham* in Kerala. There are many cases reported in which the goldsmith had failed to deliver the *tali*, the ceremonial talisman of the marriage, in time. The second allegation is that the goldsmiths adulterate the gold that is given to them for making ornaments.

This failure is, however, not deliberate, according to many traditional goldsmiths. It happens due to the sheer nature of gold as a metal and the force of circumstances. Gold is a precious metal, and village goldsmiths who are generally not well-off, cannot afford to possess it in large quantities. When an order for ornaments is placed with a village goldsmith, people usually give the exact quantity of gold that is needed to make the jewellery. But as in any other craft, the goldsmith needs some extra gold as raw material to work upon. The goldsmith, not being too rich, might not be having this extra gold at the time of taking the order. So he has to wait for a second person to place a new order. Then he takes some gold from the second order and executes the first one. Then, to execute the second order, he needs a third person to give him a fresh order and gold. This chain continues. This often causes a delay in the date of delivery of the finished ornaments. Moreover, an unavoidable nuance lurks here. Many a time the purity of the gold from different orders might not match. So, in the mixing of gold of different purities, one person might gain and another one might lose. Once this is found out by a customer, the goldsmith is declared to be a cheat. The unfortunate thing in this case is that the community as a whole has to take the brunt of the lapses of a few. It was in this way that eventually, the goldsmiths of the villages fell in trust and jewellery shops emerged in their place, mainly in towns. The shop owners became mediators between the customer and the goldsmiths. Consequently, the goldsmiths had to take up jobs in such shops in towns.

But the goldsmiths do not claim that they are always innocent. At certain occasions of extreme urgency, they admit to adulterating gold. This mainly happens when the urgency to deliver the ornaments is high and there is not enough gold with them to work upon. Another occasion of adulteration is the urgent need to raise a large sum of money for marrying off a daughter or when somebody at home falls seriously ill. Ponnappan Achari, a senior goldsmith from Ramavarmapuram, Thrissur, told me that on such occasions they are like 'cats in the custody of fish'. According to him, at night they can never sleep peacefully thinking of this valuable 'fish' at home. 'Why should we go around borrowing money when the gold is at our arm's length?' they said. In such moments, the goldsmiths fall to the strong temptation of filching and adulterating. He then explained with an ambiguous pride that to fake is much more difficult than making a normal ornament. The real gift of the goldsmith manifests in faking and this is something that gets expressed very creatively. Like a strong affect it overpowers them after a certain point. Once given to this malpractice, the goldsmiths are sometimes carried away by it. Ponnappan Achari also observed that the young 'new generation' goldsmiths do not know this art of simulation. They cannot make a total ornament, not to mention the copy of it. They are only 'jewel factory workers'. They are slaves to machines, and specialize only in parts and pieces of an ornament. They are not goldsmiths even, but only metal-cutters, wire-pullers, soldering technicians, and polishing artists. Therefore, they cannot fake a total ornament deftly. Even if they do it, it would be found out. So tradition matters a lot, not only in making attractive ornaments, but also in faking.

The metal's economic property and metallurgic qualities combine to make a different form of relationship in the case of goldsmiths, which is interesting to look into. The important thing to be taken into account here is that perhaps only gold can function as its own economic substitute, similar to the way it can function as its own fake through gilding and covering. Gold becomes its own price and wage in the conventional artisan production. Gold is perhaps the only object that shows minimal value difference between its unfinished raw material form and finished commodity state. Barring precious metals like silver or platinum, this unity of raw material and finished state does not apply to any other commodity. For example, when a tailor makes a shirt, a certain portion of the cloth is wasted in the process of conversion from the raw material state to the finished product. This wasted cloth cannot be retrieved in any viable manner. But this is not the case with gold. A certain portion of gold is wasted through processes like abrading, grinding, cutting, casting, pulling into wires, etc., during the making of jewellery. But this is not like the wasted cloth left after making a shirt, which has no value. In case of gold, one only needs to collect the gold filings and dust particles that fall off during the making of jewellery in a crucible and melt them to get a solid piece of gold again. This piece of gold carries near-equal price as the finished jewellery. This is because the real value of gold lies in its metallic state in pure form; the value addition through conversion into jewellery is insignificant compared to the high metallic value of gold. Around 85–90 per cent of the gold can be retrieved in this manner, as goldsmiths told me. Since the value of gold is very high, this small portion retrieved also has a high value. In fact, the 'wastage gold' formed the real remuneration of the artisans till very recently in Kerala. The labour charges are negligible in comparison to this remunerative 'wastage'.

Let us look further into this wastage-remuneration issue in case of the Vishwakarma goldsmiths, since it has become a political issue over and above the economic one. Kolappan Achari from Karamana, Thiruvananthapuram, explained this problem to me in a simple way. Soldering the different components of the pieces of gold jewellery is an important stage in jewellery-making, in which the raw material status of gold becomes important. The soldering material, called *mattam* (in Malayalam), should be of a lower melting point than gold, otherwise the whole thing would melt into a lump. Usually this soldering material is made by mixing gold with silver or copper. So in the final weight of the jewellery, the weight of this soldering metal is also counted. The value of these metals is negligibly small compared to gold. Copper costs roughly 40*p*. per gram and silver Rs.40 per gram, while gold costs something above Rs.2,300 per gram on an average. So the gold that is displaced in soldering carries high value. Usually, this portion called *panikkuravu* ('loss in making' in Malayalam) is given as an incentive to the goldsmith besides his labour charges. But ironically his labour charge is much less compared to the value of the wastage gold he gets. Normally this is 200 mg. for working on a sovereign of 8 g. If a goldsmith finishes a bangle of two sovereigns a day, he will get a wastage of 400 mg., the value of which will come to around Rs.900. But the formal labour charge that he gets per bangle is usually Rs.150 to Rs.200 from the gold merchant or the wholesale producer. So it can be seen that the value of the wastage is almost four times the labour charge. Here the wasted gold becomes the real labour charge, and the formal labour charge is only a nominal incentive. So an artisan goldsmith is not too keen about the formal labour charge, while he is adamant about his claim on the wastage gold. In today's scenario of mechanized, mass production of gold jewellery, the claim to wastage is denied to the goldsmiths by the gold merchants and the wholesalers for whom they work. The artisan goldsmiths are thus waging political struggles for long to get the right to wastage re-established.[21] This again demonstrates that the material quality of gold becomes important in understanding social processes concerning the goldsmiths.

Interestingly, the metallurgic complexities of gold go beyond the immediate milieu of trade and gets projected onto the political and state levels. State as an 'Apparatus of Capture' also played a dubious role in denigrating the well-to-do position goldsmiths enjoyed till mid-twentieth century.[22] The Gold Control Act declared by the Indian state in 1963, and repealed only in 1990, was the most crucial state intervention that changed their status fundamentally. The Gold Control Act was implemented by the state mainly because it felt the need to control foreign exchange outflows after the 1962 Indo-China War. Among several other provisions, it banned the public use of 22-carat gold and allowed only the transaction 14-carat gold and below. But the Act failed due to the exceptionally high demand for 22-carat gold among Indians and their refusal to surrender gold to the government. It failed in the case of the artisans also, since the government did not come out with alternate provisions to rehabilitate the goldsmiths who were thrown out of their traditional profession. The situation worsened eventually and around 260 people from the goldsmith community committed suicide in the period from 1963 to 1966.[23] Massive protests from the artisan community ensued, and finally the government was forced to make an important amendment to this Act in 1966. This was the restoration of the 22-carat gold to its old status. But the government prohibited the sale or transaction of new gold and allowed only the melting and reworking of the old 22-carat gold ornaments.

With this restitution, the concept of gold work also got redefined in the Act. The old artisan craft was suddenly transformed into an 'industry'. The Preamble to the Gold Control Act reads: 'Manufacture of gold ornaments by goldsmiths in India . . . falls within the connotation of the word "industry".' The goldsmiths were divided into two classes: the 'certified goldsmith' and the 'artisan goldsmith'. The certified goldsmith, under the Act, '. . . may make, manufacture, repair, polish, or process ornaments and may also repair or polish articles but shall not unless authorised by the Administrator so to do, make, manufacture or prepare any primary gold or article'.[24] The artisan goldsmith also performed same functions, but he was attached to a shop under a merchant. The majority of goldsmiths fell under the first category of certified goldsmiths. Shops employed one or two artisan goldsmiths just for keeping their licences and for small repair works. As M.G. Vijayan, the former president of Swarna Thozhilaly Suraksha Sangh (STSS) told me, the shop owners did a lot of illicit business during the gold control period under the label of these artisan goldsmiths, like purchasing and selling contraband gold and ornaments.

There were crucial consequences of this new system. The certified goldsmiths who formed the majority suddenly found themselves elevated to the unnatural role of the 'owners of industry' or industrialists. Thereafter, they were not supposed to work as labourers or artisans under anyone. This compelled them to move out of the shop premises, having no other place to go except their village homes. But public memory is long and the image of goldsmiths as swindlers still persisted in the villages. Except for small repair works, the villagers never approached these goldsmiths. For all major purchases they went to the shops in towns or cities. So the goldsmiths also had no other choice but to depend on the shop owners and cooperate in the illegal business they were doing.

The Gold Control Act made the position of the goldsmiths precarious; they became neither manufacturers nor labourers. They waged many struggles for getting recognized as a professional labour class with incumbent legal protection and privileges. The frontal organization in these struggles for a long time was All Kerala Gold Workers' Union (AKGWU), which was started in 1963 to resist the unfavourable provisions of the Gold Control Act. Its former leaders like E.S. Biju and N. Rajendarn were sworn to achieve the 'labour status' for the goldsmiths by fighting back the confusions created by the state and the merchants.[25] The merchants, to keep the goldsmiths out of the rights of the protected labour class, always manipulated the loopholes in the Gold Control Act. Even the courts and the labour tribunals had to give in to the lacunas in the Act. The period from 1970 to 1980 witnessed many struggles by the gold workers for getting their rights ratified as protected labourers. The most important agitations were launched in Thrissur and Alappuzha in this period. The government referred these cases to specially instituted industrial tribunals in this period.

N.K. Raveendran, the former Joint Secretary of the AKGWU, explained to me about the nuances in the verdicts of most of the industrial tribunals. A noteworthy judgement was the one made by the industrial tribunal instituted in the 1974–5 period in Alappuzha, headed by one K.P.M. Sherif. It is important to note that many gold workers themselves gave critical depositions before the tribunal that went against them. The accusation was that those who gave negative testimonies were bought out by the merchants.

There were three important points that went against the goldsmiths' cause, all of which were intimately connected to the metallurgical quality of gold. First, the mode of organization of the goldsmiths' work was different from other labourers. They did not work under the roof of a factory, owned by a factory owner. On the other hand, they were also not like a tiller or a mason who used minimum tools in his job like spades, pickaxes, or chisels—which could be owned by the employer. For goldsmiths, the most important component of their craft was the melting pot and a working place organized around it with a number of tools and chemicals. In the early times, the goldsmiths used to go to their clients' homes and work there. But as times changed, they had to use more sophisticated tools, machines, and chemicals for their work, which prevented them from resorting to such itinerant arrangements. So, as regards the work, goldsmiths became different from both the manual labourers and factory workers.

The second issue was that who would decide on the wage rate: the employee or the employer? It turned out to be that the goldsmith charged each piece according to the nature of the work. There was no fixed or standardized wage rate for any piece of jewellery as such. Even the same type of ornaments had different making charges that varied widely according to the fineness of making. For example, the cost of an ordinary ring was Rs.150. But the same ring, when studded with stones, was charged around Rs.600, which was four times more. Again, the quantity-quality problem was also present. For example, it was more time consuming to make an earring that weighed only 5 g. but with finer works in it than a plain ring of higher weight, say 12 g. In this case, the quantity was not the decisive determinant in the work. So, one charged more for the earring. There was no fixity in making charges as in the case of a factory worker or a manual labourer, who worked for fixed hours or for a fixed quantity of output. In the latter's case, the longer the hours one worked, or higher the quantity of output one generated, the more he or she was paid. But for the goldsmith, this rule did not apply.

The third issue was whether the goldsmiths were confined to one employer alone. There also the position of the goldsmiths became weak. None of them worked for a single shop or merchant exclusively. They all supplied jewellery to different shops. Therefore, there was no evidence that they were labourers attached to a single merchant from the legal point of view. The court decision thus went against the goldsmiths in the end.

Then the case was referred to the Kerala High Court. The final judgement of the high court came in 1978, which also went against the gold workers. The gist of the verdict was that they were all independent manufacturers, doing their own businesses, expending their own capital and skill. By this definition, there were no merchants in the gold trade as well. They were another group of independent manufacturers who only sold their own products and in this process took occasional help from certain other manufacturers (artisans). So the gold trade in Kerala became unique in and by itself as there were only manufacturers and 'industry owners' in it, and no labourers or artisans, in the period of the Gold Control Act.[26]

The given analysis tries to partially unravel the predicament of Vishwakarma goldsmiths with particular emphasis on the important role that gold, as a material, plays in their life. At present, the traditional goldsmiths have reached a vanishing point professionally. Their new generation have already quit the traditional haven, turning themselves into drivers, painters, construction workers, hotel employees, and so on. The general lamentation about their plight is heard from many quarters including political parties and the government. But under this clamour, the real villain, the gold, escapes; only to territorialize itself in a new hub to begin its historic journey towards destruction, which started with early history.

Notes

1. Richard Handler, 'Cultural Theory in History Today', *The American Historical Review*, vol. 107, no. 5, 2002, pp. 1514–15.
2. Christopher Tilley, *Reading Material Culture: Structuralism, Hermeneutics and Post-Structuralism*, Oxford: Basil Blackwell, 1990, p. vii.
3. Tim Ingold, 'Materials against Materiality', *Archaeological Dialogues*, vol. 14, no. 1, 2007, p. 2.
4. Ibid., pp. 3–4.
5. David Pye, *The Nature and Art of Workmanship*, Cambridge: Cambridge University Press, 1968, p. 47.
6. Alain Badiou, *Manifesto for Philosophy*, Albany: State University of New York Press, 1999, p. 144.

7. Ibid., p. 9.
8. Ibid., p. 36.
9. Alain Badiou, *Theoretical Writings*, London: Continuum, 2004, pp. 98–9.
10. Gold Demand Trends 2015, World Gold Council, p. 21. See https://www.gold.org/research/gold-demand-trends/2015, accessed on 26 May 2018.
11. Since gold is caught up in smuggling and illicit trade practices, we cannot get any reliable data about the exact volume of trade. According to office holders of Jewellery Manufacturers' Association, Thrissur alone manufactures 500 kg. gold jewellery per day. Also, 1,000 kg. of gold jewellery is traded in Kerala on a daily basis (though this data seems exaggerated). According to P.V. Jose, the chief patron of the Jewellery Manufacturers' Association, Kerala has 6,000 jewellery shops. In my own interviews with office-bearers of All Kerala Gold and Silver Merchants Association (AKGSMA), I have found that there are around 7,000 retail shops in Kerala that include unregistered ones also. Calculating from the shop sales and other sources, it can be said that around 130 tons of gold is consumed in Kerala annually. I must emphasize here that I have received starkly varying information about the quantity of annual consumption of gold in Kerala in the various phases of my fieldwork. So, precision in this data is not claimed.
12. See https://www.gold.org/research/gold-demand-trends/2015, accessed on 26 May 2018.
13. Peter L. Bernstein, *The Power of Gold: The History of an Obsession*, New York: John Wiley & Sons, Inc., 2000.
14. Timothy Green, *The New World of Gold: The Inside Story of the Mines, the Markets, the Politics, the Investors*, New York: Walker & Company, 1981, p. 1.
15. A few of the rare facts about gold's quantity and distribution are taken from the World Gold Council's literature; see www.gold.org, accessed on 23 May 2018.
16. Brian Kettell, *Gold*, Oxford: Oxford University Press, 1982, pp. 3–5.
17. The Syrian Christian copperplates depict the rights granted by the kings of Kerala to the Syrian Christian community. The languages used in these copperplates are Tamil, Pahlavi, and Vattezhuthu. Though differences in opinion exist about the exact dating of each of the copperplates, there is a consensus that some of these are dated from the ninth century.
18. V. Nagam Aiya, *The Travancore State Manual*, vol. II, Thiruvananthapuram: Kerala Gazetteer's Department, 1999, p. 126.
19. Benjamin Walker, *Hindu World: An Encyclopedic Survey of Hinduism*, vol. II, New York: Frederick A. Praeger, 1968, p. 543.
20. There is also a story about a goldsmith who made a nose ring for his mother without filching and then began to pine from remorse. He could not eat or sleep until he got it back by cutting off her nose. (Jamila Brijbhushan, *Indian*

Jewellery, Ornaments and Decorative Designs, Bombay: D.B. Taraporevala Sons & Co., 1964, p. 129.)

21. Varghese, *Swarna Keralam*, pp. 113–16.
22. Gilles Deleuze and Felix Guattari, *A Thousand Plateaus: Capitalism and Schizophrenia*, tr. Brian Massumi, Minneapolis: University of Minnesota Press, 1987, pp. 444–5.
23. T.K. Bhanu, 'Swarna Niyanthrana Chattavum Swarna Thozhilalikalum', *Souvenir of All Kerala Gold Workers' Union*, Alappuzha: AKGWU, 1980, p. 37.
24. Gold Control Act, 1963, amended in 1968, Chap. 8, p. 40.
25. In 2001, they created a record in the history of labour struggles by holding a non-stop *dharna* or siege for 171 days before the shop of the office-bearer of the Gold Merchants' Association in Kayamkulam that started on 21 February.
26. The details about the Gold Control Act and its impact on goldsmiths were gathered through conversations and interviews with a number of senior goldsmiths and office-bearers of different labour and caste organizations like AKGWU, STSS, AKVMS, KVS, etc.

3

Some Random Thoughts on Artists in the Early Middle Ages

R.N. MISRA

The early Middle Ages in Indian history is marked as a period of phenomenal growth of temple architecture and allied art activity that presuppose the existence of a group or community of artists exclusively engaged in such work.[1] The monuments and sculptures surviving from that time period and the epigraphs concerning them indicate that building temples had become a broad socio-religious movement in which donors represented a cross-section of society–from elites to commoners (including a cobbler on one instance).[2] Evolution of different styles of temple architecture, sculptures, iconography, their canon, and coming into being of several schools of *śilpa* namely, Viśvakarmā, Kaśyapa, Śukra, Tvaṣṭṛ, Manu, Māṇḍavya, etc.,[3] indicate a burgeoning state of activity with accent both on diversification and specialization.[4] It would be interesting to examine where the artists figured in these developments and whether they (mainly architects and sculptors) or their collectives could manage to alter the social and economic conditions in their favour, even as their prescribed *śudra* status remained.

Our enquiry into these issues leads us to probe into the existential reality about artists at two levels, i.e. artists in their individual capacity and artists as part and parcel of an exclusive community or a social group, and their interaction with the prevailing socio-economic structure.[5] In

* This is a revised version of my paper 'Artists in the Early Middle Ages', in *Indian Studies: Essays Presented in Memory of Prof. Niharranjan Ray*, ed. Amita Ray et al., Delhi: Caxton Publications, 1984, pp. 65–72. In this essay, I have used the standard diacritic symbols for the Sanskrit and other classical Indian languages.

both these situations, the identities of the artists are found to be surfacing and getting consistently manifest now. The notion about 'anonymity' of ancient Indian art tradition therefore becomes progressively untenable as identities continue to emerge unambiguously.[6] Independent of field data (in the form of masons' marks), our source material concerning artists, during the time period under review, consists primarily of epigraphs and literature, and in case of the latter, both secular and religious. This entire data tends to reveal their growth in various ways, marking their break from *Dharmaśastra*-imposed debilities and their ability to rise both socially and economically with dignity and honour. This was a consequence of the fact that they met the rising demand for creating different types of artwork, getting organized into guild-like collectives, and diversifying into the professional cadres of *sūtradhāra, śilpī, vijñānika*, and *rūpakāra* or into the feudal categories of *rāṇaka, ṭhakkura*, and *sāmanta*. It is through these attainments and other dispensations, which added to their expertise and authority, that they seem to have improved and uplifted their status. We may deal with some of these points in more detail.

Sporadic references to artists' 'collectives' mark an important development during the early Middle Ages, which distinguishes the period from the earlier phases.[7] Although quantitatively the information on the point is scanty, terms like *goṣṭhī, pūga*, and *gaṇa* in reference to artists seem to hint at some kind of guild organization among them. One such *śilpī-goṣṭhī* from Vārendra is mentioned in an inscription that refers to *rāṇaka* Śūlapāṇi as its *cūḍāmaṇi* (chief).[8] A Cālukyan inscription refers to *sarva-siddha ācārya*s who were well-versed in the secrets of *śrī-śilā-muḍḍe*.[9] The term may signify some organization of artists. The inscription also refers to the modalities of banishment (of artists) and their re-admission into the fold, which should indicate that functionally the artists belonging to their organizations or collectives were bound by certain codes of professional conduct that, if infringed, invited disciplinary action. Inscriptions from Karnataka refer to the artists of Sarasvatī and Deśī *gaṇa*s, where the term *gaṇa* possibly signifies a 'guild'. Scattered references to Dasojā, an artist of Balligame (Shimoga district) in Karnataka, who belonged to Sarasvatī *gaṇa*, afford details of the work done by him at different temples in Karnataka.[10] The titles like *pāthuriyā paryaṅga nāyaka, śilpī nāyaka*, and *kulapata sāmanta*, designating the *śilpī*s in eastern India,[11] similarly indicate the existence of some kind of confederation among artists, whose chiefs carried those titles.

It is likely that guilds of artists may have formed as a result of their localization in certain villages. For instance, eastern Indian inscriptions refer to the artists of Pośali, a village in Bengal. The available evidence indicates that these artists remained linked to the village for several generations. Among them, reference has been made to Mahīdhara (son of Vikramāditya), Śaśidhara, Puṣyāditya (son of Candrāditya), and Śaśideva (son of Hṛddeva)—all from Pośali.[12] It was perhaps a practice among rulers in the early Middle Ages to establish artisan villages by granting them land after some major work was accomplished. This might have been done to compensate the artists and workmen for the work that they did. It also ensured that the monument so built to suit the patron's aspirations would not suffer from neglect and remain ever supplied with skilled masons and artisans for proper maintenance. The inference is based on information concerning land grants made to different categories of artists and other workers after completion of the Konark Sun Temple. The patron prince of the temple is said to have granted 15 *mānas* (a measure) of land by the side of the 'Konākana' temple to each one of the 224 stonemasons (*pāthuriyās*) in order to establish a stonemasons' community there. Vāsudeva Mahāpātra, a master artist, was similarly 'settled' in the Gaḍaviguḍā village, and in addition to that, he was appointed the *bhoga-bisoi* of the temple. Association of artists with temples to ensure its maintenance is indicated by the Teli inscription of Korai Ravi also. It refers to administration and maintenance of a temple in which, besides temple officials, managers, dancers, and actors, painters and sculptors also find mention.[13] The existence of exclusive village settlements of skilled artists may be surmised on the basis of masons' marks from Tilori in Bhind district, Madhya Pradesh (see Plate 3.1). The village once had several temples and there were many a temple site in its vicinity as well. The masons' marks that occur at Tilori on the steps of its dried up lake are found in plenty of other contemporary or later monuments, including temples (from the tenth to fourteenth centuries) at places like Ranod, Padhavali, Mitaoli, and in the vicinity of Gwalior (Sas-Bahu Temple). These are known even from monuments of the Sultanate and Mughal periods at Jaunpur, Allahabad, Kashmir, Lahore, and many other places.[14]

The localization of artists at selected sites might have helped in the formation of 'guilds' among them.[15] So perhaps did the likes of gharanas (as in music) too, in organizing artists in specialized groups. Such specialized groups or collectives, with the institution of family at their core, seem to have been basic to artists' training. Households

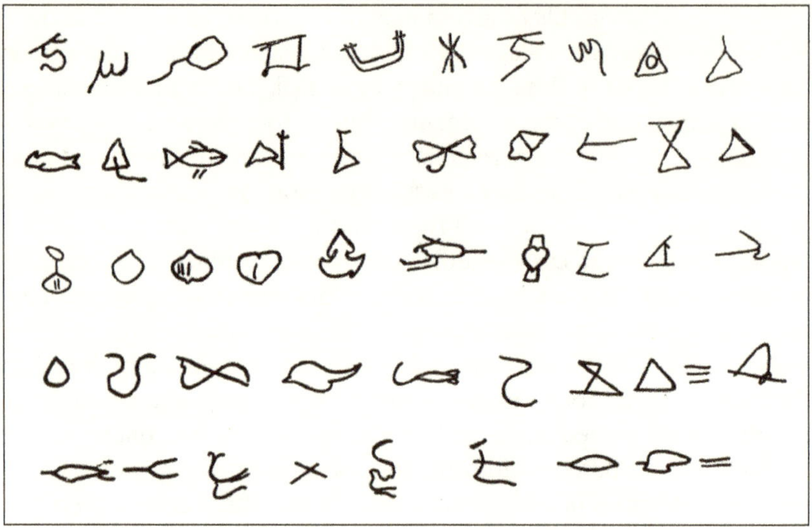

PLATE 3.1: Masons' marks from Tilori in Bhind district.

Source: Recorded by the author during a field trip to Tilori in the late 1970s; Amita Ray et al., eds., *Indian Studies: Essays Presented in Memory of Prof. Niharranjan Ray*, Delhi: Caxton Publications, 1984.

tended to become the workshop of the young artists, where the father or the elder members of the family assumed the role of a guru. Perhaps the earliest epigraphic reference to such a family is found in a pre-Kuṣāna(?) inscription from Jamalpur area in Mathura. The inscription refers to setting up of a slab at the shrine of Naga Dadhikarṇa by the 'boys', the chief among whom was Nandibala. These boys were the sons of the *śilālakas* (stonemasons) of Mathura and were known as 'Chandaka brothers' (*śailālaka bhrātṛkas*).[16] In most artists' families, training in crafts was imparted with little gender discrimination. There is evidence indicating that the *vadhūs* (daughters-in-law) were given such training and they possessed skills that enabled them to execute works with excellence. For instance, we know of *citrakāra* Śrī Sātana of the Jejakabhukti (Candella) region, whose son and daughter-in-law respectively carved the famous eleventh century images of Bodhisattva and Tārā from Mahoba.[17] The image of Tārā by Sātana's daughter-in-law is superbly executed and compels attention. It is now preserved in the State Museum, Lucknow. Information about women's engagement in art activities is also available from certain other instances from Konark and Rajasthan. In case of Rajasthan, there are references to Pāhinī, who constructed the *maṇḍapa* (pavilion), *akṣasāma*, and *damā*(?) of the temple of Bhivaḍeśvara-Śiva. In doing so, he seems to have been assisted by Jasadevī and also by *sūtradhāra* Mahīdhara and Indārka.[18] The different parts of the temple were made of bricks and stone, and the cost of construction is computed at 330 *drammas*, which possibly represents the wages accruing to Pāhinī and his associates.[19]

The foregoing details help in defining some aspects of the artists' institutional setup where their organization, inclusive of women, in terms of guilds or gharanas seems indicated. But many changes have surfaced over time in different aspects, as compared to the earlier scenario. A comparison of the categories of artists in the Middle Ages with that of even earlier times indicates:

1. disappearance of certain categories of artists like *rūpadakṣa, śailālaka, śaila-vardhakī, miṭhika, kaḍhicaka, kammantika, āveśanin, navakarmika*, and *sūtragrāhin*;
2. emergence of some new categories like *sūtradhāra, akṣaśālin* (or *arkaśālin*), and *vijñānika*;
3. continuation of some of the earlier categories like *sthapati, takṣaka, vardhakī, rūpakāra*, and *śilpī*.[20]

The period under review is also remarkable for the instances that indicate transfer of roles of the state functionaries to those of artists and vice versa. This transformation was subtle and has reference to the formation of professional and political categories of artists during the period. These developments help in defining hierarchies among artists' ranks vis-à-vis the then current bureaucratic setup and their mutual relationship.

Inscriptions from north India indicate the existence of various categories of artists, consisting of *rūpakāra, śilpī, vijñānika, sūtradhāra*, and *karmakāra*.[21] The relative frequency of references to them indicates predominance of the first four of these categories.[22] That these categories or classes were interlinked and represented some kind of hierarchy in the artists' professional setup is suggested by the case of Pālhaṇa, a master artist of the twelfth century. He is first mentioned in an inscription dated 1159 CE, when he was working as an ordinary artisan (with no titles) in the team of *sūtradhāra* Kamalasimha, building a temple of Ambikā along with a ghat and a road leading to the ghat. Afterwards, Pālhaṇa finds mention in a Candella inscription of 1165 CE, where he is described as a *pītalakāra* (brazier). Five years later, in 1170 CE, he is referred to as a *śilpī*, and two years thence, he came to be designated as a *vijñānika*. This process of acquiring recognition continued even further and in two inscriptions dated 1175 CE and 1178 CE, he is mentioned as an expert in the Viśvakarmā discipline (*vaidagdhī Viśvakarmā*). These different designations applied to Pālhaṇa indicate that they represented hierarchical positions in the ascending order. They help in linking up those different ranks and in concluding that professionally an artist (in this case, a sculptor) could rise up in hierarchy as he grew in experience and expertise.[23]

The highest position in the hierarchy seems to have belonged to *sūtradhāra*; the preponderance of references to their exalted status helps to come to this conclusion.[24] For instance, a Kalachuri inscription refers to the illustrious *sūtradhāra* Pīṭhe as having 'planned all (the structures) as Pṛthu did the earth'.[25] The *Baya Chakaḍa* refers to the appointment of Sadāśiva Sāmantarāya Mahāpātra as *sūtradhāra* (chief architect) who started the process of recruitment of at least seven different kinds of artists and craftsmen and their contingents for building the Konark Sun Temple by appointing *karmakāra*, *mūrtikāra* (sculptors), *svānśya* (stonemasons), *cūnurā* (plasterers), and *kamarakanṭa* (iron-casters). Other workers later joined the camp that was set up for those who were assigned this task.[26] They are found to have worked under the direction of the *sūtradhāra*, who allotted work, accepted or rejected the finished works and controlled the work process in various ways.

Patronage of rulers to *sūtradhāras* and their appointment to carry out specific works helped in rendering their position and rank prestigious and lucrative.[27] It is thus no wonder that elites are found competing to usurp their role as well as their designation. For instance, an inscription from south India refers to Mallavijaya, son of a *danḍanāyaka*, as the *sūtradhāra* responsible for enlarging a town.[28] Instances of those who changed their (hereditary?) profession to that of an artist can be represented by Nāgapāla, the son of *panḍita* Uhila; Jayasiṃha, the son of a *panḍita*; Yaśodhara and Sarvacandra, sons of a *bhogika*; and Cheddi, who was himself a *bhogin*, given to engraving a record.[29] An inscription dated 956 CE from Rajasthan refers to a kshatriya who took up the profession of *sūtradhāra*. Yet another inscription dated 636–7 CE from Kusuma (Rajasthan) mentions a kshatriya named Sthāvara engraving a record, a job that artists are often found to have done, in addition to their primary architectural work.[30] These instances indicate that the stigma of 'low caste' attached to artists (*śilpins*) in ancient India was gradually being dispensed with. This may be particularly true about the artists of the ranks *rūpakāra*, *vijñānika*, *śilpī*, *akṣaśālin*, and *sūtradhāra*. In certain cases, artists are found to have been invested with 'feudal' titles. For instance, Śulapāṇi, the chief of the *śilpī-goṣṭhī* of Vārendra is mentioned as *rāṇaka*; Paṇaka and Khaṇḍimalla of Odisha are similarly known as *ṭhakkura* and *sāmanta* respectively.[31]

The instances of Mallavijaya and others are not the only ones to show a transition of persons of other ranks and social status into the functional setup of the artists. Evidences showing state functionaries of subordinate status, such as *vāstavya*, *kāyastha*, and *karaṇika*, making incursions into the community of artists and discharging the latter's functions are also present. *Kāyastha* Devagaṇa,[32] who is mentioned as *rūpakāra śiromaṇi* ('the crest jewel among sculptors'), built the temple of Śiva-Bilvapāṇi at Samba (Chhattisgarh). The *vāstavya*s Vidyādhara and Puruṣottama designed and built a temple of Rāma and excavated a tank near Rewa.[33] However, it needs to be mentioned as well that a Kalachuri epigraph refers to *śilpī* Sarvānanda functioning as a *karaṇika*.[34]

There seems to be a duality in the situations representing a 'role shift' in the aforementioned cases. While one shows a *śilpī* performing the role of *karaṇika*, the other indicates *kāyasthas* and *vāstavyas* apparently surrogating to themselves the role of artists. The instances relating to the latter case may indicate that architects and sculptors had infiltrated into the ranks of *karaṇikas* and *kāyasthas*, rendering them fit for accomplishing the work that normally an artisan would do. In the instances given, it can be seen that none of these persons in the bureaucratic setup really relinquished his original role or title while performing the work that was normally assigned to masons or artisans. Alternatively, it may be suggested that a section of the bureaucratic rank and file had allotted to itself the tasks that conventionally went to artisans. This, in turn, categorically points to the scaling up of the occupation of an 'artisan', indicating that the stigma erstwhile attached to it was being gradually dispensed with, and others of diverse ranks were joining this profession because it no longer compromised their social status or position.

It would thus appear that due to the transition of architects and sculptors into the ranks of state functionaries and vice versa, different roles were getting merged into the same office, and that the persons occupying such offices could afford to switch over their functions to suit new requirements, even though their traditional functions might have continued. The emergent situation, in any case, represents mobility in the ranks of artists, indicating at the same time, an intermingling and interchangeability of activities in the aforementioned offices.

The exclusion of artists (such as *sūtradhāra*, *śilpī*, *rūpakāra*, etc.) from the royal charters, in the list of addresses,[35] and the politically neutral existence of those categories of artists even as they were being drafted in the bureaucracy, apparently presents a contradiction that can be explained by positing that 'role shifts' were selective and not on a large scale. The situation may further be explained by assuming that the artists' organizational setup was more or less exclusive, notwithstanding its coexistence with bureaucracy and power structure. Exclusivity of artists' professional categories might have been actuated by the fact that their skills were widely marketable, not being merely confined to states or potentates.

Competition among artists was stiff and it militated against their localization or their firmly settled residential status.[36] As a result, artists had to follow an itinerant or migratory regimen for work during the creative period of their careers. We have the instance of a scribe Kumarapala, whose tenure saw him collaborating with no less than six artists in a period of approximately sixteen years. This would indicate that state functionaries had a longer term of service while artists consistently kept moving out to 'fresh pastures'.[37] It also points to the lack of any regular office for artists in the state's bureaucratic setup. It may however be conceded that as a result of the artists' entry into the offices of *karaṇika* and others, and also due to the persons of other ranks and varnas joining the community of artists, the position and prestige of artists have improved. This is indicated also by the fact that they had taken over feudal positions of *rāṇaka, ṭhakkura*, and *sāmanta,* and such a rise definitely indicates their upward mobility in terms of status and position during the Middle Ages.

Certain disabilities imposed on artists—*śilpas* were traditionally assigned to the śudras in the *Dharmaśastra*—seem to have been dispensed with during this time as well. Instances are known of *sūtradhāras*, *śilpīs*, and *rūpakāras* eulogized as the 'knower of *śāstra*'. An inscription refers to Chītaku as the 'ocean of five sciences' or, 'a perfect master of sciences', 'proficient in *Śilpaśāstras*'; his younger brother Maṇḍana is described as *śāstra-japī*.[38] Artists seem to have sometimes been linked to *brāhmaṇa* priests for some guidance on religious requirements of the work at hand. This is indicated by some instances from different regions. For example, a metal image from Hatkoti (Himachal Pradesh) carries an inscription indicating that it was cast by an artist according to the prescriptions of a *brāhmaṇa*.[39] The instance of such a linkage between the two, i.e. an artist and a priest—considering that one would be a *śudra* and the other a *brāhmaṇa*—from Odisha, reveal a different story. The text of *Baya Chakaḍa* has it that when work was started at Konark for building the Sun temple, two camps were set up: one for the *brāhmaṇas* and the other for the (*śudra*) craftsmen. One of these camps, called Vedapura, was settled with the Ātreya *brāhmaṇas*, who were experts in *Śilpaśāstras*, while the other camp, known as Rūpāsa, was settled with artists and craftsmen.[40] Functionally however, the *brāhmaṇas* seemed to have had only a marginal role and significance in temple-building, for references to their activity are made only in connection with the performance of rituals. On the contrary, the primacy of artists is indicated by the quantum of work that they did, and by the decisions that they took. For instance, at a certain time, when a dispute arose on whether payment according to the contract should be made to a *śilpī* for supplying three *kanyā* (female) figures, the decision about the conformity of these figures to the canon was taken by a council of artists, without any reference to the *brāhmaṇas*. The dispute having been resolved in favour of the *śilpī* in this case, he received the payment of six gold *madha*s for the three figures.[41] The *brāhmaṇas* figure nowhere in this entire episode as the dispute was resolved by the council of artisans.

Artists seem to have been compensated for their work in different manners. Sometimes they received plots of land as reward, while at times payment was made to them in cash. Work used to be done by them on the basis of contracts also. The Malkapuram inscription of Rudrāmbā's period (1261 CE) indicates that artists enjoyed the rights of the lands granted to them. The inscription describes the activities of a *Golakī maṭha* (a Saivite monastery), which employed eight kinds of artisans—goldsmiths, coppersmiths, blacksmiths, carpenters, stonemasons, makers of stone images, potters, and *sthapatis*. The *maṭha* employed *vīramuṣṭi*s and *vīrabhadras* too, the force that carried out castration (*bījaccheda*), mutilations of skull (*śirasccheda*) and body (*kukṣicchedādi*), etc., (of the recalcitrants!) living within the property of the monastery.[42] The details in the epigraph indicate that the officials and others employed by the *maṭha* were assigned land, whose emoluments they enjoyed with the rights of ownership.

In the case of the artists employed at the Rupāsa camp during the construction of the Konark Sun Temple, payment on the basis of contracts and wages were handed out to them in cash or in kind.[43] The *Baya Chakaḍa* record that artists and other workmen received different gifts when the camp was dispersed following the completion of the project. Accordingly, the *sūtradhāra* received from the ruler 'three *krośa* of land extending from east to west in the Laṅkapada *viṣaya* as a life endowment with *dakṣiṇā*'. Another master artist Sadānanda Pattanāyaka received gift of land in Sadānandapura. Goldsmiths got land for building their houses in Sānalapura, where land was granted to 108 stonemasons also. Land measuring fifteen *mānas*—according to Alice Boner, 1 *māna* was equal to 1 acre or 4,820 sq. yds.—was given to each of the 224 stonemasons near the temple site, so as to establish a community of those artisans there. This system of giving land and wages or making payment according to the stipulated contract was probably followed in case of artists elsewhere also by other patrons. The fact that artists paid taxes is indicated by a Pallava inscription which refers to certain regulations on the matters involving such collections from artists and craftsmen.[44]

In the foregoing discussions, a valuation of the status of artists has been attempted within the framework of their professional setup. The varna-jati model does not seem to be appropriate in such a study as it groups the *śilpīs* together within the wider fold of the fourth varna and fails to recognize their distinctions, including their contribution in different areas of their activity. It has been observed that the same artists worked on sculptures or temples of different religious sects. 'Hindu' artists constructed 'Muslim' monuments and 'Muslim' artists and craftsmen were recruited for working on 'Hindu' monuments. They worked for a patron regardless of the latter's social rank, religious temper or sectarian affiliation. Discussions on these points may not be relevant here, but the points do emphasize the professional character of artists' organization and their function in the Middle Ages. By being able to alter their occupational status, income, acculturation, and prestige in their favour, artists were able to rise high in estimation and achieve social mobility, dignity, and honour. That some of them even acquired the status of feudal chiefs is conveyed by the titles that they came to acquire. Relegated to the lower ranks in the hierarchy of social order and denied privileges that others enjoyed, they were eventually able to carve out for themselves a position or status that others too vied to acquire. This reversal of roles is not without significance whether in history as a whole, or specifically in art history.

Notes

1. D.N. Jha, 'Temple as Landed Magnate', in *Indian Society: Historical Probing*, ed. R.S. Sharma, New Delhi: People's Publishing House, 1974, pp. 191–202.
2. R.N. Misra, 'Artists of Dahala and Daksina Kosala', in *Indian Epigraphy: Its Bearing on the History of Art*, ed. F.M. Asher and G.S. Gai, Delhi: IBH and Oxford, 1985, pp. 187–8; V.V. Mirashi, *Inscriptions of the Kalachuri-Chedi Era, Corpus Inscriptionum Indicarum*, vol. 4, no. ii, Ootacamund: Govt. Epigraphist for India, 1955, ins. no. 108.

3. R.N. Misra, *Ancient Artists and Art-Activity*, Shimla: Indian Institute of Advanced Study, 1975, p. 45; R.N. Misra, *Śilpa in Indian Tradition: Concept and Instrumentalities*, Shimla: Indian Institute of Advanced Study and New Delhi: Aryan Books International, 2009.
4. Specialization might have been necessitated to meet the requirements of religious sects and subsects that tried to regulate art activity according to their tenets and temper. For instance, we have *Āgama*s and their ritualistic modes that have a definite bearing on mannerisms of architecture and iconography.
5. R.N. Misra, 'Ancient Indian Artists: Organizations in Lieu of Guilds', in *Indian Art History: Changing Perspectives*, ed. Parul Pandya Dhar, New Delhi: D.K. Printworld and National Museum, 2011.
6. It has to be conceded that connecting different works with individual artists firmly would still be difficult and may have pitfalls, which need to be overcome.
7. During the earlier phases, artists usually operated within certain specific frameworks. Some of these were: (i) the varna-jati system; (ii) institutionalized religions, particularly Buddhist *samghas*; (iii) patronage of rulers, elites and commoners; (iv) state control; and (v) some sort of a quasi-guild system (Misra, 'Ancient Indian Artists'). Guilds are not specifically reported in case of architects and sculptors, unlike what is done in case of other craftsmen and artisans.
8. For the title *rāṇaka*, as also *ṭhakkura* and *sāmanta*, indicating 'clan monarchies', see Irfan Habib, 'Landed Property in Pre-British India', in *Indian Society: Historical Probings*, ed. R.S. Sharma, New Delhi: People's Publishing House, 1974, p. 285; U.N. Ghoshal, *Contributions to the History of the Hindu Revenue System*, Calcutta: University of Calcutta, 1929, pp. 241, 259–60; quoted in Habib, 'Landed Property in Pre-British India', p. 285. Habib indicates how 'new potentates' such as *sāmanta, rāṇaka,* and *ṭhakkura* emerged as dominant groups as a result of the 'territorial distribution that took place among dominant class. . . '. About Śūlpāṇi, see: Misra, *Ancient Artists and Art-Activity*, p. 43, fn. 7.
9. *Epigraphia Carnatica*, vol. V, B.1, 34; *Epigraphia Carnatica*, B.1, 36; B.1, 37; *AK*, 37, 52; *AK*, vol. VII, *SK*, 136; Ibid., Sb. 289; vol. II, 173; M. Sheshadri, 'Sculptors and Architects of Ancient and Medieval Karnataka', *Half Yearly Journal of Mysore University*, vols. XXIX–XXX, 1970–1, pp. 1–10. In these inscriptions, Dasoja is mentioned in reference to his works at Kallur (1138 CE), Shravan Belgola (1145 CE), Kanakatte (1152 CE), and Talalur (1185 CE), covering a period of forty-seven years. This might indicate existence of more than one artist of that name. Dasoja is said to have made the images of Śukabhāṣiṇī and dancing Durga at Belur, Acyutamūrti at Balligame, and Keśavamūrti at Kikkeri (A.V. Narasimhamurti, 'A Study of Label Inscriptions of the Hoysala Sculptures', in *Indian Epigraphy*, ed. F.M. Asher and G.S. Gai, Delhi: IBH and Oxford, 1985, pp. 215–20.

10. Narasimhamurti, 'A Study of Label Inscriptions', p. 216.
11. Alice Boner, 'Economic and Organizational Aspects of Building Operation of the Sun Temple at Konark', *Journal of the Economic and Social History of the Orient*, vol. XIII, no. 3, 1970, p. 262.
12. Misra, *Ancient Artists and Art-Activity*, p. 70.
13. Ibid., p. 62, fn. 134; p. 63, fn. 135.
14. See also Misra, *Śilpa in Indian Tradition*, pp. 185–206.
15. Settlement of artists at particular sites did not always restrict them to those locations only. References to itinerant artists are numerous. Occurrences of identical masons' marks after gaps of many years and in places far away from each other indicate the itinerant nature of artists who belonged to different *gharānas* or guilds. The instance of Kokāsa lineage of artists presents a typical instance of their peripatetic nature. Kokāsa is first mentioned in 1159 CE, in the team of a *sūtradhāra* Kamalasimha in the Satna region (Madhya Pradesh). Afterwards, a *śilpin* of the Kokāsa family can be traced to the Jabalpur region (Madhya Pradesh) and the most illustrious *sūtradhāra* of the (Kokāsa) family then was Chītaku; others of the family included Dityan, Maṇḍana and Manmatha. The scions moved from Satna to Chandella territory, then to Jabalpur region, and finally are located in Chhattisgarh at Ratanpur. For further reference to Chītaku and Kokāsa, see: R.N. Misra, 'Profile of an Indian Artist', in *Paroksa: Coomaraswamy Centenary Seminar Papers*, ed. Gulam Mohammed Sheikh et al., Delhi: Lalit Kala Akademi, 1984, p. 66.
16. Heinrich Luders, *Mathura Inscriptions*, ed. K.L. Janert, Gottingen: Vandenhoeck & Ruprecht, 1961, pp. 62–3. The term *śailālaka* is translated as 'actors'. We take it to mean 'stonemason' in view of the term's obvious association with *śaila* or *śilā*, meaning 'stone'. For another reference to *śailālaka*, see: Misra, *Ancient Artists and Art-Activity*, p. 15, fn. 59.
17. C. Sivaramamurti, *Indian Sculpture*, Delhi: Allied Publishers, 1961, p. 5.
18. Participation of women in art activities is also indicated by the case of Sūnā, a sculptress who 'took part in chiselling portal frames in the Konark temple' (see Boner, 'Economic and Organizational Aspects', p. 265).
19. R.N. Misra, 'A Note on Nadlai Inscription of Kelhana', in *Indian Epigraphy*, ed. F.M. Asher and G.S. Gai, Delhi: IBH and Oxford, 1985, pp. 191–2.
20. For these different categories, see: Misra, *Ancient Artists and Art-Activity*.
21. Ibid., pp. 34–53. For a *sthapati samrāt*, see D.R. Bhandarkar, 'List of Inscriptions in Northern India', Appendix in *Epigraphia Indica*, vols. 19–22, no. 1194.
22. Misra, *Ancient Artists and Art-Activity*, pp. 52–3.
23. Ibid.
24. Mirashi, *Inscriptions of the Kalachuri-Chedi Era*, ins. no. 317. *Sūtradhāra* Śambhūka is similarly said to have 'carried out' the work of building a temple dedicated to Vishnu. Mirashi, *Inscriptions of the Kalachuri-Chedi Era*, pp. 235, 311.

25. Ibid., p. 317; see also pp. 235, 311.
26. Alice Boner et al., *New Light on the Sun Temple of Koṇārka: Four Unpublished Manuscripts Relating to Construction History and Ritual of this Temple,* Varanasi: Chowkhambha Sanskrit Series Office, 1972, p. 260.
27. *Sūtradhāra* Malla has been mentioned as being a favourite of Prince Bhānu. See K.C. Jain, *Malwa through the Ages*, Delhi: Motilal Banarsidass, 1972, p. 476. The prince himself is supposed to have written *Pramāṇa-Mañjarī*, a text on iconography and architecture. For other references to *sūtradhāras* who were close to rulers, see: R.C. Agrawal, 'Some Famous Sculptors and Architects of Mewar', *Indian Historical Quarterly*, vol. XXXIII, 1957, pp. 326ff.
28. Misra, *Ancient Artists and Art-Activity*, pp. 58, 72.
29. Ibid., p. 58; *Epigraphia Indica* (hereafter *EI)*, vol. 30, pp. 266, 269. The *bhogin* named Cheḍḍi engraved this record and Jayasiṃha, a *peṭapāla* ('keeper of record box') put a *lancchita* (seal) on it. Jayasiṃha figures in the records of the Sailodbhavas of Odisha.
30. *EI*, vol. 36, pp. 48–9.
31. Misra, *Ancient Artists and Art*-Activity, pp. 71–2.
32. Mirashi, *Inscriptions of the Kalachuri-Chedi Era*, ins. no. 93. The term *kāyastha* is etymologically explained as a compound of *kaka* and *sthapati.* If this derivation is correct, then the term may be regarded as having a direct association with *sthapati* (architect).
33. Misra, *Ancient Artists and Art*-Activity, p. 61.
34. Mirashi, *Inscriptions of the Kalachuri-Chedi Era*, ins. no. 250. Likewise, a 'writer' of records claims 'adeptness in *śilpa*'. Ibid., p. 470. Several *karaṇikas*, some of them *kāyasthas*, are mentioned in the Gahadavāla records, though their connections with *śilpa* are not specifically mentioned (*EI*, vol. 4, pp. 101–24). Inscriptions also refer to *karmakāras*, explained as 'chief artisans' by D.C. Sircar (see D.C. Sircar, *Indian Epigraphy*, Delhi: Motilal Banarsidass, 1965, pp. 373–4).
35. For such lists, see Sircar, *Indian Epigraphy*, pp. 351–75.
36. Certain inscriptions from Somanathpuram, Halebidu, and Belur in Karnataka extol the virtues of particular artists while running down their rivals. For instance, Dasojā is described as 'smiter of a crowd of titled sculptors'. His son was to other titled sculptors what 'Śiva was to Kāmadeva' or what '*bheruṇḍa* was to *śarabha*' (Sivaramamurti, *Indian Sculpture*, p. 5). In north Indian inscriptions too, artists are mentioned as *śiromaṇi* (crest jewel) or *agraṇī* (foremost) among each other.
37. Misra, 'Artists of Dahala and Daksina Kosala', p. 188.
38. Mirashi, *Inscriptions of the Kalachuri-Chedi Era*, ins. no. 556.
39. I owe this information to the late Mr Karl J. Khandalavala.
40. Boner et al., *New Light on the Sun Temple of Koṇārka,* pp. 257–72. The

details in their work relate to different aspects of the artists' function in the camp during the period of construction of the Konark Sun Temple.

41. Boner et al., *New Light on the Sun Temple of Koṇārka*, p. 157; *Leaf LX*, 12.
42. D.C. Sircar, *Select Inscriptions*, vol. 2, Delhi: Motilal Banarsidass, 1983, pp. 585–7. The servile status of the artists is indicated also by the instance of a *sūtradhāra* named Sīhaṭa, who is mentioned as a *bhṛtya* (servant/dependent) of the sage Īśānajamu (*tasya karmakāro sūtradhārotra Sīhaṭaḥ*). See D.R. Bhandarkar, *Journal of Bengal and Bihar Research Society*, vol. XII, pp. 151ff. The inscription is from Jhalarapatan and is dated in the ninth century. For yet another reference to the servile status of a sculptor, his wife, and sons; see Nilakantha Shastri, *Chola Vamsa*, Delhi: Macmillan Company of India, 1979, pp. 436–7, fn. 47.
43. Boner et al., *New Light on the Sun Temple of Koṇārka*, p. 270.
44. *EI*, vol. 24, ins. no. 43, lines 18–19.

Caste and Mythologies of the Vishwakarma

4

Casting the Vishwakarma in Peninsular India

VIJAYA RAMASWAMY

The metalsmiths among the Vishwakarma group of craftsmen are famous for their casting of images. This essay turns this particular professional skill on its head to explore the social, especially, caste dimensions of the Vishwakarma community. The essay begins with an exploration of the social and ritual status of the Vishwakarma in ancient peninsular India and concludes with the legal battles fought over the caste status of craftsmen in the nineteenth and twentieth centuries.

Craftsmen, known by the generic term 'Vishwakarma'—the divine architect—played a crucial role in the economy of peninsular India in the early medieval times. The use of the term 'Vishwakarma' indicates that he was the architect of the Gods, as testified repeatedly in texts like the *Bhagavata Purana*, as well as the God of architects—whose image the craftsmen keep in their worship room and offer prayers to before the commencement of any major project. The location of Muslim craftsmen within the trope of 'Vishwakarma' craftsmen is ambiguous, because while the term these days is used as a generic term for craftsmen cutting across religious lines, traditionally the term was used only for craftsmen within the Shakta, Vaishnavite, or Saivite sectarian divisions of Hinduism.

While the rural landscape continued to dominate the economy, there was at the same time the emergence of several urban centres such as Kanchipuram, Tanjavur, Tiruchirapalli, and Madurai. These had, as their nucleus, the great temples whose construction went in tandem with the process of state formation in south India, beginning with the Pallavas in Tondaimandalam around the seventh century CE.

In medieval peninsular India, the Vishwakarma constituted a group of five types of craftsmen and were known in the Tamil region (the term 'Tamilaham' for the Tamil region found in ancient texts, included the modern Kerala region) as 'Kammāḷar', in Karnataka as 'Panchāḷar', and in Andhra Pradesh as the 'Panchananamuvaru'. However, in many of the medieval inscriptions they are also collectively referred to as the 'Rathakarar' or the 'Kammāḷa-Rathakarar'. An outstanding example of this particular nomenclature for craftsmen is the twelfth century inscription from Tiruvarur in Nagapattinam (Tanjavur district), which is a lengthy record dealing with the mixed caste status of the community, concluding with decisions by the brahmin elders on where to locate them (the Vishwakarma) in terms of the social hierarchy and in terms of their profession(s).[1] Today, they prefer to use the nomenclature 'Vishwakarma'—the divine architect from whom they claim descent. The community of Vishwakarma smiths was comprised of five occupational groups—*tattan* (goldsmith), *kannan* (brass smith), *karuman* or *kollan* (blacksmith), *tachchan* (carpenter), and *shilpi* or *kal-tachchan* (mason).

The craft persons collectively referred to as Vishwakarma today constituted a unique artisanal collective that cut through caste and class lines, having as its constituents the humble blacksmith and carpenter, the affluent *sthapati* who was the mason cum architect, and also the *tattan* or *pon kollar* (goldsmith). The primary identity of crafts persons stemmed from their community, rather than their caste identity. Majority of the medieval inscriptions emphasize that artisans belonged to the Vishwakarma *kula* or the Kammāḷar *kula* (*kula* meaning community), rather than detailing his caste affiliation. Inscriptional evidence makes it amply clear that despite belonging to different professions and jatis, these craftsmen claimed a collective identity that transcended caste and class to form the larger community of crafts persons. The Vishwakarma are thus a unique example of five disparate caste groups coming together in a new community identity, developing the contours of caste, and re-integrating itself into the caste system and ritual hierarchies.

This essay seeks to explore the very complex trajectories taken by the caste question in the context of the Vishwakarma community. In an attempt to trace the complexities of this issue, the essay not only looks at the ancient past of the Vishwakarma craftsmen, but also at its reflection in the more recent past. For instance, the Vishwakarma sought brahminical status and went to court in many regions—the long-drawn dispute between the Vishwakarma and the brahmin communities, which began in the early twentieth century at Chittoor in Andhra, being the best known. The claims of the Vishwakarma were bitterly contested by the brahmin community who however, lost the case in the Chittoor court. This essay therefore zigzags between the distant past and the recent past/present in order to understand the caste question.

In focusing entirely on the Vishwakarma, one also attempts to answer an oft-repeated question—why did the Kammāḷa-Rathakarar consist only of these five categories, i.e. the three types of smiths, the mason-architect, and the carpenter, and no other? The logical answer would be that it was these five groups who were primarily engaged in the temple-building activities that revived under the Cholas in the eighth and ninth centuries. This type of construction did not involve the mere erection of shrines, but the building of entire temple townships spread over vast areas, such as the Srirangam temple at Tiruchirapalli. The Kammāḷar, weavers, and merchants used to live in the streets on the four sides of these temple complexes.

The term 'Vishwakarma' begins to appear in inscriptions referring to the smiths from the eleventh and more specifically from the twelfth century onwards. The precise nomenclature used is 'Vishwakarma *kula*' or 'Vishwakarma *kulaja*'. The Chebrolu inscription of CE 1118, the Nadindla inscription of CE 1141, and the Tellapur inscription dated CE 1417 state that the smiths and sculptors belonged to the Vishwakarma *kula*.[2] Although different nomenclatures have been used for this community in the medieval period, commencing from the eighth century records till the seventeenth century records, this essay will generally address them as 'Vishwakarma'.

Geographical Location of the Vishwakarma

What emerges on the basis of epigraphical evidence is that at least during the time of Raja Raja and Rajendra Chola, the poorer artisans (called *kizh kalanai*) lived in the *kammanachcheri*, which in terms of its geographical proximity was usually coupled with the *paraichcheri* (place where the paraiyas lived). Interestingly, both these, along with *vannarachcheri* (washermen's street) and *tindachcheri* (area of the untouchables), are mentioned as *iraiyili*, i.e. tax-free lands. This evidence recurs in an entire block of inscriptions dated between the tenth and eleventh centuries from Tanjavur.[3] The reference to the artisanal *cheris* (settlement or habitation) is followed by the reference to *paraikkulam* and *kuzhi*, i.e. ponds and wells of the Paraiyas, as well as the *sudukadu* or cremation grounds. The extent of social differentiation prevailing in the early medieval times and the significance of this fact in terms of the geographical location of the craftsmen is reflected in an inscription of Raja Raja from Tanjavur. It refers to the Vellan *sudukadu*, the cremation ground of the dominant cultivating caste, as distinct from the Parai *sudukadu*, the burning ground of the low caste.[4]

Inscriptional evidence indicates that the areas where the *kammanachcheris* were located, ranged from *brahmadeya* (villages conferred on brahmins) settlements like Karimangalam and Panamangalam, to the Vellan *vagai* or non-brahmin villages like Kizh Vadugakkudi, Kizh Palaru, Ingaiyur, and others.[5] *Kammanachcheris* were also found in *nagarams* such as Tiruttengur.[6] Another important point that emerges from inscriptional evidence is the connection between status and location in relation to the two terms—*purambadi* and *ullalai*. For instance, a record of Raja Raja, also from Tanjavur, mentions that while the *teru* (street) of the *agambadaiyar* (shepherds), *anaiyatkal* (elephant mahouts), and *villigal* (musicians) were a part of *purambadi* or outer city, the *saliya teru* (weavers' street) was a part of *ullalai* or inner city.[7] By this criterion, the *kammanachcheri* stood 'outside' and therefore it may be deduced that the artisans ranked far below the weavers during the Chola period.

It is therefore clear that till the early medieval period, roughly up to the eleventh century, artisans were perceived to be of low caste, with their habitational site being located alongside the Paraiyas, who were deemed to be of low caste (even outcaste) in regions of medieval Tamil Nadu, especially in Cholamandalam and Pandiamandalam, from where many of the inscriptions recording their presence have been found. In Kerala (medieval Keralam), the '*ainkudi* Kammāḷar' or the Kammāḷar of five groups, were seen as migrants and therefore socially inferior to the original inhabitants of the region.

While the available evidence for the early medieval period clearly indicates both the carpenter and the blacksmith to be a part of the hereditary village community, there might have been some efforts on their part towards social and geographical mobility that were effectively blocked by social legislation. For instance, the assembly at Tribhuvani in the erstwhile district of South Arcot states with respect to the carpenters and some other village functionaries in a record dated CE 1113: 'They (the carpenters) should take up such services in the village only. Those who engage themselves in these services beyond this village will be considered to have transgressed the law, to have committed a fault against the great assembly and to have ruined the village.'[8]

Another determinant in defining the caste status of the artisans was the changing dynamics of craft technology. The evidence from the reign of Raja Raja suggests that these Rathakarars had a fairly low status within the caste hierarchy during the Chola times. Thus, the social mobility of the craft groups depended, among other things, on their importance to the economy and the changing nature of both the use of basic craft materials and tools as well as artisanal technology. For example, it has been pointed out by R.N. Misra, in the context of northern India in the early medieval period, that the importance of the *takshaka* or *kashtagara* (carpenters), honoured in ancient India as *rathakara*, was supplanted by that of the stonemason or *shilpi* as the essential building material changed from wood to stone in the post-Mouryan period.[9] Perhaps a similar explanation would hold true for southern India as well. While carpenters, the makers of wooden chariots used in temple rituals, continued to have a social and religious significance, they were socially superseded by the architects/sculptors called *shilpi*. The latter began to command more respect in society and this is reflected in their donations to temples and the fact that these *aasari* (craftsmen) were signatories and witnesses to many of the activities of the temple trustees, is recorded in stone and copperplate inscriptions.

While positing the argument that a change in the primary building material (from wood to stone) may have modified or altered social hierarchies, it is important to note that despite the social stratification that existed between the different categories of craftsmen, the beginning of the era of temple constructions in southern India (eighth century onwards), integrated both carpenters and stoneworkers in the massive enterprise of temple construction and installation of deities. Thus, the collective community identity of the Vishwakarma held together, despite sharp differences in caste status.

A third dimension to the social status of craftsmen is the process of urbanization, which, though connected closely to the emergence of temple townships, also went beyond it to encompass the capital towns/administrative towns called *talai nagaram*, mercantile towns called *nagaram*, port towns called *pattinam*, and military towns called *padaividu*. Most of the metal-workers, the masons/sculptors, and the architects (whom the records refer to as *shilpachariyar*), along with the weavers and the oilmen, participated in the process of urbanization, especially in the emergence of temple towns, in a manner that put them in an advantageous position vis-à-vis other artisanal groups, which were a part of the traditional village community. Those caste groups among the Vishwakarma, especially the goldsmiths, sculptors, and carpenters, who migrated to towns and became a part of temple-centred urbanization, seemed to have enhanced their status and gradually became a part of the *ullalai*, rather than the *purambadi*. It must however be emphasized that the term 'urbanization' here is not being used in its modern sense, but in a much more limited sense, since the dividing line between town and country was not very sharp in medieval India. In fact a more convenient term for this period would be the portmanteau word 'rurban', a term coined by Richard Fox which Frank Perlin has most effectively used in his article 'Proto-Industrialization and Pre-colonial South Asia'.[10] It must be noted, however, that this nomenclature to characterize early medieval towns was first used by Richard Fox,[11] without fully exploring its ramifications for the emergence of urbanism. The early medieval period also saw the rise of *nagarams*, which have been translated as 'market towns'.

Inscriptions from the tenth century onwards, which marked the commencement of extensive temple-building activities under the later Cholas, provide evidence of the location of smiths around the *tirumadaivilagam* or temple town, and their participation in the urbanization process. It would be obvious from the Srirangam temple in Tiruchirapalli and the Brahadisvara temple in Tanjavur that these temples were huge architectural complexes with numerous shrines and enclosures, which developed as centres of large-scale trade and craft activities. Every temple had masons, architects, metalsmiths and carpenters attached to them in a permanent capacity and they seem to have lived in and around the *tirumadaivilagam*. The best example of this would be the employment of various categories of smiths at the Brahadisvara temple according to Raja Raja's inscriptions dated CE 1011.[12]

Situating the Vishwakarma: The Artisans and the Craftsmen

The caste status of the Vishwakarma as a collective body, as well as the differentiation and stratification that existed among them in pragmatic terms, depended upon the nature of their role or function, which, in turn, was linked to their physical or geographical location. It would be erroneous to treat craftsmen as a monolithic unit despite their banding together as the 'Vishwakarma'. The distinction between an artisan and a craftsman may seem 'fuzzy' because of the shifting nature of their occupations, but it is nevertheless important to make this distinction. Unless one is aware of the complex layers that underlay craft development in early medieval India, it is possible that one (a perceiver/researcher/historian) may impose one's own teleological vision as an 'orientalist' and 'imperial', or do what the Marxist historians did by imaging the medieval craftsman as a static, immobile figure, enmeshed within a 'honey-combed' caste structure. One of the ways of breaking up this discourse is to look at the producers of craft objects as being distinct from the producers of purely utility commodities such as bricks, which are unvarying in terms of the production process or appearance. Is the man routinely laying bricks or being employed as a workman in the construction of a dam, an artisan or a craftsman? Would the hereditary maker of ploughs in a village have the same position in economy and society as the icon-maker? Inscriptional evidence clearly indicates that artisans and craftsmen represented two different kinds of economies, both of which existed parallel to each other. While the maker of ploughs would exist in the village community with relative physical immobility, socio-economic security, and comparatively static living standards, the metal craftsman, benefiting from the temple economy and an expanding clientele, would be more mobile and have greater opportunities for improving his income while at the same time facing greater economic risks. His risks would primarily arise from the withdrawal of patronage or the decline of temple centres with the fall of dynasties—as in the twelfth and thirteenth centuries with the decline and fading out of the Chola state, or the uncertainties occasioned by the decline and fall of Vijayanagar and the Deccani states. Thus it can be said that while every craftsman was an artisan, every artisan was not a craftsman, because his relationship to the economy, both in terms of his location and function, differed significantly from that of his urban counterpart. To give an example, there were two distinct hierarchical categories even among the goldsmiths. At the lower level was the small-time *tattan*, essentially catering to a custom-determined market, working on a piece-wage and living at the subsistence level. They can be seen even in the present century in south India, sitting at street corners, eking out a living by repairing chains or ornaments as well as piercing ears and noses (a must for women and the girl child among many south Indian communities). At the higher level was the big-time goldsmith, referred to in the inscriptions as *perum-tattan* (literally 'great goldsmith')—indicating a master-craftsman employing apprentice goldsmiths, catering to a fairly wide market, and forming a part of the urban setup.

Another question that comes to mind when one looks at the plethora of historical material on the Vishwakarma is the precise character of this grouping. What is the link between the jati structure or caste system within which the categories of craftsmen (among others) are said to be located and the Vishwakarma community, which is obviously cutting across caste lines? For long, beginning with theorists like Max Weber and Karl Marx, caste has been regarded as a major factor for India's economic and technological backwardness. The classic statement by Marx that crafts in the Indian context 'either petrify into castes or ossify into guilds',[13] was taken up by historians like Morris D. Morris to argue for a situation of technological stasis in the craft structure. Marx, commenting on the fineness of the Dacca muslins, in fact concludes on a note of irony by saying, 'It is only the special skill accumulated from generation to generation and transmitted from father to son that gives to the Hindu, as it does to the spider, this proficiency!'[14] Here I have endeavoured to point out that the functioning of the Vishwakarma as a community comprising five socially and economically differentiated jatis shows that the ground situation, at least in south India's craft history, was much more complex. The situation in ancient south Indian societies was comparatively fluid and community solidarity in certain situations may have taken precedence over jati solidarity. Caste distinctions certainly continued and craftsmen in the rural setting seem to have been known by their individual jati affiliation, rather than as members of the Vishwakarma community. It is in the context of temple-building, where these five craft groups worked in such close coordination, that the concept of 'Vishwakarma *kula*' seems to have predominated over that of separate caste identities. This can be deduced by the location of the inscriptions referring to the 'Vishwakarma *kula*' in the early medieval times, whether one is looking at the Cholas, Pandyas, or Eastern Chalukyas.[15]

Having argued for a more open interpretation of craft groups cutting across caste and embracing the wider notion of craft community, one cannot logically push forward this argument to state that the five jatis within the Vishwakarma community were exogamous. No evidence is forthcoming, one way or the other, in this regard. However, working backwards from the Kallidaikurichchi inscription of the seventeenth century,[16] which records the legal dissociation of the five jatis at the behest of the *tattan*, one could presume that the five castes may have been exogamous up to that point. If economic status was a factor, then the Vishwakarma goldsmiths located in the temple townships would have much more in common (in terms of forming matrimonial alliances) with the affluent smiths settled there than with their poor village counterpart. Although one can deduce the fluidity of caste boundaries among these craftsmen, in the absence of more concrete evidence it is not possible to determine as to how open the Vishwakarma community was to social and familial interaction among these five disparate jati categories.

Name Analysis of Craftsmen

An oft-expressed question by historians, whether they are looking at the arts/aesthetics aspect or the economic aspect, is whether craftsmen in those times worked in total anonymity, or did they sign their names on what they had crafted. In a society where individual identity was, or seemed to be, submerged under caste or community identities, it was not usually the practice of the craftsman to sign his name on his product. Therefore, the instances where such names are available in the records either below a piece of sculpture or beneath a hero stone, or on an engraved inscription become an invaluable source of information in understanding the location of the craftsman in the medieval social milieu. This section studies these names and their social implications.

The majority of inscriptions merely give the name of the engraver such as Revachari, Samundachari, etc., or if the record is from Andhra or Karnataka, the names are usually suffixed by the term 'Oja', such as Dasadomoja, Malloja, etc. An alternate nomenclature to 'Achari' is 'Bhatta'. For instance, an inscription from Badami states that Sri Chandra Kirtiya Bhatta made the sculpture of Durgadevi.[17] The nomenclatures 'Acharya' or 'Achari/Asari' and 'Bhatta' or 'Bhattar' are noteworthy because of the fact that although all craftsmen in south India are located as shudras within the varna order, they were using a suffix usually attached to the names of brahmins. In fact, 'Bhattacharya' is regarded as the highest even among brahmins. It is a fairly common Bengali brahmin surname. Does this indicate the influence of Sanskritization and brahminization from a very early period in south India? The inscriptional evidence definitely points that way. It is worth observing here that the term *karmiyar* is again used in inscriptions ambiguously for both brahmin priests and for craftsmen. Even now, the south Indian Viswakarma *kula*, the name by which the Kammāḷar prefer to be known these days, use the Dravidian versions of these nomenclatures—'Pathar' for 'Bhattar', and 'Asari' for 'Achari'.

The names of the craftsmen themselves vary between Tamil names and Sanskritized names. While Tamil names end with the nomenclature 'Devan' (e.g. Muvendavelar Devan, Achchappan Devan, etc.), all Sanskritized names invariably carry the suffix 'Achari' (e.g. Baladevachari, Somachari, Revachari, etc.). However, in the face of as yet inadequate evidence about these names and the fixing of their geographical locations against a historical setting, mere categorization of these names do not provide us with much information.

Canonical Constructions and Caste and Ritual Location of the Vishwakarma

In terms of their social and ritual status, the origin of the Kammāḷa-Rathakarar was defined as being that of a mixed caste, primarily *anuloma*, i.e. born of a high-born father and low-born mother. In the Tiruvarur inscription of the twelfth century from Pandyakulantaka Chaturvedimangalam[18] (Tanjavur district) and another record from Rajasraya Chaturvedimangalam from Uyyakondan Tirumalai[19] (Tiruchirapalli district) of the same period, it has been found that the brahmin assembly determined the status, rights, and duties of the Kammāḷa-Rathakarar. Based on the *Dharmasastras*, such as *Narada Sutra, Shukra Niti*, and the *Smritis* of Yajnavalkya, Gautama, Maskara, and Bhima, they arrived at the consensus that the Rathakara were primarily *anuloma*, being born of *Mahisha* (vaishya) male and *Karana* (shudra) female. According to some texts, as *anuloma* they could perform the *upanayanam* (the sacred thread ceremony) and *sandhyavandanam* (the special worship of the sun at dawn, dusk and high noon) but silently (*tushnim eva*). Yajnavalkya however forbids them all sacred texts, except those relating to architecture and sculpture like *Agastya Vastu Shastra* and *Visvakarmiya*. Specifically, they had the right to build temples and to sculpt the images of gods.

The *Vaikansa Dharma Sutra* however defines their status as *pratiloma*, i.e. born of a high caste vaishya mother and a low caste shudra father, and says that they were fit only to perform menial tasks like feeding and training horses. The *Smartyarthasara* of Sridhara Bhatta (a south Indian text assignable to 1150 CE) states that a Kammāḷa-Rathakarar born of a *Mahisha* man and a *Karana* woman was in fact a *pratiloma*, and hence no more than a menial artisan. The second major inscription from Uyyakondan (Tiruchirapalli) makes a clear distinction between the *anuloma* Rathakarar and the *pratiloma* smiths who were aspiring towards privileges like *upanayana* (the sacred thread) accorded to the superior Rathakarar.

One could therefore conclude from the rather ambiguous and confusing evidence presented in inscriptional records, especially in the two mentioned, that a Kammāḷa-Rathakarar could be classified as *anuloma* or *pratiloma* depending on the nature of his job, thus providing ritual sanction for the socio-economic differentiation that already existed among the prosperous architects and jewellers on the one hand and the poor village smiths on the other.

Caste Mobility and Caste Conflict in Later Medieval South India

The change in fortune of weavers and smiths with the advent of the Vijayanagar Empire is a striking one. Commercial expansion under the active patronage of the Vijayanagar kings was reinforced by the opening up of new markets with the establishment of the East India Companies. Cloth, for example, was no longer a primary item of barter for spices or Arab horses as in the Chola period, but a commercial product in its own right. The new-found economic prosperity of the weavers and smiths is reflected in the nature and quality of the donations made by them to the temples, temple donation being a primary index of social status in the medieval period. The temples responded by conferring important ritual privileges on these groups and it is significant to note that while in the Chola period there is not a single instance of the conferring of *sangu* and *tandu* (conch shell and palanquin) honours on the weavers, there are more than a dozen such inscriptions in the Vijayanagar period for the Tondaimandalam region alone, between the fifteenth and sixteenth centuries.

The desire for enhanced social status among the artisans was a major factor in the Left Hand-Right Hand (*idangai-valangai*)[20] conflicts and schisms. Each artisan group, claimed for itself, ritual recognition and privileges, and in this it was challenged by rival caste groups. An artisan caste that had registered its higher status by obtaining flags and symbols, assiduously sought to prevent others from obtaining the same, which led to conflicts. These conflicts took place within the framework of the *idangai-valangai* categories. Just as the varna system marks a horizontal division of human society, the *idangai-valangai* division marks a vertical division of the south Indian society.

Rivalry in the *idangai* was usually between the Kammāḷar and the Kaikkolar. A record from Virudhachalam (South Arcot district) registers the decision of the *Nattavar* (the heads of the *nadu*) to withdraw the privileges of *parivattam* and *pavadai* from the Kammāḷar, which they had acquired in imitation of the weavers of certain regions of South Arcot like Senji, Padaividu, and Tiruvannamalai. This was apparently done on the insistence of the weavers.[21] Dissensions seem to have risen even amongst the smiths during this period, and evidence indicates that the goldsmiths increasingly dissociated themselves from the other sections, a process that is evident in their claim for exclusive privileges. In the early seventeenth century, at Kallidaikurichchi in the Tirunelveli district, the smiths finally separated from each other. The inscription records the order of Virappa Nayaka, which stated that the Kammāḷar should not intermingle any longer (*udankoota vendam*). It meant that the five groups of craftsmen who constituted the Kammāḷar could no longer inter-marry among themselves. The writ is said to be a privilege granted to the Kammāḷar goldsmiths in the presence of their chief, Kulasekhara Asari, indicating that the separation of the smiths was at their own instance.[22] The record, however, does not give the reason for this separation.

Society in the Vijayanagar period was in a state of flux. The higher artisan castes, the sat-shudras, had been the chief beneficiaries of urbanization and the expansion of markets—both foreign and domestic. Increasing economic prosperity resulted in their bid for a better social status that revealed itself, unlike in the medieval north, not in caste negation but in caste exaltation. This urge operated in a peculiar fashion. On one hand the artisans sought to overcome ritual restrictions imposed on them due to their low caste status by raising themselves to the level of the brahmins. On the other hand, they assiduously tried to maintain a differential status and even ceremonial pollution in relation to the other shudra castes who were lower to them in the social hierarchy. This dichotomy is best revealed in the observation of the seventeenth century traveller John Fryer:

> But the most insolent were the artificers; as the engravers, refiners, goldsmiths, carpenters, and the like, who behaved themselves not only disrespectfully to their superiors, but tyrannically to those of a viler rank. . . . Whereupon they jointly conspired their ruin and with that their own slavery, taking the Moors to their assistance who not only reduced the usurpers to composition . . . but they also took power into their own hands which though despotical the Gentus endure. . . .[23]

This observation provides a hint of the future history of the artisans in the aftermath of the Vijayanagar Empire. The Vishwakarma grouping seems to have provided one of the flashpoints for conflict in later medieval and early modern times over the burgeoning divisions between right-hand and left-hand communities. Fryer's comment can be applied with even greater justification to the rule of the East India Company in the seventeenth century. Exploiting the caste factor was one of the primary devices through which the colonial masters maintained their hegemony over the artisans of the Black Town.

Origin Mythologies of the Vishwakarma

The dialectical relationship between craft jatis and Viswakarma *kula* is clearly established through their mythologies and oral traditions. The oral traditions of the smiths consist of—(a) origin myths, (b) craft related oral traditions, and (c) ritual status related traditions. Interestingly, although these are basically 'soft evidence', some of these oral traditions assume the form of 'hard evidence' when they are found in the medieval inscriptions. For instance, an inscriptional record dated 1111–12 CE from Macherla in Palnad Taluk, Guntur district of Andhra Pradesh, links the Vishwakarma to Brahma, the divine creator.[24]

Many of the origin myths can be found in the *Vishwakarma Puranam* written in Tamil.[25] The work does not have an author and different stories and local legends seem to have been incorporated into it—some of these dating back to the pre-Vijayanagar inscriptions. It was most probably written during the period of the East India Company in the eighteenth century, because of the fact that there are occasional references to the Company's rule. For example, it says that while at the beginning of time the smiths could think objects and buildings into existence, now they had to work on the basis of musters.

The *Vishwakarma Puranam* states that Brahma and Vishwakarma together created the universe. In their own version of the 'Big Bang Theory', the artisans claim that the five natural elements formed an enormous egg that burst forth like thunder and the universe came into being. Shiva and Vishnu emerged from the blue space and created Vishwakarma and Brahma, respectively. Vishwakarma had five faces representing the three smiths (in fact according to the text, of the colour of the faces were also gold, copper, and black), the mason, and the carpenter. Vishwakarma then made tongs out of the power emanating from Brahma and Vishnu and joined it with the nail called Rudram or Shiva. He called this 'kuradu', which is an important tool of the smiths.

This origin myth also makes the point that Vishwakarma was born wearing the sacred thread 'similar to what the Brahmins wear around their shoulder'. This statement made it obvious that one of their major purposes was to claim brahaminical status. The Vishwakarma artisans I have interviewed in 1986 in the course of my field interviews, told me that even then *avani avittam* or thread changing function was among their most important ceremonies.

The *Vishwakarma Puranam* also mentions that Vishwakarma wrote the *Mayanool*, which is the science of architecture. It contains the details of indigenous hand measurement systems (*kadam, ma, yojanai,* etc.) and refers to the importance of mathematical and astrological calculations in the construction of buildings.

The origin myths of the Vishwakarma also get recorded by the Vishwakarma craftsmen themselves, in inscriptions which are found alongside the images sculpted by them. It was usually in the context of their role as engravers and sculptors that the names of craftsmen, accompanied by panegyrical notes on their origin and skills, occur in epigraphical records. The inscription on a *Naga* pillar in the courtyard of the Chennakesava Temple in Macherla in Palnad Taluk, Guntur district, dated 1111–12 CE (referred to earlier), states that the smiths had descended from Vishwakarma, who was the son of Brahma. He is also said to be the father-in-law of Sun, converting the rays emanating from him into divine weapons, like the discus of Vishnu. The record begins by referring to the eight *Nagas* (serpents)—Sesha, Vasuki, Takshaka, Karkota, Abja, Mahmbja, Sankhadhara, and Kulika. Macherla is also stated to be the site of a sacred temple to Adityesvara, the Sun God (sometimes claimed to be the son-in-law of Viswakarma, as mentioned already). The craftsmen are credited with the construction of this temple as well. The inscription further states that the Vishwakarma smiths made images of gods and were experts at cutting/crafting the linga of Shiva, constructing the four kinds of *prasada* (mansions) based on the directions they faced along with their innumerable subforms, and used their knowledge of geometry (Sanskrit *yamitro*) in *Vastusastra*, or the science of sculpture, and in 'gracefully handling the tools of their profession'.[26]

The Vishwakarma community sports a banner with the image of Hanuman even to this day. Offering an explanation for this, the *Vishwakarma Puranam* states that Vishwakarma was the divine architect who accompanied the victorious army of Rama to Ilangai, i.e. present Sri Lanka. He rebuilt Sri Lanka after it was burnt by Hanuman and as a symbol of Rama's triumph, his army began to fly the *Hanumatkodi* or Hanuman flag.[27] An inscription from Dindigal, which carries the spurious date 1365 but refers to Tirumalai Nayakar and seems actually to belong to the seventeenth century, also mentions that *Hanumatkodi* was the banner adopted by the Kammāḷar called the 'Anju Jatiyar' in the inscription, meaning the five castes of craftsmen..

The knowledge of architecture and the science of calculation found in the *Mayanool* makes it a holistic science for which the *Vishwakarma Puranam* uses the term 'Visvapooranam'. The text states that Vishwakarma or Vishwabrahma, also known as Jagadguru Mayan, '*who is a Brahmin*' [emphasis mine], with inputs from Brahma, sage Mareechi, Angirar, Pulattiyan, Ganapati, Brighu, Takshan, and Dharma Devathai created the text *Mayanool*.[28]

There are several points of interest here in understanding the cosmological view of the craftsmen. It is curious that though divine figures like Ganapati and Dharma Devathai (the reference may be to Yama, who is regarded as the god of dharma) provided assistance in creating *Mayanool*, the text brings in the artisanal caste *takshaka*, i.e. carpenters and Pulattiyan, Pulayan being low caste service providers usually associated with death rituals. Besides these, the text mentions brahmin sages such as Athreyi, Brighu, and Angirar, who are neither divine nor mortal figures, but are spiritual personalities.

From such heights, the Vishwakarma community fell into abject poverty and lost the right to use the *Hanumatkodi*, because of the curse of Agastya. The *Vishwakarma Puranam* is suggestive in locating this curse in Agastya's jealousy towards Vishwakarma, since the former was regarded as the authoritative source of the science of miracles while the latter was the ultimate authority on material creation such as buildings.[29]

The most important oral tradition of the Kammāḷar is the story of the magnetic fort, the *Kanta Kottai*. The main purpose of this story seems to be to show the high ritual status enjoyed by the smiths once upon a time and their subsequent fall in status. This happened as a result of—(a) the destruction of the *Kanta Kottai* or magnetic fort, and (b) the curse of the Agastya (the curse syndrome is common to many of the artisan castes).

One popular version of this oral tradition, which is found recorded in the *Vishwakarma Puranam*, is that the five artisans of the Vishwakarma *kula* were, once upon a time, entirely in the service of the gods. Since they were celibates, they had conserved their *veerya*.[30] They therefore possessed the power of creating things by merely imagining them. As an example of this, an invincible fort that they made out of lodestone can be cited. The location of this fort is said to be on the shore of 'Ilangapuri'. As a result of its magnetic powers, the weapons thrown by enemies stuck to the fort walls and could not penetrate within. The principal enemy of the Vishwakarma was a king called Karunakaran, who is said to have derived his authority from the Chola raja. He placed several beautiful women (in some versions they are brahmin women) in the fort, who married the Vishwakarma, thus destroying their spiritual powers obtained through *veerya*. They revealed the secret of the fort to these women, who conveyed it to the enemy king. This was the use of a particular kind of grass (*Panicum antidotale*), which was poisonous and could burn up the fort. The fort was consequently blown up and the Vishwakarma were scattered in all directions and forced to work for ordinary mortals—making weapons, ploughs, houses, temples, and even small things like pins and needles.[31]

Certain points of this story are extremely significant to the economic historian or the craft specialists. The first is the reference to the lodestone fort. Hamilton Buchanan, for instance, has mentioned the finding of laterite and magnetite, i.e. lodestone, in iron mining sites. Besides the awareness of its magnetic properties, lodestone may also have been used in the process of smelting iron. Francis Buchanan, an eighteenth century traveller, in his survey of Karnataka,[32] records the statement of Karnataka smiths that they use lodestone in their smelting furnaces since its melting point is higher than that of iron ore. The second point is the use of the poisonous grass, which is described as *haraka* (English panicum) in the Kannada version and *varagu* in the Tamil version. This has been identified as a variety of wild millet, which can be highly poisonous if not properly processed. After processing, it was eaten in the form of pancakes.

A most extensive survey of the different versions of the *Kanta Kottai* from the region of Karnataka was undertaken by the Dutch anthropologist Jan Brouwer, who wrote an authoritative book on the Vishwakarma/Panchala community of Karnataka titled *The Makers of the World*.[33] In this book, he presents two leading versions—the northern one from Konnurpanta and the southern one from Skantakal in Mandya district. The Konnurpanta version emphasizes on the purity of life and immense Vedic knowledge of the Vishwakarma. It also states that the Vishwakarma had to leave the protection of the fort in order to sell their goods, showing that they were still shackled by the economic bind of producers and consumers.

The story, as with the version cited earlier, juxtaposes the brahmins as the main antagonists. Sage Vedavyasa, the quintessential brahmin *rishi*, is said to have cunningly got his daughter married to the doorkeeper of the magnetic fort, which would enable her to get the knowledge of the *haraka* grass necessary for destroying the fort. The girl is successful in her mission and the Vishwakarma are scattered to the four winds. The southern (Mandya) version cited by Brouwer essentially came up in the context of a court case between the brahmins and the Vishwakarma in the Chittoor District Court in CE 1818. The legal and social context was in the repeated efforts in the eighteenth-nineteenth centuries, on the part of the Vishwakarma, to be recognized as brahmins.

The ritual curse becomes operative in the last part of the story, the foundations of which have already been laid in another mythological story. Long ago, the balance between northern and southern India was upset and the Vindhyas began to dip downwards. Shiva ordered Sage Agastya to go down towards the south and hold up the Vindhyas. He was very reluctant to do so and said that he would go only if he could see his own face. The Vishwakarma craftsmen came to the aid of a perplexed Shiva and polished a brass plate so much that it reflected the face of Agastya. Thus was made the first mirror! Agastya was now forced to comply with Shiva's command. But in retaliation, he cursed Lord Vishwakarma and his people that they would be scattered to the four winds. One very interesting aspect of this 'curse' story is that even now the method of crafting mirrors of polished brass (probably the kind of mirror made to enable sage Agastya to see his own reflection) remains with the 'Vishwabrahmana', i.e. the Vishwakarma caste. Though craftsmen claim that it goes back into antiquity, the local craft groups are unable to provide any timeline to the crafting of these mirrors. Aranmulai in Kerala is a place that still boasts of the production of these mirrors.

Legal Battles over the Caste Identity of the Vishwakarma

The past of the Vishwakarma is firmly embedded in their present. This part of the essay will therefore seek to understand the caste status of the Vishwakarma through the legal battles that were fought by them in the course of the twentieth century, claiming for themselves a brahminical status. These battles are also important in understanding the ways in which the Vishwakarma were re-inventing themselves and their past by publishing extensively on the scriptural evidence of their caste status and compiling a record of their legal battle through various courts in staking a claim to the brahminical caste identity. One such compilation was made in Gujarati by Gopala Vamana Sharma and was titled *Viswakarma ane tena Vanshaj.*[34]

The various epistemological constructs of the Vishwakarma caste identity (the iconic representation of God Vishwakarma is envisaged as a five-headed/faced one with a single body) has been discussed in the *Vishwakarma Brahmana Vamsa Prakasikai.*[35] This was written, or rather compiled by T.M. Devasikamani Acharya in 1950,[36] although the process putting together the oral traditions on Vishwakarma began as early as 1903. In the beginning of the century, C.R. Subharaya Acharya kindled his interest in bringing together the collective memories of the Vishwakarma. In 1928, when he invited a gathering of the elderly and the knowledgeable among the Vishwakarma, Devasikamani Acharya distributed a set of forty questions regarding the origins and community traditions of the Vishwakarma. Among the responses was a comprehensive one from Kundalur K. Subramanya Acharya, which was eventually published in the Vishwakarma community journal *Visva Kalanidhi.*[37]

The debates and discussions that eventually led to the publication of *Vishwakarma Brahmana Vamsha Prakasikai* were foregrounded by a case in the Chennai High Court in 1885 and again in 1919, around the issue 'Are Vishwakarma Dvija?' (or, 'are the members of the Vishwakarma community to be classified as brahmins'?). Sri Kavishekara Pandita Vattepadi Niranjana Shastri represented the Vishwakarma, who had petitioned the court to grant them brahminical status. The Chief Justice Trotter asked if the Vishwakarma had a canonical text like the Bible for the Christians, so that their claims could be authenticated. Devasikamani Acharya's *Viswakarma Brahmana Vamsa Prakasikai* brings together these legal debates over the Vishwakarma's caste identity and status. Devasikamani briefly reports on the judgements delivered in the legal battles between brahmins and the craft groups over their social/ritual status in various district courts at places such as Velur, Salem, and Chennai in present-day Tamil Nadu and Masulipatnam, Guntur, and Chittoor in present-day Andhra Pradesh.[38] It must be noted that these areas came under the Madras Presidency during the colonial period.

The Vishwakarma of the Gujarat region also came out with a seminal work titled *Vishwakarma and tena vanshaje-pramanabadh gauravgrantha* compiled by Gopalji Vaghji Sharma. This text quotes in detail the judgement given in the Guntur district court in 1911–12. The issue arose because the Vishwakarma craftsmen performed the *prana pratishta* (literally breathing life into the idol) or installation ceremony at the twin temples of Proleramma and Pathpatalamma constructed by them. Usually, this ritual is performed by brahmins. The plaintiff Janapati Pattabhirama Sastri argued that as defined by Manu, a brahmin is one who is born into the brahmin varna and by this criterion the Vishwakarma are not brahmins. Therefore, they had no right to perform this ritual. The defendants were led by Voleti Lakshmayya and Nandigama Kaseepathy. The judgement pronounced by C. Ranganayakulu, the Additional Munsiff, held that:

> ...having regard to the evidence of custom and usage and to the procedure laid down in Gargeya Agamam that the community [the Vishwakarma] to which

the defendants belong, has a prominent part, whether or not an exclusive part, in the *Prana Prathishta* ceremonies and the installation referred to could not have profaned the temple even if it were a God of higher status. . . . Much less, therefore, can it be said that there has been any profanation with regard to the said temples. I find the issue in the negative and against the plaintiff.[39]

The most notable of the many cases fought between the brahmins and the Vishwakarma is the one at the Chittoor district court. The plaintiffs/complainants were the brahmins who charged the Vishwakarma community with making false claims to 'brahminhood' in 1885. After dragging on for a number of years, the decision was finally given in favour of the Vishwakarma community in December 1915, entitling them to 'brahminhood'.

It is important to conclude this section with a somewhat curious development that has taken place after India's independence, which puts a new light on the caste question of the Vishwakarma community. In what appears to me as something of a downward mobility, the Vishwakarma, who had fought and won a long drawn legal battle to be accepted as 'brahmins', are now tilting in favour of reservations in education and employment sectors, which is generally given to the backward classes. While the Vishwakarma of Tamil Nadu, Andhra, and Kerala are now under the OBC (Other Backward Castes) category, the Vishwakarma of Karnataka, are seeking a further 3 per cent (within the total 15 per cent) internal reservation within the OBC quota. This nature is in contrast to their earlier history of Sanskritization and their legal triumph in getting brahminical status.

Conclusion

This essay has attempted to map the origin, growth, and changing phases of the Vishwakarma community. I have endeavoured to show how the great temple building era in southern India, commencing from the eighth century onwards, led to the emergence of the craftsmen as key players in the process of medieval urbanism. The development of temple townships also led to the peculiar grouping of the Vishwakarma as representing only the five professions directly involved in temple building—the masons, the carpenters, and the three kinds of smiths. The essay also makes it clear that this collective term for the five kinds of craftsmen had its origin in inscriptions going back to eleventh-century Andhra and subsequently found in the other regions such as Tamil Nadu.

Who were these craftsmen and where did they live? These questions have been addressed by geographically locating the craftsmen within the rural and urban sectors of the medieval economy and society. Logically, the essay sets forth the difference between the humble artisan and the temple craftsmen and concludes with the observation that while every craftsman was an artisan, every artisan was not a craftsman.

Contrary to the popularly held notion that traditional craftsmen did not sign their names, this essay has argued that they left their imprint on their creations in myriad ways—sometimes by inscribing their names, sometimes by giving a panegyric account of their genealogies, and sometimes by engraving the tools of their profession in the stone inscriptions.

The discussion on the caste and social status of the Vishwakarma brings together all the evidence given in the sections on geographical location, urbanization, function, etc. The section titled 'Canonical Constructions and Caste/Ritual Location of the Vishwakarma' looks at the imaging of these craftsmen within the *Dharmasastra* traditions, which also formed the basis of many of the decisions recorded in medieval inscriptions by the brahmin community. These canonical positions have been juxtaposed with instances of caste mobility and caste conflict in medieval south Indian societies from the period of the late Cholas (roughly thirteenth century) till the period of the Vijayanagar Empire (fourteenth to seventeenth centuries).

The last section deals with the process of Sanskritization among the Vishwakarma community, resulting in numerous court cases in the nineteenth century. This concluding part is foregrounded by the analysis of the origin mythologies of the Vishwakarma craftsmen which imaged them as being superior to the brahmins since they were 'Vishwabrahma' who were endowed with the sacred thread from birth. My final reflection however, is that, despite their many legal successes in asserting their brahminical status, today the caste question among the Vishwakarma has come a full circle with the community constitutionally seeking reservations.

Notes

1. *South Indian Inscriptions* (hereafter *SII*), vol. XVII, no. 603. This remarkable inscription is in Sanskrit and has lengthy passages which are quotes from the Dharmasastras and the writings of law-givers like Yajnavalkya, in an attempt to determine whether the Rathakarar are *anuloma* or *pratiloma* castes and whether they should be allowed to perform rituals like sacrifices

or be allowed to wear the sacred thread. This record has been analysed by J.D.M. Derrett. See J. Duncan M. Derrett, 'Two Inscriptions Concerning the Status of the Kammalas and the Application of Dharmashastra', in *Professor K.A. Nilakanta Sastri Felicitation Volume in commemoration of his 80th birthday*, ed. S. Ganesan, Madras: Prof. K.A. Nilakanta Sastri Felicitation Committee, 1971, pp. 34–55.

2. *SII*, vol. VI, no. 117; *SII*, vol. VI, no. 673. Some of these records have been analysed by E. Sivanagi Reddy. See E Sivanagi Reddy, 'Shilpin in Early and Medieval Andhra', unpublished mimeographed text, presented at the Second International Seminar on Mayonic Science and Technology, Thiruvananthapuram, 1997, p. 10.
3. *SII*, vol. 16, insc. no. 2, p. 67; *SII*, vol. 2, insc. no. 4, lines 1–27, pp. 14–16; pp. 65, 67–8 refers to *kammanachcheri*, *paraichcheri*, and *tindachcheri*. For evidence from inscriptions on this point, I would like to draw attention to K. Suresh Kumar, 'Caste and Community in Early Medieval Tamizhagam: From circa sixth century AD to thirteenth century AD', unpublished PhD thesis, Centre for Historical Studies, Jawaharlal Nehru University, 2012. Seminal to the issue under discussion is page 95 in the third chapter 'Social Stratification in Early Medieval Tamizhagam', where he defines and describes *paraichcheri*, *kammanachcheri*, *tindachcheri*, and other residential localities within a habitus. More specifically, see the fifth chapter 'Space and Identity of Paraicheri and Teendacheri', pp. 148–81 for further elucidation of social hierarchies and the location of artisanal communities within them.
4. *SII*, vol. II, no. 5.
5. *SII*, vol. II, part I, nos. 4 and 5.
6. *SII*, vol. II, part I, no. 5.
7. *SII*, vol. II, part 4, no. 94.
8. *Annual Report of Epigraphy* (hereafter *ARE*), 205 of 1918–19 of the period of Kulottunga Chola.
9. This point has been made by R.N. Misra in his book. See R.N. Misra, *Ancient Artists and Art-Activity*, Shimla: Indian Institute of Advanced Study, 1975.
10. Frank Perlin, 'Proto-Industrialization and Pre-colonial South Asia', *Past and Present*, issue no. 98, 1983, pp.30–95.
11. Richard G. Fox, Kin, *Clan, Raja and Rule: State-Hinterland Relations in Preindustrial India*, Berkeley: University of California Press, 1971.
12. *SII*, vol. II, no. 66.
13. Karl Marx, *Capital*, vol. I, English translation of the third German edition by Samuel Moore and Edward Aveling, edited by Friedrich Engels, Moscow: Foreign Languages Publishing House, 1957, pp. 339–40.
14. Ibid., p. 340.
15. One unique inscription from Varikunta in Cuddapah district says that a Boya (tribal community) named Tippana (which was obviously a non-

Vishwakarma) built the local temple for a lump sum payment of 20 rukas (P.V. Parabrahma Sastri, 'Inscriptions of Andhra Pradesh—Cuddapah District', *Epigraphical Series*, no. 15, Hyderabad: Government of Andhra Pradesh, vol. II, no. 107). The inscription is a late one, dated CE 1529, but it points to a certain degree of social flux that was most likely a post-Chola phenomenon. See E. Sivanagi Reddy, 'Shilpins in Early and Medieval Andhra', p. 7, for the citing of this inscription.

16. *ARE*, 309 and 378 of 1916; Report 1917, para 55.
17. *ARE: Bombay-Karnatak Inscriptions*, 223 of 1927–8.
18. *SII*, vol. XVII, no. 603, Thiruvarur, Nagapattinam Taluk, Thanjavur district.
19. *ARE*, 479 of 1908 from Uyyakondan Tirumalai, Tiruchirapalli Taluk and district.
20. Southern India did not have a fourfold varna system. In northern India, society was metaphorically divided according to the *Purusha Sukta* into—brahmin (the head), kshatriya (the arms), vasishya (the thighs), and shudra (the feet). In sharp contrast to this fourfold division, the south Indian society was divided vertically into the left hand and right hand castes. This division excludes the brahmins but divides the rest of society comprising agricultural and artisanal castes into shudras and vaishyas, who are classified as either 'left hand' or 'right hand'.
21. *ARE*, 293 of 1928–9.
22. *ARE*, 309 and 378 of 1916–7; Report 1917, para 55.
23. John Fryer, 'Declares our Course from Johanna to our landing at Mechlapatan', in *A New Account of the East Indies and Persia in Eight Letters, 1672–1681*, London: Hakluyt Society, 1909–15, vol. 1, p. 82.
24. *ARE*, 575 of 1909.
25. *Vishwakarma Puranam*, Mackenzie Manuscripts, Wilson Collection, no. 72, handwritten manuscript in the India Office Library, London.
26. *ARE*, 575 of 1909–10.
27. *Vishwakarma Puranam*, p. 2.
28. Ibid., pp. 2–5.
29. Ibid, p. 5.
30. This refers to the conservation of the semen. According to Hindu tradition, this is supposed to bestow great power.
31. *Vishwakarma Puranam*, pp. 6–7.
32. The technology of smelting of iron is described at length in Francis Buchanan, *A Journey from Madras through the Countries of Mysore, Canara and Malabar*, vol. I, London: W. Bulmer and Co., 1807, pp. 171, 318–25; and vol. II, pp. 437–40. Jan Brouwer cites the description in Buchanan regarding the specific point about the higher melting point of magnetite in his article.
33. Although multiple oral versions of this community tradition exist, an excellent textual analysis is to be found in Jan Brouwer writings. See Jan Brouwer, 'The Story of the Magnetic Fort', in *The Makers of the World:*

Caste, Craft and Mind of South Indian Artisans, Bombay: Oxford University Press, 1995. Also see Jan Brouwer, 'The Story of the Magnetic Fort', in *The Leiden Tradition in Structural Anthropology: Essays in Honour of P.E. de Josselin de Jong*, ed. J.A.J. Karremans et al., Leiden: E.J. Brill, 1987. This is not to say that this is the only authentic version, since other oral traditions differ from it in significant respects.

34. Gopalji Vaghji Sharma *Vishwakarma ane tena Vanshaj: Pramanabadhdha Gaurav Granth*, Anjar, Kutch: Dipak Printers, 1958. I am grateful to Kirin Narayan of the Australian National University, Canberra, for providing me with this material on the court cases fought by the Vishwakarma to establish their brahminical identity.
35. I am very grateful to Amutha Charu Sheela Chandrasekeran, the granddaughter of Devasikamani Acharya, for sharing with me her grandfather's writings on the Vishwakarma community, especially the *Vishwakarma Brahmana Vamsa Prakasikai*, *Brahma Vamsa Brahmana Perumaigal*, *Vishwabrahmaneeyam*, and *Vishwa Brahma Vamsha Sandyavandanam*.
36. T.M. Devasikamani Acharya, *Vishwakarma Brahmana Vamsa Prakasikai*, Chennai: Sadhu Publications, 1950.
37. The author gives no publication details of this journal, which seems to have gone out of publication during the pre-independence period of India.
38. Devasikamani, *Vishwakarma Brahmana Vamsa Prakasikai*, pp. 198–201.
39. The detailed judgement of the Guntur district court is given in *Vishwakarma ane tena Vanshaj*, pp.138–51.

5

Dynamics of Diversity and Inclusion

The Case of the Vishwakarmas

JAN BROUWER

Introduction

The Vishwakarma perspective is not only significant for the understanding of the crafts and the history of the community, but also for the understanding of Indian culture and its history as a whole. To gain insight into how a culture has been constituted, an examination of the exceptions within that culture is called for.

This has been the starting-point for my studies on the Vishwakarma caste of artisans of Karnataka. The sources used for these studies were their oral tradition—different myths (including the origin myth), settlement stories, riddles, and proverbs; my personal participation in each of their crafts during which I even learned the secret crafts lexicon (language?); and published material, indigenous or academic.

In the Vishwakarma origin myth, their main problem is formulated as an inner conflict between the ideal of autonomy and the reality of interdependence. In this sense, they are no different from the other Hindus. What makes them different is that they break into Nature (to obtain principal raw materials), transform Nature faster than Nature herself can, resulting in cultural products for others. Thus, they are different from the others on account of their activities. Hence, it is not surprising that there is no single point of reference for them in the indigenous sociological theory of varna categories.

* I wish to thank Dr Mark Avery for the lengthy discussions on Advanced Cross-Cultural Dynamics. I also thank Wim Kluft (the Hague) and Vikram Shankar (Bangalore) for comments on an earlier draft. The usual disclaimers apply.

In what follows, I shall first describe the general culture in which they live. Consequently, the questions that arise are how the Vishwakarmas operate in this context and how this is expressed in their view.

My perspective is that of an anthropologist, who uses both universal and culture-specific (Indic) categories to explain the matter. I feel that the study of the Vishwakarmas has a wide-ranging significance in the complete understanding not only of traditional factors as the Scriptural Tradition and the Traditional Practices but also of the interface between (system of) modernity and (process of) indigenous knowledge.

Hindu Cultural Context of the Vishwakarmas

Taking the risk of being called an essentialist, I would like to view the whole as a logic system. In the core of the logic system, it is all about reaching *moksha* (liberation of the soul). A Hindu is alone in this pursuit of *moksha*—so it is all about 'me'. At that level (attainment of *moksha*), the illusion of 'me' (*maya*) is gone and only the *Paramatman* (supreme soul) remains. To reach that level, there are a few rules: come pure, come alone, all is god, and all is me.

J.C. Heesterman refers to this level as the transcendent order.[1] It stands in direct contrast to the mundane world that we live in. Thus, one wants to go to the transcendent order from the mundane world (where one is). The transcendent order is timeless. There is no past, present, and future. I call this concept of time the 'perpetual present'.

The transcendent order is the realm of authority (not of power), where no distinctions whatsoever exist. The original *mathas* and true renouncers of the world (*sannyasis*) represent this order in the world. The *mathas* and the *sannyasis* are the sources of most, if not all, Vedic and classical texts. Together, they represent the transcendent order in the mundane world and thus all these texts are located outside the mundane order.

For the mundane world, a person who has reached the transcendent order is a person of values who is elevated, set apart, or even worshipped. In the mundane order, the rules are also different. First, one has to strive for autonomy, which implies the protection of not only one's own but also of others' individuality. The first rule (autonomy) is diametrically opposed to the second rule—survival. In other words, to reach *moksha* as an autonomous individual, one has to strive to outlive the others. However, an autonomous individual cannot survive alone in this world; he needs others, and this leads to interdependency. This logically leads to the third rule—anarchy—especially if autonomy and survival are read together with reference to the location of the texts.[2]

These three rules, read together with the concept of time as being the 'perpetual present', does not encourage change and innovation. However, the fourth rule—narcissism—challenges the lack of change and innovation.[3]

Thus, the transcendent order of virtues, the order of authority, is the reference for the mundane world of vices, the order of power. In the mundane world that is the realm of power, 'might make[s] right', where the individual is in his 'My Space', and all else is the undifferentiated environment. However, the texts classify almost everything: flora, fauna, people, and things. The Vishwakarmas are an exception to this. They have classified all of the natural environment in detail.[4] The world does not distinguish between flora, fauna, and humans as much as it distinguishes among humans aimed both at one's own autonomy and survival. Survival cannot be achieved with autonomy; it implies interdependency. Then, the necessary but loathed interdependency is compromised with 'me' in 'this place' negotiated with genealogy.[5]

Then logically, the 'game'[6] of matching the ideal with the real in the market place of the mundane world is played significantly different from the game in the modern state, for, in the modern state, there is the conjunction of authority and power. This generates a direct relationship between power and responsibility across social domains. But in traditional India, the Scriptural Tradition and the Traditional Practices, together comprise the indigenous knowledge system. Here, authority is separated from power, and that generates an indirect relation between power and responsibility across social domains. Responsibility here is articulated in terms of indebtedness of one to another. Multiplied across all domains or levels of society simultaneously, it generates, what industrialist Baba Kalyani has called, a 'trust deficit'.[7]

The Vishwakarmas

Within the context of the Vishwakarma caste, the Vishwakarmas have visualized the aforementioned general ideal into the image of Lord Vishwakarma, having five heads and five pairs of arms, where each head and each pair of arms represent one of their five craft groups. As such, the idol should not be worshipped, and the dependence of all crafts on the products (tools) of the blacksmith is precluded by this representation. However, an individual Vishwakarma, in this world, depends on others for making his crafts and for the marketing of his products. Thus, his survival demands social relationships and market operations.

On the crafts level, the view of the Vishwakarmas shows a ritualization of crafts. The principal raw materials are considered to be the *brahmanda*, or the universe, while the finished products are seen as images of *vishwa*. The initial stage is followed by the breakdown of nature, when the main raw materials are considered to be Mahakali. It represents the form that the Goddess Mahalakshmi assumes on the dissolution of the universe. If, however, the crafts are considered individually, iron (Kali) can be said to stand in opposition to gold (Lakshmi).

On the caste level, the view of the Vishwakarmas shows a discontinuity between caste (ideal of autonomy, non-violence, and completeness) and subcaste (reflecting the necessity of interdependence and violence).

Conflict of Values

The collective title for the craftsmen communities—Vishwakarma—was found on a Ganga copperplate inscription. This and later epigraphic references suggest that the construct was conceived or (re)activated at times of technological change, or of an increased need for artisans. In the nineteenth and twentieth centuries, particularly since the census operations[8] began in 1851, this root paradigm has been reactivated.

On the ground level, the caste is seen in terms of a dichotomy of a pure and a less pure category—pure in the sense of being exclusive, having minimum relationship with others, and impure in the sense of being inclusive, having maximum relationship with others.[9] There are considerable contextual variations in attributes expressing the two categories. The contexts of both the categories of the dichotomy vary significantly spatially, while they also vary over time.

At the state level, the dyadic conflict of caste is seen in the myths as well as in the ritual connections of the Vishwakarmas. They can all be traced back to the local ruler of the time. Stories and cults of their holy men appear to be indigenous tools to supersede the dyadic conflict. As we have already seen, the Vishwakarma caste consists of two categories held together by the image of Lord Vishwakarma on the ideological level and Goddess Kali in the lived-in order. Each category comprises two subcastes. One category is pure, exclusive, brahminical, and as such, represents 'authority'. The other category is less pure, inclusive, kingly, and as such, represents 'power'.[10]

The Vishwakarma oral tradition shows how they play the game

under the impact of opportunity/threat from outside. In each region of Karnataka, there are four subcastes of which two follow the exclusive model (brahminical orientation) and two that follow the inclusive model (kingly orientation). For example, in southern Karnataka, the 'authority' category comprises the Sivachar subcaste (comprising all Vishwakarma crafts and is market oriented) and the Uttaradi subcaste (only goldsmiths and priests of the Kali temples). The 'power' category, on the other hand, comprises the Kulachar subcaste (comprising only three crafts and is the sponsor of the Kali temples) and the Matachar subcaste (only coppersmiths and is market oriented).

In the Vishwakarma myths of southern Karnataka, they appear more brahminical. Here, they frequently collide with the brahmins. In the Vishwakarma myths of northern Karnataka, however, they appear more violent; they are presented as those who can solve problems, and thus appear as ideal kings. With the oncoming of the Modern State, and specifically after the economic restructuring of the 1990s, a realignment of internal caste organization among the Vishwakarmas has been witnessed.

Indigenous Mechanism to Cope with Rapid Change

In the foregoing paragraphs, the culture system logic was described with special reference to the Vishwakarmas. Comparing the ideal with the real shows a conflict of values. The system, however, has its own mechanism to cope with such conflicts. Let us see what happens in the case of a rapid change. In the transcendent order of *moksha*, god is in his own box, there 'god is you'. It is the order of the ideal brahmin. In the world, this order is represented by the *sannyasi*. Thus, in the world, *moksha* and the ideal brahmin (together, 'authority'), combined with the capacity of the king's achieved position ('power') and the authority of brahmin's mirror,[11] each isolated to their own means, creates the need for a 'trickster'[12] to bend the rules and deal with the unknown, uncontrolled—'not us'. Thus, in the world, we see the creation of priesthood and local deity, the 'trickster' legitimating rule bending/unlocking the gridlock, embodying the negotiating tensions, and the shifting/arbitrary nature in local games. In the Hindu worldview, there is a split between the transcendent and mundane, and the same must be established in the (lived-in) world with brahmin, king, and a third element, which may be a goddess (in various cultural or natural forms), or a guru.[13] The critical difference is that the transcendent remains inert and unreachable.

The eighteenth century in India was not a period of 'decline' and 'native mismanagement' as stated by some, but a period of rapid social and economic change. Christopher A. Bayly demonstrates the adaptability of the eighteenth century economy in his writing.[14] In his *Land and Sovereignty: Agrarian Society and Politics under the Eighteenth-century Maratha Svarajya*, André Wink shows that the hierarchical relationship between the Chhattrapathi rulers and the Peshwa ministers changed from one in which the brahmin's authority ranked higher than the king's power to one in which the authority and power became aligned.[15] The rise in power of the Peshwas was visible in the fact that both the positions of king and minister became inherited. The threat of the Mughals (an opportunity?) can be considered in this case as the trigger for this change. It was in this period that we see increased monetization and the cash nexus that reached its culmination in the later eighteenth century.[16]

As has already been seen, the indigenous way of coping with threats or opportunities is firstly introducing a third element to the first element of authority and the second element of power. The third element is the 'trickster'; in our example, the Goddess Kali. Second, instead of retaining the hierarchical relationship between authority and power and introducing a third element, the relationship between authority and power can be changed from hierarchical to one of alignment. If one now reverts to the concept of *moksha* as mentioned, social relationships require another way to cope with threats and opportunities, besides introducing a third element. The main rule is 'to come alone', i.e. without any attachment to the world, or rather, the chosen way to prosperity and ultimate liberation demands an individual's detachment from the material world. Basically there are two options to achieve this either independently or in combination. First, for survival, an unavoidable social relationship between two individuals is mediated by a third element, which can be a deity or an institution; and second, it can be made incidental by the use of money.

In the modern definition of money, the concepts of salary, profit, and loan bind the employer to the employee, the employee with the work, the work with the salary, and the debtor with the creditor. The enterprises are organized around a series of single, stranded relationships that are only indirectly related at the production level. Money induces no relationship between the seller and producer that extends beyond the functional transaction, while, in the indigenous view, it terminates the relationship between the giver and receiver of money. This follows directly from the dominant world view that does not allow social relationships.[17]

Money then, is the instrument used to negate social relationships or to make them incidental. What matters here is that there is much more than money in a transaction, which is more than just a functional exchange. Objects and subjects are not very clearly segregated, and in that they reveal their intricate nature. If an exchange does not contribute anything, it is only an expression of what interpersonal relations have already constituted—as Jean-Claude Galey has argued in the context of land tenures.[18]

Elsewhere, I have written:

> Consequently, a loan is not meant be repaid. Receiving a loan itself constitutes the debtor and creditor, while its repayment would actually involve the terminating quality of money and thus dissolve the relationship. Similarly, a salary or share in the enterprise's profit cannot be seen as a payment for the work done, as it would establish a relationship between employer and employee. In the case of the goldsmith and the Shroff it is the Goddess who receives the money and in the case of the employee it is his home.[19]

In the twentieth century, an equally serious opportunity/threat occurred, some of which were—the independence of a nation that had never before existed, the sudden opening up of a country's economy to the world, rapid growth in the IT sector, access to newer technology and new forms of organization that led to unimaginable wealth, etc. These elicited a response from the traditional pair of authority and power similar to hierarchy plus a third element or alignment. Through this, the Hindu tradition shows its own mechanism of coping with rapid economic change.

The key points of insight that can be gained from this are: power and authority do not have to be combined if they are aligned, and opportunity and/or threat create situations of crisis that give rise to the need for alignment of power and authority.

These dynamics may now be briefly illustrated by three cases: the Hindus of Surinam, the Vokkaligas (a dominant farming community) of Karnataka, and the Vishwakarmas of Karnataka.

Surinami Hindus

In Surinam, the Hindus were unable to duplicate the caste system as the immigrants were widely distributed, with small numbers at one place. Everyone had a non-negotiable contract with plantation owners that brought him or her there. Services and goods were remote for everyone, so they all survived through the local markets and Chinese goods. Caste endogamy was unviable, as was purity and food restrictions from traditional India. Brahmin *pundits* and Muslim clergy bound the community families together. The brahmins now played the role of heads of associations (a new category enabled by the government), and then later, these *pundits* became heads of political parties as the Indian interest group emerged within Surinam.

Vokkaligas of Karnataka

The British instituted laws that allowed organized societies and associations between 1910 and 1950. Associations formed around categories of 'what you do', in this case—ploughing (*okka* [K] is plough). This new category led to the practice of exogamy within smaller caste groups of peasants, who were now suddenly in this new, superimposed category. Once this new category was formed, over time, authority was handed to a *matha*, run by a brahmin figure elected from within the category (not a 'certified brahmin' from outside). The *matha* stood as an incarnation of the ideal state of the category. A political party (Janata) also emerged, representing the category that had been superimposed on otherwise segregated, smaller peasant caste groups.

Vishwakarmas of Karnataka

The Vishwakarmas perceived the modern state as both an opportunity and a threat imposed from the outside, consequent to which, new subcastes emerged from within the main caste. Later, there was both fission (breaking away of subcastes) and fusion (combination of subcastes in alliances) within the caste itself.[20] This, in turn, led to new opportunities as well as threats created by the new underlying order, e.g. new practices of endogamy, ideas of purity, and certain rules and rituals regarding food.

Threats and Opportunities and the Response Process

The following ideas emerged from all three cases, which point to a relatively consistent response process.

A situation, such as a new opportunity or threat that can only be dealt with through collective action on a new level that triggers the creation of a new idea of 'task', furthers the need for association.

We then see the dynamics affecting power and authority at two different levels. (a) Territorial dynamics: unstable environment of opportunity/threat—special interest groups emerge within the association over time; the association splits as these special interest groups unite. (b) Genealogical dynamics: stable environment and no opportunity/threat.

In a stable environment, power and authority are strictly separated. *Mathas* emerge, as do leaders. It is consistently an outside force that creates the new categories. The relevance of the outsider's categories was 'benefits', which now became accessible to those within the new boundaries—the boundary 'salience' being critical here.

On the strategic level, one can see that the one who sets up these new categories changes the game, rules the game, and essentially owns the game. The otherwise fragmented subcastes, now united in the new category, play the game of the modern state (the outsider). The outsider can organize itself in such a way that the subcastes ultimately win. The insiders are willing to pay tribute to the outsider, who set up the superimposed categories, if the insiders (as defined by the new, larger category) can benefit from the outsider's larger system. These categories, with greater unity between subcastes, segregated by historical dynamics, cannot 'emerge' from within—higher forms of unity must be superimposed from outside.

The Vishwakarma Situation

Historically, the Vishwakarmas have no point of reference in the indigenous sociological theory of the varna categories. They responded by claiming either the brahmin or kshatriya status. I see this response as being one to an opportunity/threat from outside. This is because, in the society, they are not recognized as having a clear status. The others (communities) do not really know how to classify them and hence, how to behave with them. In many situations they are often avoided, even in institutions such as universities.

Taking the caste as a whole, one can thus see the concepts of power (inclusive, kingly) and authority (exclusive, brahminical) in alignment within the caste. For all Vishwakarmas, their rallying point is the Goddess Kali.[21]

Let me illustrate this with the case of the Vishwakarmas of southern Karnataka. Here, the Vishwakarma caste comprises four subcastes: Sivachar, Uttaradi, Kulachar, and Matachar. The Sivachar and Uttaradi subcastes substantiate the concept of authority, while the Kulachar and

Matachar substantiate the concept of power. The agreed internal ranking of these subcastes from high to low is: Sivachar, Uttaradi, Kulachar, and finally Matachar. On the authority side, the Uttaradi rank lower as they deliver the priests to the Kali temples. On the power side, the Matachar rank lower as they are strongly market oriented.

Power and authority are necessarily segregated and necessarily arbitrated. They are segregated because either, left to itself, is chaos and, so to speak, freeze; they are arbitrated because the logic of each excludes the logic of the other, while both are practically necessary.

The substance of power is local and permeated with political manipulations and backroom politics. By contrast, the substance of authority supersedes distinctions and shows supra-local connections with acquaintance-level connections. It creates confusion and complexity by bringing in an outside factor that it can negotiate with, but that no one else knows what to do with. It deconstructs a situation and that ability to deconstruct gives it the right to choose what it will focus on, out of an arbitrary list.

The indigenous tactic to cope with modernity here is to predict how the inclusive category will deconstruct it, often by bringing in an outside factor, complement it on its ability to see that factor (thus making it impossible for it to contradict itself) and then capture that authority and turn it back on the inclusive category by incorporating it into a solution. The response then is, 'There, we have customized modernity to our needs.'

The role of the goddess in this context is both social and economic. The goddess is a storehouse of knowledge that could blow everything up if it were let out to play both sides of the game privately and turn up publicly on the side of the winners.

In the modern times, one can observe a reorganization to cope with the opportunity/threat. There is a differential response to modernity. The Kulachars are increasing their inclusiveness; the Matachars are rapidly leaving the crafts and entering into modern contract-based professions; the Sivachars are adopting modern manufacturing techniques; and the Uttaradis are leaving priesthood and taking up other occupations.

Concurrently, the various Vishwakarma *mathas* (often local) have agreed on the formation of an apex body, and one *matha* that will oversee all the local ones. At the same time, the subcastes are in the process of forming a political association to voice their problems vis-à-vis the modern state. The image of Lord Vishwakarma has also made its entry into the Kali temples and is being worshipped.

Simultaneously, there is a trend of genealogical integration of

Kulachars and Matachars, while the Uttaradis are intermarrying with a similar subcaste of central Karnataka. However, the Sivachars remain as exclusive as they were.

In other words, the Vishwakarma response to modernity is no longer confined only to a brahmin claim and Scheduled Caste status call. At the same time, we also find fusion and fission of subcastes, i.e. realignment of subcastes in each region.

Thus, while power is being shifted to a political association, authority is increasingly being vested in the guru of the supreme *matha*. Thus, power and authority are being taken out of the caste context and being placed in alignment above the subcastes.

The traditional calls for the brahmin status or the Scheduled Caste status are vanishing. Thus, where in the premodern, stable period, power and authority were strictly separated, in the modern state itself, these concepts are combined—they are in alignment in a situation of rapid change.

Conclusion

The initial situation of the Vishwakarmas resembles the general situation of all Hindus in both the historical and contemporary contexts of rapid change and increased monetization. By identifying the concepts—authority, power, and trickster—behind the subcastes, the indigenous mechanism of coping with opportunity/threat could be found. Extending the analysis to wider historical and contemporary contexts, the study of the Vishwakarmas, unlike the study of any other caste in the subcontinent, contributes to the understanding of India as a whole.

Thus, at a time of increased monetization and expansion of the market, one can see an alignment of power and authority. The development is clear: the shift from hierarchical system in positions of power and authority to the alignment of these two goes hand in hand with a shift in importance from the goddess to either a male deity (Maruti) or a guru, i.e. from female to male.[22]

Having moved to the concepts underlying practices, a prophesy may be formulated: further monetization and expansion of the market shall lead to further alignment of the concepts of power and authority, juxtaposed to the combination of power and authority of the modern state, and an increase in importance of gurus as the representation of institutions of socio-economic mediation.[23]

Notes

1. J.C. Heesterman, *The Inner Conflict of Tradition: Essays in Indian Ritual, Kingship and Society*, Chicago: University of Chicago Press, 1985.
2. If the texts belong to the mundane world, they would act as guidelines to prevent anarchy. But if they are perceived as being located in the transcendent order, the world is left to itself, i.e. left to interdependency. With autonomy and survival playing a central role (in order to attain *moksha*), this will lead to chaos.
3. On the basis of an analysis of texts and empirical observations, certain rules can be abstracted. For the transcendent order, they are—come pure, come alone, all is god, and all is one (or, 'me'). For the mundane order, they are—autonomy of the individual, survival of the individual, anarchy, and narcissism. Behaviour is based on the striving for individual autonomy. This means that one has to survive first; but if everyone does so, it leads to anarchy and thus the culture as a whole has mechanisms to prevent this, among different castes. Unbridled individualism means a high degree of narcissism. Only when this narcissism is in conjunction with taking responsibility does it lead to innovation.
4. Jan Brouwer, 'Riddles of Raw Materials: An Exploration of the Artisans' Views of Stones and Wood', *Man in India*, vol. 67, no. 2, 1987, pp. 147–59; Jan Brouwer, 'Artisans' Oral Tradition as a Resource of History', in *The Resources of History: Tradition, Narration and Nation in South Asia*, ed. Jackie Assayag, Etudes Thematiques, vol. 8, Paris and Pondichery: École Francaise d'Extrême-Orient and Pondichéry Institut Francais de Pondichérry, 1999, pp. 213–32; Jan Brouwer, 'Trees for Timber and Trees for the Forest: Aspects of Indigenous Knowledge of Wood and Stone in Karnataka, India', in *Man in the Forest: Local Knowledge and Sustainable Management of Forests and Natural Resources in Tribal Communities in India*, ed. Klaus Seeland and Franz Schmithüsen, New Delhi: D.K. Printworld, 2000, pp. 345–60.
5. I define genealogy in opposition to territory as all that is not territory, and thus, all that has to do with people. The individual can never survive alone (autonomously), others (kin and the right choice of affines taken together genealogically) are always necessary. This demands a compromise to the ideal.
6. By 'game', I refer to a set of rules by which the participants play to achieve a given goal. The rules for attaining *moksha* are vastly different from the rules for doing business in the marketplace; also, the rules that govern the marketplace of India are different from those that govern the global or the Western marketplace.
7. Ajay Shukla, 'Building Strong Global Competitive Advantage in Defence Manufacture is an Achievable Goal: Baba Kalyani', *Business Standard*, 10 September 2013, see http://www.business-standard.com/article/economy-policy/building-strong-global-competitive-advantage-

in-defence-manufacture-is-an-achievable-goal-baba-kalyani-113091001025_1.html, accessed on 24 April 2018.

8. For the first time in South Asian history, people were asked their caste name, profession, and other details in a systematic way. This created an unprecedented awareness of categories hitherto unknown.
9. Jan Brouwer, *The Makers of the World: Caste, Craft and Mind of South Indian Artisans*, Delhi: Oxford University Press, 1995.
10. J.C. Heesterman described the two models of emancipation to attain *moksha*. The brahminical model of exclusiveness minimalizes social relationships and investments are largely done in oneself. The kingly model of inclusiveness maximizes social relationships and investments are largely done in people.
11. The degree of authorization that the king has is not more than that of a brahmin seen in a mirror. This is what Heesterman has called the conundrum of the king's authority.
12. The elements 'authority' and 'power', being in principle mutually exclusive, require a third element to make the structure work. A trickster is a character that exhibits a great degree of intellect or knowledge and uses it to play tricks or otherwise disobey normal rules and conventional behaviour. He or she fills the void between authority and power.
13. Jan Brouwer, 'The Goddess for Development. Indigenous Economic Concepts among South Indian Artisans', *Social Anthropology*, vol. 5, no. 1, 1997, pp. 69–82.
14. C.A. Bayly, *Rulers, Townsmen and Bazaars: North Indian Society in the Age of British Expansion, 1770–1870*, Cambridge: Cambridge University Press, 1983.
15. André Wink, *Land and Sovereignty: Agrarian Society and Politics under the Eighteenth-century Maratha Svarajya*, Cambridge: Cambridge University Press, 1986.
16. Ibid., p. 331.
17. Jan Brouwer, 'Conflict between Modern and Indigenous Concepts in the Small Enterprise Workplace: A Proposal', *Social Anthropology*, vol. 8, no. 2, 2000, pp. 181–208.
18. Jean-Claude Galey, 'Creditors, Kings and Death', in *Debts and Debtors*, ed. Charles Malamoud, New Delhi: Vikas, 1983, p. 100. Also see Akos Ostor, *Culture and Power: Legend, Ritual, Bazaar and Rebellion in a Bengali Society*, New Delhi: Sage Publications, 1984.
19. Brouwer, 'Conflict between Modern and Indigenous Concepts', p. 195.
20. Jan Brouwer, 'The Latecomers: A Case Study of Caste and Subcaste of Goldsmiths in Karnataka, South India', in *Ritual, State and History in South Asia: Essays in Honour of J.C. Heesterman*, ed. A.W. van den Hoek et al., Leiden: E.J. Brill, 1992, pp. 433–55.
21. The position of Goddess Kali is to be seen from two levels. On the worldly

level, she represents the raw materials, while on the cognitive level, she is the mediator between the categories of power and authority.

22. This can be observed in Mediterranean cultures about 2,000 years ago and more recently among the weavers of Karnataka. In the traditional setting, they lived and worked in towns and worshipped their goddess, Banashankari. During the past 25 years, they have gradually moved to the industrial areas out of town, where they worship the male deity Maruti.
23. This theme is being worked out by my co-author Dr Mark Avery and me in our book on Indian culture and corporate business—*The King's Game: Creating Value in a Culture* (forthcoming).

APPENDIX

The Vishwakarma Origin Myth

In the origin story—the 'Fort Story'—all Vishwakarmas lived in a strong, magnetic fort, which could not be destroyed by anything. The inhabitants of the fort were pure and united. They did not know distinctions such as that between life and death; they were immortal. However, the fort is besieged, resulting in mixed marriages, a fire, consequent escapes, and the origin of endogamous subcastes (of different descent lines). The inhabitants of the fort manufactured their products secretly at night, and during the day its doors opened automatically to deliver the goods to the world. This narrative expresses the Vishwakarma ideal of autonomy and completeness, while it gains significance through the homology between Lord Vishwakarma and the Vishwakarmas in the real world. The ideal Vishwakarma is autonomous, because he is the *Parabrahma* and above Brahma. All others, including the brahmins, depend on the Vishwakarmas of the real world, while Lord Vishwakarma has no relationships at all: he simply 'is'. He is self-contained, an image of autonomy. In the world, this is expressed as a 'kingly' aspect of not being subordinate, and of being socially and ritually independent. The ideal of completeness conceptualizes the universe as being composed of a static male and a dynamic female constituent part. The Vishwakarma craftsman himself, being the worldly counterpart of the heavenly Vishwakarma, is thus an image of the universe itself. Through the imagery of the tools, the craftsman conceptualizes his workshop also as an image of the universe and finally, his (main) finished products are images of the world. (For a detailed analysis, see Jan Brouwer, *The Makers of the World: Caste, Craft and Mind of South Indian Artisans*, Delhi: Oxford University Press, 1995.)

6

Who is Vishwakarma's Daughter?

Divine Kinship and Goddess Randal Worship in a Gujarati Artisan Community

KIRIN NARAYAN

Side by side, golden flames steadily burn from two ghee lamps, making present the doubled goddess, Randal Ma, as food offerings are laid before her. For larger celebrations, she is invited in the form of two metal pots filled with water, each balancing a coconut. In the past, faces were made on these coconuts by molding clay and adding cowry eyes and cowry mouths; now her identical faces are painted on flat strips of printed paper or plastic, or sculpted in twin heads of brass or silver. Two, four, six, eight . . . even one hundred and eight: multiple twinned sets of goddesses may be swathed in red and green garments and decorated with jewellery. In a room fragrant with offered flowers, incense, and food, women sing and dance their welcome.

The scenes I describe are familiar to members of the Gujar (or Gurjar) Sutar community of hereditary carpenters with ancestral roots in Kutch, western Gujarat. Like Hindu artisans and craftsmen in many other regions of India, they see themselves as 'Vishwakarma-*putra*, sons of Vishwakarma', emphasizing their descent from the deity. In a range of localities, languages, and dialects across India, written and oral myths affirm this connection between Vishwakarma and his male progeny. Ethnographers,[1] historians,[2] and art historians[3] have all pointed to the patrilineal mythological grounding of the artisans' identity. However, the importance of Vishwakarma's daughter to some hereditary craftsmen communities remains largely unexplored.

This essay offers a preliminary and provisional sketch of the myths and contemporary rituals surrounding Vishwakarma's daughter, who in Gujarat is especially known as Randal Ma. Her other names include Ranna De, Ranna Devi, and even Ravi Randal, because of her marriage to Ravi, the Sun God. Even as she is considered a relative by hereditary craftsmen, she is also worshipped across many Gujarati communities, who may regard her as a *kuldevi* or family goddess, granting blessings for fertility.[4] I wrote about some aspects of Vishwakarma's mythology in *My Family and Other Saints*,[5] a family memoir. Like the memoir, this essay emerges from interest sustained across years as a partial insider. I describe how mythology is transmitted by individuals and groups as family folklore, yielding insights into how mythological kinship relations may continue to inform contemporary social relations. Though Randal Ma is a regional deity found only in Gujarat, the worship of this doubled goddess is also a reminder of a larger connection between Vishwakarma and goddess worship in different regions of India.

Vishwakarma's Daughter

A popular north Indian poster displayed in many artisans' homes, workshops, and on factory floors depicts Vishwakarma enthroned: a white-bearded, four-armed, crowned patriarch, encircled with a wide halo containing tools. Gathered respectfully beside him are his two-armed human sons. Since Vishwakarma is mostly represented as having five (*pānch*) sons, members of hereditary artisan communities are sometimes called 'Panchalas' or 'Panchabrahmas'. Using Vishwakarma as a surname, some groups also reaffirm a genealogical connection with the god. This patrilineal ancestral link has also been historically used sometimes to claim brahmin status, with some artisans terming themselves 'Vishwakarma Brahmans' or 'Vishwabrahmans'.[6]

Vishwakarma's daughter Randal Ma can be found in poster art as well, though mostly in Gujarat and through the Gujarati diaspora. She is represented from the torso up as two beautiful identical twin goddesses, joined at the shoulder, wearing red saris with green blouses. She is bedecked with dangling gold earrings and layers of glittering gold necklaces, as golden rays extend brightness beyond her two covered heads. Randal Ma is unique among goddesses in her doubled form, and a range of oral and written stories explain this unusual iconography.

I begin by reproducing a lightly revised retelling of the story of Randal Ma, as it appears in *My Family and Other Saints*. Reconstructing events in my family in the early 1970s from the perspective of a young half-American child, I had pieced together the story from the different oral versions I had encountered.

Vishwakarma Dada had four sons. He also had a daughter, Randal (We call her Randal Ma since she's a goddess). She has two names: Samjna [symbol/name] and Chhaya [shadow].

Daughters, you know, must be married away. Vishwakarma Dada had constructed the Sun's chariot for riding through the heavens, and he thought that the Sun would make a good groom. So Vishwakarma Dada arranged his daughter's marriage to the Sun.

Randal Ma lived with the Sun and bore him children, but this life was difficult for her. The Sun was hot and bright. So Randal Ma placed Chhaya, her own shadow, in charge of everything in the house. Then she herself went off to the jungle to meditate. She turned herself into a mare because she didn't want anyone to disturb her.

At first, the Sun didn't notice that his wife was gone because the shadow was identical. Even the children didn't see any difference from their mother. But then, when she was serving food, one of the children who was making trouble, kicked her. She got so angry that she cursed his leg. When do mothers curse sons? The boy, Yama, suspected that she was not really his mother and alerted his father, the Sun.

The Sun could not completely undo Chhaya's curse. But he questioned her, and she confessed who she was. Then the Sun went to Vishwakarma Dada to ask where Randal Ma had gone.

Vishwakarma Dada told the Sun, 'How is she to live with you when you are so hot and bright?'

'What am I to do? This is my nature,' the Sun said.

So Vishwakarma Dada offered a solution: 'You can let me shave off some of your brightness.'

The Sun agreed, and his father-in-law put him on a lathe and shaved away some of that light. From those fragments of Sun, all the shining weapons of the various gods were forged: Vishnu's discus, Shiva's trident, and all the other weapons later used in the great battles against demons.

Then the Sun went to find Randal Ma in the jungle. She was praying peacefully in her mare form. He became a stallion and they danced together. They had more children, including the horse-faced twin gods who heal people—the Ashwins.

Because she existed in her own form and the form of her shadow, we worship Randal Ma with two faces. For special pujas we bring at least two coconuts and balance them in pots. We give them clay faces with cowries for their eyes and mouths, and we dress them in red saris. Then we say Randal Ma has come to visit.[7]

Older Gujar Sutar mythology and iconography often feature four sons, rather than the five acknowledged elsewhere in India—the divergence being sometimes bridged by enumerating four groups of carpenters, and then adding that Vastu (the principle of building) was an adopted son. Increasingly, though, the names of the five sons as primordial ancestors of different crafts groups are understood in accordance with a wider pattern across India: Manu (blacksmith), May (carpenter), Tvashta (copper/brass worker), Devagna (goldsmith), and Shilpi (sculptor). In the 1970s, when I first recall hearing this story, not only were the sons still seen as four, but Randal Ma too was still visiting households in the form of coconuts with painted clay faces crafted by the women themselves; later, as I will show, other mass-produced forms for these faces became more popular.

This story I just sketchily reproduced echoes across time through many media, and has been written about at length by Sanskritists intrigued by a riddle verse (*brahmodya*) that first appears in the *Rig Veda* (*c.*1200–1000 BCE). The riddle in *Rig Veda* X.17 describes the daughter of Tvastar, the divine maker and shaper, who is married to the Sun; the mother of Yama, she disappears, with an identical form put in her place, and she gives birth to the Ashwin twins after abandoning two sets of twins: her name 'Saranyu' is offered as the riddle's solution.[8] This Saranyu from the *Rig Veda* is also known by other names in the epics and Puranas, especially Samjna (symbol), accompanied by Chhaya (her shadow) or Savarna (her identical self). Wendy Doniger in particular has traced versions of the story all the way towards a contemporary English language mythology-based comic book in the *Amar Chitra Katha* series,[9] and she offers a nuanced feminist discussion of the story's many versions in light of other motifs of doubling and splitting in Hindu and Greek mythologies.[10] In these accounts, Randal Ma is described more as a mythological character than as a powerful goddess who might descend into presence even today.

Retellings and embellishments of Vishwakarma's daughter's story continue to surface in an assortment of media, including Vishwakarma Puranas, caste publications, pamphlets associated with temples, newspapers, and websites—all sites that may then re-enter the oral tradition and move across languages. For example, in one of my old notebooks, I find an undated written account, in English, of my father's sister's retelling of a story in Hindi, deriving from her reading of a Gujarati newspaper article about the Tapti River that flows from central India towards the coast of Gujarat. Here is my translation of Chandaphui's retelling, for which I unfortunately do not know the exact year or source.

> Tapti is the Sun's daughter. The first wife of the Sun had six children: Vaivasvata Manu, Yama, Yamuna, Ashwini twins and Raivanya [Revanta]. The second wife was the shadow double of the first (because of the Sun's fierce heat).

The Sun's wife had gone back to Vishwakarma's house. He asked, 'Why are you alone?' He said, 'If you've done something wrong, I won't keep you.'

Then she went to the jungle to do austerities (*tap*). But she had made the shadow double who bore four children: Shani, Tapti, Vishti and Savarna Manu. Tapti became Tapi, the river and sister of Shani, like Yamuna river is the sister of Yama. The Tapti river's birth is on the seventh day of the bright half of Ashadh.

This version depicts Vishwakarma questioning his unnamed daughter for leaving her husband, the Sun. The story also connects her austerities (*tap*) to Tapti, the daughter born from her shadow and mentions another child Vishti, also born to the shadow—who I have never heard of before or after. Usually, in contemporary retellings, Vishwakarma's grandchildren, born through his daughter's marriage to the Sun, are described in sets of three:

1. To the original daughter: the fraternal twins Yama (the lord of Death) and Yami (the Yamuna river), along with Vaivasvata Manu (primary to the current era or *manvantara*);
2. To the shadow form: the fraternal twins Shani (the planet Saturn) and Tapti (the river), along with Savarna Manu (primary to the coming era);
3. To the mare form: the identical twins—Ashwini Kumars (horse-headed physician gods), and Revanta (the deity of horsemen).

Women retelling the story of Randal Ma's marriage sometimes include other characters too, like Randal Ma's mother, i.e. Vishwakarma's wife, and the Sun's mother. For example, they speak of how Randal Ma's mother was concerned that her daughter would be married to a god who would be away all day long. Since the mother was reluctant to agree to the marriage, Randal Ma had to be won through a trick. For this, the Sun's mother came to his (the Sun's) aid. The tale of this trick was retold by Pramila-ben, Chanda-phui's sister-in-law, sometime in the 1990s:

Surya Bhagavan (the Sun God) really wanted to marry Randal Ma. He saw that she was very smart. He really wanted to marry her. So he told his mother to go to her in the form of an old woman and loan Randal Ma a clay griddle (*ṭhīkrī*). His mother told Randal Ma's family, 'I'm giving this to you on loan. You must give it back whole. If not, you'll have to give us your daughter (*ḍhīkrī*).' This was a trick.

They kept the griddle very carefully and used it well. But Surya Bhagavan sent his blazing heat and the griddle cracked. When his mother went to take it back it was cracked. So she asked for the daughter. This was how Randal Ma was given in marriage to the Sun.

The play here is between the words for griddle (*ṭhīkrī*) and daughter (*ḍhīkrī*). In a published variant, at the very moment that Randal Ma is returning the griddle, the Sun aims a ray into the eye of a male buffalo, who becomes agitated, sending Randal Ma running. The griddle is broken as a result and Randal Ma's mother had to concede her daughter in marriage.[11]

Some retellings of Randal Ma's doubling underplay her pursuing of spiritual aspirations in the jungle. Like the newspaper article I just cited, these may instead highlight women's ambiguous rights to their natal homes after marriage. In one version recounted in English to me by a female relative in a Mumbai apartment in 2013, Vishwakarma questions his daughter about her return, and she then obligingly goes back to her husband's house to keep him company, along with her shadow.

> She was married to the Sun. But the Sun was too bright and she made her shadow, Chhaya, to stay with the children, and she went back to her father's house. After a while Vishwakarma thought: why is she here when she's married? He said to her, 'Shouldn't you go home?' So then she went back and the Sun realized that the other Randal had been a shadow. He said, 'Now you both stay here together.'
>
> That is why we honor her in the form of two, though she's actually one goddess. People say that this is why we all have shadows. Now that Randal has made a shadow, these shadows are always with us when we walk in the sun.

This retelling transformed the story into an etiological or explanatory myth, explaining why everyone has a shadow. Every shadow thus becomes a reminder of the shadow created by Randal Ma.

Community Rituals for Randal Ma

'She's a daughter, so she's always invited first,' explained Alka-ben, another Mumbai-based Gujar Sutar member, when asked about Randal Ma. 'We're in the Vishwakarma lineage, so if there's anything good in the family then first she is called. If there's any good news, or an occasion, then it will gain "good vibrations" with her visit.'

While a woman might honour Randal Ma by lighting two ghee lamps and offering rotis with milky rice pudding (khir) in her own household puja, Randal Ma often becomes a focus for a wider community celebration. Vishwakarma is particularly worshipped by the Gujar Sutars on *amāvāsya* (new moon) days, and also from the fifth to the thirteenth days of the bright half of the lunar month of *Magh* (rather than 17 September, as standardized with the solar calendar for worship in other parts of India). Randal Ma, however, can be worshipped any time through the year. As she is married to the Sun, her special weekday is Sunday. For reasons I have not yet learned, she may be especially invited for a mass celebration on the first Sunday in the month of *Bhadrapad*.

In the second half of the nineteenth century, network-based mass migrations took many Gujar Sutars to cities like Karachi and Bombay, where they adopted new professions associated with colonial urban expansion: leaving carpentry, they became engineers, contractors, and architects. The worship of Vishwakarma's daughter as a goddess who is honoured like a daughter returning home, and welcomed by her gathered family, appears to have become an important way to recreate community celebrations in these cities. Such an occasion is variously known as 'welcoming the pots' (*loṭā tedvānu*), 'welcoming the Mother' (*Mātājī tedvānu*), or 'welcoming Randal' (*Rāndal tedvānu*). Randal Ma is routinely honoured to gain blessings for important life events, like a seventh month ceremony for a pregnancy, a wedding, or other happy occasions. She may also be welcomed in observance of a vow to honour her (*māntā*) if she has granted a particular request. Her rituals can also be incorporated into the spring Navaratri, or 'Nine Nights to the Goddess', where her identity merges with mother goddesses more generally. On all these occasions, Randal Ma is invited to 'descend from the sky' and grant blessings.

Born in Karachi in 1929 and living in Ahmedabad at the time of our conversation, Pramila-ben explained the practices of her time for giving Randal Ma form. Set atop two water pot, coconuts were crafted with faces of clay.

> You give her two faces of white clay. Then you take cowry shells to make her eyes and lips. You outline her eyes with kohl and you stain her lips red. Then you dress her up in a nice sari and give her ornaments: earrings, nose rings, necklaces. When you worship her, she arrives for a 24-hour visit and grants blessings. It's really as though she is there! Then, just the way we send off our married daughters, we say farewell, and we lay those coconuts to rest in the earth where *tulsi*, the sacred basil Goddess, grows. The clay came from the earth and it returns to the earth.

Just as a daughter is never sent away from her parental home on Wednesdays, because the Gujar Sutar celebrants are from Vishwakarma's family, Randal Ma too cannot be summoned on a Tuesday and bid farewell on a Wednesday. If called on a Tuesday, she must be sent back that very day, or else hosted until Thursday.

While Pramila-ben is of the generation that recalls making the goddess's faces from organic materials, in recent decades, it has become customary to use brass or silver faces (*mohrā*). These faces are heavy and valuable, and are usually owned collectively, along with the metal pots or lotas. For the Kutchi Gujar Sutar community in Mumbai (though not in other cities that I am aware of), Randal Ma's faces, pots, the metal frame for constructing a canopy, a stool, and suitcases filled with clothes and jewellery circulate among different households in the community, and are kept for a year at a time in the home of a particular family. In 2009, in a cramped apartment in Matunga, Mumbai, I was shown how Randal Ma's things had been stored amidst other family possessions. In the course of my questioning, the women hosting Randal Ma balanced the lovely silver faces atop the pots and then dressed them up as twins. I learned that during that year, anyone in the community who wanted to invite Randal Ma would have to come and collect her from the family in whose care she was, and at the end of the year, that family would also host a large function for the community to worship the goddess together. One woman, who had recently hosted Randal Ma and was visited by other families borrowing the goddess through the year, observed that such centralization in the community was perhaps done partly to avoid too many competing rituals, especially since fellow celebrating women must be assembled for the ritual to be considered complete. Equally, one could see the goddess's circulation as a way for community members to re-affirm their connection to each other and their divine lineage alike.

For every twin pair representing the goddess, a group (*gorni* or *goyni*) of either young girls or married women, is assembled. The required number of women is fourteen: a number perhaps associated with the light and dark halves of a lunar month, or perhaps with a doubling of the seven horses that carry the Sun's chariot. These women represent the goddess and are honoured with food, particularly, khir served with wheat rotis (for a fuller meal, this would include rice, a dal, and vegetable dishes made with chana and potato). Then the feet of the women are washed and anointed with red vermillion (kumkum). Also, each woman is given gifts—for example, a package of *chāndlā* (bindi) worn by auspiciously married and marriageable women, a handkerchief, bangles, nail polish, a metal dish of some sort, fruits, and money. Alka-ben explained the dynamics of keeping track of this worship:

> To invite her you must call fourteen women and make fourteen *roṭis*. Married women or else unmarried girls are worshipped. Each one puts her foot on the low wooden stool (*pāṭlā)* and her foot is then washed and the right toe is worshipped with water, milk and then water again and little *kumkum*. You

mark the stool each time with a *chāndlā* of *kumkum* to keep track. When there are fourteen marks you know you have finished. Then you put the water on the eyes or touch it to your tongue, and you finish the *vrat* that way.

Songs sung at this time list the names of all the women participating in this *pūjā*, establishing a continuity between the goddess and her celebrating women relatives. During the waving of lights for *ārati*, women may become possessed, and certain individuals are known for the goddess entering their body (*angmā āve che*). When other communities welcome Randal Ma, they particularly invite women from carpenter families in the hope that they may embody this goddess. A possessed woman is filled with tremendous strength, dancing with energy, her head whirling and hair coming loose. Randal Ma may speak through her to answer questions posed by members of the gathered group. Sometimes a few women may become possessed. As Alkaben explained—'Women have *shaktī*, energy. They have a supportive presence. Women are *shaktī* and so we do their *pūjā*. Wherever women are respected, Lakshmi is there.'

In addition to circular *garba* dances in Randal Ma's honour, women dance to simulate the movement of a galloping horse (*ghoṛo khundvānu*). As the folklorist Hasu Yagnik writes, 'two or more pairs of women bent [*sic*] down from the waist, and jump in the manner as they are horse riding...when the body is bent down, it makes a shape like a horse, and the dance is performed by strutting like a horse.'[12] As my cousin Yeshu explained, 'You become a horse, you hop like a horse and it makes the Mataji happy.' Dance scholar Purnima Shah, working with brahmin communities who invite Randal Ma, describes this dance performed in those settings by one woman as the 'Hamchi' as—'a vigorous rhythmic movement resembling the stomping of a horse.'[13] As she observes, 'This movement is a symbolic representation of the romantic interlude between Surya and his consort Randala in the form of a horse and mare.'[14] Thus, a segment of the ancient myth of the goddess is recreated through the horse dance.

The Ties of Kinship

In addition to stories told within and between families, a key node for the transmission of mythological tales about Vishwakarma and his descendents has historically been the genealogist, who, among Gujar Sutars, is known as the Bhat or Barot. When the Bhat is invited to a home, he comes carrying his *chopḍo*—a handwritten genealogical manuscript wrapped in oilcloth. If the *chopḍo* is to be opened for a reading, it must be worshipped first and given an offering of cash.

My elder sister had the forethought of making a cassette tape of a Bhat's reading in Ahmedabad sometime in the 1980s. In 2013, I quickly reviewed the contents with a retired Gujar Sutar builder with a wide-ranging set of interests that included the history of the caste.[15] I offer a quick summary from the notes that pertain to Vishwakarma's daughters:

> Vishwakarma made the circuit for the Sun or Surya with the twelve signs of the zodiac and he designed the *nakshatra* (lunar mansions). He established the northern and southern hemispheres, and the equator. He made the architectural science (*vāstu*) according to the intensity of the Sun, to guide the opening for the Sun's energy and the circulation of air.
>
> He had two daughters, Ranna Devi and Brihasmati. Ranna Devi was given in marriage to Surya who was gifted with a chariot. Brihasmasti was married to King Priyamvrit and she became jealous that her husband wasn't given a chariot. Then Vishwakarma gave this other son-in-law a chariot too. As the king tried to follow the Sun, his wheels scoured the earth, making seven continents and seven seas.

These two daughters reappear in a closely related variant in the *Vishwakarma Purana* from Mathura. In this version, they are called Ratna Devi and Brihasmati, and are produced from their divine father's two hands.[16] Ratna Devi is married to the Sun, while Brihasmati chooses King Priyashree or Priyavrat. This version also describes how the Sun's wandering in his chariot establishes the structure of days, months, seasons, and a wider cosmology, while the other son-in-law's chariot produces the seas and continents on the earth. The creative actions of the 'Universe-Maker' Vishwakarma, then, continues not just through his sons, but also through his daughters and sons-in-law, as they give the current universe its form.

In 1991, my aunt Chanda-phui invited the son of the storytelling Bhat (mentioned earlier) to her house in Ahmedabad. This son, Narendra Barot, arrived on a motorcycle with the *chopḍo*. As he was offered tea, he chatted, telling some general stories about the history of the caste, and recalling how his father had once travelled just after the monsoon season to patrons within and outside Gujarat. With his permission, I set up a small tape recorder. When the Bhat unwrapped and opened up the book, he worshipped it and we honoured its presence with offerings (of incense, fruit, and cash). He chanted mantras and recited verses, interspersing these with oral interpretations in Gujarati mixed with Hindi, for my benefit. He then moved into swift currents of narrative, flowing from the creation through the four great eras of time, washing forward towards ancestors tied to historical kings, and emerging towards recent entries in genealogical records of my father's patrilineage.

The Bhat began by recounting a time when there were no boundaries or distinctions between things (*ante nati bhed nati*) until and Brahma experienced the desire to create; how the basic elements (*mahātattva*) were made, and combined; and how each human being is also a microcosm of this larger creation. The Bhat then moved through further stories of the creation of different gods and sages, including Vishwakarma himself. After telling many other myths relating to Vishwakarma and his sons, the Bhat returned to the daughters. One of his stories describes the daughters' key role as Vishwakarma's sons moved from making things simply from the power of mantras to actually using metal tools in the Kali Yuga. I present this story, interweaving a translated account from the Bhat and the comments of the women chopping and cleaning vegetables some years later, listening to his voice from a cassette player that I had set up.

Randal Ma and Brihasmati went home after marriage, and their brothers honored them with great respect, and delighted them with gifts. As they were both preparing to leave, Randal Ma gave her brothers a boon. 'Brothers, in Kaliyuga, when you build and use iron, even if you pierce yourself and blood flows, you won't get tetanus (*dhanurvātā*).'

[Here the women paused to reflect on home treatments involving jaggery and *ajwain* seeds that can be smeared on cuts to keep tetanus at bay.]

She gave this boon. The four sons thought, 'In Kaliyuga, our own sons will do this work and they'll need the right tools.' They went to their father Vishwakarma to ask for his help.

['This work is in our blood!' commented Pramila-ben, 'We keep these tools in our house. On Vishwakarma's day those who do carpentry especially worship their tools. I'll show you all the tools in posters of Vishwakarma!']

Vishwakarma said, 'On Mount Abu, there's a blacksmith (*lohār*). He has the bones of a huge demon (*daitya*) buried there. He'll make you tools from those bones.'

The four brothers went to Mount Abu. They went and stayed with the blacksmith. 'Make us tools,' they requested.

He said, 'I have a Devakanya, a divine girl, here. One of you should marry her. Then I'll craft tools for you.'

The older brothers married the youngest one to her according to all the proper rites. Then the blacksmith made them tools from the bones of the demon. [The Bhat began to recite a list that is difficult for us, unfamiliar with names of tools, to follow]. From the skull he made a huge anvil, from the ribs he made drills, from the elbow a set square, ten fingers into chisels and so on.

[Other tools are mentioned that I can't understand and my female relatives can't explain].

The four brothers took these instruments to their father Vishwakarma, and they also saw their sisters off. Randal Ma said, 'Those who invite me at least once a year will never be hungry.' She gave them these boons, that her brothers will never be hungry as they have these building tools, and they won't get tetanus.

Though this story starts with two daughters, they rapidly merge into one. Randal Ma's boon to prevent tetanus inspires her brothers to recognize the need for tools in the future, and to consult their father on how to procure them. Vishwakarma sends them to the blacksmith on Mount Abu, a high mountain in Rajasthan, just across the border of Gujarat. Just as Vishwakarma is the donor of a chariot to his son-in-law, the Sun, the blacksmith suggests linking himself to the brothers through the relation of father-in-law before granting them the right tools. Made from the bones of a demon, these tools are crafted through the blacksmith's furnace.

While tools are clearly central to the artisans' livelihood, my older female relatives' commentary on the story focussed less on the acquisition of tools and more on the issue of the ongoing relationships between brothers and married sisters. I wrote down their comments in a continuous scribble:

We should always invite Randal Ma. But brothers don't always remember their sisters. Randal Ma is our married daughter, our married sister, and we should honor her the way we honor the daughters of a house. She gives us happiness. If nothing else we should invite her to our home at least once in a lifetime. She grants wealth, happiness and prestige. She's Vishwakarma's daughter, after all, and she gave her brothers this boon! She is a Goddess, and she should be honored as a Goddess. The boon she gave is true. It's still going, it hasn't shattered. . . .

Just as Randal Ma and her sister helped the sons of Vishwakarma in gaining tools, goddesses are associated with granting tools in different regions of India. For example, Jan Brouwer notes that artisans in Karnataka emphasize on how they consider their tools to be manifestations of Goddess Kali,[17] and Nita Kumar reports that metalworkers worship 'anvils, bellows, workplace and all tools' in domestic pujas for Goddess Durga in Benares.[18] Brouwer presents two narratives that emphasize how the powers of Kali and Shiva are together present in the tools and the process of making of the tools. In one myth, the primordial blacksmith makes the anvil his right knee, his left hand the tongs, his right hand the hammer, thus crafting the first tools; the right and left sides, Brouwer argues, are tied to Kali and Shiva.[19] In another myth, Shiva asks Vishwakarma to make an image of him, but he keeps changing his form. As a result, each day, the previous work is rendered incorrect. Kali helps by suggesting that Vishwakarma set up four mirrors instead, so Shiva might glimpse himself. Finally, Shiva recognizes his present self in the image.

> In gratitude, he gave himself and his weapons to Visvakarman. Paramesvara himself is the anvil, his *damaru* the hammer, the *trisula* the forceps, his snake the measuring tool. Mahakali herself became the furnace and her vehicle the bellows. Thus in the workshop of the Visvakarmas the whole universe (*brahmanda*) is represented, according to our father.[20]

While the Gujar Sutar account mentions the bones of a demon rather than the body of a primordial artisan or metamorphosed deities, the accounts merge around the goddess's involvement with prior forms being dramatically transformed into tools with the potential to craft new forms.

The association between Vishwakarma and goddess worship is also present in Bengal, where Vishwakarma Jayanti may be celebrated in conjunction with the worship of the Goddess Manasa or Monosha. Arguing that these rituals enact kinship relations of care, Bear has shown how shipbuilding artisans observe a cooking ritual or *rannā* puja to the Snake Goddess Monosha in their homes, even as they celebrate Vishwakarma puja with feasts and family visits in the shipyard.[21]

As Pramila-ben said, reflecting on stories about Randal Ma, these were also about 'taking and giving' (*len-den*) and that exchanges of gifts—which included daughters—consolidated relations. 'There is a certain kind of fate in these relations too,' she reflected. This applied also to relations between Vishwakarma communities, as representatives of Vishwakarma's sons, in their continued engagement with their sisters/aunts. For as Chanda-phui—my father's sister—once responded when I asked her about Randal Ma, 'The love between a brother and a sister is very strong. So of course a sister loves her brother's children. That's why Randal Ma helps us.'

Randal Ma in Comparative Context

I now move beyond the specificity of Gujar Sutar worship of Randal Ma to contemplate the worship of this doubled goddesses within a wider comparative perspective.

First, while Randal Ma is honoured as a returning daughter by artisan communities, other Gujarati communities also host her as a goddess.[22] At such events, her identity as the Sun's wife and the fertile mother of many children can be emphasized more than her status as Vishwakarma's daughter. She is especially honoured at ceremonies in the seventh month of pregnancy to ensure a safe delivery. The Maher community, based in Leicester, UK, for example, offers instructions on how to welcome her on a webpage titled 'Randal Mataji na Lota'—the Pots of Randal Ma. Besides, YouTube clips abound with devotional songs to Randal Ma, complete with images from her temples. As a fertility goddess, she grants children to childless women from diverse backgrounds—not just artisan communities.

Second, Randal Ma also is worshipped in shrines and temples, including those of the Sun. Yagnik suggests that the worship of Randal Ma in Gujarat appears to be linked with the Solanki dynasty and describes images of Randal Ma reaching back to the twelfth and thirteenth centuries;[23] similarly, Shah cites an inscription dated 1237 CE, and mentions 'Rannade' at the Jayaditya temple to Surya and Randal in Kheda district, near Khambhat.[24] While there is apparently a shrine to Randal Ma in Rander (seen to be a corruption of her name) near Surat (as associated with *suraj*, or sun), most of Randal Ma's shrines are in the Saurashtra peninsula—an area where Kutchi Gujar Sutars often took brides from (and interestingly, among these Kathiawari Sutars, Randal Ma is more likely to be kept in everyday household worship rather than by special invitation). One of Randal Ma's main temple is at Mota Dadhva or Randhal-na-Dadhva near Rajkot, and is known as 'Randal's Doors' (*Rāndal no dvāro*). However, in a case of further doubling, there appear to be other more minor temples in different districts and villages also named Dadhva. Her granting of boons gives her the epithet *Dadhvā-ni dātār*—the generous donor of Dadhva.[25] Interestingly, in being represented with identical heads and torsos, she bestows these boons without any iconographical reference to hands. In these temples too, the goddess is honoured by feeding circles of fourteen women or girls with khir and rotis.

Third, Randal Ma's doubled form is closely related to at least another Gujarat-based iconographical representation of the goddess. This is the Gujar Sutar's *kuldevi*, Chamunda of Chotila. At the temple atop the hill of Chotila outside Surendranagar, the Goddess Chamunda is worshipped in a doubled form, also fused at the shoulder. However, unlike Randal Ma, who is shown only from the torso up, Chamunda is represented from head to toe. In this case, the doubling is given a different interpretation, associated with a story in the *Durga Saptashati* epic. (The epic describes how, when the goddess Chandika was enraged by two demons, Chanda and Munda, the fearsome and tempestuous Kali burst from Chandika's brow. Together, Chandika and Kali killed the demons. When Kali offered Chandika the two severed demon heads, Chandika playfully gave Kali the name 'Chamunda'. Joining the names 'Chanda' and 'Munda' and the peaceful and fierce forms of the two goddesses who destroyed them, the name 'Chamunda' plays on doubles.) Images of Chamunda of Chotila are regularly kept in Gujar Sutar households for worship. The possible link between Chamunda Mata and Randal Ma as two doubled goddesses was echoed when I asked the old Bhat about the two faces of Randal Ma, and he linked her to the peaceful and fierce forms of the goddess associated with the power of the creator Brahma and the destroyer Rudra. 'The Mataji is both Brahmani and Rudrani,' he said, 'though they are still the same core energy (*mūl shakti*).'

Fourth, as a Gujar Sutar woman living in Maharashtra pointed out, doubled goddesses are also worshipped for Gauri puja, associated with Ganesh Chaturthi in Maharashtra. These identical twin goddesses, sometimes known as 'Jyeshta' (Older) and 'Kanishta' (Younger), may be summoned with the same metal faces as those used for Randal Ma. Further research is needed to understand this link better.

Fifth, the iconographical motif of the doubled goddess may be evidence of ancient connections through trade, tools, and migrations between Gujarat and regions to its north-west. For example, I was astonished to confront a twin goddess, joined at the shoulder, in the Smithsonian Museum at Washington. This image is thought to date from Jordan in the seventh millennium BCE[26] and is an example of the larger range of ancient double goddess figures from the Eurasia region stretching from the Balkans and Turkey towards India. In her popular book, *The Double Goddess: Women Sharing Power* that assembles this iconographical evidence, Vicki Noble offers a feminist perspective on these doubled goddesses, suggesting that they represent women sharing power and the sacred potential of female bonding. While this interpretation does not fully fit the mythology of Randal Ma, all these comparative contexts point intriguingly to the need for further research.

Conclusion

While the sons of Vishwakarma are highlighted in most popular representations in different regions of India, in this essay, I have moved beyond patrilineal narratives and kinship relations that connect artisans' occupations to their divine ancestor. Shifting the focus to Vishwakarma's daughter, as she is worshipped in Gujarat, brings to light how Vishwakarma's daughters and their marriage alliances also continue Vishwakarma's work of creating the universe. In addition, this reminds us of a larger connection between Vishwakarma and goddess worship in regions beyond Gujarat.

As the daughter of Vishwakarma, what does Randal Ma's doubling mean to artisans? Through her perfectly identical resplendent heads and torsos, Randal Ma seems to celebrate a larger creative theme of self-replication that does not depend on the skill of the hands. Much like her artisan father, brothers, and their sons, Randal Ma crafts something of herself that will have an independent life: her own shadow double. Yet she does so without a reference to hands.

I wonder whether this doubling may be viewed as an insight into the creative process that connects the artisans' inner engagement with the objects that they craft. For example, in a remarkable documentary film *Vaastu Marabu* (1991) that explores the metaphysics of creativity from the perspective of artisans, the master sculptor Ganapati Sthapati describes his own creative experience. 'I saw the image within me take shape outside,' he explains in Tamil. 'Feelings do take forms. When I saw this I realized that the figure that stood before me was really myself. In a flash I understood the statement from my tradition, "The sculptor becomes the sculpture."' Reflecting on this correspondence between inner vision and outer form, I was reminded of Randal Ma's doubled self.

The doubled form also echoes other doubles in the artisans' worldview. For example, based on his work with the ironworkers in Karnataka, Brouwer has described the Vishwakarma (he writes 'Visvakarma') communities' worship at temples of Kalika Kamatesvara to assert that 'the goddess is, in the Visvakarma cultural ideology and on the ground, a crucial asset of collective identity and communicative action'.[27] He makes a link to the distinction made between '*finishing* a work and *completing* a work' (emphasis in original),[28] so that the finished product, delivered to a patron, is not completed until a final ritual action is done, using black materials (such as black pupils added to the eyes of a sculpture) that invokes the goddess. He writes, 'The incomplete and imperfect product is metaphorically seen as Life, while the complete and perfect product is viewed as Death. The Black Goddess stands between Life and Death, thus protecting the artisans through her communicative actions.'[29] Doubling, then, can also be a way of bringing together differences.

Randal Ma's doubling stands not just for artisanal creativity but procreativity as well. As a fertile mother in her various forms, she grants children to those who pray to her. She is thus a goddess of fertility not just for the artisans, but for all other communities who honour her. Her wider cult of worship for fertility extending beyond the Vishwakarma community in Gujarat—and also her association with the doubled Chamunda Mata—is a reminder of how the Vishwakarma mythology becomes connected and adapted to larger regional forms of goddess worship.

Gujar Sutars who no longer engage in professions that involve working with their hands, continue to honour Vishwakarma as a form of ancestral continuity. His daughter Randal Ma's presence remains important for any moment of transition needing blessings and reassurance, and her identity as a divine relative merges with that of other benevolent, auspicious goddesses. Women are central to organizing the invitations to bring Randal Ma from the sky, her iconography and stories linking to their own identities as daughters, sisters, and wives. Also, her stories highlight women's concerns with the ongoing issues of visiting and gifting within and between families joined through blood and through marriage. This preliminary essay suggests the need for further ethnographic work among female descendents of Vishwakarma, starting from his daughter, and continuing towards contemporary women in hereditary artisan communities.

Acknowledgements

I thank all the relatives who talked to me through the years about their experiences of worshipping Randal. I also thank the readers of this essay, whose comments were invaluable: Kalpesh Bhatt, Ken George, and Maya Narayan. I am grateful to Vijaya Ramaswamy for including me in this volume, though I did not have the good fortune to participate in the conference from which this volume emerges. This essay was largely written before I had the opportunity to begin fieldwork under the auspices of the American Institute of Indian Studies Senior Fellowship and the Australian Research Council (Discovery Project Award DP170104212, 'Building India: Religion, Craft, and Infrastructure in Contemporary Asia'). I am extremely grateful for the fieldwork support that has allowed me to give this essay a final polish, and I look forward to future opportunities to revisit and expand on the issues raised here.

Notes

1. Laura Bear, '"This Body is Our Body": Vishwakarma Puja, the Social Debts of Kinship and Theologies of Materiality in a Neoliberal Shipyard', in *Vital Relations: Modernity and the Persistent Life of Kinship*, ed. Susan McKinnon and Fenella Cannell, Santa Fe: School for Advanced Research Press, 2013, pp. 155–78; Jan Brouwer, *The Makers of the World: Caste, Craft and Mind of South Indian Artisans*, Delhi: Oxford University Press, 1995; Renaldo Maduro, *Artistic Creativity in a Brahman Painter Community*, Berkeley: Center for South and Southeast Asian Studies, 1976; Samuel Parker, 'Making Temples/Making Selves: Essentialism and Construction in the Identity of the Traditional South Indian Artist', *South Asian Studies*, vol. 129, no. 1, 2003, pp. 125–40; T.R. Singh, 'Analysis of Some Panchabrahma Myths', *The Eastern Anthropologist*, vol. XXI, no. 1, 1968, pp. 11–20; George Varghese K., 'Globalisation Traumas and New Social Imaginary: Visvakarma Community of Kerala', *Economic and Political Weekly*, vol. 38, no. 45, 2003, pp. 4794–802.
2. Vijaya Ramaswamy, 'Vishwakarma Craftsmen in Early Medieval Peninsular India', *Journal of the Economic and Social History of the Orient*, vol. 47, no. 4, 2004, pp. 548–82.
3. Alka Hingorani, *Making Faces: Self and Image Creation in a Himalayan Village*, Honolulu: University of Hawaii Press, 2013; Stella Kramrisch, 'Traditions of the Indian Craftsman', *Journal of American Folklore*, vol. 71, no. 281, 1958, pp. 224–30; Tryna Lyons, *The Artists of Nathadwara: The Practice of Painting in Rajasthan*, Bloomington and Ahmedabad: Indiana University Press and Mapin Publishing, 2004.
4. Purnima Shah, 'Randala Ritual: Women's Heritage and Identity in Gujarat, India', in *Ritual, Heritage and Identity: The Politics of Culture and Performance in a Globalised World*, ed. Christiane Brosius and Karin M. Polit, New Delhi: Routledge, 2011, pp. 165–201.
5. Kirin Narayan, *My Family and Other Saints*, Chicago: University of Chicago Press, 2007.
6. Narayan Ravaji Shastri Kshirsagar, *Vishvabrahmakulotsaha or History of Vishvabrahmins*, Poona: Kalika Prasad Press, 1921; A.E. Roberts, *Visvakarma and his Descendents*, Calcutta: All India Vishwakarma Brahman Mahasabha, 1909.
7. Adapted from Narayan, *My Family and Other Saints*, pp. 94–5.
8. Maurice Bloomfield, 'Contributions to the Veda III: The Marriage of Saranyu, Tvastar's Daughter', *Journal of the American Oriental Society*, vol. 15, 1893, pp. 172–88; Wendy Doniger, 'Saranyu/Samjna: The Sun and the Shadow', in *Devī: Goddesses of India*, ed. John S. Hawley and Donna M. Wulff, Berkeley: University of California Press, 1996, pp. 137–53; Wendy Doniger, *Splitting the Difference: Gender and Myth in Ancient Greece and India*, Chicago: University of Chicago Press, 1999; Stella Kramrisch, 'Two:

Its Significance in the Ṛgveda', in *Indological Studies in Honor of W. Norman Brown*, ed. Ernest Bender, New Haven: American Oriental Society, 1962, pp. 109–236.

9. Doniger, 'Saranyu/Samjna: The Sun and the Shadow'.
10. Doniger, *Splitting the Difference*, pp. 43–55.
11. Hasu Yagnik, *Folklore of Gujarat*, tr. N.M. Kansara, New Delhi: National Book Trust, 2002, pp. 29–30.
12. Ibid., p. 156.
13. Shah, 'Randala Ritual', p. 173.
14. Ibid., pp. 173–4.
15. Kirin Narayan, 'Narrating Creative Process', *Narrative Culture*, vol. 1, 2014, pp. 109–23.
16. Ayodhyanath Chaturvedi, *Shree Vishwakarma Purana*, Mathura: Jagdish Printing Press, 1989, p. 163.
17. Brouwer, *The Makers of the World*, pp. 141–5.
18. Nita Kumar, *The Artisans of Benares: Popular Culture and Identity 1880-1986*, Princeton: Princeton University Press, 1988, p. 203.
19. Brouwer, *The Makers of the World*, pp. 142–3.
20. Ibid., p. 144.
21. Bear, '"This Body is Our Body": Vishwakarma Puja, the Social Debts of Kinship and Theologies of Materiality in a Neoliberal Shipyard'.
22. Shah, 'Randala Ritual'.
23. Yagnik, *Folklore of Gujarat.*
24. Shah, 'Randala Ritual', p. 167.
25. Yagnik, *Folklore of Gujarat*, p. 29.
26. See also Vicki Noble, *The Double Goddess: Women Sharing Power*, Rochester, Vt.: Bear and Co., 2003, pp. 33–4.
27. Jan Brouwer, 'The Communicating Goddess of the Artisans', in *The Social and the Symbolic*, ed. B. Bel et al., New Delhi: Sage, 2007, p. 232.
28. Ibid., p. 241.
29. Ibid., p. 245.

Northern Perspectives on the Vishwakarma

7

Artists and the Early Art-Activity

R.N. MISRA

The artist in ancient India was not an isolated institution; in the social hierarchy he belonged to a general class of artisans engaged in various crafts. Historically therefore, his position and craft have to be related to a kindred group of artisans and their occupations. An enquiry into the existence, function, and organization of artists in ancient India ultimately leads to a body of data in which different categories of artisans are found clubbed together in one general group called *śilpīn*. Likewise, the term *śilpa* has a wide connotation and it includes within its ambit various crafts, skills, and occupations. This necessitates an enquiry into different crafts in relation to the word *śilpa*, with a view of making a brief survey of some aspects of crafts along with its practitioners, in a historical perspective.

The earliest occurrence of the word *śilpa* is found in the *Saṃhitās*[1] and *Brāhmaṇas*.[2] In these, it has been used to define a variety of acts or activities, such as manual arts and crafts, ceremonial acts and rites, artistic work, and so on. In the *Naighanṭuka* (III.7), it connotes a form or a shape. In the *Brāhmaṇas*, the word is used in the sense of work of art, e.g. 'They recite *śilpas*. These are the works of art of the gods; in imitation of these works of art, here is a work of art accomplished—an elephant, a goblet, a garment, a gold-object, a mule-chariot are works of art.'[3] In the *Kauśītaki Brāhmaṇa* (XXIX.5) are enumerated the threefold *śilpas*—dancing, music, and singing. The *Pañchaviṃśa Brāhmaṇa* has the word *śilpatva*, indicating a state of being variegated or decorated.[4] The diverse usage of the word *śilpa* clearly indicates that the acts requiring skill in certain performances, such as singing, dancing, compiling hymns, and

* I have used the standard diacritic symbols for the Sanskrit and other classical Indian languages.

other diverse art-activities, were broadly known as *śilpa*. Even in the realm of dramatic arts, the word has significance in a form of drama which was known as *śilpaka*.[5]

The term *śilpa* denotes 'ceremonial act' in the *Āśvalāyana Śrautasūtra* (VIII.4.5–8; IX.10.11; XI.2) and in this sense it is close to *kāru* (from the root *kṛ*), which in the Vedic context, stands for a maker or an artisan, a singer of hymns or a poet. In a reference in the *Rig Veda*, Vishwakarmā, a god of creation, is mentioned as *dhātu-karmāra*, while *karmāra* alone refers to artisans and artificers.[6] Vishwakarmā is supposed to create things out of *dhātu*, i.e. 'raw material', and the act is known as *sanghamana*.[7] The process of cutting, shaping, and painting has been often explained in the texts by the root *takṣ*.[8] For instance, Tvaṣṭā is sometimes described as a god who *tatakṣa*, 'sharpens', the Vajra (thunderbolt) of Indra.[9] The correspondence of Indra and Tvaṣṭā in the creation of some forms is mentioned in the early texts. Indra creates a form by his inner power, while Tvaṣṭā brings forth a form by chipping and carving, an act that has been described as *rūpa-piṃśana*. These activities may significantly be taken under the wider connotations of *śilpa*. Besides, these references also shed some light on the practical aspect of the skill required in the practice of crafts.

As regards the types of occupations or *śilpas* (crafts), the *Saṃhitās* and *Brāhmaṇas* have preserved relevant material. The Vedas bring out in clear profile craftsmen like *takṣaka* or carver, *rathakāra* or chariot-maker, and *karmāra* or blacksmith. The list of occupations and crafts grew in the post-Vedic period. While the *Rig Veda* knew only of the *karmāras*, *takṣakas*, weavers, tanners, and the *rathakāras*,[10] the later Vedic texts enumerate many other occupations. The *Vājasneyī Saṃhitā* (XXX.6.21) and the *Taittirīya Brāhmaṇa* refer to various categories of artisans: chariot-makers, carpenters, potters, smiths, jewellers, etc. Such an increase in the categories of trades that generally fall under *śilpas*, indicates a greater degree of economic activity that consequently brought about development. The growth in the number of crafts as well as their practitioners continued even in the post-Vedic period.[11]

During the early Vedic phase, it seems that even though the social status of some of the artisans, particularly the *takṣakas* and the *rathakāras*, tended to vary, the artisans as a class enjoyed a respectable position in the society. The *Atharva Veda* (III, 5.6) cites that some of those engaged in various crafts belonged to the *Viś*, an Aryan community. The special place of *takṣakas*, *rathakāras*, and *karmāras* and their administrative responsibilities have been indicated in certain other texts. They were designated as *ratnins* and assigned important roles in the coronation ceremonies of kings.[12] Moreover, the agricultural Vedic society found immense use of the products made by the craftsmen in both agriculture and war. As a result, it can be concurred that the craftsmen must have commanded respect of the society. The crafts during this period were neither restricted to śūdras (as it happened later) nor was their practice stigmatized.[13] These points, among other things, define some of the fundamental traits of crafts during the Vedic period.

When stone came into use, the *takṣakas* of the Vedic times transformed their techniques and contributed to the growth of art-activities. During the early stages, they were primarily concerned with woodcraft. As regards the other *śilpas*, pointed out earlier, they grew in number in the post-Vedic times. The Buddhist texts enumerate various other occupations that came into prominence with the advent of the usage of stone. In the *Majjhima Nikāya* (I.85), the number of such occupations is twelve. The *Dīgha Nikāya*,[14] the *Mahāvastu*,[15] and the *Milinda Pañho*[16] have long lists of occupations and indicate the organization of craftsmen's guilds. About classification of crafts as high or low, the *Vinaya Piṭaka* says:

> Craft [*sippa*] means: there are two (kinds of) crafts: low craft and high craft. Low craft means: the craft of basket makers, the potters' craft, the weavers' craft, the leatherworkers' craft, the barbers' craft or whatever is disdained . . . despised in these districts—that means low craft. High craft means: reckoning on fingers (*muddā*), calculation (*gananā*), writing (*lekhā*), what is not disdained . . . what is esteemed in these districts—this means high crafts.[17]

The *Dīgha Nikāya* (I.51) lists all crafts except that of the leatherworker under the category of *puthu* (ordinary) crafts, and the list includes crafts even like *gananā*, *muddā*, *lekhā*, etc., which have been mentioned in the *Suttavibhānga*[18] as high crafts. The *Dīgha Nikāya*[19] has also made a distinction between those who were regarded low by birth and those who followed 'low' professions. But on the basis of such random statements, which are often contradictory, it is difficult to draw a hard and fast line to delineate a distinction of birth between those who followed different types of crafts.

While a complete correspondence of crafts with lower castes is difficult to establish in the Buddhist texts, the *sūtras* almost exclusively associate crafts with the śūdras. The *sūtras* rule that in the absence of any other means of livelihood, the śūdras may take to the various *śilpas*. Gautama holds this view while dealing with *śilpavṛtti*, i.e. practice of *śilpa*, as a means of the śūdras' livelihood.[20] The artisans seem to have started losing their pre-eminent position in the post-Vedic period and eventually the craftsmen such as *rathakāras* and *takṣakas*, who were of supreme importance during the Vedic age, lost their prerogatives and were relegated to the ranks of śūdras.[21] By about the sixth century BCE, the śūdras seem to have got largely associated with diverse types of *śilpas*, and it became customary to designate individuals according to the crafts they practiced. Richard Fick has classified the practitioners, belonging to the 'despised castes', of various crafts but he indicates a state of society which admitted certain casteless professions, particularly those that had a better guild organization.[22]

However, it will be far from correct to assume that the practice of crafts was limited only to persons in the lower strata of society. There are instances of persons belonging to higher castes practicing crafts. A *Jātaka* tale has the anecdote of a brahmin who earned his living from making carts, and thus plied the trade of a *vardhakī* (carpenter).[23] The *sūtras* usually frowned upon such cases of individuals belonging to higher castes taking to professions of lower castes. Baudhāyana, in this connection, has ruled that a brahmin tending cattle, or living by trades, or by working as an artisan should be treated like a śūdra.[24] Keeping aside such disapprobation, one notices a fluidity in respect of the practice of crafts by groups of people, high or low in social hierarchy. In a growing society, the artisans had enormous utility and the *śilpas* had a special role to play in the growth of economy as well as in urban patterns of life. In such circumstances, it is no wonder that quite often one comes across instances of people of various social ranks practicing different crafts. The Buddhist texts offer evidence to the extent that *gahapatis* (householders) were engaged in various crafts.[25] In their social status, the gahapatis of the Buddhist texts were equivalent to the vaiśyas of the orthodox *varṇa* system. The *Anguttara Nikāya* (III.363) refers to a *gahapati* who earned his living by *sippādhittāna*, i.e. the practice of art and craft. The institution of the *gahapatis* itself seems to have come up as a result of the prosperity of artisans, several of whom swelled the ranks of *gahapatis*.[26] Such cases clearly indicate the upward mobility, both in social and economic spheres, of the artisans. In Vātsyāyana's *Kāmasūtra*, among the virtues of a *nāyaka* (cultured man), the knowledge of various *śilpas* gets special mention. The *nāyaka* was supposed to be adept in *śilpas*.[27] Reference to the need of having a solitary place where a person could hone his skill in carving various objects, indicates the popularity that certain *śilpas* enjoyed amongst the higher sections of the society.[28] The *Lalitavistara* likewise indicates that proficiency in *śilpas* was inculcated amongst the princes of ruling families. Reference is made in the text to the hesitance of Śākya Daṇḍapāṇi in giving his daughter in marriage to Prince Siddhārtha, as the latter was not proficient in *śilpas*.[29]

In the aforementioned works, the word *śilpa* has different connotations, covering occupations, skills, and crafts. These references also establish a close relation between the artisans practicing different *śilpas*. In fact, the mutual correspondence of artisans is vividly expressed throughout ancient social history. At a later stage, this correspondence of different *śilpīs* was formalized. A parable in the *Brahmavaivartta Purāṇa* (I.10) relates how, as a result of a blessing from Brahmā, Vishwakarmā, who was born in a brahmin family, married the Apsarā Ghṛtāchī, who was reborn as a milkmaid; and out of this union came *jātis* such as tailors, potters, carpenters, as well as the *jātis* adept in the *tantra-vidyā*. This parable in the *Brahmavaivartta Purāṇa* thus seeks to interpret a common descent as well as the equivalence of different craftsmen.

How the sculptors and architects fared in this general class of *śilpīs*, and when they came to have a distinct class of their own is another important question. The question may be answered by splitting it into parts relating to the pre-Mauryan and the post-Mauryan times. To a great extent, the evolution of a distinct class of stonemasons must have depended upon the extensive use of stone for building purpose, which happened sometime during the rule of the Mauryas. Before the Mauryas, monuments were scarce and evidence meagre; so it has been surmised that wood, ivory, and other materials of perishable nature must have been in use for art-activities during that time. In these activities, the *takṣakas*, *vardhakīs*, and *karmāras* must have played an important role.[30] With the coming into use of stone for building, these artisans might have changed their techniques to suit the new requirements. This can be confirmed by references to the *takṣakas* and *vardhakīs* in the canons of iconography, written during the medieval period.[31] For instance, the *Mayamataṃ* (V.13–14) refers to four types of *śilpīs*: *sthapati*, *sūtragrāhin*, *takṣaka*, and *vardhakī*. Elsewhere, the same text defines *takṣaka* as an artisan who was required to fashion stone, wood, or bricks in the construction of buildings.[32] Such references clearly point towards a transformation of techniques and medium of artists, even though their designations continued to be the same.

That artists such as smiths and carpenters were involved in art-activity is proved by other references too. A *Jātaka* story refers to a prince who invited a *kammāra-jeṭṭhaka* (chief of goldsmiths) to make a female figure out of a given quantity of gold.[33] The *vaḍḍhakīs* and their activity find mention in several *Jātaka* stories. The *Alinachitta Jātaka*

(II, 156) refers to a *vaḍḍhakīgāma*, i.e. a village of carpenters, with 500 such carpenters. These carpenters, it is said, collected wood from forests, made 'things' out of these for use in various types of buildings, including the multistorey ones, to the choice and satisfaction of their clients. After completing a particular job, the carpenters started the cycle of collecting raw material and building objects, all over again.[34] Specific references to workers in stone during the pre-Mauryan period are very scarce. V.S. Agrawala, however, has indicated their existence as well as their participation in the building activities of the Achaemenian king Darius.[35] Agrawala says that the artists of Gandhara find mention in an Achaemenian inscription that acknowledges their contribution in the building of a palace at Susa.

More positive evidence about the stonemasons can be dated to the Mauryan times. The *Arthaśāstra* is of great use in this respect. It refers to various types of artisans engaged in building activities and their remuneration and protection provided by the state. Other information concerning artisans is also available in this text. It gives details concerning the artisans' remuneration, which varied according to the skill of the concerned person. According to this scale, a salary of two hundred *paṇas* for the *vardhakī* (chief architect) appears to be equivalent to that of a physician or a *rathakāra*.[36] The *Arthaśāstra* also has a term *kāru*, which generally designates artisans, whose different classes find mention in the text.[37] These references are of great assistance in identifying an independent class of artisans, specifically connected with architecture and sculptural art. The *Milinda Questions* (section 330) specifically refers to a 'city-architect', who lays out and raises a city and 'when the city was fully developed he might go away to another district'. This reference to the architect's mobility is important and to some extent it may explain why, in the Buddhist texts, although various other *śilpīs* have often been mentioned, architects and sculptors in particular do not get proportionate mention. It may also be surmised that probably these artists did not have such guilds as other craftsmen had, due to their mobility. Consequently, references to them are not as frequent as to those who were better organized.

With the acceleration in tempo of the building activities during the Mauryan period, artists began to receive greater attention. The stonemasons no longer remained anonymous or completely aligned to the kindred group of craftsmen. They seemed to have obtained a distinct niche in the class of artisans, which probably helped in salvaging their trade from obscurity. The emergent socio-economic situation following the Mauryan rule must have added its share in the advent of artisans specializing in building activities. The control on economy, production, and crafts as well as the growing inland and overseas trade during the Mauryan-Sātavahana era opened up new avenues for crafts and craftsmen. The religious fervour of the newly affluent classes in urban centres such as Mathura, Sanchi-Vidisa, and Nasik led to raising religious edifices. All these developments had their natural consequences on the tone of building activities and on the craftsmen engaged in them. The accent now was on the use of stone for building edifices or sculptures.

The vast administrative organization of the Mouryas had successfully harnessed the skill of craftsmen on a grand scale. The introduction of stone revolutionized art-activity. The impact of these transformations was felt in various parts of the country and the epigraphs available from Mathura, Bharhut, Sanchi, Gaya, and western and eastern coastal India help in understanding the degrees of such impact and the consequent transformation in the techniques and medium of artists. The epigraphs have expressions like *silākarmanta* or *śailakarma*, indicating that the activity had come to be known as 'stonework',[38] in contradistinction to work in wood, ivory, or metals. The sculptors are mentioned as *rupakāra*, *śailavardhakī*, *aveśani rūpadakṣa*, etc., all of which point to the growth of new factors in the realm of art-activity. The inscriptions also offer prolific references of small or big excavations and constructions or carvings, such as setting up of caves (*selaghara/leṇa*) or the facades of caves (*gharamugha*), stone pillars (*śilā-laṣṭi*) or their bases and so on.[39] Many important and extensive excavations, e.g. caves, *upasthānaśāla* (hall of reception), cells, and quadrangular dining halls find mention in the inscriptions. These are in addition and complementary to smaller things such as 'benches for sitting', 'walk', etc.[40] Sometimes, the donors took pride in commissioning works which they regarded as 'marvellous' and which were indeed so. For instance, an inscription from the Buddhist cave at Karla records the 'establishment of the cave dwelling, the most excellent on the Jambudvipa'.[41] Besides the edifices and their architectural components mentioned already, the inscriptions also record setting up of images,[42] or stone pieces decorated with carvings—the latter described as *śailarūpakarma*.[43] The exclusiveness of the stoneworker has been conveyed by qualifying him as *śailavardhakī*, which probably purports to indicate the distinctiveness of the stonemason in comparison to the ordinary *vardhakī*. The use may alternatively indicate the transformation of techniques and medium of the craftsmen, with the change in the medium of art.[44]

In addition to the evidence from epigraphs, evidence from the texts also suggests the growth of different classes of artists. The *Mahāvastu* refers to various classes of artists and their fields of specialization. Those figuring in its list are: *chitrakāraka* (painters), *vardhakī-rūpakāra* (carpenters), *kārupatrika* (carvers), *pustakāraka* (modellers of clay), *pustakarmakāraka* (plasterers), *lepaka* (decorators), and *sthapati-sūtrakāra* (architects).[45] These different terms signify that in the realm of stone carving and architecture, different classes of artists formed specialized groups. The *Manu Saṃhitā*[46] attempts to set up a hierarchy of artists related to building activities and mentions the *sthapati* (master architect), *sūtragrāhin* (surveyor-designer), and *takṣaka* (sculptor, carpenter, and painter) in relation to each other. In this hierarchy, the *sūtragrāhin* has a special relationship to the master architect in the sense that the former either has to be the son or a disciple of the latter. We have two terms here, *sūtragrāhin* and *sūtrakāra*, which are important and indicate designations which were to become more important in the post-Gupta times. The word *sūtragrāhin* has been explained as having referred to a surveyor-designer,[47] while *sūtrakāra* has been sometimes explained as having referred to a '(cotton-)spinner'.[48] However, on the analogy of the Sanskrit *sūtrakarma*, i.e. 'rule-work' or 'carpentry', it has been suggested that the whole compound in the *Mahāvastu* would seem to mean 'a builder working by rule' or a 'builder-carpenter'.[49] It may be added here that 'working by rule' was an idea limited not only to carpentry, but was also used in case of the stonemasons. The use of stone brought about a transformation in the building materials, though not so much in the building methods. The liberal use of wood in early monuments, such as the cave temples of western India, or even the principles of construction (e.g. pillars of wooden posts, pillars tilted inwards at the top in order to support the overhanging roof, and so forth) indicate a continuation of the older experience.

It has been surmised that some of the schools of *śilpa* had started taking shape in the early centuries of the Christian era. But the role of artists in the evolution of such schools is not clearly defined. On one hand, the information derived from the canons of iconography seems to relate the evolution of such schools to the prominent *āchāryas*, or to the craftsmen like Maya and Vishwakarmā;[50] on the other hand, Tārānath (a Tibetan lama) relates the development of the schools of art to the Nāga and Yakṣha artisans who, he says, were employed by the Mauryas for building their edifices. The relevant passage from Tārānath reads as follows:

> In the ancient period, the human artists possessed miraculous power and their artistic creations were astounding. In the *Vinaya Vastu*, etc., it is clearly said

that the statues made and pictures drawn by them created the illusion of being real objects. For about a hundred years after the *parinirvana* of the Teacher (i.e. the Buddha), there were many artists like them.[51]

As none of them were there afterwards, the celestial artists appeared in human guise and made eight wonderful images for worship in Magadha, like those of the Mahābodhi and Mañjuśrī-dundubhīśvara (an epithet of Amoghasiddhi Buddha). The *caityas* of the eight sacred places and the inner boundary wall of *vajrāsana* were built by the Yakṣa artists during the period of Aśoka, and the Nāga artists built many images during the time of Nagārjuna.[52]

Evidently, the information given by Tārānath is anachronistic in case of the images mentioned by him, for these images are untraceable in Indian art, till the time of the Kushanas. However, the tradition about the artists of the Mauryan period cannot be dismissed summarily. There is independent evidence, from Patanjali (dating from the middle of the second century BCE) as well, about the Maurya's involvement in making images for the collection of money.[53] That the making of images was a source of livelihood is also indicated by the *sūtra* of Pāṇini and the commentaries on it.[54] The Mauryas popularized (animal) sculptures and their making, and along with it, the artists came to have a permanent place in the legend of making sculptures, which is important even though the specifics of Tārānath's statement may not be true. It has been suggested that the *nāgara* (northern) style may have stemmed from the innovations by the Nāgas.[55]

Apart from what is known from the literary texts, a fair amount of information about the artisans and their role in building activity, is available in the ancient inscriptions. A large number of such inscriptions are from Mathura, Bharhut, Sanchi, and many regions of western and eastern India, viz., Kuda, Kanheri, Karla, Amaravati, Jaggayyapeta, etc. Most of these places were flourishing urban centres and served as important trading posts for overseas or inland trade in various commodities. The consequent prosperity and affluence explains the circumstances responsible for evolution of art and architecture at such places. It seems that in the evolution of the local idiom of art, the resident artists of different places helped in accomplishing a major breakthrough. In fact, the art evidence clearly indicates the development of local styles that evolved into distinct schools of sculpture, e.g. the Mathura school, the Western Indian school, and the Amaravati school. A comparison of the motifs of artworks as well as the sculptural styles clearly indicate that though there were distinct schools at different centres, mutual influences with respect to motifs, subjects of reliefs, the technical aspects of carving reliefs, the practice of accompanying labels with the reliefs, etc., among the various schools are clearly discernible.

We thus have a phenomenon in the realm of architecture and sculptural art, which accommodates the cognate styles as well as distinct ones. This leads to the conclusion that experiments and the skill obtained at one particular place did not necessarily remain localized to the place of origin. Rather, they spread to regions far and wide.[56] This, in its turn, is indicative of some sort of an organization of the artists that probably included both the resident and the itinerant artists. The epigraphs afford evidence regarding both the types of artists. The localization of building activity at different centres such as Mathura and Bharhut may indicate the existence of resident artists, and such artists may ultimately have led to the organization of the kindred group on a more efficient basis, even as the itinerant artists may have helped in the dissemination of the art idiom. The epigraphic data suggests that these classes of artists working in stone had come into existence by the second century BCE. As regards the resident artists, an inscription from Mathura records the dedication of a *silapatta* (stone slab), in the temple of Dadhikar.na[57] (Nāga) 'by the sons . . . of *śailālaka*, "stonemasons", [of] Mathura'.[58] These artisans are praised as Chandaka brothers, and the chief among them was Nandibala. The inscription offers information regarding the artists of Mathura. Another artisan of Mathura was Gomataka, a pupil of Kuṇika, who claims to have made the famous Parkham Yakṣha image.[59] Yet another pupil of Kuṇika, Nāga is known from a Mathura inscription as the maker of an image of Yakṣiṇī Lāyāva.[60] These inscriptions show that the artists' occupation was already in the process of specialization. In the case of the Chandaka brothers, it was practiced by all the brothers and Chandaka, the eldest among them, was the most reputed for his craft.[61] Similarly, in the case of Kuṇika and his disciples—Gomataka and Nāga—the phenomenon of specialization may be inferred from their teacher-disciple relationship. Further evidence about such relationship is available from other regions also, and will be mentioned at the relevant places. Among the resident artists, reference may also be made to the *dantakāra* (ivory carvers) of Vidisa, mentioned in a Sanchi inscription. This inscription records that the *rūpakamma* (carving) on a portion of the south gate was done by the *Vedisaka* workers in ivory.

Of greater number and importance are inscriptions pertaining to the itinerant artists, which have come to the fore from Sanchi, Ramgarh, and Jaggayyapeta. One of the earliest of such inscriptions has come from Ramgarh (Jogimara cave) and it refers to a *lūpadakha*, i.e. sculptor, Devadina (Devadatta) who was a native of Varanasi and a lover of Sutanukā, a *devadasikye* (temple servant).[62] An inscription from Sanchi[63] refers to an artisan(?)—Visakama (Vishwakarmā), a native of Ujjayinī. Another Sanchi inscription,[64] on the top architrave of the south gate of the main *stūpa* records that the work was the gift of Ānanda, who was the foreman of the artisans of *Rājan* Siri Sātakarṇi. This architrave has an outstanding depiction of the story of *Chhaddanta Jātaka*, whose equal in style could not be achieved on any other gate of the Sanchi Stupa. Sanchi was under the rule of the Sātāvahanas, whose centre of power during this time seems to have been located in the western part of Maharashtra. In the case of Ānanda, we have a clear evidence that the artist belonged to another region, but accomplished his work at Sanchi.

Evidence regarding the itinerant artists also comes from certain inscriptions of Jaggayyapeta, in Andhra Pradesh. These inscriptions refer to an *āveśani*, 'the foreman among artisans', namely Siddhārtha, who made a gift of five entrance pillars at the *dāra* (door) of the *Mahāchetiya* at Velagiri.[65] Siddhārtha was a resident of the village Mahākamdurura while his father Nāgachandra, who also was an *āveśani*, resided in Nadatura, in the province of Kammaka. Besides indicating that the artist's profession was hereditary, the inscriptions also refer to their mobility, i.e. physical movement from one place to another.

There are inscriptions which refer to artists alone, without any reference to the places to which they belonged to, e.g. the inscription referring to *rūpakāra* Budharakhita of Bharhut.[66] Similarly, the inscriptions of Sanchi refer to two such artisans—Artha and Abhaya.[67] These cases are unlike an Amaravati inscription that refers to an artist (whose name has disappeared), who was a native of Vīrapura and the son of Dharmadeva.[68] There are several other cases in which the artists find mention, e.g. the *vaḍhakī* Svāmin, the son of Venuvasa of Dhenukāṭaka, who made the *mugha* (door) of the cave at Karla[69] of Baluka (or Balaka) at Kondane.[70] Some of these inscriptions indicate that craftsmen belonging to other fields like ivory-carving, carpentry, etc., also joined the ranks of the stonemasons.

Information is also available regarding the artists' setup and organization. Individual artists, as we have seen already, were known as *rūpakāra*, *rūpadakṣa*, *karmika*, *śailālaka*, etc. Sometimes they were designated as *śailavardhakī*.[71] These terms might also have designated their occupational classes, just as work on stone was known as *śailakarma*.[72] Among the artists of authority, the *navakarmikas*[73] and *āveśanins*[74] figure prominently. A Sonari inscription refers to the *navakarmika* (overseer) Dharmagupta, a pupil of Ārya-Prasannaka; a

Bharhut inscription mentions the *navakarmika* Ārya-Riṣipālita who is also styled as *bhadanta* (monk or elder) and *bhāṇaka* (preacher). A Kanheri inscription gives a long list of *navakarmikas*, describing them as *bhadantas*; their names are—Achala, Gṛihala, Vijayamitra, Bodhika, and Dharmapāla. The merchant Apareṇuka also occurs in this list of overseers, but his role cannot be exactly established. The inscription adds that the work of excavating the cave was 'executed' by *bhadanta* Bodhika, the pupil of *bhadanta* Seumla, and that in this work he acted as overseer (*uparakhita*) of the *sela-vaḍhakin*, 'stonemasons'; the *nāyakamisa*; the *kaḍhichakas*; the *mahākaṭakas*; the *miṭhika*, 'polisher'; and the *khadaraki*. This inscription is invaluable in explicating the functions of different types of artists engaged in the completion of a monument. An Amaravati inscription refers to a *thera* (elder) living at Rājagiri, styled as a *bhadanta*, called Buddharakṣita, who was the *navakamaka* of the Chaityakas (a Buddhist sect).[75] The Nagarjunakonda inscriptions of the time of the Ikṣvākus similarly refer to certain *navakarmikas*. For example, there was the student Ānanda, a *navakarmika*, who knew the *Dīgha Nikāya* and *Majjhima Nikāya* 'by heart' and who established the foundation of the *Mahāchetiya*;[76] then there were the three *thera-navakarmikas*, viz., Chaṃḍamukha, Dhammanandi, and Nāga, who supervised the work of building edifices such as a *chaitya* and a *vihāra*, a *bodhi* tree, shrines, cells, pillars of a *maṇḍapa*, a hall for religious practices, a tank, a veranda, and other things at different places. The inscription also mentions that the work was accomplished by the stonemason Vidhika: '*selavaḍhakisa Vidhikasa kamman ti*'.[77]

These records indicate that the work of excavating the Buddhist edifices was supervised by the members of the Buddhist Church and that these members sometimes functioned as pupils of other theras, who might have been master architects in their own right. In any case, the latter proposition indicates a situation conducive to the specialization of crafts and to the development of individual schools of sculpture and architecture.

In the *Mahāvaṃsa* (XXX. 98), an overseer of work is designated as *kammādhiṭṭhāyaka*. The appointment of the *navakarmikas* by the Church may have been necessary for the purpose of observing ecclesiastical specifications in the Buddhist edifices, and also for the simple reason that the people so appointed possessed the requisite technical skill for the job. Evidence suggesting both is available. The *Cullavagga*[78] specifies rules regarding the buildings and the objects of use by monks and nuns, and it can be guessed that ecclesiastical supervision might have been enforced to ensure proper adherence to these norms. As regards the eligibility of monks in supervising the building work, they seem to have earned it on account of their skill in that area of activity. Artisans were seeking and getting admission into the Buddhist Church and such artisans-converted-monks might have continued to use their skill even after joining the Buddhist Church. The status of such monk-artists in the Church was in no way inferior to any other member of the Church. In the texts, the specificities of the usage of speech have been defined and it was ordained that a monk's former occupation ought not to be mentioned to humiliate him.[79] A passage in the *Samaññaphala-sutta* of the *Dīgha Nikāya*[80] also indicates that persons of different occupations[81] joined the Buddhist Church in order to escape the rigours of the brahminical caste system. The passage records a dialogue between the Buddha and Ajātaśatru, in which the latter asks the Buddha of the advantages in becoming a recluse. The Buddha describes the advantages and interposes whether a monk, even though he might have earlier been the king's slave, would or would not receive respect from the king. To this, Ajātaśatru replies that he would be respected. Such craftsmen-turned-monks, as mentioned in the *Dīgha Nikāya*, might have been useful in the building of Buddhist monuments.

Besides the Church, the overseer of work, or its 'executer', was also appointed by other authorities or persons. In a Banavāsī inscription[82] of the time of *Rājan* Viṣṇukaḍa-Chuṭukulānanda Sātakarṇi, mention is made of a princess who donated a *nāga*(?), a tank, and a *vihāra*. Mention is also made of the *kamaṃtika*, or 'superintendent of work', in this case a minister—Skandsvāti. Similarly, the Junagarh rock inscription of Rudradāman cites the instance of the minister Suviśākha, who executed the work of restoration of the Sudarśana Lake after a storm.[83] From these two examples, it follows that if the work undertaken by some person required independent execution, that was possible and in such a case, the Church may not have had the responsibility of supervising the project.

Āveśanins also occur in the inscriptions as artists of authority. In the Sātavāhana-Ikṣvāku inscriptions, this term occurs quite a few times, once in the case of Ānanda, at Sanchi; thrice in the case of Siddhārtha, an Ikṣvāku artisan and his father Nāgachandra; and once in the case of an artist whose name has disappeared from the inscription.[84] Siddhārtha, in his inscription, gives the details of his family also. The *āveśanin* Nāgachandra and Nagilā were his parents; Samudrā his wife; Buddhi his brother; Kṛṣṇā his brother's wife; Mūlaśrī his son; Nāgabuddha his daughter; and Nāgaśrī, Chaṇḍaśrī, and Siddhārtha his brother's progeny. The relevant inscriptions mention only Nāgachandra and his son Siddhārtha as *āveśanins*, and there is no direct evidence whether their occupation was followed by all the other male (and female) members of the family. But there is sufficient evidence in the inscription to suggest that the profession was hereditary. This information is equivalent to the one relating to the teacher-disciple relationship amongst the *navakarmikas* mentioned earlier.

The term *āveśanin* has been usually translated as 'foreman among the artisans'. The lexicons explain *āveśan* as *śilpiśala*, manufactory (or workshop). On the analogy of *akṣaśālā* mentioned in the *Arthaśāstra*[85] and in its commentary, the word *āveśani* may be explained as manufactory. Alternatively, *āveśanin* may imply a title or position acquired by an individual who possessed great artistic merit. The resourcefulness of the *āveśanin* is supported by the fact that at least in two of the cases where reference has been made to them, they are mentioned as having been involved in making an important structure. Ānanda, the *āveśanin* at Sanchi was associated with making the *toraṇas* when the work was started.[86] Likewise, the *āveśanin* Siddhārtha of Jaggayyapeta inscription is associated with the making of five *āyaka* pillars on the eastern gate of the Mahāchetiya of the Buddha, at Velagiri.[87] In any case, the reference to *āveśanin*, i.e. the chief artist, points towards the existence of *āveśan* for the training of artisans or making objects of art, as commissioned by the royal or other donors. Such workshops find mention elsewhere also. The *Bṛhatsamhitā* of Vārāhamihira refers to *śilpālaya*; the *Brahmavaivartta Purāṇa* to *śilpagṛha*; and the commentary of Kullūka on Manu, to *śilpageha*.[88] The *Kāmasūtra* provides us with the information that persons of taste, who practiced *śilpa* in their own houses, used to have such workshops—*ekāṃta cha takṣatakṣana-sthānaṃ*.[89]

The task of building edifices or excavating monuments was well organized. The extant monuments usually indicate a premeditated design and its execution in which probably every single architectural part, including motifs and reliefs, was predetermined and made according to a layout previously defined.[90]

Before starting the actual work on some edifice, it was possibly customary to prepare a design. An instance of this is found in the *Mahāvaṃsa*.[91] Similarly, in the *Thūpavaṃsa*,[92] there is the instance of King Duṭṭhagāmanī Abhaya, who expressed a desire to build a 'palace similar to a celestial mansion'. He assembled the Order of Monks and asked them to prepare a 'drawing of a mansion made upon a linen cloth...'. Thereupon, the Order sent eight *bhikkhus* who went to the abode of thirty-three *devas* and saw 'a jewelled palace, twelve *yojanas* high and forty-eight *yojanas* in circumference, which was adored with thousand pinnacles, was nine-storied, and provided with a thousand chambers . . . and which floated in the air'. They made a drawing of it with vermillion upon a linen cloth, and on their return, gave it to the Order of Monks, who sent it to the king. When the king saw it, he was glad at heart and had the *lohapāsāda* ('brazen palace') built in the style of the drawing.[93] It is said that the design for the *lohapāsāda* was prepared by the theras after the *vimāna* (palace) of a *devatā*, namely Vīraṇi.[94] Such designs find mention as *varṇaka* or *hastalekha* in the texts of the Gupta or post-Gupta times. *The Uttara Naiṣhadha Charita* mentions that the entire feminine world created by Brahma is a *hastalekha*, a 'preliminary attempt', to the final shaping of the beauty of Damayantī.[95] However, more important are the details in the *Mahāvaṃsa* and *Thūpavaṃsa*, which set out the whole process of making of certain buildings, including the great *stūpa* and these details are of invaluable significance.

These texts mention that artisans were gathered on drumbeats and a skilled mason was selected from among a number of masons who were properly interviewed regarding their capacity to undertake the work. The king's men and the *theras* went around places collecting the necessary metals, stones, and bricks for use in the construction of the *stūpa*. All the work was paid for, and if somebody stealthily contributed something, he was detected and amply compensated for his gift. The aforementioned texts also deal with the motifs and legends carved on pillars and railings of the *stūpa*. These details give a comprehensive idea about the mode of construction of the *stūpa*, the roles of different participants (e.g. the chief architect, masons, donors), the decoration and its motifs, the mobilization of men and money for collecting necessary building materials, and so on.[96] The elder Indagutta, 'who was gifted with six high faculties, most wise, directed all this, being the superintendent of the building.'[97]

In the early reliefs, the artisans at work are also depicted at times. One really wonders whether only the ordinary chisel and hammer, as depicted, were the important tools of sculptors and masons. The *takṣaka* and the *vardhakīs* used their *sūtra* (threads), for measuring. A *vardhakī-haṣṭa*, a measure of forty-two inches, finds mention in texts.[98] In the reliefs of Bharhut, however, we have a depiction of two figures of *rūpakāras* (sculptors), carrying 'dagger-like' chisels in their hands; they seem to be clearing irregular rocks, preparatory to some excavation. One of them stands on the flat ground, while the other stands on a nail pierced through rocks, which serves as his working platform. Both the persons are shown, carrying on their backs, baskets which contain their other tools (see Plate 7.1). The coping stone depicting the scene was acquired from Bhatanwara in Satna district of Madhya Pradesh and is now in the National Museum, New Delhi.[99] A figure of a scribe, in relief, has been found from Nagarjunakonda.[100] The figure here holds a similar iron stylus with a large, round head for a convenient grip. C. Sivaramamurti identifies him as a royal scribe 'shown here as casting

PLATE 7.1: Bharhut inscription depicting two *rupakāras*

the horoscope of Siddhārtha . . .'; the relief might as well represent a sculptor.

The *Thūpavaṃsa*[101] gives details of the making of the relic chamber. These details throw light on the process of raising edifices. When the king asked the skilled *iṭṭhakā-vaḍḍhakī*, i.e. the brickmason, as to how will he make the relic chamber, the mason replied, '. . . I shall pound [the sand] in mortar, and have it sifted with winnowing basket, and crushed in mill, and then I shall do the work with a hundred workmen, throwing down only one *ammaṇa* [a measure of capacity] of dust in one day'.[102] Elsewhere, in the same text, is an account of the starting of work on a *stūpa*. It describes different stages of work and the various articles of use in the preliminary stages of the work. Such processes as clearing the place and laying of stone by the king's soldiers inside an elephant wall (i.e. a basement or a platform with figures of elephants); breaking of the stone into pieces, which were 'stamped down by great elephants' with their feet encased in heels'; spreading of butter clay on the pounded stones; spreading of bricks over it; 'over the bricks, a rough cement, over that cinnabar stones, over that a network of iron, over that sweet-scented sand . . .'[103] and so on are described. The description is no doubt exaggerated, for the excavated *stūpas* in India hardly reveal such material in the order described; but there is enough in the description to show that the edifices were raised with meticulous care and effort.

As regards the artisans of lower categories, engaged for routine work, mention may be made of the *sela-vadhakin* (stonemason); *mahākataka*,[104] *kaḍhichaka*,[105] and *miṭhika* (stone polisher). All these words occur in a Kanheri inscription cited earlier. In a Sanchi inscription, there is a reference to *karmika* (labourer[?]), which juxtaposed to *navakarmika*, may explain itself as referring to a worker of lower ranks, engaged in the construction of buildings. Quite often labourers had to be employed if the task to be accomplished was big. The *Thūpavaṃsa* cites the case of a skilled mason who wanted to employ 500 workmen for achieving his task. The *Mahāvaṃsa* also refers to the *iṭṭhakā-vaḍḍhakī*.[106] The existence of such specialized classes in different departments of building activity indicates that crafts were becoming more and more diversified, leading to specialization. In this process of specialization, many factors like acquisition of greater skill through successive stages of the practice of crafts, or teacher-disciple relationship, or hereditary factors, may have contributed their share. One may often wonder over the fact that in the early inscriptions, the different terms designating artists are not identical to those that occur in the texts. Moreover, the texts mention classes of artisans such as *sthapati* and *sūtragrāhin*, for which the inscriptions have an entirely different set of terms. However, on several terms, e.g. *karmāra*, *karmakāra*, *vardhakī*, etc., the texts and inscriptions complement each other. It may be suggested that since inscriptions relate to the actual activity, and texts offer evidence mostly on the theoretical aspects, the former should be taken as more important and concrete in defining the practical aspects of ancient art-activity.

While plying their trade, the artisans came into contact with individuals belonging to various sections of society. The composition of these sections and their relations with artists are examined here. The donative inscriptions from different places, like Bharhut, Sanchi, and Mathura, offer evidence regarding donors, their ranks and social status, the region they came from and also their share in making of the relevant monuments or parts thereof. Several hundred such donative inscriptions relating to the gifts of caves, *stūpas*, *vihāras*, etc., as well as their parts or decorative motifs, indicate how the people competed with each other for receiving the merit of participation in the construction of a monument. In terms of the commissioning of new edifices, the donors belonging to different social or professional strata in society stood as equal partners in the ventures, which were executed by workmen and their superintendents. Evidence regarding the donors, as found in the early epigraphs, seems to suggest that the building activity gathered momentum, encouraged not by any single resourceful class of the society, but as a result of a ubiquitous interest of different classes of people towards a common end. In a situation like this, the artists, who did the actual work and enlivened the aspirations of the devotees, must have risen in status, even though they belonged to a lower strata of the society. Their relation with different classes of people is clearly established in the inscriptions, which besides indicating the enthusiasm of persons of different social standing, in building or excavating monuments, also point to the combining of different sections of society at the same level, ignoring thereby the caste and class distinctions. As such, the social implications of such religious fervour and enthusiasm are enormous.

The evidence regarding the donors may be examined on two planes—an overall general survey with regard to the classes of donors and their donations at different centres of art-activity, and the specific donor-monument equation. With regard to the first, we find references to the participation of different sections of the society, including kings, chiefs and the members of their families and administration; kṣatriyas and brahmins; persons of occupationally middle ranks, viz., bankers, *śreṣṭhīs* (chiefs of occupational guilds); and commoners like ploughmen, perfumers, smiths, carpenters, sculptors, etc. Sometimes, such donations represented corporate gifts, which were meant both for small and big works. For instance, a Junnar Buddhist cave inscription[107] refers to the gift of a seven-celled cave and a cistern by the guild of corn dealers. In another case, Sivama and the members of his family commissioned a cave in which different members of the family took credit for different works, e.g. stone carving through the gift of his sons, pillars through the gift of his daughters, etc.[108] Among the smaller gifts of corporate type, in which more than one person were involved, reference may be made to an Amaravati Buddhist inscription that records the 'gift of a slab with a filled vase [*punaghaḍaga paṭa*] by the leatherworker Vidhika . . . and by his son Naga, together with their relatives'. Any number of such examples may be quoted here, these two instances being only indicative. Besides the corporate gifts, there are scores of examples of gifts by individuals combined with guilds or those by individuals alone. Thus we have recorded instances of individual donors such as kings, the members of their families, and the members of administration (like ministers, commanders, royal scribes, royal physicians, etc.).[109] In the construction of the *stūpa* of Bharhut, we have references to the donations of *toraṇa* (gateway), *vedikā* (railing), and *śilākarma* (stonework) by the royal personages.[110] The Nagarjuna cave inscriptions of the Mauryan King Daśarath refer to the gifts of the *Vāhiyaka*, *Gopikā*, and *Vadathika* caves to the Ājīvika monks.[111] In western India, which was under the rule of the Mahārathis and Mahābhojas, who were the feudatories of the Kṣaharātas and the Sātavāhanas, there are inscriptions indicating the chiefs' munificent gifts, as well as those of their families. It is interesting to observe that sometimes the important personages came together with people from other classes and made a corporate gift for excavation and maintenance of some monuments. For instance, a Kuda inscription records the gift of a cave by three persons—two of them belonged to the royal family of the Bhojas and the third one was a *lekhaka* (scribe) of the Mahābhoja.[112]

Among the individual donors of lesser ranks, mention may be made of a *gaṇikā* named Vasu (daughter of the courtesan Loṇaśobhikā) who set up a shrine, an *āyāgasabhā*, a reservior and stone slabs; a metal worker, member of a guild, who set up an image of Sarasvatī; and several others like a ploughman, a gardener, a perfumer, a weaver, a dyer, and so on.[113]

The categories are diverse, and seem to include persons of all possible professions and social ranks. Sometimes, the members of lower occupational classes joined with merchants to make a donation, as did a perfumer along with the merchants in making a gift of a pavilion, at Amaravati.

From such instances, it clearly emerges that the activity of raising monuments was not limited only to upper classes; in fact, the financial status mattered more. There are instances of men of various occupational classes being instrumental in the excavation of caves, while other instances relate how the more important personalities sometimes took credit only for partial excavations, like a cistern. It seems that different occupations (*śilpas*) were becoming quite remunerative, and a class of traders practicing various *śilpas* had emerged more resourceful, and at the same time, willing to contribute to such activity. The Kanheri inscriptions seem to support this suggestion.[114] Within this class of traders, the largest share in such donations goes to the merchant class. Of the class-wise break-up of the donative inscriptions here, two epigraphs refer to a princess of the Mahābhoja family; one each to a minister, a physician and a jeweller; six to the community of monks, nuns, *theras*, and *theris*; and all the rest to the *gahapatis*, merchants and traders, and the members of their families. Many of these inscriptions record corporate gifts in the sense that either more than one person combined to raise the monuments, or that the work was so financed that the merit might be incurred by more than one member. The Kanheri inscriptions also suggest that all the donors did not belong to the same region; in many cases they came from places such as Sopara, Chaula, Dhenukataka, and Kalyana.[115]

The interaction of the different classes of people for building specific edifices indicates the same pattern as detailed earlier. To be clearer on the point, we may refer here to the evidence from the Karla inscriptions.[116] Of the twenty inscriptions from the Buddhist cave at Karla, two refer to the Sātavāhana kings Gautamīputra Sātakarṇi, and Vāśiṣṭhīputra Śrī Pulumāvi. One inscription records the gift of Rṣhabhadatta, the son of Dinika and son-in-law of the Kṣatrapa King Nahapāna; while another records the gift of a pillar by Mitradeva, the son of Rṣhabhadatta. Of the inscriptions concerning the Mahāraṭhīs, the local chiefs, one records the erection of a lion pillar, a gift of Mahārathī Agnimitra, son of Gauptī; another gives details of the gift of a village and a cave to the local *saṃgha* by Mahāraṭhī Somadeva. Other epigraphs indicate that the *selaghara*, 'the most excellent one in Jambūdvīpa' was 'established' by the banker Bhūtapāla who hailed from Vaijayantī. The contributions for different parts in the cave came from several persons, e.g. the perfumer Siṃhadatta from Dhenukāṭaka commissioned the making of the *gharamugha* (this was made by the *vaḍhakī Svāmin*); the elephant motif and the upper and lower *vedikā* before the elephant were carved through the gift of the *thera* Indradeva; three pairs of sculpted figures were donated by the monk Bhadrasena; another *vedikā*, made by Nandika, was donated by a woman whose name has not been specified; the pillars were made through donations from the Yavanas Sihādaya and Dharma, both from Dhenukāṭaka; and the other pillars were the gifts of individuals such as Bhāyila, the mother of the householder Mahādevanaka, and the preacher Svātimitra who hailed from Sopara. There are two more epigraphs, one recording some unspecified gift by a nun and the other referring to a female disciple of a *bhadanta*, who paid for a cistern.

From these inscriptions, it is easy to find out the extent of participation of different classes of people in the excavation of the Karla Buddhist cave. Those who contributed included the local chiefs, the king's relatives, bankers, perfumers, householders, *theras*, nuns, foreigners, and also artisans. Here also, we have the information that the people who helped in excavating the cave, in many cases, came from distant places (Vaijayantī, Dhenukāṭaka, Sopara, etc.). Examples of such contributions at the centres of art-activity, by persons coming from different places are available at most of the ancient art centres.[117] This evidence, coupled with that of the mobility of artisans from one place to another, might be profitably evaluated for explicating the pattern of spread of art styles and idioms. It seems that the work executed at one place did not represent only a local movement; it had the participation of people living far beyond the region where it was located and such people, including both donors and artists, in the course of their movement, might have helped in dissemination of the art idioms developed at the original districts of art-activity.

Notes

1. *Kāṭhak*, 2.3; 37.9; 48.1; *Paippalāda*, I. 92.2; 4.3.2; *Taittirīya*, 1.2.2.1; 6.1.2.3; 5.5.22.1; *Kaṭha*, 1.15; *Mādhyandin*, *Śukla Yajur Veda*, 4.9; 24.5; 29.58; *Maitrāyaṇī*, 1.2.2.
2. *Śatapatha*, 14.9.9.33; 1.1.4.3; 3.2.1.5; 14.9.4.32; *Aitareya*, 6.27; 6.38; *Gopatha*, 2.6.7.9; *Śānkhāyana*, 25.12, 25.13, 29.5; *Taittirīya*, 2.7.15.3; 3.33.2.1; *Taittirīya Araṇyaka*, 1.7.1; *Tāndya*, 16.4.3; 16.4.8–9; 9.15.2.
3. *Aitareya Brāhmaṇa*, VI. 27.
4. Monier Monier-Williams, *Sanskrit-English Dictionary*, New Delhi: Manohar, 2006, s.v. 'silpatva'; Tarapada Bhattacharya, *A Study on Vāstuvidyā: or Canons of Architecture*, Patna: United Press, 1947, p. 26.

5. Monier Monier-Williams, *Indian Wisdom: Or Examples of the Religious, Philosophical, and Ethical Doctrines of the Hindus*, p. 468.
6. *Rig Veda*, X, 72.2; *Atharva Veda*, III, 5.6; *Manu*, IV, 215.
7. *Rig Veda*, X, 72.2; quoted in V.S. Agrawala, *Indian Art: A History of Indian Art from the Earliest Times up to the Third Century A.D.*, Varanasi: Prithvi Prakashan, 1965, p. 40.
8. *Rig Veda*, I, 162.6, *taṣṭṛ*; *Rig Veda*, I, 61.4; I, 105.18, 130.4; a *rathakāra* who used wood for joining and making of chariots, is called *takṣaka* in the *Maitrāyanī Saṃhitā*, IV, 3.8.
9. *Rig Veda*, I, 32.2; I, 85; X, 48.
10. *Rig Veda*, IV, 35.6, 36.5; VI, 32.1, *Takṣaka*; X, 72.2; VIII, 5.38.
11. R.S. Sharma, *Śūdras in Ancient India: A Social History of the Lower Order Down to circa A.D. 600*, Delhi: Motilal Banarsidass, 1958, pp. 27–8, 49, 70ff.
12. Ibid., pp. 49ff. The *rathakāras* and *karmāras* were close to the king, according to a passage in the *Atharva Veda* (III, 5.6); but later on, the *karmāras* were replaced by the *takṣakas*. In terms of antiquity, *takṣakas* were older than *rathakāras*, for the *rathakāras* came to fore mainly in the later Vedic period.
13. Ibid., p. 28; also *Vājasneyi Samhitā*, XVI, 27; *Kāthak*, XVII, 13; *Maitrāyaṇī*, II, 9.5; *Taittirīya*, IV, 5.4.2.
14. *Dīgha Nikāya*, I, 51.
15. See translated version of *Mahāvastu*: J.J. Jones, tr., *The Mahavastu*, vol. III, London, 1956, pp. 112ff, 443ff.
16. See a translated version of *Milinda Pañho*: I.B. Horner, tr., *Milinda's Questions*, 2 vols., London: Luzac and Co., 1964. There is a mention of a list of about eight crafts and occupations in section 331.
17. I.B. Horner, tr., *The Book of Discipline* (*Vinaya-Piṭaka*), vol. II, London: Luzac and Co., 1957, pp. 176f.
18. Ibid.
19. In T.W. Rhys Davids, tr., *Dialogues of the Buddha*, vol. I, London, 1951, pp. 100, 102. 'One may cite here the case of *rathakāra* and *chammākara*, "leatherworker". *Chammākara*, occurs in the *Suttavibhānga* (*Book of Discipline*, II, 176) among the low crafts, while *rathakāra* is among low kinds of birth; and there seems to be no correspondence between kinds of low births and kinds of low crafts such as would enable one to say that a man of such and such birth follows such and such trade'. Horner, tr., *The Book of Discipline* (*Vinaya-Piṭaka*), vol. II, p. 173, fn. 7.
20. *Gautama Dharmasūtra*, X, 60; *Manu*, X, 99.100; Pāṇini, in certain *sūtras*, e.g. IV, 2.62, V, 4.95, also refers to *śilpī*, *kāruśilpī*, and *chāruśilpī*; R.P. Kangle, ed., *The Kautiliya Arthaśāstra*, Delhi: Motilal Banarsidass, 1965, I.3.8.
21. Sharma, *Śūdras in Ancient India*, pp. 27–8, 48–51.

22. Richard Fick, *The Social Organisation in the North-East India in Buddha's Time*, tr. S.K. Mitra, Calcutta: University of Calcutta, 1920, pp. 267–336.
23. *Jātaka*, IV, 207.
24. *Baudhāyana Dharmasūtra*, I, 5.10.24; *Vaśiṣṭha Dharmasūtra*, 11, 27; *Gautama Dharmasūtra*, X.67. Haradatta, commenting upon Gautama recognizes the social equivalence of a śūdra and a brahmin performing an occupation allotted to a śūdra. But he adds that a śūdra doing his allotted work should not be despised by those who follow the non-Aryan occupations. Such injunctions implicitly indicate that certain occupations were generally identified with the śūdras. But at the same time, they indicate that the situation was flexible enough to admit persons of higher castes into these professions.
25. For *gahapatis*, see Fick, *The Social Organisation in the North-East India*, pp. 253ff; H. Luders, 'A List of Brahmi Inscriptions', *Epigraphia Indica* (hereafter *EI*), vol. X, 1912, pp. 1–179, nos. 193, 201 202, 449.
26. *Dīgha Nikāya*, III, 281; *Uvāsagadasāo*, p. 184; quoted in Sharma, *Śūdras in Ancient India*, p. 88.
27. *Kāmasūtra*, VI, 1.12.
28. Ibid., I, 4.4; III, 3.16.
29. When Śuddhodana asked for the marriage of Daṇḍapāṇi's daughter to Siddhārtha, Daṇḍapāṇi is described as having said: '*asmākaṃ chayaṃ kuladharmaḥ śilpajñasya kanyā dātavyā naśilpajñasyeti; kumāraścha na śilpajño . . . tat kathama śilpajñahaṃ duhitaraṃ dāsyāmi*' ('Our family's *dharma* is to give away our girls [in marriage] only to those adept in *śilpas*. Since Kumāra [Siddhārtha] is not so endowed, therefore how can we, the knowers of *śilpa*, give our daughter [in marriage] to him?'); see S. Leffmann, ed., *Lalitavistara*, Halle: Buchhandlung des Waisenhauses, 1902–8, p. 143.
30. Sharma, *Śūdras in Ancient India*, pp. 27–8, 49–51.
31. *Mahabharata*, V, 255; *Ramayana*, II, 80.2; quoted in P.K. Acharya, *An Encyclopaedia of Hindu Architecture*, vol. 7 of Manasara Series, London: Oxford University Press, 1946, s.v. 'sthapati', p. 581.
32. *Mayamatam*, V, 20.
33. *Jātaka*, V, 282; quoted in Fick, *The Social Organisation in the North-East India*.
34. *Jātaka*, II, 405 and IV, 159, for *vaddhakigama*. The *Samuddavanijja Jātaka* refers to a village of 1,000 carpenters in which each group of 500 had a chief.
35. V.S. Agrawala, *Studies in Indian Art*, Varanasi: Vishwavidyalaya Prakashan, 1965, p. 121. About the origin of stone architecture in India, see T.P. Bhattacharya, *The Canons of Indian Art*, Calcutta: Firma K.L. Mukhopadhyay, 1963, pp. 300ff.
36. *Arthaśāstra*, V.3.12; V.3.16. The text prescribes two hundred *paṇas* for *vardhakī* and only a hundred and twenty *paṇas* for *karusilpis*. Also see

J.N. McCrindle, ed. and tr., *Ancient India as Described by Megasthenes and Arrian*, Calcutta: Chuckervertty, Chatterjee & Co., 1926, p. 86, fragment 34. In the section on *kārukara-rakṣaṇaṃ*, the *Arthaśāstra* (IV.1.2–4; IV.1.65) lays down rules protecting the artisans and guarding them from troubles. Also see *Arthaśāstra*, IV.2.18.

37. *Arthaśāstra*, IV.1; IV.1.65.
38. *Luders' List*, nos. 687, 350.
39. Ibid., nos. 1087, 1090, 962. Several other objects are mentioned in the inscriptions, e.g. *puṣkariṇī* (tank), *udapana* (reservoir), garden, *gaṃjāvāra*(?), *pujā-śilā-prākāra* (stone enclosure for a place of worship), *chakrapaṭa* (slab with a wheel), *pādukāpaṭa* (slab engraved with a pair of feet), *svastikapaṭa* (slab with a *svastika*), and *harmya* (temple). See *Luders' List*, nos. 82, 6, 1253, 1217, 1282, 1287, 23. A Sanchi inscription (*Luders' List*, no. 350) contains an imprecation against him 'who takes away or causes to be taken away the stone-work . . . or causes it to be transferred to another temple. . .'.
40. *Luders' List*, no. 988.
41. Ibid., no. 1087.
42. Ibid., nos. 114, 115.
43. Ibid., no. 1045.
44. Jones, tr., *The Mahāvastu*, vol. III, p. 112, see esp., p. 443, where this list occurs with certain modifications.
45. Ibid., p. 444.
46. *Manu Saṃhitā*, VI.47–8; also see M.K. Dhavalikar, 'Sri Yugandhar—A Master Artist of Ajanta', *Artibus Asiae*, vol. XXXI, no. 4, 1969, p. 308, s.v. 'editor's note'.
47. *Manu Saṃhitā*, VI.47–8.
48. *Sacred Books of the East*, vol. XXXVI, 1965, p. 201; *Milinda Paňho*, section 331.
49. Jones, tr., *The Mahavastu*, vol. III, p. 112; also see *sūtradhyakṣa* in Kauṭilya's *Arthaśāstra*, II, 23.1ff, *sūtrakrīdā* in *Kāmasūtra*, I, 3.15. The epigraphic evidence tends to indicate that *sūtragrāhin* was eliminated and a new class, *sūtradhāra*, came into being in the post-Gupta era.
50. T.P. Bhattacharya discusses the earliest nature of *Vāstuśāstra* and the originators of the different schools of architecture and art. See Bhattacharya, *The Canons of Indian Art*, pp. 87ff; Acharya, *An Encyclopaedia of Hindu Architecture*, s.v. 'sthapati'.
51. D.P. Chattopadhyaya, ed., *Taranath's History of Buddhism in India*, Shimla: Indian Institute of Advanced Study, 1970, p. 347.
52. Ibid.
53. *Mauryaiḥ-hiraṇya-rthabhitaiḥ-archā-prakalpitāḥ*, see J.N. Banerjea, *The Development of Hindu Iconography*, Calcutta: University of Calcutta, 1956, p. 40.
54. Pāṇini, *Jīvikārthe-cha-paṇye*, V.3–99; Banerjea, *Development of Hindu*

Iconography, p. 391, states that on the authority of commentaries regarding the *Mahābhāṣhya* and the Kāśikā, one may assume that these objects which were meant for livelihood, were however, not for sale.

55. See also Bhattacharya, *The Canons of Indian Art*, pp. 309f. His reasons are different.
56. For the Bharhut and Mathura, and western and eastern Indian early idioms of art and their cognate character, see M.G. Dikshit's article in *Indica*, vol. VIII, pt. 1, 1971, pp. 1ff; A.K. Coomaraswamy, *History of Indian and Indonesian Art*, New York: Dover Publications, p. 27.
57. *Luders' List*, no. 85; this temple of Dadhikarṇa finds mention in another inscription from Mathura (*Luders' List*, no. 63), which records the 'dedication (on the pillar) by Devila, the servant (or priest) at the temple of Dadhikarṇa. . .'.
58. Luders translates *śailālaka* as 'actors', so does the *Amarakosa* (in Śūdra-*varga*, 11, 12). However, this translation is not borne out by the context of the inscription at Mathura, as it has reference to *śilā* (stone). Also see J.J. Jones, tr., *The Mahavastu*, vol. II, London: Luzac and Co., 1952, p. 444, fn.7; F. Edgerton, *Buddhist Hybrid Sanskrit Grammar and Dictionary*, n.d.
59. *Luders' List*, no. 150.
60. R.P. Chanda, *ASIAR*, *1922–23*, p. 165; Agrawala, *Studies in Indian Art*, p. 118. G. Buhler says that a sectarian distinction among artists of Mathura cannot be established and it is possible that the same set of artists were commissioned to create the stonework related to different sects, e.g. Buddhist, Jain, and Hindu.
61. *Luders' List*, no. 150.
62. Ibid., no. 921.
63. A. Cunningham, *Bhilsa Topes: Buddhist Monuments of Central India*, n.d., p. 151; *Luders' List*, no. 173.
64. J. Marshall et al., *Monuments of Sanchi*, vol. I, ins. no. 398, which states: '*rañosiri Sātakanis avesanisa Vāsiṭhīputrasa Ānandas dānaṃ*' ('[This is] a donation of Ānand, the foreman of the artists of King Vāsiṣṭhīputra Sātakarṇi.').
65. *Luders' List*, no. 1002. The Jaggayyapeta Buddhist pillar inscription is a record of the time of *Rājan* Mādharīputra Śrī Vīrapurisadatta of the Ikṣvākus; also see *Luders' List*, no. 1203–4.
66. H. Luders, 'Bharhut Inscriptions', revised by E. Waldschmidt and M.A. Mehendale, *Corpus Inscriptionum Indicarum* (hereafter *CII*), vol. II, pt. 2, 1963, p. 36; *Luders' List*, no. 857. This *rūpakāra* may have had something to do with the 'creation of a gateway (*toraṇa*) and stonework (*silākammanta*) by Dhanabhūti . . .' which finds mention in another Bharhut inscription (see *CII*, vol. II, pt. 2, pp. 11ff; *Luders' List*, no. 687).
67. Marshall et al., *Monuments of Sanchi*, vol I, ins. nos. 199, 448. Both find mention as *karmika,* which, like *navakarmika*, 'architect', may have some relevance in relation to artisans.

68. *Luders' List*, no. 124.
69. Ibid., no. 1092; also see *sela-vaḍhakī* (stonemanon/sculptor), *EI*, vol. XX, 1933, ins. F, line 4, p. 22; *iṭṭhakā-vaḍḍhakī* (brick mason); *Mahāvaṃsa*, XXIX, 5, 30.
70. *Luders' List*, no. 1071.
71. Ibid., no. 987.
72. Ibid., no. 350; also *EI*, vol. XX, p. 22; *Luders' List*, nos. 1045 (*śailarūpakarma*), 345 (*rūpakarma*), 687 (*śilākammaṃta*), 1087 (*selaghara*); also see *EI*, vol. XX, ins. no. B4 for *sela-khambha* and *śaila-maṇḍapa*.
73. *Luders' List*, nos. 154, 773, 987, 1250; *EI*, vol. XX, pp. 17ff, ins. nos. C1, C2, F.
74. The different forms of the word *āveśanin*, occurring in the inscriptions are *āvesani*, *avesani*, *avesaṇi*. These can be found in the inscriptions from Jaggayyapeta, Sanchi, and Amaravati. See *Luders' List*, nos. 1202–4, 346, 1298.
75. *Luders' List*, no. 1250.
76. *EI*, vol. XX, p. 17, ins. no. Cl; also p. 20, ins. no. C2.
77. Ibid., p. 22, ins. no. F, line 4.
78. I.B. Horner, tr., *The Book of Discipline* (*Vinaya-Piṭaka*), vol. V, London: Luzac and Co., 1963, pp. 204ff.
79. Horner, tr., *The Book of Discipline* (*Vinaya-Piṭaka*), vol. II, p. 173. Reference has been made here to various crafts, though not specifically to the sculptors or masons.
80. *Dialogues of the Buddha*, vol. I, pp. 68ff, 76ff.
81. Occupations are enumerated here.
82. *Luders' List*, no. 1186.
83. Ibid., no. 965.
84. Ibid., nos. 346, 1202–4, 1298.
85. Kauṭilya's *Arthaśāstra*, II, 13.1. *akṣaśālāyāṃ suvarṇādhyakṣaḥ*: the commentary explains *akṣaśālā* as *akṣaśālā-eti-suvarṇa-ādi-parikarma-āvasthanasya samajnā*, i.e. *akṣaśālā* is the name of the chamber in which artistic work of gold and other metals is carried out. See *EI*, vol. XXIV, 1938, p. 182. *akṣaśālin* as an officer finds mention in several inscriptions from eastern India. See *Bhandarkar's List*, nos. 1497, 1498, 1500–2.
86. Vidya Dahejia discusses the dates and sequence of the different *toraṇas* of the main stupa at Sanchi and expresses some doubts as to the priority of the south gate in relation to the dating of other gates. See V. Dahejia, *Early Buddhist Rock Temples: A Chronological Study*, London: Thames and Hudson, 1972, pp. 187ff.
87. *Luders' List*, no. 1202. It dates back to the time of the Ikṣvāku *Rājan* Mādharīputra Śrī Vīrapurisadatta (third quarter of the third century).
88. Monier-Williams, *Sanskrit-English Dictionary*, s.v. '*śilpa*'.
89. *Kāmasūtra*, I, 4.4. *śilpīśālā* finds mention in the *Mayamataṃ*, LXVIII, 50.

90. Dahejia, *Early Buddhist Rock Temples*, pp. 135f. She also describes the process of cutting a cave from start to its finish and the time taken in such work. Dahejia, *Early Buddhist Rock Temples*, pp. 136f.
91. *Mahāvaṃsa*, XXVII, 10, 18.
92. B.C. Law, tr., *The Legends of the Topes*, Bibliotheca Indica, no. 1553 n.s., Calcutta: Royal Asiatic Society, 1945 p. 64.
93. Ibid., pp. 64ff.
94. *Mahāvaṃsa*, XXVII, 10, 18; Law, *Legends of the Topes*, pp. 64ff.
95. *Purākritis sainaṃ imaṃ vidhātuṃ abdhu vidhātuḥ kila hastalekhaḥ*: see C. Sivaramamurti, *Indian Sculpture*, Delhi: Allied Publishers, 1961, p. 9. The other synonyms of *hastalekhaḥ* are: *varṇaka*, *hasṭolaka*, and *pāṇḍulekha*. Also see Sivaramamurti, *Indian Sculpture*, p. 9, pl. 2. In the temples of Khajuraho, there are miniature representations of pillars or *mandapas*, etched on the surfaces for the reference of artisans.
96. Law, tr., *Legends of the Topes*, pp. 73–84.
97. Ibid., p. 84; *Mahāvaṃsa*, XXX, 98–9.
98. Monier-Williams, *Sanskrit-English Dictionary*, s.v. '*vardhakī hasta*'.
99. Museum antiquity no. 68.163; cf., R.C. Agrawala, 'Unpublished Bharhut Reliefs in the National Museum, New Delhi', *Lalit Kala*, vol. 14, 1969, p. 54, plate xx, fig. ii.
100. C. Sivaramamurti, 'Indian Epigraphy and South Indian Scripts', *Bulletin of the Madras Government Museum*, vol. 4, 1948, p. 33, fig. 13.
101. Law, tr., *Legends of the Topes*, p. 73.
102. Ibid.
103. Ibid., p. 69.
104. Probably an artist or artists engaged in ivory work; *kaṭaka* means ivory.
105. The word is difficult to explain. Buhler has pointed out that in Gujarat, a word *kadiyo* (which is close to *kadhichaka*) is still in use for bricklayers. See *Archaeological Survey of Western India*, IV, p. 76. *kadhichaka* may alternatively be derived from *kathi*, meaning kaolin, which may help to explain *kadhickaka* as a stonecutter, stone painter, or stone polisher.
106. The workmen in building trade in Ceylon were known by a collective name *vardhakī*, '. . . but within this group there are several sub-groups: the carpenters (*dāru-vaḍḍhakī*), the bricklayer (*iṭṭhakā-vaḍḍhakī*), the worker in stucco (*cunna-vaḍḍhakī*), and the worker in stone (*śilā-vaḍḍhakī*). They seem to have been organized as a caste-like body of artisans with a *nagara-vaḍḍhakī* at the head'.
107. *Luders' List*, no. 1180.
108. Ibid., no. 1045 (Kuda cave inscription).
109. Ibid., nos. 1253 (minister); 1266 (general); 271, 1045; 1190 (royal scribes), 1191 (royal physician); also refer to the Yavana Heliodorus (the ambassador of Antialkidas, an Indo-Greek king of north-west), who set up a Garuda pillar at Besnagar; *Luders' List*, no. 669.
110. *CII*, vol. II, part 2, ins. nos. 1, 2, 3, 4, 12.

111. *Luders' List*, nos. 954–6.
112. Ibid., nos. 1079 (Bhaja), 1100 (Karla), 1021, 1186, 1052 (Kuda), 1054 (Bedsa), 1186; also, nos. 943–4 (Pabhosa inscriptions).
113. Ibid., nos. 1037, 102, 54, 1084, 1121, 756, 1210, 1230, 38, 39, 331, 32, 1230.
114. Ibid., nos. 984–1034.
115. This analysis of Kanheri inscriptions is based on the *Luders' List* and takes into account those cases where the details of donors are accurately mentioned (see *Luders' List*, nos. 984–1034). The period of the Kanheri caves and their inscription in the Hinayana phase, is roughly 90–181 CE. See Dahejia, *Early Buddhist Rock Temples*, p. 184.
116. For the inscriptions of the Buddhist cave at Karla, see *Luders' List*, nos. 1087–107.
117. Dahejia, *Early Buddhist Rock Temples*, p. 142.

8

Artisans during the Sultanate Period

An Epigraphical Study

PUSHPA PRASAD

Inscriptions are the scattered but authentic pages of history, often used for dealing with problems of political and dynastic history. Additionally, they also bear evidence on the work and skills of artisans over the years. The inscriptions found within the limits of the Sultanate period contain considerable material of this nature. Much has been written by R.N. Misra, who explored ancient inscriptions for evidence on the work and skills of artisans on one hand, and on the other hand by Lallanji Gopal, R.S. Sharma, B.N. Yadav, and others about craft and industries. Here, my purpose is to illustrate this kind of evidence available on artisans or craftsmen by testifying the inscriptions where the relevant data are available.

To begin with, the terms *silpi* and *silpin* are generally applied to any skilled work or worker and by definition, it tends to denote all kinds of crafts, skills, and occupations.[1] The category of an 'artisan' is a complex one. There are fundamental variations between artisans or craftsmen according to craft, and within each craft, according to the process of production and the nature of the product. However, broadly speaking, on the basis of their sites of work, four major types of artisans and craftsmen existed in India—those within peasant villages who received fixed wages in kind; those settled in separate villages of their own; those settled by kings, chiefs, and religious institutions in their seats of authority; and lastly independent artisans residing in different areas of a city.[2]

A specimen document from the fourteenth century in the *Lekhapaddhati* divulges to us that in a small village, there were five categories of artisans and craftsmen, or the *panca-karuak*, which included the *sūtradhāra* (mason), the *lohakara* (ironsmith), the *kumbhakara* (potter), etc., who received handfuls of produce at the time of harvest from individual peasants.[3] However, a fifteenth century literary account *Kanhadade Prabandha* by Padamanabha offers additional information. It mentions that during the course of military expeditions, a large number of craftsmen and artisans, such as *udas* (who made the roads passable), *sutars* (carpenters), *silavatas* (stonecutters), *sunars* (goldsmiths), *luhars* (blacksmiths), *kanskaras* and *trambahidas* (bronze and copper utensil makers), *karus* (stonemasons), *tirangars* (arrow-makers), and thousands of *chamars* (leather workers) were engaged. They marched along with the army and thus formed an integral part of the royal compaign.[4]

Historically, in a professional set-up of artisans and craftsmen, changes are evident in their functional categories during the Sultanate period. In the text of the inscriptions dated tenth century onwards, *rupadaksa, sailalaka, sailvardhaki, kamantika, navakramika*, and *sutragrahin* are no longer heard of, while new ones such as *sthapati takshaka, silpi, rūpakara, sūtradhāra aksaslin*, and *vijnanika* began to be mentioned. It is, however, possible that in many cases the change might have been one only of nomenclature, rather than of skill or status.

The craftsmen of this period blended the native styles—the traditional Hindu techniques and Islamic conception of ornamentation. It consequently gave rise to the fusion of forms. In the context of architecture, the skill of Indian craftsmen, particularly in ornamenting the stone, was unquestioned. Works on architecture refer to a number of villages and towns where various categories of artisans and craftsmen were settled within the dominions of different rulers.[5] Epigraphic evidence suggests that artisans belonging to different categories and with different sets of skills settled in the villages and mingled with others in everyday life in the medieval period.[6]

The *sūtradhāras*[7] occupied a special place amongst the artisans, since they performed works of varied nature. The literary texts and inscriptions, dated particularly from the sixth century onwards, refer to them consistently.[8] They performed different roles and had different functions related to the construction of monuments and engraving of inscriptions. They emerged as the executor of edifices and buildings like temples, pillars, mosques, forts, stepwells, and others.

In the evolution of Indo-Islamic architecture, the Qutab Minar stands chronologically next to Quwwat-ul-Islam Mosque. The Qutab serves as a minaret and is therefore a formal part of that mosque. The Nagari inscriptions in the Qutab relate to repair works carried out on it from time to time, and gives us the names of an architect, a carpenter, and several masons.

On a yellowish stone of eighth course on the third balcony of the Qutab is found an inscription that says the masons Nana, Salhe, Lola, and Lashman were employed for repair work in 1368 CE.[9]

An inscription to the left of the entrance in the fifth storey records that the Minar was renovated during the reign of Sultan Firuz Shah Tughlaq in 1369 CE. The work is said to have been completed by the grace of Sri Vishwakarma (the divine architect). The masons involved in this renovation were Nana, Salhe, and Chahad—the son of Devapala, while Dharmavanani was the *darukarmakara* (carpenter).[10] The name of the *silpi* (architect) is not found. Professor M. Mujeeb has suggested that Lashman, Nana, Saleh, and Chahad, mentioned in these inscriptions, were in fact the master masons under whom the repairs were carried out.[11]

An inscription of 1542 CE on the face of the eighth angle on the left side of the second balcony records the name of a *sangtārash* (stonecutter) Sikh, the son of Hira.[12] Here, the use of the Persian word for a stonecutter is interesting. Though the inscription is dated in the post-Sultanate period, it is actually of an early period, i.e. of the reign of Sher Shah (1540–5).

A bilingual inscription on a pilaster in the north wall of Karimuddin Mosque at Bijapur, dated Saka year 1242 (1320 CE), records that the *sutaru* (carpenter) Revaiya from Salehaitage (Salotagi, near Bijapur) built the mosque. In return, the Malik gave him a field in the village Bitur, the measurement being 24 *nitens* with 24 cubits, and made it free from taxes and other obstructions.[13]

An inscription of Baroda dated Vikram Samvat year 1396 (1340 CE) records that during the reign of Muhammad Bin Tughlaq, a mosque with a well at the village Karkhadi in Lata *desa* was constructed by order of the king and the stonemason who built it was Mokhaka, the son of Kheta.[14]

In Jaunpur, an inscription found on a slab near the first niche on the southern side of the eastern gate of the Atala Mosque tells that Patman, the son of Vaisaihava, was a *sūtradhāra* apparently working at the mosque in 1376 CE.[15] The name of the same mason is repeated in another inscription found on the right jamb of the northern door outside the same mosque. It would suggest that Patman was the chief mason employed to construct this mosque.

Another undated fourteenth-century Nagari inscription, found on the face of the fifth octagonal pillar in the middle row of the north-west cloister of the Lal Darwaza Mosque, also at Jaunpur, records that Kamau, the son of Visadru, was the chief *silpi*.[16]

A Nagari inscription dated VS year 1462 (1405 CE) has been found on the marble pillar of the northern balcony in the entrance gate of Adhai din ka Jhonpra Mosque at Ajmer. It records the name of the *sūtradhāra* Dharma of Bundi. The *sūtradhāra* had measured the monument—172 *hath* and 167 *hath*.[17] Thus, not only was the mason a Hindu, but he belonged to a distant place in Rajasthan.

A bilingual inscription[18] from Baroda, dated VS year 1462 (1405 CE) records that the construction of the wall of the main entrance of Jami Masjid and the excavation of a stepwell at Vatapura has been done by Miranatha, the son of Mira Taksha belonging to the Mira family (i.e. Mer community).[19]

Again, an inscription dated VS year 1545 (1488 CE), on the compound wall of a mosque near Moti Magri at Udaipur of Bhilsa district, records that the mosque was constructed during the reign of Gyasuddin of Mandu, when Sher Khan was the governor of Chanderi. It gives the names of *sūtradhāras* . . .(?)—the son of Satalu, Maharu, Pumamu, Dalhana, Narasingh, and Chittamana.[20]

A Sanskrit influenced Gujarati inscription, dated VS year 1308 (1251 CE), has been found on a pillar in the Ahmad Shah Mosque at Bhadr in Ahmedabad. The pillar is to the right of the pulpit and faces the latticed gallery. The inscription belongs to the reign of Visaladeva. It records the gift of a trellis window in the Utteresvara Temple at Mahimsaka by one Pethad, a servant of Sodaldevi, and tells us that the *updrasta* (overseer) was Rauta Malla and the *sūtradhāra* was Sumana.[21]

Similarly, another inscription is engraved on the two faces of the third octagonal pillar in the first row of the north-west cloister of the Lal Darwaza Mosque at Jaunpur. It is dated Plava Samvat year 1353 (1296 CE). The purpose is to record the construction of a temple of Padamesvara on the north side entrance of Visvesvara Temple at Kashi (or Kashi Vishwanath Temple) by Padamsadhu.[22]

An inscription dated VS year 1272 (1215 CE) from Manganana (Parbatsar Tehsil) records that during the reign of Sultan Samasdin of Yoganipura, a stepwell was built by *sūtradhāra* Asala and stonework and the shaping of stones was done by *silavata* Jahada.[23]

An inscription from Batiyagarh, Damoh district (Madhya Pradesh), dated 1328 CE records that a local ruler Jallal (Jalal), son of Isaka (Ishaq), built a *gomath* (cowpen[?]), a stepwell, and a garden at 'Batihadam'. The *sūtradhārai* (principal masons) were Bhojuk, Kamadeva, and Hale of the Silapatta *vamsa*.[24]

A Sanskrit inscription has been found at Asarava, a suburb of Ahmedabad in a well, called 'Dada Harir Vav' (Dada Harir stepwell). The inscription is dated 1458 CE and belongs to the reign of Sultan Mahmud Shah I (or Mahmud Begda).[25] The lady Bai Harir, who got the well constructed, is described as 'the general superintendent of the kings harem' and later as 'the religious [devotee]' and 'chief councellor of the king'. Bai Harir had the well built at Harirpur, a village (named after herself) to the north-east of Ahmedabad to alleviate the suffering of men, beasts, birds, and plants, and to please God. Thus, the well was constructed by a very highly placed Hindu lady (in the Sultan's employment), and the work was carried out by a royal officer—Malik Sri Bihamad—a Muslim. Those who actually worked on the well were Hindus. Their names are mentioned as *gajadhara* (mason) Vaisya, *gajadhara* Vira and his servants, *gajadhara* Deva, Sri Girana, Mahant Saya, and Mahant Vira.

Two inscriptions, one on a pillar at the Jinmata Temple, dated VS year 1534 (1478b CE) and other at the Harsha Temple (inscription engraved on the left side of the entrance), dated VS year 1535 (1478 CE), record that during the reign of Gyasuddin (of Mandu), Kunda, Udha and Kola, sons of Champa of the Mori caste and Hola, son of Parsa, came there to pay the homage to the deities. They belonged to the family of *silavata* or stonecutters.[26]

The inscription[27] in the niche to the left of the steps in a stepwell at the village of Singhpur in Mungoali Tehsil (Guna district), dated VS year 1535 (1479 CE), informs that the stepwell was constructed by Rajmati *bhatini*, the daughter of Bhairavadasa; son of Uvara; and son of Chajjala of Sirohanagar (Siroha). It claims that several Muslim rulers of different regions sent gifts to Rajmati for the construction of the garden, temple and stepwell. These are named as Sher Khan of Chanderi, Gyasuddin of Mandoa (Mandu), Hussain Sahi of Jaunpur, Barbak Shah of Pandua (Pandu), Tughlaq Sahi of Thatta and Qutubuddin of Gujarat. Among the donors are also included an unnamed king of Bidar (also designated Sultan of Bahmani), and a Sultan of Delhi. The named rulers are not exactly contemporaneous, though it is possible that the said gifts came over a long period, say from 1440 to 1470. The *karigars* (masons) were Vurahmata, Sukhumala, and Dashana.

It is of much significance that the Sanskrit and Nagari inscriptions set up by Hindu architects or masons should have been so freely allowed to be installed in the mosques. The inscriptions contain invocations in traditional Hindu style, for example, *Om Svasti* (prayer for auspiciousness), the references to Vishwakarma (the divine architect) and Ganapati (Ganesh), Mamgala Mahasri (god controlling fortune, felicity), and *Om Namaha Sivaya* (salute to Shiva) appear. Such invocations in a mosque would be considered anathema by the orthodox Muslim theologians. Yet, their presence suggests that a different sense of what is appropriate in mosques prevailed 600–700 years ago.

Besides, all these are in keeping with the tradition of masons' inscriptions put on Hindu structures like temples, pillars, images, and stepwells. Amongst the masons, the names Rama and Suprata occur in the inscriptions of Kalinjar and Ajayagarh fort. As regards Rama, he is mentioned as both a sculptor and a mason, and is credited with the building of the temple of *Nilakanth* and with the making of the image of *Nilakanth* Mahadeva.[28] A Kalinjar fort inscription (dated 1201 CE) of the Candella dynasty refers to the architect Padama, who was more competent than and superior to all architects and was the favourite of the King Paramarddi. Rama, also the builder of a well and the *mandap* (pavilion) at Ajayagarh fort during the reign of Viravarman, is described as having the skill of a *vaidagdhi* (master) in his craft (1261 CE).[29] A Kalinjar fort inscription records that Manuvijaya was the main architect in 1506 CE,[30] when certain repairs were carried out. In other inscriptions of 1240–60 CE, Palhana, Jayasimha, and Pratapasimha are mentioned as architects.[31]

An inscription from Dabhoi dated VS year 1311 (1253 CE) records the names of the officials, architects, and masons related with construction of a temple. The guardian of the fort Vaidestri was the son of Chandasimha (whose name is not recorded). The *sutra* Vamadeva, son of Sahadeva, built a Sun temple called Mulasthana, and Madan, who belonged to the Vishwakarma race, constructed the walls of the extensive temple. Devaditya was the main architect of the temple and was famous in the first rank of masons.[32]

The Kalachuri inscriptions offer varied information about the masons as well. Balsimha was regarded as the 'foremost among the masons', while Pitha is eulogized as being conversant in architecture and as the planner of several edifices (1155 CE).[33] An inscription of 1216 CE mentions the masons Surak, Kamalsimha, Namadeva, Maheswara, and Ananta—the son of Galhana. The mason Chhitaku, who belonged to the Kokasa family, is said to have been well known for his proficiency in the *Silpasastra* and mastery of sciences. Both his father Manmatha and his younger brother were well versed in astronomy by the favour of Vishwakarma, according to an inscription of 1495–6.[34]

Few inscriptions have been engraved on the Kirti Stambha, here and there, at Chittor. They are dated VS years 1495, 1499, 1507, 1510, and 1515 (i.e. 1438, 1442, 1450, 1453, and 1458 CE).[35] These epigraphs recorded the names of architects and masons during the reign of Rana Kumbha. They are Narad and Jaita—the sons of *sūtradhāra* Lakha; and Napa, Punja, Bhima, Chuthi, and Puma—the five sons of Jaita. The *maha-pratoli* (main gateway), and *ranapoli* (royal ward) of the Samadhisvara Temple, the Kirti Stambha—were all constructed by these masons. One of the inscriptions mention that Jaita was the main architect, well versed in *Vastusastra* by the grace of Vishwakarma. It seems that this family has a long association with the ruling monarch and are well versed in their profession. In the Kumbhalswami Vaishnavara Temple at Chittor, which was constructed in the fifteenth century, the architect Jaita, along with his two sons, figure amongst the decorative portrait sculptures adoring the temple.[36] An inscription dated VS year 1515 (1458 CE) from Achalgarh Fort on Mount Abu records the names of *sūtradhāras* from Mewar, i.e. *vijnam sūtradhāra* Deva, *sūtradhāra* Mihipa, Deva, Hala, Padohampa, Jala, and Danakala.[37]

The emergence of guilds during this period, which was an important development, also furnish the information on varied aspects of the artisans' lives. Although the inscriptions provide scanty information on this point, they appear to have been organized into guilds called *sreni desi* and sometimes *goshti*. Inscriptions of Chamba and Garhwal reveal that *srenis* were also called *prakritis*.[38]

Bayachakad[39] (a thirteenth-century account book of the Konark Sun Temple) provides exact information on the organization of workmen and their relationship with their patron, administrators, artisans, and labour forces. It enumerates the work process and also provides the merits and qualifications of all those who collaborated in the construction of the Konark Sun Temple. Further, it records that the artisans and craftsmen were organized into corporations that were based on religious and technical initiation, which clearly defined the common rules for training imposed on its members, but at the same time, constituted a professional community.

It appears that guilds had a local character concerned only with the men of a certain profession, residing in a particular area. A Gwalior inscription from the tenth century[40] recorded that two perpetual endowments were made by the members of the guild of oil mills headed by their *mahattakas* (chiefs) who dwelt in Sri Sarvesvarapura, and the members of the guild of the gardeners with their chiefs, who dwelt at the top of Gopalgiri. Some epigraphs from Chamba also indicate the local character of the artisans' organizations. The Sai inscription records that *baladhara* Chh...ka(?) superintended the work of the artisans. Likewise, Nayak was the head of the masons at Kangra.[41]

Epigraphs also reveal that due to localization in certain villages, the craftsmen passed on their work from generation to generation and received the grants from their patrons to complete the tasks assigned to them. From the inscriptions of Chittor, it has come to light that the architects and masons had associated themselves with the ruling family and received certain grants.[42] *Bayachakad* informs that land grants were made to different categories of artisans and craftsmen. The patron-prince is said to have granted 15 *mana* of land beside the Konark temple to each of the 224 stonemasons and established a centre of the stonemason community.[43]

It has been noted that artisans invested their own money and materials for the construction of the temples. The Nadlai inscription of Kelhana, dated VS year 1228 (1172 CE), records that the *mandapa*, *akshasama*, and *dama* of the temple of Bhivadesvara (Shiva) was constructed by Pahini, son of *sūtradhāra* Mahadua, and his wife Jasadevi. They worked with stones and bricks, and their construction cost 330 *drammas*. He was helped in this pious work by *sūtradhāra* Mahidara and Imdaraka.[44]

The Cintra *prasasti* of the reign of Sarangadeva, dated VS year 1343 (1287–8 CE), states the remuneration for some of the benefactions. Verse 50 informs that the guild of gardeners furnished two hundred white roses and two thousand fragrant oleander *kanavira* (blossoms) daily. Further it mentions that the illustrious Chaturjataka (an official) who wore the garland of faith in god (Shiva) made over to the gardeners in the exchange market(?) for their daily furnishing of the quantity flowers (required) for worship.[45]

The Anavada stone inscription of the reign of Sarangadeva, dated VS year 1348 (1291 CE), records a gift (or rather an offering, to god Krishna) by five classes of people of the town, one of which is the local *mahajanas*. Some of them were *sresthis*. Besides, there were also goldsmiths, braziers, ship owners, and members of the Vanjara community. Further, it states that one *pali* from the *ghada* or jar of ghee was granted by a seller (belonging to the Vanjara community).[46]

The Khalari stone inscription of VS year 1471 (1451 CE) records that Devapala, a *mochi* (shoemaker), the son of Sivadas, built a temple of Naryana along with a *mandapa*.[47]

Inscriptions reveal that the artisans made donations for the maintenance and upkeep of the religious institutions individually, as well as through their corporate organizations. The Kaman stone inscription (786–905 CE)[48] records the donations and endowments made from time to time by the artisans. It reveals that the *kumbhakara srenyas* (guild of potters), living in Kamyak, received a sum of money in advance and agreed to pay a permanent cess of one *pana* per wheel, to be paid monthly by each of its members. In the fourth part of the same inscription, it is again stated that the guild of gardeners living in Kamayaka, in consideration of a sum of money paid in advance, was to supply permanently sixty garlands, of which thirty-four were to be delivered at the temples of Vishnu and the remaining twenty-six at the temples of Chamunda. It also mentions a guild of artisans, who in return of a sum of money received in advance, made a permanent endowment and every artisan who worked in the place had to pay one *dramma* per month. A worker of conch shells named Bhadra, was donated, by means of a written deed, two *avaris* (enclosures) facing the west.

The Siyodani inscription records a large number of donations made at different times from 903 to 969, by merchants and artisans in favour of brahminical deities at Siyodani.[49]

An inscription from Bijapur district, dating to the twelfth century, belonging to the reign of Kalachuri King Bijjala, records the gifts made by guilds of oilmen, guilds of artisans, as well as by basketmakers and mat-makers, for the benefit of the Hanumat Temple.[50]

Oilmen contributed from the products of oil mills, and worked in the villages to get religious or other endowments. Thus, in Mathura *prasasti* of the reign of Vijayapala, dated VS year 1207 (1149–50 CE), it is stipulated that on each machine (i.e. oil mill) a *pali* was to be levied from the garland maker and a fourth part from each *mapaka* (grain dealer).[51]

The Bhatera copperplate inscription of Govinda Kesavadeva mentions that a donation of 246 houses and 375 *halas* of land was made by the prince to God Shiva. In this grant, few houses belonged to the *kasya* (bell-metal worker), *rayaka* (washerman), *navika* (boatman), and *dantavara* (ivory worker).[52]

A Kolhapur inscription[53] reveals that the leatherworker gave a pair of sleepers every six months, the basketmaker gave one *mora* every year and the cobbler gave one strap every six months at the time of the Chaitra and the Dipavali festivals.

The profession of *sūtradhāra* was in all probability, a much respected profession. A family that produced many illustrious *sūtradhāras* has been referred to as an auspicious family.[54] Sometimes, Lord Vishwakarma himself has been styled as the *sūtradhāra* of the universe, as he is the creator of the world. Thus, Lord Gokarnasvami has been referred to as 'the master (*guru*) of things movable and immovable, the architect (*sūtradhāra*) for the creation of all the worlds'.[55] The *sūtradhāras* also styled themselves as *pitalhara*, *lohakara* or *ayaskara*, *hemakara*, *silakuta*, *rupakara*, and *vijnanika*, i.e. brazier, blacksmith or coppersmith, goldsmith, stonecutter, sculptor, and simple artisan.[56] From the tenth century onwards, the status of artisans seems to have improved as some of them enjoyed lofty titles, e.g. *acarya*, *sūtradhāra pitamaha*.[57] Sajjan, a potter, was even appointed the Governor of Chittor by Kumarpal of Gujarat.[58] Further, a *mochi* is said to have built a temple.[59]

There are several inscriptions in which the term *sūtradhāra* is used in the context of an engraver.[60] However, the inscriptions do not imply that other artisans or craftsmen were not available for this job. The workmanship and skill of the *vijnanika*, *silpi*, and *rūpakāra* made them options for the work of engraving letters on stones or on copperplates. In the context of the *silpi* category, mention might be made of an inscription that refers to Punasimha, the son of Nahad, as the engraver of Cintra *prasasti*.[61] The Salimpur stone inscription of Jayapaladeva of Kamrupa was engraved by Somesvara, the *silpin* Magadhah (Maghadhan artist). The inscription records, 'Just as a lover [paints] with rapt attention his own mistress by means of colour decoration, so Somesvara, the Magadhan *silpi* incised [with rapt attention this *prasasti* by means of a division of letters].'[62] There are other inscriptions as well, where the qualities and proficiency of other engravers are recorded. The *silpi* named Karnbhadra is referred to as 'one whose engraving was neat and who was intelligent, courteous and an accurate workman'.[63] The plates of Bhotavarman, dated 1396 CE, refer that the *thathera* (brazier) Rupunu was the engraver of copperplates.[64]

Inscriptions sometimes refer to a relationship between the *sūtradhāras* and other ranks of artisans. A Kalachuri inscription says that the artisan Mahidhara engraved the letters of the inscription after the *sūtradhāra* Pithe had worked out the relevant portions of the text of the inscription on the rock on which it was to be engraved.[65] The Chirwa inscription of the Guhila King Someswar Singh, dated VS year 1330 (1272/1273 CE) is said to have been engraved by Kelisimha with the help of *silpi* Delhan.[66]

An inscription dated VS year 1362 (1305 CE) has been found, which belonged to a stepwell at Jaipur. This was written by Sivaraja, who called himself 'vyas'. Vyas was an official designation of a brahmin employed by Rajput kings for reciting and explaining the epics.[67]

It seems that with an increase in experience, the status of an artisan also tended to rise. Different steps in their promotion are indicated in the inscriptions. For example, one Palhana worked in different capacities with the passage of time, which probably suggests that some norms existed in order to determine the status of an artisan. This was perhaps on the basis of his proficiency and skill. Five inscriptions during the reign of Paramarddi (Chandella ruler) engraved in a span of twelve years by Palhana, are noteworthy in this respect. In the Semra plate (1165–6 CE), he calls himself a *pitalhara*; in the Icchawar plate engraved five years later, he is designated as a *silpi*; and in the Mahoba plate of 1172 CE, he calls himself *vijnam* (skillful artist). In the other two inscriptions, the Pachar and Charkari plates (1175 and 1177 CE), he mentions himself as *vaidagdhi Vishwakarman* (expert in the craft of Vishwakarma). It seems that the successive stages of Palhan's rise point to the stages of an artisan's hierarchical mobility, starting from *pitalhara* to *silpi* and finally to *vijnam*.[68]

The hereditary character and family lineage of few famous architects and sculptors are recorded in a fifteenth century inscription from Mewar. During the reign of Rana Mokal, Vasa and Visala—the two sons of Nana and grandsons of Vijala—were mentioned as *sūtradhāras* and sculptors in the Samidesvara temple at Chittor. Further, Phana and Karana, the sons of Hada, are also mentioned as sculptors.[69]

Rana Mokal also invited Mandana, a native of Gujarat, who was an expert on sculpture and architecture, and granted him Rs.30. However, it is not clear from the copperplate whether it was a gift or was given as a wage. The names of Mandana's younger brother Nath, and his son Isar, are also mentioned in the inscription.[70]

A fifteenth-century inscription from Ratanpur records the lineage of four artisans of the Kokasa family, namely Manmatha and his three sons Chhitaku, Mandana, and Dityana, all of whom were well versed in their profession.[71]

Another fifteenth century inscription from Chittor mentions the name of *sūtradhāra* Lakha and his two sons, Jaita and Narada. Napa, Punja, Bhima, and Chautha, who were the sons of Jaita, are also mentioned in the inscription. The name of Jaita, along with those of his sons, are again repeated in a sixteenth-century inscription.[72]

In this context, certain exceptions among the artisans may also be pointed out. In the Kalachuri inscription of 1167–8 CE, the sculptor Devagana, who constructed the Bilvapani temple is described as *rupakara siromani* ('crest-jewel among sculptors'). On the other hand, the *sūtradhāra* Sampula is merely described as the engraver of the record, and in another inscription, he is mentioned as a *rūpakāra*, not as a *sūtradhāra*.[73]

Epigraphical evidences suggest that the profession of an artisan was not limited only to the male members in the families. Women also acquired the skill and excelled in their work. An inscription of the Chahamans of Nadol in Rajasthan, dated VS year 1228 (1172 CE), refers to Pahini, along with his wife Jasadevi, in the context of the construction of the *mandapa*, *akshasama* and *dama* of a Shiva temple.[74] *Bayachakad* mentions that women were employed for lighter work, e.g. for plastering walls, for cleaning and polishing floors and other stonework, for filling the cracks and joints between stones with a mixture called *karala*, for tempering iron chisels in oil and water, for cutting wooden pegs, etc. Only one woman named Suna Pathuriani is mentioned as a sculptress.[75] Sati Burj at Thera Rawat village in the Agra district records that during the reign of Sultan . . . (the name is lost), Uma, the daughter of Vasudeva, committed Sati and *sutradhari* (female mason) Sirma set up the pillar.[76] It should be noted here that the women artisans were paid lower wages than the men.

Some inscriptions also state that in the construction and renovation of the temples, artisans from other communities were also employed. For example, *Bayachakad* records the participation of the renowned Shuja Mohammed of Bhadraka was ordered for smelting iron for the Konark Sun Temple, and that he received 40 *madha* (Leaf VI, 17) as payment for his work. Similarly, Surkhan Mohammed received 210 silver 'Badshah' *sikkas* taken in war for supplying 250 *palas* of lead to admix to the iron. Again, Shuja Mohammed worked with Basu Ojha for making iron channels of different sizes (Leaf VI, 25). He also worked in casting iron girders with others and received a *dupatta* and two strips of *phutta* (a cloth) for a *jama* (Leaf XXIII, 14; XXIV, 1).[77]

Inscriptions and literary accounts give meagre information about the wages of these craftsmen/artisans. They received payment in both cash and kind. According to the Kendupatana plate of Narasingh II, dated Saka year 1217 (1295 CE), the coppersmith and engraver of the plate received 'one *Vatika* of mixed homestead and water covered land for doing this job'.[78] A fourteenth-century document of *Lekhapaddhati* records that five artisans received handful of grains from the threshing floor.[79] Further, the traditional model documents in *Likhanavali* from the fifteenth century reveal that the writers' fees was generally one or two *rupya tanka*.[80] Exclusive information on the wages of artisans is found in the *Ain-i Akbari* (1595) by Abul Fazl, which is a chronicle of Akbar's court.[81]

Most of the inscriptions, while recording pious endowments, tend to view the artisans as a part of temple complexes. They are seen catering not only to the needs of brahminical temples, but of other denominations also, such as of Jain temples, monasteries, and even to the needs of saints.

The socio-economic status of the artisan class can be judged on the basis of the donations made by them to the temples or at the times of festivals. Their position seems to come immediately below that of the merchants. On the other hand, they certainly appear to bear a heavy burden of taxation, just next to peasants. Artisans also paid market dues and cesses upon the sale of their articles. Their conditions thus had a dual aspect. Artisans employed by their ruling classes and chiefs sometimes achieved a higher status; but outside of such employment, their conditions varied very greatly. Further, artisans and craftsmen seem to have been truly professional—the same artisans worked on sculptures or temples of different religious sects. Hindu artisans constructed Muslim monuments and Muslim artisans and craftsmen were recruited for working in Hindu monuments. So, hiring an artisan or a craftsman may simply have been a question of the customer's preference.

Notes

1. The term *silpin* is derived from the word *silpa* and means art or craft. See also, M. Monier-Williams, *A Sanskrit-English Dictionary*, Oxford: Clarendon Press, 1979; R.N. Misra, *Ancient Artists and Art-Activity*, Simla: Indian Institute of Advanced Study, 1975, pp. 2–6.
2. See Max Weber, *The Religion of India*, tr. and ed. Hans H. Gerth and Don Martindale, Glencoe, Ill.: Free Press, 1962, p. 95; also see by B.N.S. Yadava, *Society and Culture in Northern India in the Twelfth Century*, Allahabad: Central Book Depot, 1973, p. 267.
3. C.D. Dalal and G.K. Srigondekar, eds., *Lekhapaddhati*, Gaekwad's Oriental Series, vol. XIX, Baroda: Oriental Institute, 1925. For English translation, see Pushpa Prasad, tr., *Lekhapaddhati: Documents of State and Everyday Life from Ancient and Early Medieval Gujarat*, New Delhi: Oxford University Press, 2007, p. 98, doc. no. 24.
4. Padamanabha, *Kanhadade Prabandha*, tr. V.S. Bhatnagar, New Delhi: Aditya Prakashan, 1991, p. 79.
5. Yadava, *Society and Culture in Northern India*, p. 267.
6. *Epigraphia Indica* (hereafter *EI*), vol. II, ins. no. XV; ins. no. XVI, pp. 9ff; vol. VII, p. 85; J. Philippe Vogel, ed., *Antiquities of Chamba State*, vol. I, Calcutta: Superintendent Government Print, 1911, pp. 162, 166, 193.
7. The term *sūtradhāra* stands for the person holding a thread, cord, string line, and performing various crafts. See Radhavallabha Tripathi,

'Sūtradhāra', in *Kalattavakosha: A Lexicon of Fundamental Concepts of the Indian Art*, vol. II, ed. Bettina Bäumer, Delhi: Motilal Banarsidass, 1988, pp. 321–2.

8. The term occurs frequently in inscriptions from sixth century onwards. One of the earliest references to *sūtradhāra* occurs in a fifth century inscription in Ajanta Cave XV, and in an inscription of Panduvamsi kings of south Kosala. See also M.K. Dhavalikar, 'Sūtradhāra', *Annals of Bhandarkar Oriental Research Institute*, vol. III, 1971, p. 216. The variants of the term are *sutrabhrit*, *sutradhatri*, and *sutradharin*; we also get *sūtradhāra pitamaha* and *gajadhara* as the synonyms of *sūtradhāra*. See D.C. Sircar, *Indian Epigraphical Glossary*, Delhi: Motilal Banarsidass, 1966, pp. 108, 329.
9. Pushpa Prasad, *Sanskrit Inscriptions of Delhi Sultanate 1191-1526*, Delhi: Oxford University Press, 1990, pp. 33–4.
10. Ibid., pp. 34–5.
11. M. Mujeeb, *Islamic Influence on Indian Society*, Delhi: Meenakshi Prakashan, 1972, p. 118.
12. Prasad, *Sanskrit Inscriptions*, Appendix A, p. 216.
13. M. Nazim, *Bijapur Inscriptions*, vol. 49, Memoirs of the Archaeological Survey of India, New Delhi: Archaeological Survey of India (hereafter ASI), 1999, p. 25.
14. *Annual Report of Indian Epigraphy* (hereafter *ARIE*) *for 1961-62*, 1966, C.1311; also see *Bulletin of Baroda Museum and Picture Gallery*, vol. XII, 1955–6, pp. 33–5.
15. Prasad, *Sanskrit Inscriptions*, pp. 179–81.
16. Ibid., p. 181.
17. A. Cunningham, *Four Reports made During the Years 1862–65*, vol. II, Varanasi: Indological Book House, 1992, p. 259, plate LXXV, no. 9; R.L. Mishra, *Inscriptions of Rajasthan*, Udaipur: Himanshu Publications, vol. IV, 2006, p. 138.
18. *ARIE 1959–60*, B.188.
19. The Medas formed an important section of the population and, though living in the forests and mountains, were as influential as any other caste (Dasharatha Sharma, *Early Chauhan Dynasties*, Delhi: S. Chand and Co., 1959, p. 25). G.H. Ojha regards them as the descendants of Sakas and seeks some similarity between the words Mer, Meda, and Mihira (Dasharatha Sharma, *Rajasthan Through the Ages*, Bikaner: Rajasthan State Archives, 1966, p. 15). According to J.M. Campbell, 'the wilder cattle-dealers and the craftsmen alone continue the name Gurjjars and even with them the name is not popular.' So, the Medas, under name Mihiras, were the leaders of Yeta; or the white Huna hosts had adopted Rajput and other names and left the title Meda or Mher to a few of the wilder sections of their people in Sindh, Kathiawar, and Rajaputana (James M. Campbell, *Gazetteer of*

the Bombay Presidency, vol. IX, pt. I, Bombay: Government Central Press, 1901, pp. 463, 492–4).

20. *Annual Report of the Archaeological Department Gwalior State*, Gwalior: Alijah Darbar Press, vs 1986/1929–30, Appendix D, ins. no. 4.
21. H.C. Ray, *The Dynastic History of Northern India*; vol. II, p. 1033, fn. 4, Delhi: Munshiram Manoharlal, 1973; *EI*, vol. V, pp. 102–3.
22. Prasad, *Sanskrit Inscriptions*, pp. 149–52.
23. Govardhan Srimali, *Rajasthan ke Abhilekh*, vol. I, Jodhpur: Maharaja Mansingh Pustak Prakash, 2000, p. 213.
24. Hira Lal states that Silapatta, known as the Silawat caste, still exists in the vicinity of Damoh; *EI*, vol. XII, p. 46.
25. H.B. Blochmann, ed., *Indian Antiquary* (hereafter *IA*), vol. IV, Delhi: Indological Book Reprint Corporation, Antiquarian Booksellers & Publishers, n.d., p. 367; J.E. Abbott, 'Bai Harir's Inscription at Ahmedabad AD 1499', *EI*, vol. IV, 1896, pp. 297–300.
26. Ratan Lal Mishra, *Epigraphical Studies of Rajasthan Inscriptions*, Delhi: B.R. Publishing, 1990, pp. 106, 108.
27. Pushpa Prasad, 'A Curious Step-well Stone Inscription of V.S. 1535', *U.P. Historical Review: Journal of History*, vol. 4, 1987, pp. 72–81.
28. Cunningham, *ASI*, vol. XXI, pp. 35–49; *EI*, vol. I, pp. 320–30; XXX, p. 166.
29. *Journal of Asiatic Society of Bengal*, vol. XVII, 1848, p. 313; *EI*, vol. I, p. 328.
30. Edwin T. Atkinson, *Statistical, Descriptive and Historical Account of the North-Western Provinces of India*, vol. I, Allahabad: North-Western Provinces Government Press, 1874, p. 466.
31. Cunningham, *ASI*, vol. XXI, pp. 142–8; *IA*, vol. XVII, pp. 224, 230–4; H.C. Ray, *Dynamic History of Northern India*, vol. II, Delhi: Munshiram Manoharlal Publishers, 1973, p. 725.
32. *EI*, vol. I, pp. 21–32.
33. V.V. Mirashi, ed., *Corpus Inscriptionum Indicarum* (herefater *CII*), vol. IV, pts. I–II, pp. 204, 230, 235, 311, 317, 324, 336, 441, 456, 556, 561, 573, 586, 652.
34. R.N. Misra, *Śilpa in Indian Tradition, Concept and Instrumentalities*, Delhi: Aryan Books International, 2009, p. 67.
35. *Indian Historical Quarterly*, vol. XXXIII, 1957, pp. 326–7. Balaraja, the youngest son of Jaita, is mentioned in another inscription, dated vs year 1547 (CE 1490); *PRAS of Western India, 1903-4*, p. 41; Ibid., pp. 39–40, 56, ins. no. 2056. *Sūtradhāra* Narada, another son of Lakha, is also mentioned. *JBBRAS* (old series), vol. 23, p. 49.
36. C. Sivaramamurti, *Indian Sculpture*, Delhi: Allied Publishers, 1961, p. 7.
37. Srimali, *Rajasthan ke Abhilekh*, vol. V, pt. 1, p. 328.
38. Vogel, ed., *Antiquities of Chamba State*, vol. I, pp. 162, 166, 193. Also, *sreni* and *prakriti* appear as synonymous terms in Sri Hemachandracharya, *Abhidhanachintamani*, ed. Nemichandra Sastri and Haragovinda Sastri, vol. III, Varanasi: Chaukhamba Sanskrit Series Office, 1996, verse 378.

39. Alice Boner et al., eds., *New Light on the Sun Temple of Koṇārka: Four Unpublished Manuscripts Relating to Construction History and Ritual of this Temple*, Varanasi: Chowkhamba Sanskrit Series Office, 1972, p. xlii.
40. *EI*, vol. I., pp. 154–62.
41. Ibid., p. 115; Vogel, ed., *Antiquities of Chamba State*, vol. I, ins. no. 35, p. 236.
42. G.N. Sharma, *Rajasthan ke Itihas ke Srota*, vol. I, Jaipur: Rajasthan Hindi Granth Akadami, 1973, pp. 141–4.
43. R.N. Misra, 'Artist in the Early Middle Ages', in *Indian Studies: Essays Presented in Memory of Professor Niharranjan Ray*, ed. Amita Ray et al., Delhi: Caxton Publications, 1984, p. 66.
44. *EI*, vol. XI, p. 48.
45. Ibid., vol. I., pp. 277–9; *kanavira* is the Prakrit and vernacular form of Sanskrit *karavira*.
46. *IA*, vol. XLI, pp. 20–1.
47. *CII*, vol. IV, pt. II, pp. 575–9. Mochi Dariya also built a mosque at Didwana in 1686 CE, according a Persian inscription. *ARIE 1969-70*, D.141.
48. Kaman is situated 35 mi. north-west from Bharatpur and about 40 mi. from Mathura. *EI*, vol. *XXIV*, pp. 324–36. An eighth century inscription from Gwalior records a perpetual endowment to receive oil lamps from the chief of the guild of oil millers and its members. It states that the members of the guild of gardeners, including its chief, were to give fifty garlands daily of such flowers that were available in a particular season (*EI*, vol. I, p. 154). The potter's guild dates back at least to the first century CE, as one can notice an investment by this guild in a record from Nasik. *EI*, vol. VIII, p. 89, ins. no. 15.
49. Siyodani is situated near Gwalior and this inscription has been found at Siron Khurd, about 10 mi. north-west of the town. The inscription consists of two parts, with the first part mentioning a large number of donations.
50. *EI*, vol. V, pp. 9–23.
51. *EI*, vol. I, p. 287.
52. *EI*, vol. XI, p. 41.
53. *EI*, vol. XIX, pp. 40–1.
54. *EI*, vol. XII, pp. 44–7.
55. *EI*, vol. IX, p. 33.
56. *EI*, vol. I, p. 328; vol. III, p. 374; vol. IV, p. 170; *IA*, vol. XVI, p. 208; vol. XVII, pp. 227, 230, 236; vol. XVIII, pp. 17, 237.
57. *EI*, vol. I, pp. 207–14; *IA*, vol. XIX, p. 249.
58. *EI*, vol. II, pp. 42ff.
59. *CII*, vol. IV, pt. II, pp. 575–9.
60. *EI*, vol. VI, pp. 202–3; vol. II, p. 13.
61. *EI*, vol. I, p. 287.
62. Ibid., vol. XIII, p. 295; See also *CII*, vol. IV, pt. I, p. 317.
63. *EI*, vol. II, p. 354.

64. Vogel, ed., *Antiquities of Chamba State,* vol. II, pp. 31–2.
65. *CII*, vol. IV, pt. I, p. 317.
66. *Bhandarkar's List*, no. 573.
67. *EI*, vol. XXI, p. 190; R.L. Misra, *Inscriptions of Rajasthan*, vol. III, Delhi: Himanshu Publications, 2006, p. 162.
68. *EI*, vol. IV, pp. 156, 170; vol. XX, p. 128; vol. XVI, pp. 9–10.
69. *The Indian Historical Quarterly*, vol. XXXIII, no. 1, 1957, pp. 321–2.
70. Ibid., pp. 323–4.
71. *CII*, vol. IV, pt. II, pp. 441, 456, 556f; 490; 515, 543, 556ff; 573, 579, 586, 626. For the other engravers and masons from central India, see *Bhandarkar's List*, nos. 1329, 1876, 1887.
72. *Rajputana Museum Report, 1924-25*, pp. 3–4.
73. *CII*, vol. IV, pt. II, pp. 490–515.
74. An eleventh century inscription from Mahoba records that the image of the Buddhist goddess Tara was built or painted by the daughter-in-law of Sri Satana, a painter. *Memoirs of the ASI*, no. 8, p. 3; *EI*, vol. XI, p. 48.
75. See also, Boner et al., eds., *New Light on the Sun Temple of Koṇārka*, Leaf X, Leaf IV, p. 6.
76. Prasad, *Sanskrit Inscriptions*, p. 178.
77. Boner et al., eds., *New Light on Temple of Koṇārka.*
78. *Vatika* is a land measure of twenty *manas* in Odisha. Sircar, *Indian Epigraphical Glossary*, p. 368; *EI*, vol. XXVIII, p. 189.
79. Prasad, tr., *Lekhapaddhati: Documents of State and Everyday Life*, p. 98.
80. Vidyāpati Thākur, *Likhanavali*, ed. and tr. Indra Kant Jha, Patna: Indrālaya Prakāśana, 1969, pp. 92, 94–5.
81. Abul Fazl, *Ain-i Akbari*, vol. I, tr. H. Blochmann, Delhi: Aadiesh Book Depot, 1965, pp. 235–6.

9

Mughal Artisans at Work and at Home

SYED ALI NADEEM REZAVI

Artisans were known to be creative individuals, who worked together in guilds or coalitions in order to bring their crafts to the public, while maintaining a position in the society. Typically, the term artisan was used to describe a person who made products or provided services and who either had his own business or worked for the business of others.

In the West, the owners of these businesses were referred to as masters, while the workers were referred to as apprentices or journeymen. The masters held a higher status in social circles as compared to the workers. Eventually, they formed 'guilds', which were made up of several artisans, who were consequently able to wield more power, get better protection, and secure a higher status by grouping together. The guilds protected the members from outside competition, while the members followed certain criteria and standards to maintain their status.

This essay attempts to reconstruct some rudiments of the professional and social life of these artisanal classes under the Mughals in India. What was their social status? Were they, like their European counterparts, or those during the ancient period in India, organized in guilds? Did they have some self-perception? How did the state and society perceive them? What remuneration did they receive for their endeavours? Were they static or were they mobile, moving to places which would provide them a steady market for their labour and expertise?

Since there is a paucity of information, not much has been devoted to this theme over the years. However, there is some information available on at least two categories of the artisanal class: those involved in building or construction works, and those involved in the textile sector. On the first, we have accounts such as Abul Fazl's *Ā'in-i Akbari* and the documents relating to constructions from Rajasthan—the

Arhsatta Imarati and the *Kamthana Bahis*. Abul Fazl includes a notice (*Ā'in-i Imārat*) on the craftsmen involved in this industry, which provides their wages and mentions the materials used for construction. His list of personnel starts with the *gilkār* (plasterer) and ends with the *ābkash* (water carrier). For the artisanal classes of the textile sector, our major sources of information are the English factory records and other European accounts.

Artisans of the Building Industry

The actual construction work was carried out by the *mi'mār*. A perusal of the sources shows that the term *mi'mār* denoted a mason. The word was also frequently used to refer to the chief or the supervisor of the masons. The chief architect, under whose supervision the other architects constructed the Agra Fort, is called a *mi'mār* by Gulbadan Begam in her memoirs.[1] Abdur Rahim Khan-i Khanan too, had in his service, a *mi'mār* who had no parallel.[2] Similarly, the Shahjahanabad Fort was completed under the able directions of Ustad Ahmad and Ustad Hamid, who were expert *mi'mārs*.[3] These master masons had under them a number of ordinary masons, whose job appears to have been fixing bricks or stones with the help of mortar. The master masons, in fact, were the real builders. Their expertise extended even up to estimating the prices of buildings and lands. For instance, Lachhmi *mi'mār* at Mathura was officially assigned the task of estimating the price of a private house during the early phase of Aurangzeb's reign.[4] The *mi'mārs*' importance and affluence can be deduced from their portrayal in Mughal miniatures, where, while directing the building work, they are depicted to have been fully clad from head to toe.[5] It was the job of the architect not only to choose the site of construction, but also to draw the *tarh* (plan) of the building to be constructed. A *manshūr* (document) pertaining to the appointment of a *mi'mār*, given by Abu'l Qasim Namakin, mentions the preparation of *tarhi* (drawing of plan) as one of the functions of the *muhandis* (architect).[6] A *Babur Nama* painting, commissioned during the reign of Akbar, depicts an architect holding a rectangular grid in his hands, which presumably contained the *tarh* of the garden that was being constructed. A number of men are depicted holding a long rope, following the instructions while measuring the garden.[7] Among the qualifications required for being a *mi'mār*, the document given by Abu'l Qasim Namakin mentions a very good knowledge of mathematics and geometry, besides expertise in the 'art of construction'. He would head a team of professionals comprising the *gilkārān* (clay workers), the *khisht malan* (bricklayers), the *sangtarāshan* or *sangtarāsh* (stonecutters), the *durūdgarān* or *durūdgar* (carpenters), the *khisht puzān* (brick burners), and the *āhak puzān* (limeburners).[8]

Another official of this department was the *mushrif-i 'imārat-i pādshāhi*, who was the accountant.[9] The last important officer was the overseer, who would supervise the actual construction. The miniatures depict both these officers, the first with a notebook and pen, and the second with a mace in his hands.

Next in importance was the *sangtarāsh* and the *najjār* or *durūdgar*, depending on whether the building under construction was made of stone or wood. While dealing with the positive aspects of the Indian society, Shaikh Zain Khan Khawafi comments on the abundance and easy availability of *sangtarāsh*. He says:

> They are far more numerous and exceed in number than those of any other country . . . in the royal edifices at Agra 680 stonecutters who are the natives of the city, have been at work every day in special departments of the governments, and in laying in the foundations of the buildings of Fathpur Sikri, Biana, Dholpur, Gwalior, Kol, and, in carrying out the imperial command, as many as 1491 stonecutters worked daily. Moreover, every one of the pillars of the government (grandees) who erect buildings of stones, employ a large number of the stonecutters in the same way.[10]

Babur too had alluded to the large number of *sangtarāsh* in India and had written that these stonecutters were also sent to other countries.[11] Abul Fazl in the *Ā'in-i Imārat* mentions two categories of *sangtarāsh*, viz., the *naqqāsh*, who was the tracer or carver, and the *sādahkār* or the plain stonecutter, whose only job was to cut and fix stones.[12] Depictions in the Mughal paintings point to the comparatively superior position of the *naqqāsh* over the *sādahkār*. The *Akbar Nama* paintings show the carvers to be better dressed than the stonecutters.[13] The stone was first handed over to the *sādahkār*, who would cut it into the required shape. It was then handed over to the *naqqāsh*, who would trace the required floral or geometrical design before handing it over to the *parchīnkār* (engraver) or the *mambatkār* (embosser) as per need. For carving out more intricate designs, the stone was handed over to the *gultarāsh* (carvers of floral designs).[14]

The *najjār* or *durūdgar*[15] had the responsibility of constructing doors and windows. Some of the European accounts mention the existence of wooden houses, which were built by the *durūdgars*.[16] Even Abul Fazl mentions wooden structures that were built by these artisans.[17] In his chapter on buildings, Abul Fazl thus mentions them (the carpenters) just after the stonecutters. According to him, the carpenters were divided into two groups. The first group of *durūdgar* appear to be those who shaped and chiselled the wood. He further subdivides this group into five categories. The second group, which he calls *sādahkār* or simple workers, who probably just shaped the planks, are divided into three categories. The man responsible for sawing the logs of wood was called *ārah-kash*.[18] The need for carpenters for making windows must have been considerably high due to the high cost of glass for the panes.[19] Abul Fazl also speaks of the *pinjarasāz*, the lattice and wicker workers who probably decorated the windows with their art.[20] Whenever glass was used in buildings, the services of the *tābdān tarāsh* were required.[21]

A building which was under construction could not be completed without the presence of artisans who had expertise in digging and bricklaying. Thus, the Persian sources have innumerable references to *beldārs*.[22] A lofty building, being constructed with stones and bricks, needed the service of the *beldārs* to dig its foundation. Then again, the mason, busy in his work, needed the help of certain artisans to prepare the bricks and bring them to him. Thus, Abul Fazl divides the *beldārs* into two further categories. The first were those who helped in the construction of walls and the second were the ordinary diggers.[23] When the bricks had to be cemented with the help of lime mortar, the services of a *gilkār* were required. Presumably then, the *gilkār* was a kind of mortar maker.[24] Another cementing material which was in vogue at that time was prepared with the help of *surkhi* or pounded bricks. This work of pounding the bricks and mixing it to prepare mortar was performed by the *surkhikob* or the pounder.[25] The tiles which were used in roofing the houses of the middle income group, were prepared by the *khisht tarāsh*.[26] From the Mughal paintings, it appears that most of these workers were ill-clad and went about—as can be seen in the present times—in a semi-clad condition, with only a loincloth and piece of cloth used to carry the load.

Salary, Wages, and Status

The actual work of construction was carried out by workers designated *mi'mār*, *gilkār*, *sangtarāsh*, and the *najjār* or *durūdgar*. Depending on the material of construction, a particular number of members from each group would be employed.

Except the *mi'mār*, the wages of the others are mentioned, ranging from 2 *dāms* (40 *dāms* = Re.1) to 7 *dāms* daily.[27] The *mi'mār* was paid higher. During Aurangzeb's reign, a *mi'mār* was paid a salary between

12 and 26.60 *dāms* per day.[28] As far as the stonecutters and carvers are concerned, we find that a stonecutter doing plain work was earning 5 *dāms* per *gaz* of stone during Akbar's reign.[29] The carvers, on the other hand, were paid 6 *dāms* per *gaz* for their labour under Akbar. The wage of the *ārah-kash* depended on the quality of the wood which he was sawing. Thus, the sawyer of sisam wood was paid 2½ *dāms* per *gaz*, and the one working with nazhu wood drew a payment of 2 *dāms* per *gaz* of wood. On the saw, the *ārah-kash* was helped by a labourer who was employed on a daily wage of 2 *dāms*.[30]

The bricklayers were given 3 to 3½ *dāms* for common work. If they were asked to work for the construction of the walls of fortresses with battlements, they were paid at the rate of 4 *dāms* per *gaz* of work. For all other walls, they were given 2 *dāms* per *gaz*. If a *beldār* dug foundations, he got 2½ *dāms* per *gaz*, while the *beldār* whose job was to dig ditches was given ½ *dām* per *gaz*.[31]

A perusal of these wages and salaries points towards a differentiation within the ranks of the professionals and artisans, which probably arose due to their levels of acquired skill and expertise. It also appears that under the administration of Akbar, the highest daily wage given to an artisan of the building establishment was 7 *dāms* and the lowest was 2 *dāms*. The piece wages on the other hand, varied between 100 *dāms* to ½ *dām* per *gaz*.

The depiction in the Mughal miniatures also establishes the respective positions of the people involved in construction work. A total of nineteen categories of craftsmen have been mentioned by Abul Fazl. Each of these categories is further divided into a number of sub-categories, depending on the job and expertise of the craftsmen. Again, 'minor inscriptions', in the form of names, dates, and symbols, provide information on the artisans. For instance, some light is thrown on the personnel involved in the construction of buildings at Fathpur Sikri by the inscriptions left behind on individual pieces of stone. From these, one comes to know not only of the actual names of some of the builders, but also gets information as to who they were.[32]

Residential Housing

In most of the Indian towns, we are informed, these artisanal classes and other common people, including the members of the inferior ranks of society, lived in 'lowly huts and tiny cottages'.[33] Fr Rodriquez, in a letter to Fr Quadras, comments that in the towns between Belgaum and Bijapur, the dwellings were huts that were 'inferior to those the bulls have in our country, and in some parts the pigs'.[34] In the town of Burhanpur, and the entire area around it, according to Thomas Roe, the houses were built of mud. In fact, we hear that in this area, there was 'not a single house for a man to rest in'.[35] Similarly, in Bengal, all such houses were constructed of 'mudd, dug out of the ground'.[36] In southern India also, most of the houses were of made of mud, and these, as John Fryer mentions, mostly belonged to the 'Hindus who also plastered their floors with cow dung'.[37] In Surat as well, there were quite a few houses built with clay mixed with cow dung. Sometimes, brushwood was also used to provide support to the houses.[38]

Abul Fazl's *Ā'in-i Imārat* mentions *chhapparbands* (thatchers), whose wages were 3 *dāms* per day or 24 *dāms* per 100 *gaz* of thatching done, indicating thereby, the economy of such roofing.[39] In Delhi, there were a large number of small structures built of mud and thatched with straw, in which the troopers and a multitude of servants and camp followers, which included the artisanal classes, lived. These thatched roofs were supported by a layer of 'long, handsome, and strong' canes, while the mud walls were covered with 'fine white lime'.[40] In Agra and Masulipatam also, the houses of artisans were commonly built with mud walls covered with a thatched roof.[41] Thatched houses in great numbers are also mentioned at Narwar near Gwalior, and Patna.[42] The mud structures at Lahiri Bandar in Sindh, we are informed, were 'supported with such poore tymber that it is a wonder how they stand'.[43] At Thatta, Antonio Boccaro says, ordinary houses were made entirely of poles covered with a mixture of straw and mud. This straw and mud plaster over the poles made the walls hard.[44] Similarly, at Toke in Maharashtra, houses with walls of bamboo framework were plastered with mud or cow dung.[45]

In his list of artisans employed in the building establishment, Abul Fazl mentions *patalband* (reed binders), who were employed to thatch the houses. Such reeds, we are informed, were also varnished to give them longer life and durability. Abul Fazl uses the term *lakhira* for those employed in varnishing the reeds.[46] There are also a number of references in our sources regarding *patalbandi* (reed thatching). For example, at Surat, reeds were used along with palm leaves for thatching houses.[47]

Yet another type of structure in which artisans and other such classes may have lived was the one in which the houses were constructed using bamboo or wood. Jean-Baptiste Tavernier mentions a large number of carpenters' houses near Dacca, which were nothing but 'miserable huts' constructed of bamboo, with a covering of mud over them.[48] Such use of interlacing in mud walls provided the strength needed to hold the huts in the wet climate of Dacca. Some of the houses in Surat were built with bamboo interwoven with reeds.[49] Similar bamboo houses were also found in Delhi and Patna.[49] These bamboos were shaped and cut to size for use in building by a group of experts known as *banstarash*.[50] Abdul Qadir Badauni says that at Patna, such thatched structures covered with wood or bamboo roofs were generally known as *chhapparband*.[51] The technique of joining the bamboo sticks to make a cage or frame, to be covered later with thatch or mud, could be accomplished in quite a few ways. According to Abul Fazl, the lattice and wicker worker could apply six techniques. The *pinjarasāz* could accomplish his job either by fastening strips of bamboo with strings into a dodecagonal, or by giving it a twist of a dozen circles, or *duazdih gird*. The third method was to make a hexagon.[52] The most frequent shape that was given was that of a criss-crossed wattle, popularly known as *ja'fari*.[53] Yet another form was the chessboard style of making small squares. The most intricate style was of joining the bamboo sticks by interweaving them.[54] Popularity of and accessibility to these techniques and styles can well be alluded from the respective wages that a *pinjarasāz* got by applying one of these methods. The lowest per day wage was that of a lattice worker applying the chessboard style, while the one expert in interweaving the bamboo sticks drew the highest wages.[55] These wages might suggest the type of binding of bamboo sticks that a member of an artisanal class or a common man would choose while constructing his house.

On the other hand, Tavernier maintained that the *banya* merchants and artisans dwelt in houses passed on 'from father to son', which was the reason why most of the houses owned by them were made of stone and brick.[56] According to William Finch, most of the brick houses of '*banyas*' and 'handicraftsmen' were not only fair and high, but had carved windows and doors as well.[57] In Lahore, these brick structures were higher than those at Agra and Delhi.[58] In 1610, Finch found that the city (Lahore) was mostly inhabited by merchants and handicraftsmen who had buildings (houses) 'faire and high', constructed generally of bricks. He remarks that these structures also had 'carved windows and doors'.[59] In fact, at Lahore, Niccolò Manucci informs us that the 'houses are lofty, some having eight stories'.[60]

Artisanal Mobility and Migration

The Mughal period was a period of monetization and urban development that resulted in hectic building activity and demand for textiles. Different sources testify to the frequent migration and a healthy mobility of the people of the artisanal classes from one place to another, mostly for work. For example, according to Abul Fazl, a large number of master craftsmen were called for imperial building enterprises in Agra and Fathpur Sikri. We are only informed that craftsmen from areas like Gujarat and Rajasthan were employed in the enterprise. Irfan Habib, basing himself on the information available in Persian sources, reaches a figure of 5,000 to 8,000 craftsmen employed in the construction work at Fathpur Sikri.[61]

The establishment of cities as primary centres of production for long-distance trade could be established only by the immigration of craftsmen. Thus, when a sixteenth century poet of Bengal, Mukundaram Chakrabarti, gave an imaginary account of the establishment of a mythical city, he particularly described the settlement of Muslim migrants there, who included *julahas* or weavers, *kagozias* or papermakers, and so on.[62] Likewise, when Mahmud Beghra, the Sultan of Gujarat (1458–1511), established Mahmudabad, it is stated by an eighteenth-century historian that large numbers of artisans and craftsmen came to settle there and made the textile products of Ahmedabad and Mahmudabad famous all over the world, especially in 'Iran, Turkey, and Syria.'[63]

According to Mughal regulations, newcomers to a town were required to offer sureties, but this was done apparently to discourage thieves and other undesirable elements. Any consideration of protecting the local craftsmen against outsiders does not seem to lie behind this regulation.[64] Indeed, far from discouraging the immigration of artisans, local authorities always tended to encourage it. Everyone, as reported by Wellebrand Geleynssen in 1629, was 'free to settle here (Ahmedabad) and live by his craft or his business without molestation or interference by anyone.'[65] As an evidence of this fact, an imperial order issued in 1672 to the officers of Gujarat can be cited, which prohibited them from realizing unauthorized cesses from the cotton-dressers and oil-pressers who had recently come to Gujarat from other places and opened shops there.[66]

Occasionally, a change in taste of the consumers of craft products resulted in the demand for new or different products, which, in turn, induced the migration of specialists in the crafts. Connected with this was the emergence of new techniques in making crafts, which would diffuse along with their practitioners, a phenomenon very common in early modern Europe as well.[67]

An illustration of this comes from the reign of the Akbar (1556–1605). He was keenly interested in shawls from Kashmir and over a thousand workshops of Kashmir shawls were therefore established in Lahore.[68]

Apparently, this could be done only by bringing a large number of shawl-weavers from Kashmir to Lahore. Similarly, for manufacturing Persian carpets, weavers migrated from Iran to India. Such a community of Persians was found settled in the Godavari district of Andhra Pradesh in 1679. They made high quality carpets, and claimed to have come to India over a hundred years earlier (i.e. in the sixteenth century).[69]

If certain techniques remained confined to any particular caste, this was not owing to any official policy of the Mughal government, which generally seems to have been averse to the monopoly of any craft by any group. For example, when, in the Ahmedabad mint, the Srimal caste of smelters and wire-drawers did not let others follow the profession, an imperial order was issued that their monopoly should be disregarded since no one could stop anyone from following any profession, by law.[70] Naturally, this would also encourage migration, since the artisans knew that they could establish themselves in their trade at any new place.

Since textile-making had particularly developed in India as a craft, the weavers specialized in a number of different techniques. Specialists in a particular technique of weaving would therefore move to areas where such products were in demand. This mobility most probably continued till the nineteenth century, when Lancashire gravely devastated the entire profession in India. Before that time, however, there are multiple instances of weavers' migrations.

Painters too formed a class of immigrants. Of the Iranian immigrants, whose paintings have survived, there is now an authoritative record,[71] and one need not say more about it. There were specialists in the related arts, who also migrated from Iran to India. An example of such a painter was Muhammad Amin, an expert in margin and tabular presentations as well as tracing, who invented the technique of tracing in seven colours and also introduced the use of mica paper. He trained Mullah Muhammad Husain of Herat[72]—another immigrant.

An interesting question that can be put forward in this context is whether this mobility and migration also involved a change in caste status. Was it motivated by a desire for 'Sanskritization', which, according to the definition of M.N. Srinivas, means elevation in status through a shift to the rituals and customs of upper castes?[73] Such 'Sanskritization' might have been easier for the skilled craftsmen. For instance, at a new place, where their previous position was unknown, they might have used their relative affluence to get recognition of a higher position in the society.

There are some evidences to answer this question. A carpenter caste, the Chaptegaras, who migrated from Konkan to the Madras Presidency, not only started putting on the sacred thread, but also began to employ brahmin priests for their rituals![74] The analogous carpenter caste of Charodi from the Kanara district followed the same practice on moving to Madurai.[75] These claims were seldom disputed in the immigrants' new homes, but they were generally not assimilated in the local caste hierarchy or treated socially at par with the residents, as may be seen in the case of the Saurashtras.

The Muchaveru shoemakers, who in the seventeenth century came along with the Mughal noble Qasim Khan from Ajmer to Karnataka, pretended to be of the kshatriya caste. They were, however, not allowed even to eat or intermarry with the local painters and weavers, who too had come from Rajputana to Karnataka. They were yet allowed the 'privilege' of the Rajput caste, such as polygamy and domestic seclusion of women.[76]

Migrations were sometimes, indeed, a form of protest or way of escape for the artisans against acts of oppression and tyranny. For instance, when, in 1636, the Mughal 'governor' at Baroda resorted to a forcible procuring of cloth at prices dictated by him, the weavers refused to do so and departed for Surat. They were well on their way, when the governor finally relented and persuaded them to return.[77] This incident confirms the fact, already noted, that the Mughal government did not generally impose any restrictions on the movement of the artisans, and they could not be forced to stay at any particular place. However, the British rulers, when they obtained authority, sought to exercise control on the movement of the artisans. Thus, when in 1776 the weavers of Palaiyam village (near Cuddalore), having been reduced to the state of wage labourers by the English East India Company, migrated to neighbouring districts under the Nawab of Arcot, the British compelled the Nawab to issue orders for their seizure and return. The Nawab, however, protested that 'it is contrary to the customs of the country'.[78] Only those who emigrated to Pondicherry, where the French were setting up weavers' settlements, could escape the Company's clutches.

Professional 'Guilds' or 'Family Organizations'

Guilds in ancient India were a unique and multifaceted form of organization, which combined the functions of a democratic government, a trade union, a court of justice, and a technological institution. The trained workers of the guilds provided a congenial atmosphere for work. They procured raw materials for manufacturing goods, controlled the quality and price of the manufactured goods, and located markets for their sale.[79] According to Romila Thapar, the distribution of work was not only organized in terms of the classes of artisans living in the town, but also in terms of the physical occupation of the different classes residing in different parts of the town. Each *sreni* had its own professional code, working arrangements, duties and obligations, and even religious observances. Matters relating to wider areas of dispute were sometimes settled by the *srenis* among themselves. Social mobility among such *srenis*, where an entire group would seek to change its ritual status on the basis of an improvement in its actual status, were more frequent, since the economic opportunities for improving the actual status would be more easily available, particularly in periods of expanding trade. It is not coincidental that the greatest activities of heterodox sects and of religious movements associated with social protest were in the periods of expanding trade.[80] These guilds appear to have existed in India at least up till the early medieval period.[81] The existence of a guild has, however, been contested for the Mughal period.

A large number of Persian documents, as well as the medieval structures down to the nineteenth century, reveal a number of curious marks and symbols carved or drawn along with names of certain individuals [see Plates 9.1(a), 9.1(b), and 9.1(c)]. It appears that there was the practice of artisans to draw a sign or mark along with their signatures. The symbols in the documents, as compared to the symbols in structures, usually appear along with the signatures of the various witnesses who are testifying the deed, which is being put up in a court of law, be it a *hiba nama* (gift deed), *bai'nama* (sale deed), or a *rahn nama* (mortgage deed). A larger number of marks and symbols, sometimes accompanied by the names of individuals, are found inscribed on almost all the stones of the medieval monuments, be it at the Qutub complex or the Taj. Similar symbols are found on most of the surviving coins of the medieval period. A clue as to what these marks and symbols were is provided by a stray remark of Manucci, when he is writing an account of Emperor Jahangir. I quote:

> It happened one day that he (the Emperor) was on the banks of the river (at Lahore) and saw a pot carried down the stream. He ordered that this pot should be produced before him. It was found to contain a dead body cut into pieces. Orders were given for the officers of justice to discover the culprit, with warning that if they did not find him, all of their heads would be cut off. Among the other expedients they resorted to, one was to order every potter to deliver one pot, and by examining the marks on these, they hoped to trace the vendor of

the pot in question. It is customary in the Mogul country for every potter to put his own special mark on his pots. It was thus that they caught the culprit.[82]

From this remark of Manucci, it becomes manifest that: every potter had a mark put on the pot which he created; each potter had a mark which was individual to him; and if one saw the mark, one could identify through it, its owner. This would thus mean that the marks put on the pots were the professional marks of the master craftsmen. The surviving evidence, in the form of legal documents and individual stone slabs of various structures, point to the fact that the traditional system of using professional marks was not confined only to the potters—it was far more prevalent than what historians have so far thought.

Let us first take the symbols and signatures found on legal documents. For this case study, I have taken into account three sets of original legal documents. The first two are a set of documents preserved in the National Archives of India (Delhi) dealing with the sale, purchase, and mortgage of houses at Cambay.[83] The third is a set of the Bhandari documents of Batala, which have been reproduced by J.S. Grewal.[84]

The Cambay documents mostly consist of sale, mortgage, and gift deeds of the properties of the Hindu *banya* merchants of Gujarat. These

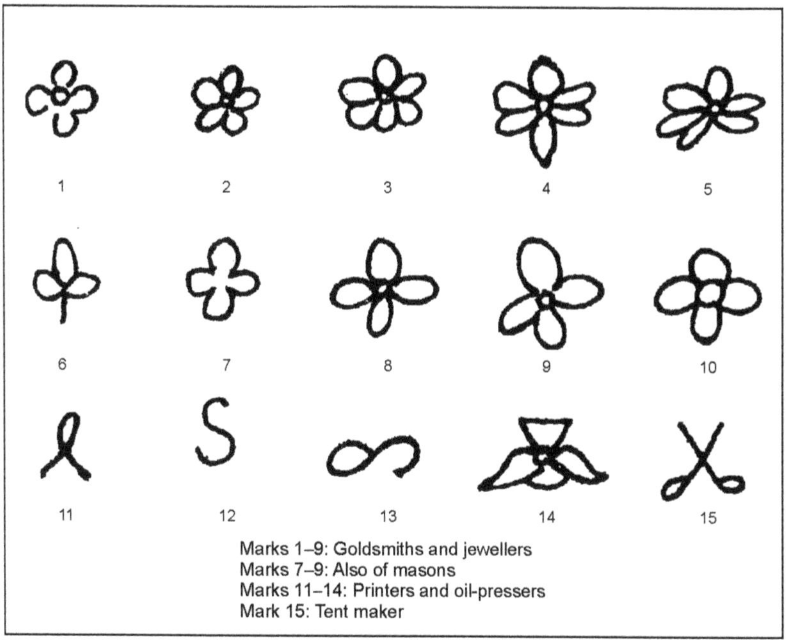

PLATE 9.1(a): Marks of professionals found on legal documents (set 1)

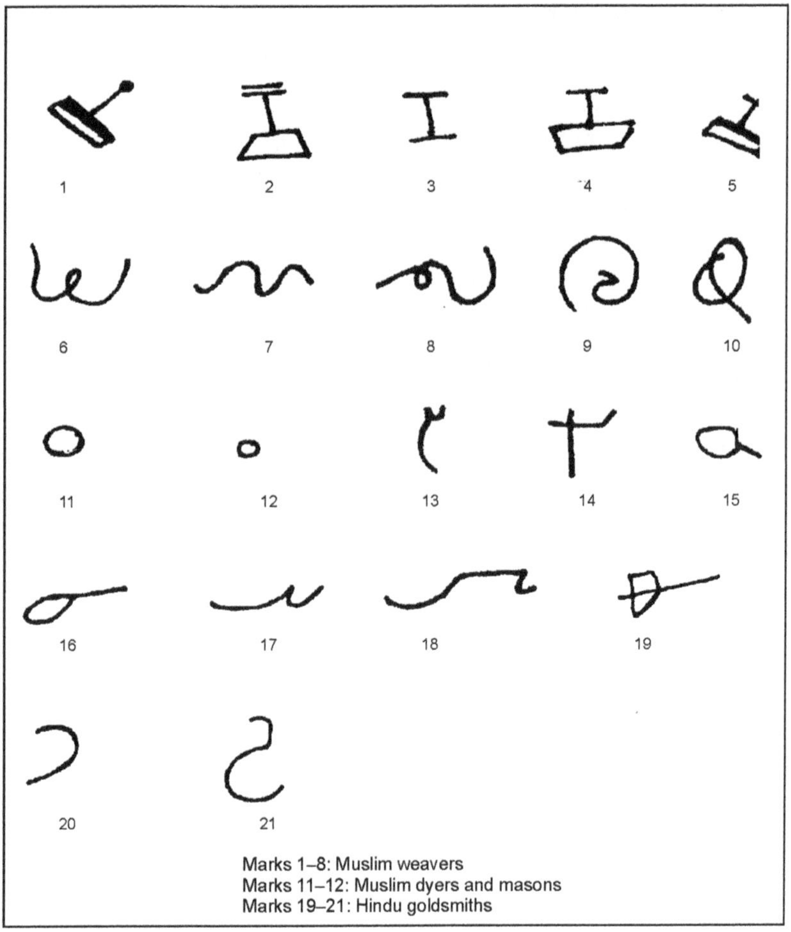

PLATE 9.1(b): Marks of professionals found on legal documents (set 2)

legal documents contain the signatures of a large number of *gavāh* (witness), some of whom are women as well as Muslims. Almost all of the witnesses and signatories belonged either to a group of petty merchants (*banya, baqqāl*) or were professionals like *bunkers* (weavers) and *zargars* (goldsmiths). A few of them were also *zunnārdārs*, i.e. brahmins.

It is interesting to note that the symbols and marks, or *alāmat-i dastakhat*, put beside the names of the *zunnārdārs, banyas*, and *baqqāls*, are invariably in the form of a swastika, a symbol with religious affiliations, especially in the Indian subcontinent. But it is interesting to note that each swastika mark is different from the other.[85] No two swastikas in these documents are similar. These swastikas are both in

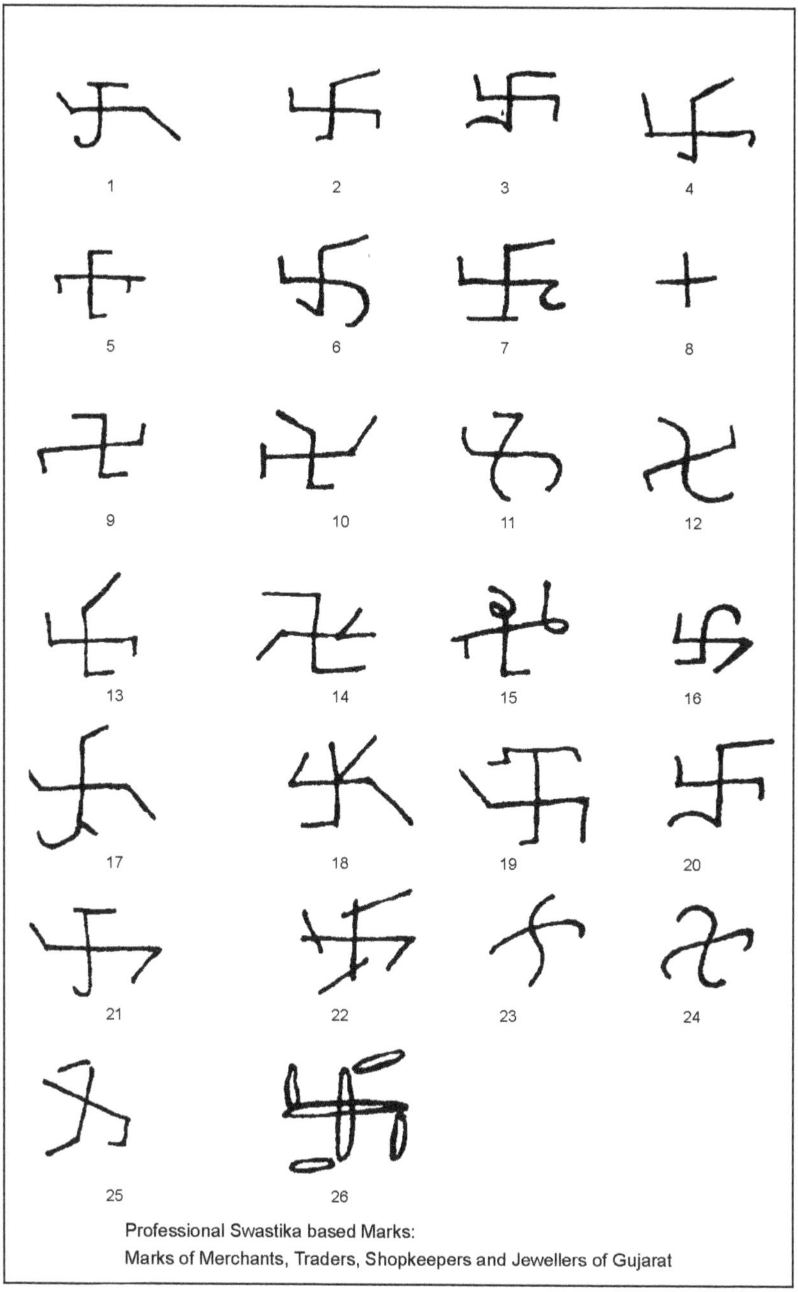

PLATE 9.1(c): Marks of professionals found on legal documents (set 3)

Indo-Aryan and German style. It is quite obvious from the way they have been drawn that a conscious attempt was being made to customize them for exclusive use. Similarly, against the names of the persons professing the weaver's craft, the symbols are in the form of their instruments of trade, as well as wavy lines connoting, perhaps, the cotton yarn.[86] The few goldsmiths that occur in these documents supplement their names with either marks of flower buds[87] or, in one case, the slim goldsmiths' hammer.[88]

In the Batala documents, without fail, a floral mark is applied without fail along with the name of a *zargar* or *jauhari* (jeweller). Just as it was in the case of the swastika marks of the Cambay merchants, each flower in this case is individualistic in appearance.[89] A hook-like or S-shaped design appears along with the names of *telis* (*kunjadgar*) or oil-pressers.[90] The *chhapagar* (printer) has a distinct mark betraying his profession as well.[91] In another document, a *khemadoz* (tent-maker) is represented by a pair of open scissors drawn near his signature.[92] The same document represents two *mi'mārs* with two different floral symbols, while one *mi'mār* has the same mark as stonemason's at Fathpur Sikri. The same mark, but a little larger in size, is also used for a dyer.[93] All this would mean that each profession, and within it, each professional, would have his own mark through which he could be distinguished.

As in case of the documents, marks and symbols made their appearance on buildings as well. Here, they represented the master mason or master stonecutter. This tradition of carving and putting marks and symbols was not unique to one period or region only. It was a tradition quite well known and practiced widely over the world.[94] Among the Romans it was a common practice to stamp bricks with their marks and dates, through which students of architecture can pinpoint the period in which a particular structure was built.[95] In ancient Sri Lanka, the buildings had certain marks on their walls and ceilings, which have been ascribed to masons.[96] In medieval Europe, the masons' marks served multiple purposes. Having a mystical meaning, their primary purpose was to denote the work of each mason employed in hewing or preparing stones for any building. These marks on the stones also helped in deciding the payment that each man could have for his work, as it could be measured without dispute. In case the work was badly done, the superintendent or the chief architect also came to know whom to blame and penalize for the fault committed, through these marks.[97] Lastly, according to a view, these marks could also be used at times to identify the kind of stone on which it was made.[98]

This tradition was popular in India since at least the Mouryan period, and a number of Sultanate structures are known to have them.[99] Individual stones of various structures belonging to the medieval period, including those of the Mughal era, likewise, contain a large number of masons' marks. What strikes one is the remarkable similarity of these marks, in whichever country or place they may be found. Further, all these marks are in the range 1–6 in. in length, the majority however being 2–3 in. long.

Unlike in the West, the monuments of the Mughal period also contain, in abundance, the names and signatures of those who probably were the primary ones responsible for building them.[100]

They might as well be termed the 'guild marks' of a profession, which carried on year after year, reign after reign. When one finds references that for the building of complexes such as Fathpur Sikri and the Taj Mahal, craftsmen and artisans came all the way from places like Gujarat and Rajasthan, one might assume that they came under the leadership of the master craftsmen, to whom they were tied either by family loyalty or by professional links. Thus, the different characters in the signatures vary, while the marks, representing caste or professional groups, recur.

Perceptions

Let us now deal with how these artisanal classes were perceived by the contemporaries.

According to Abul Fazl, 'the people of the world' were divided into four classes, or *tabaqa*—the warriors who had the nature of fire; the artisans and merchants, who held the place of air; the learned, like the philosophers, physicians, arithmeticians, geometricians, and astronomers, who corresponded to water; and the peasants and cultivators, who might be compared to earth.[101] Elsewhere, Abul Fazl ranks all professions into just two classes, placing the warriors at the higher level, and the peasants and other professionals at the lower level. He then goes on to state that the Greeks had classified professions into three types—noble, ignoble, and middling. The noble professions were those based on the use of reason, contributing to far-sightedness and administrative competence; those based on knowledge, such as writing or oral eloquence; and those based on the strength of heart, such as the military profession. The three types of ignoble professions were those that were against the interests of the people, like hoarding; were contrary to sobriety, such as buffoonery; and were detestable, such as the professions of the barber, tanner, and sweeper. The middling professions, on the other hand, were divided into essential, such as agriculture; those that one could live without, such as cloth dyeing; basic crafts, such as carpentry and metalwork; and secondary crafts, such as weighing and tailoring.[102]

This esteem awarded to artisanal classes is reflected in one of Akbar's recorded statements as well: 'An artisan who rises to eminence in his profession has the grace of God with him. Holding him in honour amounts to worship of God.'[103] That at least Akbar held the artisans in high esteem is also reflected through certain other facts as well. For one, it is known that Akbar himself was not averse to take up the work of the artisans himself. Thus, as Fr Antonio Monserrate astonishingly remarks: 'Zelaldinus [Akbar] is so devoted to building that he sometimes quarries stone himself, along with the other workmen. Nor does he shrink from watching and even practicing, for the sake of amusement, the craft of an ordinary artisan.'[104] A similar account of Akbar's perception of this class is found in the description of Akbar, given by another Jesuit, Fr Pierre du Jarric: 'At one time he would be deeply immersed in state affairs, or giving audience to his subjects, and the next moment he would be seen shearing camels, hewing stones, cutting wood, or hammering iron, and doing all with as much diligence as though engaged in his own particular vocation.'[105]

This attitude of Akbar is further discerned through Akbar's dealing with an artisan, as recorded in a few official documents. Three farmans survive, which relate to a certain Ustad Ramdas *rangrez* (dyer), the prefix 'ustad' indicating that he was a 'master' dyer. The first farman, dated 7 April 1561, assigns Ramdas the revenues of a village near Agra in lieu of his salary. The next year, probably on his retirement, he was given a further grant of 21.73 ha. of land in the same locality. This grant, according to the second farman, was made against his personal petition to the emperor against a person (named Darayya) who had accused him of insanity and had not paid him back his loan. The third farman, issued in 1569, directs the local revenue collector to make Darayya repay the loan and to take him to the local *qazi*, to extract an undertaking that he shall not harass Ramdas again.[106] This preferred attitude towards artisans appears to have dissipated after Akbar's death.

While writing his biography in 1641, Banarsidas, a Jain trader, refers to the artisanal classes as 36 lowly clans or *pauni* of shudras. These, according to him, were:

sīsgar (glassmakers), *darji* (tailors), *tanboli* (betel leaf sellers), *rangbāl* (painters), *gwāl* (milkmen/herders), *bādhai* (carpenters), *sangtarāsh* (stonecutters), *tēli* (oil-pressers), *dhobi* (washermen), *dhunia* (carders), *kandoi, kahār* (palanquin-bearer), *kāchhi, kalāl, kulāl, māli* (gardener), *kundigar, kāgdi* (papermaker), *kisan* (cultivator), *patbuniya, chitera, bighera, bāri, lakhera* (reed-maker), *thathera* (blacksmith), *rāj* (mason), *patuva, chhaparbandh* (thatcher), *nāi* (barber), *bhār-bhuniya* (roaster), *sunar* (goldsmith), *luhar* (ironsmith), *sīkligar, hawāigar, ghīwar,* and *chamār* (tanner).[107]

After a few decades, when Muhnot Nainsi compiled his statistical work *Marwar ra Pargana ri Vigat*, he provided the information that in Merta, the whole town was arranged in a hierarchical order: it was first the brahmins (priests), then the Kayasthas (clerks), the Rajputs and warriors or *sipahi*, followed by a category designated as *pavan jati* (working caste), where the houses of fifty other casted, artisanal, menial, and mercantile are enumerated.[108]

However, it is noteworthy that from fifteenth century onwards, one begins to witness artisans assuming the garb of religious preachers and asserting the dignity of their profession in the eyes of God. A notable example of this practice is given by Tulsidas (*fl.* 1570), the author of *Ramcharitmanas*, who noted that during his days: 'Low-caste people such as oilmen, potters, untouchables, fishermen, watchmen and distillers simply shave their heads and turn into mendicants, at the loss of their wife or household goods.'[109] Namdev (cloth printer) and Kabir (weaver), who were artisans as well as religious figures, can be cited as similar examples.

In 1603, when the *Guru Granth Sahib* was compiled by the fifth Guru, it contained the verses which bring out the defiant perception of the artisan's own proximity to God:

In Gobind [God], Gobind, Gobind was Namdev's heart absorbed;
A calico-printer worth half a *dam* became worth a *lakh*
Abandoning weaving and stretching thread, Kabir devoted his love to God's feet; Though a weaver of low family he obtained untold virtues.
Ravidas who used to remove dead cattle, abandoned worldly affairs
Became distinguished, and in the company of saints obtained a sight of God.
Sain, barber and village drudge, well known in every house
In whose heart the Supreme God dwelt, is numbered among the saints.
Having heard all this, I a Jatt [peasant], applied myself to God's service
I have [now] met God in person and great is the good fortune of Dhanna.[110]

The notable Muslim theologian, Abdul Haqq Muhaddis-i Dehlavi (*fl.* 1600) records a conversation that took place between his father and grandfather, as early as in 1522, in which the former was told by the latter that Kabir deserved respect as he was a *muwahhid* (monotheist), being neither a Muslim nor a Hindu.[111] Abul Fazl too reserves wholesome praise for Kabir and finds him to be of 'broadness of path and elevated of vision' and his verses containing truth.[112] Such praise of Kabir also suggests a curious indifference in the higher circles of the Mughal elite to Kabir's lowly artisanal affiliations, and a willingness to exalt and share common truths with him, although he himself rejected their religion (indeed, all religions) in toto.

Notes

1. Gulbadan Bano Begam, *Humayun Nama*, repr. Lahore: Sang-e-Meel Publications, 1966, p. 14. For the English translation, see A.S. Beveridge, tr., *The History of Humayun*, London: Royal Asiatic Society, 1902, p. 97; See also Abul Fazl, *Akbar Nama*, vol. II, Calcutta: Asiatic Society, 1907, p. 247.
2. Mullah Abdul Baqi Nahavandi, *Ma'asir-i Rahimi*, ed. Muhammad Hidayat Husain, vol. II, Calcutta: Asiatic Society of Bengal, 1910, pp. 610–11.
3. Muhammad Waris, *Badshah Nama*, vol. I, transcribed copy from the MS at Raza Library, Rampur, p. 38.
4. *Mathura Documents*, dated 10 *Jamadi* I, 5th r.y. of Aurangzeb.
5. See for example, 'Workmen Erecting a Palace', n.d., *c.*1600, gouche on paper, IS.95-1965; 'Construction of Fathpur Sikri', *Akbar Nama*, fol. 2-1896, 86 / 117; 'Construction of Fathpur Sikri', *Akbar Nama*, fol. 2-1896, 91 / 117; and *Akbar Nama* paintings depicting the construction of Agra Fort preserved in Victoria and Albert Museum, for example, 'Construction of Agra Fort', *Akbar Nama*, fols. 2-1896, 46 / 117 & 2-1896, 45 / 117.
6. Abu'l Qasim Namakin, *Munsha'āt-i Namakīn* MS, Aligarh Collection, Maulana Azad Library, Aligarh Muslim University, fol. 133(b). See also Ishtiyaq Ahmad Zilli, tr., *The Mughal State and Culture 1556-1598: Selected Letters and Documents from Munshaat-i-Namakin*, Document 19, New Delhi: Manohar, 2007, pp. 60–1.
7. *Babur Nama*, Victoria and Albert Museum, London, no. IM.276-1913.
8. Namakin, *Munsha'āt-i Namakīn*, fol. 133(b).
9. A.J. Qaisar, *Building Construction in Mughal India*, Delhi: OUP, 1988, p. 11.
10. Shaikh Zain Khan Khawafi, *Tabaqat-i Baburi*, tr. S. Hasan Askari, Delhi: Idarah-i Adabiyat-i Delli, 1982, p. 134.
11. *Babur Nama*, ed. A.S. Beveridge, London: Luzac and Co., 1971, fol. 291(b).
12. Abul Fazl, *Ā'in-i Akbari*, vol. I, Lucknow: Nawal Kishore, 1882, p. 117.
13. *Akbar Nama* paintings 'Construction of Fathpur Sikri' and 'Construction of Agra Fort'.

14. For their separate skills, see Abdul Hamid Lahori, *Badshah Nama*, ed. K. Ahmad and A. Rahim, vol. II, Calcutta: Asiatic Society of Bengal, 1868, p. 324; Mirza Beg, *Ahwal-i Taj Mahal* MS, Research Library, Department of History, Aligarh Muslim University.
15. Abul Fazl used the term *durūdgar* for them. See Abul Fazl, *Ā'in-i Akbari*, vol. I, p. 117.
16. Francisco Pelsaert, *Jahangir's India: The Remonstratie of Francisco Pelsaert*, tr. W.H. Moreland and P. Geyl, Cambridge: W. Heffer and Sons, 1925, p. 34; Francois Bernier, *Travels in the Mughal Empire AD 1656-1668*, London: Archibald Constable, 1891, p. 398.
17. Abul Fazl, *Ā'in-i Akbari*, vol. I, p. 562. For the use of wood in houses and its importance, see Hidayatullah Bihari, *Hidayat-ul Qawaid* MS, University Collection, Azad Library, Aligarh Muslim University, fol. 40(b). For the expert carpenters of Calicut, see Pyrard, *The Voyage of François Pyrard of Laval*, tr. and ed. Alfert Gray, vol. I, London: Hakluyt Society, 1887, p. 403.
18. Abul Fazl, *Ā'in-i Akbari*, vol. I, p. 117.
19. John Fryer, *A New Account of East India and Persia in Eight Letters: Being Nine Years Travels, Begun 1672 and Finished 1681*, Delhi: Periodical Experts Book Agency, 1985, p. 92.
20. Abul Fazl, *Ā'in-i Akbari*, vol. I, p. 117.
21. Ibid., p. 118.
22. See for example, *Babur Nama*, ed. A.S. Beveridge, fol. 291(b); Khawafi, *Tabaqat-i Baburi*, p. 115; Lahori, *Badshah Nama*, vol. I, p. 323; Ali Muhammad Khan, *Mirat-i-Ahmadi*, ed. Syed Nawab Ali, vol. 1, Baroda: Oriental Institute, 1928, p. 276; M.A. Naeem, ed., *Mughal Documents: Catalogue of Aurangzeb's Reign*, vol. I (1658–63), Hyderabad: State Archives, Government of Andhra Pradesh, 1980.
23. Abul Fazl, *Ā'in-i Akbari*, vol. I, p. 117.
24. Ibid. Interestingly, he is placed first in the list of artisans employed in building establishment.
25. Ibid.
26. Ibid., p. 118.
27. Abul Fazl, *Ā'in-i Akbari*, pp. 117–18.
28. Naeem, ed., *Mughal Documents*, vol. I, document nos. III/347, III/358, III/595, III/890, III/976, IV/300, IV/560, IV/794, IV/1091, IV/1195, V/839, V/959, V/1713, V/1922, and V/2051. I have converted the wages quoted in rupees into *dāms*.
29. Abul Fazl, *Ā'in-i Akbari*, vol. I, p. 117.
30. Ibid.
31. Ibid.
32. See Syed Ali Nadeem Rezavi 'Identifying the Builders: The Mason's Marks and their Signatures', in *Fathpur Sikri Revisited*, New Delhi: Oxford University Press, 2013, pp. 176–203.

33. Fr Antonio Monserrate, *The Commentary of Father Monserrate, S.J., on his Journey to the Court of Akbar*, tr. J.S. Hoyland (annotated by S.N. Banerjee), London: H. Milford, 1922, p. 219.
34. See also John Correia-Afonso, 'Bijapur Four Centuries Ago as described in a Contemporary Letter', *Indica*, vol. 1, 1964, p. 83.
35. Account of Sir Thomas Roe in Samuel Purhcas, ed., *Hakluytus Posthumus or Purchas his Pilgrims*, vol. IV, Glasgow: James MacLehose & Sons, 1905, pp. 323, 443.
36. Streynsham Master, *The Dairies of Streynsham Master, 1675–1680: And other Contemporary Papers relating thereto*, vol. II, ed. R.C. Temple, London: John Murray, 1911, pp. 92–3.
37. Fryer, *A New Account of East India and Persia*, p. 199.
38. Jean-Baptiste Tavernier, *Travels in India*, tr. V. Ball, vol. 1, New Delhi: Oriental Books, 1977, p. 6; G. Careri and M. de Thevenot, *Indian Travels of Thevenot and Careri*, ed. S.N. Sen, New Delhi: National Archives of India, 1949, p. 163. For reference to similar houses in Nandurbar, near Surat, see R.C. Temple, ed., *The Travels of Peter Mundy in Europe and Asia, 1608–1667*, vol. II, London: Hakluyt Society, 1914, p. 44.
39. Abul Fazl, *Ā'in-i Akbari*, vol. I, p. 117.
40. Bernier, *Travels in the Mughal Empire*, p. 246.
41. Account of William Finch in Purchas, *Purchas his Pilgrims*, vol. IV, p. 75; Fryer, *A New Account of East India and Persia*, p. 27. For reference to the large number of mud and thatched houses in Masulipatam, see T. Sreenivas, 'Old Masulipatam', *The Journal of the Hyderabad Archaeological Society*, 1918, p. 42.
42. Tavernier, *Travels in India*, vol. 1, pp. 42, 51, 100.
43. W. Foster, ed., *English Factories in India: 1634-36*, Oxford: Clarendon Press, 1911, p. 124.
44. Fr A. Meersman, tr., 'Antonio Boccaro's Description of Sind', *Journal of Sind Historical Society*, vol. IV, 1944, p. 201.
45. M.S. Mate, *Maratha Architecture, 1650 A.D. to 1850 A.D.*, Poona: University of Poona, 1959, p. 28.
46. Abul Fazl, *Ā'in-i Akbari*, vol. I, p. 117. For a discussion of such professionals and their wages, see Rezavi, *Fathpur Sikri Revisited*, pp. 21–5.
47. Tavernier, *Travels in India*, vol. 1, p. 6; J. Ovington, *A Voyage to Surat in the year 1689*, ed. H.G. Rawlinson, London: Oxford University Press, 1929, p. 95. In Rajasthan too, there is evidence that in 1694, reeds were used in construction work. See *Arhsatta Imarati* preserved in Bikaner Archives, Bikaner (MF, Research Library, Department of History, Aligarh Muslim University). I am thankful to Dr Sumbul Halim Khan, now an Associate Professor in the Department of History, who brought this information to my notice and helped me in deciphering the documents.
48. Tavernier, *Travels in India*, vol. 1, p. 105; Ovington, *A Voyage to Surat*, p. 95.
49. Tavernier, *Travels in India*, vol. 1, pp. 78, 100.

50. Abul Fazl, *Ā'in-i Akbari*, vol. I, p. 117.
51. Abdul Qadir Badauni, *Muntakhab-ut Tawarikh*, vol. II, Bib. Ind. Calcutta: Asiatic Society, 1968, p. 182.
52. Abul Fazl, *Ā'in-i Akbari*, vol. I, p. 117.
53. Peter Mundy mentions the use of such wattle and thatch style for houses and huts in Patna. See R.C. Temple, ed., *The Travels of Peter Mundy*, p.364.
54. Abul Fazl, *Ā'in-i Akbari*, vol. I, p. 117.
55. Ibid.
56. Tavernier, *Travels in India*, vol. 1, p. 46.
57. Ibid.
58. Tavernier, *Travels in India*, vol. 1, p. 77; Monserrate, *The Commentary of Father Monserrate*, p. 160.
59. Account of William Finch in Purchas, *Purchas his Pilgrims*, vol. IV, p. 52.
60. Niccolò Manucci, *Storia Do Mogor; Or, Mogul India 1653-1708*, tr. William Irvine, vol. II, London: John Murray, 1907, p. 173.
61. Irfan Habib, 'The Economic and Social Setting: Akbar and Fatehpur Sikri', *Marg*, vol. XXXVIII, no. 2, 1987, pp. 79–80.
62. Mukundaram Chakrabarti's *Chandimangal*, cited in J.N. Das Gupta, *Bengal in the Sixteenth Century, A.D.*, Calcutta: University of Calcutta, 1914, pp. 91–2.
63. Ali Muhammad Khan, *Mirat-i-Ahmadi Supplement*, ed. Syed Nawab Ali, Baroda: Oriental Institute, 1930, p. 7.
64. Abul Fazl, *Ā'in-i Akbari*, ed. H. Blochmann, Calcutta: Asiatic Society of Bengal, 1867, p. 284. See especially, Abul Fazl's explanation of the regulation (which he says he proposed to Akbar in 1582) in the *Akbar Nama* (for full translation of the passage, see S. Moosvi, *Episodes in the Life of Akbar: Contemporary Records and Reminiscences*, New Delhi: National Book Trust, 1994, pp. 87–9). Those without sureties were not in any case to be turned away but put up in inns in an earmarked zone (Abul Fazl, *Ā'in-i Akbari*, vol. I, p. 284; Khan, *Mirat-i-Ahmadi*, vol. 1, p. 169).
65. W. Geleynssen, 'Verclaringe ende Bevinding', etc., extracts tr. W.H. Moreland, *Journal of Indian History*, vol. IV, 1925–6, p. 75.
66. Khan, *Mirat-i-Ahmadi*, vol. 1, p. 287.
67. On this, see C.M. Cipolla, *Before the Industrial Revolution: European Society and Economy, 1000-1700*, 3rd edn, London: Routledge, 1993, pp. 157–9.
68. Abul Fazl, *Ā'in-i Akbari*, vol. I, p. 104.
69. Streynsham Master, *The Diaries of Streynsham Master*, vol. II, p. 171.
70. Khan, *Mirat-i-Ahmadi*, vol. 1, pp. 292–3.
71. S.P. Verma, *Mughal Painters and their Work: A Bibliographical Survey and Comprehensive Catalogue*, Delhi: Oxford University Press, 1994.
72. Mullah Abdul Baqi Nahavandi, *Ma'asir-i Rahimi*, ed. M. Hidayat Hosain, vol. III, Calcutta: Asiatic Society of Bengal, 1931, pp. 1679–80.
73. See M.N. Srinivas's essays on 'Sanskritization' in M.N. Srinivas, *Social Change in Modern India*, Indian edn, Hyderabad: Orient Longman, 1989.

74. E. Thurston and K. Rangachari, *Caste and Tribes of Southern India*, vol. 2, Madras: Government Press, 1909, p. 22.
75. Ibid., p. 23.
76. F. Buchanan, *A Journey from Madras through the countries Mysore, Canara, and Malabar*, vol. I, London: T. Cadell & W. Davies, 1807, pp. 302–3.
77. Foster, ed., *English Factories in India*, p. 290.
78. Madras Public Proceedings 1778, 240/45, Nawab to Governor, 22 May 1778, quoted from S. Arasaratnam, 'Trade and Political Dominion in South India, 1750-1790: Changing British-Indian Relationships', *Modern Asian Studies*, vol. 13, no. 1, February 1979, p. 35.
79. For guilds or *srenis* in ancient India, see for example, Romila Thapar, *Asoka and the Decline of the Mauryas*, Delhi, Oxford University Press, 2000, p. 73; Upinder Singh, *A History of Ancient and Early Medieval India: From the Stone Age to the 12th Century*, New Delhi: Pearson Longman, 2008, pp. 404–6.
80. Romila Thapar, *Ancient Indian Social History: Some Interpretations*, Hyderabad: Orient Longman, 1996, pp. 130–3.
81. Herman Kulke and Dietmar Rothermund, *A History of India*, New York: Routledge, 1998, p. 118.
82. Niccolò Manucci, *Storia do Mogor: Or Mogul India, 1653–1708*, vol. I, London: John Murray, 1907, p. 174.
83. 'Cambay Documents' preserved in the National Archives of India (NAI), collection nos. NAI, 2695 and NAI, 2702.
84. J.S. Grewal, *In the By-Lanes of History: Some Persian Documents from a Punjab Town* (hereafter *Batala Documents*), Shimla: Indian Institute of Advanced Study, 1975.
85. See for example, NAI, 2695/ 1, 3, 6, 14, 16, 28, 30, 31, 32, 33, 36; NAI, 2702/ 4, 5, 7, 8, 12.
86. For example, NAI, 2695/ 5, 29; NAI, 2702/ 8.
87. NAI, 2695/ 4.
88. Ibid., 2695/ 34.
89. *Batala Documents*, nos. IV, XII, XVI.
90. *Batala Documents*, nos. XIII, XV, XXIII.
91. Ibid.
92. Ibid.
93. Ibid.
94. See for example, George Godwin, 'Something About Mason's Marks in Various Countries', *Transactions, Royal Institute of British Architects*, session 1870–71, pp. 135–44; J.A. Smith, 'Exhibition of Mason's Marks, Copied from Melrose Abbey, Dryburgh, Jedburgh, etc. etc.', *Proceedings, Society of Antiquaries of Scotland*, vol. IV, 1863, pp. 548–53; H. Treziny, *Architecture et societe de l'archaisme grec a la republique romaine, 1980*, Collection de l' Ecole Francaise de Rome, vol. 66, no. 11, Centre National de la Recherche Scientifique, 1983, pp. 111–13.

95. See Bradley Hudson McLean, *An Introduction to Greek Epigraphy of the Hellenistic and Roman Periods from Alexander the Great down to the Reign of Constantine (323 B.C.–A.D. 337)*, Ann Arbor, Mich.: University of Michigan Press, 2002; R.H.C. Davis, 'Catalogue of Masons' Marks as an aid to Architectural History', *Journal of the British Archaeological Association*, series III, vol. 17, 1954, pp. 43–76.
96. H. Parker, *Ancient Ceylon*, London: Luzac and Co., 1900, pp. 640–7.
97. Patrick Chalmers, Esq., 'On the Use of Mason-Marks in Scotland', *Archaeologia: Or, Miscellaneous Tracts, Relating to Antiquity*, vol. XXXIV, 1852, pp. 33–6.
98. M.J. Walhouse, 'Archaeological Notes', *The Indian Antiquary, A Journal of Oriental Research*, ed. J.A.S. Burgess, vol. IV, 1875, p. 303.
99. Ibid., pp. 302–5.
100. The survey of the masons' mark in Agra was conducted by the author in 1989. For details, see Syed Ali Nadeem Rezavi, *Fathpur Sikri Revisited*, New Delhi: Oxford University Press, 2013, pp. 176–202; also see Syed Ali Nadeem Rezavi, 'Marks and Symbols of Professionals on Mughal Mouments', in *Sacred Landscapes in Asia: Shared Traditions, Multiple Histories*, ed. Himanshu Prabha Ray, IIC Asia Project, New Delhi: Manohar Publishers, 2007, pp. 107–68.
101. Abul Fazl, *Ā'in-i Akbari*, vol. I, pp. 3–4.
102. Abul Fazl, *Ā'in-i Akbari*, vol. II, p. 291.
103. Ibid., p. 229.
104. Monserrate, *The Commentary of Father Monserrate*, p. 201.
105. Pierre du Jarric, *Akbar and the Jesuits*, tr. C.H. Payne, London: Routledge, 1926, p. 28.
106. See Irfan Habib, 'Three Early Farmans of Akbar in Favour of Ramdas, the Master Dyer', in *Akbar and His India*, ed. Irfan Habib, Delhi: Oxford University Press, 1997, pp. 270–93.
107. This is an extract from the translated version of Banarsidas's *Ardhakathānaka*. See Mukund Lāṭha, tr. & annot., *The Ardhakathānaka: Half a Tale*, Jaipur: Rajasthan Prakrit Bharati Sansthan, 1981, verse 29, p. 226.
108. Muhnot Nainsi, *Marwar ri Pargana ri Vigat* (*c*.1664), ed. Narain Singh Bhati, 2 vols., Jodhpur: Rajasthan Prachya Vidya Pratisthan, 1968–9.
109. F.S. Growse, tr., *The Ramayana of Tulsidas*, Allahabad: Government Press, North-Western Provinces and Oudh, 1978.
110. This is a translation of an extract from *Guru Granth Sahib*. See M.A. Macauliffe, *The Sikh Religion: Its Gurus, Sacred Writings and Authors*, vol. 6, Oxford: Clarendon Press, 1909, p. 109.
111. Abdul Haqq Muhaddis, *Akhbarul Akhyar Fi Asrarul Abrar*, Delhi: Matba Muhammadi, 1913–4, p. 306.
112. Abul Fazl, *Ā'in-i Akbari*, vol. I, pp. 393–433.

Southern Perspectives on the Vishwakarma

10

The Place of the Kammāḷa in the Agrarian Society of Tamil Nadu, *c.*600–1600 CE

Y. SUBBARAYALU

The term Kammāḷa (Kaṇmāḷa and Kaṇṇāḷa being variants) denoted, in Tamil inscriptions and literature from the eleventh century, different artisans—*tachchan*, who worked in stone and wood; *kollan*, who worked in iron; *taṭṭān*, who worked in gold; and *kannān* and *kañchakāran*, who worked in copper and bronze. According to context, the term may denote either the whole group of artisans or an individual member. Until the eleventh century, the individual terms (*tachchan*, *kollan*, etc.) were used to specify a particular artisan. Thereafter, the term Rathakāra[1] was also used as an alternative term for Kammāḷa. Again, from the fifteenth century, the designation *pañchāḷattār* or *pañchānattār*, meaning 'the five people', was additionally used to denote them collectively. Initially, the artisan communities were considered to be a fraternity of three groups, namely *tachchan*, *kollan*, and *taṭṭān*.[2] In the later centuries, the number increased to five, and hence the term *pañchāḷattār* came into use.[3] In the Kannada region, the five groups were denoted by the term *pañcha-kāruka*.[4]

Unlike the landed and warrior groups, the artisans do not get prominent mention until in the twelfth century. This should be attributed largely to the bias in the inscriptions, which were concerned mostly in recording land grants to temples and other religious institutions. In the inscriptions, a few specific references to artisans occur in the context of engraving records on stones or copperplates and in the context of receiving land shares in a newly created brahman settlement. There are also some artisan donors.

In early Tamil literature (*c.* first to third centuries CE), the artisans are appreciated for their work in making iron weapons and vehicles for transportation, in constructing palatial buildings with ornamental woodwork and paintings, and in making jewellery in gold. Their prominent presence in urban centres like Madurai is understood from the *Silappatikāram*, a Tamil epic of about the fifth or sixth century.[5] This poem mentions that a royal goldsmith serving the Pandya king had, in his workforce, several talented smiths.

From the sixth century onwards, erection of rock-cut and free-standing stone temples gained popularity in various parts of Tamil Nadu. There is, however, no information on the artisans who have contributed their expertise and labour to the erection of those temples. Another thing to be noted is the parallel rise of the Bhakti movement from the seventh to ninth centuries. People from various walks of life are believed to have joined this religious movement, embracing both the Saiva and Vaishnava sects. Interestingly, among the seventy-five Bhakti saints (Vaishnava *Āḻvār* and Saiva *Nāyanār*), there is no Kammāḷa artisan, though there are three Saiva saints from other non-agrarian groups—a potter, a washerman, and a fisherman.[6] Though this phenomenon needs some explanation, there is some evidence to say that the Kammāḷa artisans had recognition in the society as writers or engravers of royal records on copperplates and stones in those centuries. For example, in three Pallava copperplate records, the writers were carpenters (*kāshṭakāri* or *tachchan*); in another case the writer was a goldsmith; and in the fifth one it was an ironsmith.[7] All these persons, being in the service of the king, were bestowed with titles indicating royal connection as well as elite position among their groups. Some of them were also found to be related: a goldsmith's son was a goldsmith, an ironsmith's son was an ironsmith, and so on. This, in turn, implies that the artisan families had been carrying on their occupation hereditarily. There were, however, exceptions to this practice. For instance, there is evidence of a father-son pair serving in the Pandya court in about 900 CE,[8] where the father was the writer/engraver of a copperplate record and the son was the composer of the Tamil section of the same record. The latter can be easily considered an accomplished poet from the way he has composed the record—an example of highly ornate Tamil poetry. It seems he had a good knowledge of Sanskrit too. It is thus no wonder that he was given the title 'Pāṇḍi-Tamiḻ-ābharaṇan', i.e. 'one who wears Tamil as his ornament and who is honoured by the Pāṇḍi (Pāṇḍya) king'.

In north India, we come across *śrēṇis* (guilds) of artisans and other craftsmen besides traders, in the early medieval period.[9] Similar instances are, however, very rare in south India. But there seems to have existed some sort of separate artisan quarters in urban centres.

Thus, we hear about a quarter called *aimmanai-chēri* in Kanchipuram, wherefrom came two carpenters, working for the royalty, within an interval of about sixty years.[10] We get clear information about the residence of Kammāḷa people only in the time of Rāja Rāja I (985–1014). Two of his inscriptions from the Big Temple (Brihadisvara Temple) at Thanjavur throw light on this aspect. It has been found that in most of the non-brahman villages, there were separate residential quarters for the landowning people (mostly Veḷḷāḷa) and for the others who were either agricultural labourers or craftsmen. While the main village was occupied by the former, the hamlets were occupied by the Kaṇmāṇa or Kammāṇa (same as Kammāḷa), the Paṟaiya, the Īḻava, and a few others. But not all villages had these hamlets of craftsmen and labouring groups. Out of the thirty-three villages for which social data is available, some seven villages had hamlets for the Kammāḷa artisans.[11] Almost the same pattern is noticed in a copperplate grant of 1050 CE relating to the creation of a new brahman settlement in the eastern part of the Thanjavur delta.[12] There we get nine Kammāḷa hamlets for a total of forty-five villages. In both the cases, the proportion roughly comes to one Kammāḷa hamlet for every five villages. However, it is difficult to estimate the number of households in each of these hamlets. In any case, the artisans of these hamlets would have fulfilled the production needs of the surrounding villages. The aforementioned brahman settlement was made by clubbing forty-five old settlements, for settling 730 brahman families brought from various other settlements in and around the Kaveri delta. To cater to the needs of this new settlement, some 133 professional people were also brought in. They included 37 Kammāḷa artisans, besides doctors (4), astrologer (1), potters (22), musicians (10), bards(?) (5), bangle merchants (5), oil-pressers (3), herders (3), washermen (10), water distributors (3), barbers (18), the Paraiya (2), and a few others. The Kammāḷas included 8 carpenters, 7 ironsmiths, 20 goldsmiths, and 2 coppersmiths. Some of these professionals were from the local settlements and others were brought from outside.[13] Many of the goldsmiths came from outside, perhaps due to the lack of local talent in the field.

The goldsmiths had better prestige and visibility among the Kammāḷas from early centuries. The goldsmiths' workshop was known, in south Indian inscriptions, as *akkasāle* (in Kannada) or *akkasālai* (in Tamil),[14] which by extension also denoted the communities of all the Kammāḷas. Gold was the most precious metal used for making jewellery and also for minting coins. In larger commercial transactions, gold was used as bullion and therefore there was always some necessity to test its purity. Naturally, the services of the goldsmiths would have been in high demand in all the settlements. A touchstone was kept in many of the bigger settlements for testing gold. For the Chola government, particularly during the twelfth and thirteenth centuries, the tax on goldsmiths or *taṭṭār-pāṭṭam* was an important source of commercial income.[15] Taxes on ironsmiths and carpenters are only rarely found,[16] because their services, though very essential for the agrarian society, did not have much commercial importance. Actually, the artisans were, for long, considered as service providers to the agricultural and commercial communities. In social ranking, they were treated as lower to the latter community. This may be understood from the way they are addressed in some public gatherings: *nam paṇichey-makkaḷ*, i.e. 'our servants'.[17] Occasionally, they were also given the label of *kīḻ-kalanai*, meaning the lower castes.[18]

The large number of temples that came up from the tenth century onwards required the labour of a large number of artisans, like the stonemasons, carpenters, smiths, and so on. This was certainly an opportunity for the Kammāḷas to get a boost in their social position. Like many other low-ranked communities, they started asserting their position in one way or the other. Patronizing temples or shrines of their own was one of the ways. The earliest instance of this kind is found in Nagapattinam. It is in this important port town of the Cholas that a Buddhist *vihāra* was erected by the Srivijaya king in about 1006, with the permission of the Chola King Raja Raja I. Around 1100, the Kammāḷas erected within the same complex, another *vihāra* named after their workshop/community as *Akkasālai-perum-paḷḷi* ('the great *vihāra*', called after the *akkasālai*).[19] It is said that the Buddha image enshrined therein was to be adored by all the members of the Eighteen-*Vishayam*. The Eighteen-*Vishayam* is one of the names for the big south Indian merchant corporation called *Ayyavoḷe*-Five Hundred. This would, in turn, support the fact that the Kammāḷas were closely associated with the merchant corporation.

As noted already, the Kammāḷas were also known as Rathakāras from the twelfth century onwards. In some inscriptions of the twelfth–thirteenth centuries, the Rathakāras are given a lengthy attribute that may be translated as 'the four categories of Rathakāra engaged in six kinds of work in three kinds of *paḷḷi* or workshops'.[20] However, this being a conventional description, we cannot literally interpret the attribute. The numbers three, four, and six cannot be considered to be exact figures; they would only mean that there were several kinds of artisans in the Rathakāra fold. Three of the Rathakāra inscriptions, dated 1118, 1169, and *c.*1200, respectively,[21] need special attention. They are somewhat similar in nature; they record the Rathakāras' attempt to decide their social standing in the varna system. They approached some learned *bhaṭṭas* (brahmans) for deciding their caste credentials in the light of the *Dharmaśāstra* prescriptions. The scholars, after much deliberations on the basis of the *smritis*, *āgamas*, and Puranas, as well as some (unspecified) commentaries, decided that the Rathakāras can be considered to constitute a proper *anuloma* caste and therefore they were entitled to perform certain Vedic rituals (in the context of erection and consecration of buildings), besides carrying on with their noble occupations, namely, the making of sacrificial implements, statues, palaces, temples, chariots, carts, and several other things. J. Duncan M. Derrett, who discussed the contents of these inscriptions, thinks that they depict one of the earliest attempts on the part of the Rathakāras to challenge brahman dominance in certain ritualistic fields.[22] For the time being, the brahman scholars gave a satisfactory solution to the Rathakāra aspirations that the *anuloma* Rathakāras were entitled to the noble occupations prescribed in the *Dharmaśāstras*. It was also asserted that if there were some artisans doing menial jobs they must be considered as *pratiloma* people.

Apart from the deliberations as to the *anuloma* status of the Kammāḷa, the inscriptions also suggest the fact that the Kammāḷas, like any other contemporary landed and commercial elite, started to make solidarity meetings at wider, supra-local levels, and to assert their social importance.[23] This is clearly the message of an inscription dated 1264 CE, found at Alangudi in the Thanjavur district, almost at the fag end of the Chola rule.[24] The Sanskrit verse at the beginning of this Tamil inscription is much mutilated, but the fact that it refers to Vishwakarma can be deciphered. The subsequent passage (in the inscription) is a sort of eulogy to the Rathakāras, praising their good qualities and occupation. After that is given the information that the Rathakāras of several *vaḷanāḍu* (localities) and *nagara* (towns) assembled at the Shiva temple and decided to collect some money from each member of the community to erect their own pavilion in a nearby grove, and to celebrate an annual festival there for the deity of the Shiva temple. From the names of the localities, it can be said that the Rathakāra members represented some sixteen *vaḷanāḍu* that covered the entire Kaveri delta and some adjoining territory, which actually formed the Chōḻa-*maṇḍalam*, the central territory of the Chola state.

The solidarity assemblies just mentioned suggest the rising importance of the artisan communities in the society. From the thirteenth century onwards, the collection of commercial taxes, particularly those on weavers and goldsmiths, is found to be more important in the collection of revenues than before.[25] This phenomenon becomes more conspicuous in the fourteenth–fifteenth centuries, when the economy becomes fully monetized under the Vijayanagar state. At this juncture, the society is perceived as having two distinct parts, one agrarian and the other commercial (including the craftsmen). The craftsmen were collectively called the *paṭṭaḍai* people and were encouraged by the king and his subordinates to settle in temple centres and newly created townships or *pēṭṭāi*.[26] Among the craftsmen, the weaver communities, particularly the Kaikkōḷa, figure prominently. The rise of the weaver communities is more or less a south Indian phenomenon, with some centres of concentration in the northern part of Tamil Nadu.[27] Though the presence of the Kammāḷas is not attested prominently in inscriptions, their parallel rise in the society can be understood indirectly, as their technical expertise and service should have been necessary for the making and maintenance of the weavers' looms, etc. Naturally, they associated themselves closely with all the basic producers in the society under the banner of *Valaṅgai-Iḍaṅgai* (Right Hand and Left Hand) division in the early half of the fifteenth century, when the latter rose in revolt against the Vijayanagar government in order to oppose tax exploitation.[28] So far, this is the earliest evidence of the inclusion of Kammāḷas in the dual division, though the *Valaṅgai-Iḍaṅgai* division in its formative stage is present from about 1200 CE.[29] The Kammāḷas are also found forming big assemblies of their own in the fourteenth and fifteenth centuries for the purpose of celebrating some temple festivals by collecting voluntary contributions from every household of their community spread over wide areas.[30]

In spite of their growing power and social position, the Kammāḷas were always at the mercy of the ruling class, including the chief landholding groups, and had to remain vigilant to protect their privileges and rights. This fact can be inferred from a series of inscriptions put up in 1572–3. They record that the main landholders and the local chiefs of the Tiruvadi-*rājya* (same as the Vaḻudilampaṭṭu-*rājya*) took an oath in the name of the king and the superior *nāyaka* in the locality, not to collect unjust levies that had been imposed by their predecessors upon the three groups of the Kammāḷas of their area.[31] It is also mentioned that the decision was taken on the basis of the information provided by the Kammāḷa representation that such levies had not been imposed on their brethren living in Paḍaivīḍu, Señji, Tiruvaṇṇāmalai, and Kānchipuram *sīmais*. These four localities comprised the territories of Paḍaivīḍu and

Chandragiri *rājyas*, occupying the northern part of Tamil Nadu and the adjoining Andhra districts. This information also shows that the Kammāḷas could come together from over a wide area, spreading over three *rājyas*, for achieving some common social goal. In this, they followed the lead of the Kaikkōḷas of the same *rājya* who petitioned to the local Vijayanagar Governor in around 1500 and obtained some privileges and rights that their brethren had been enjoying in the Kanchipuram area.[32]

Notes

1. This term occurs in north India much earlier in Vedic and *Dharmaśāstra* literature.
2. *Annual Report on Epigraphy* (hereafter *ARE*), 1914, no. 153; 1922, no. 65; 1929, no. 293.
3. The term is wrongly spelt as *pāñchāḷattār* in T.V. Mahalingam, *Administration and Social Life under Vijayanagar, Part II: Social Life,* 2nd edn, Madras: University of Madras, 1975, pp. 20–1.
4. S. Gururajachar, *Some Aspects of Economic and Social Life in Karnataka, A.D. 1000–1300*, Mysore: Prasārānga, University of Mysore, 1974, p. 159.
5. U.V. Saminathaiyar, ed., *Silappatikāram*, Madras: U.V. Saminathaiyar Library Publications, 2001, pp. 137–8.
6. M. Rajamanikkam, *Periyapurāṇa Ārāychchi*, Chennai: Avvai Publishers, 2002.
7. T.N. Subramanian, ed., *Thirty Pallava Copper Plates*, Madras: The Tamil History Academy, 1966, pp. 169, 196, 245, 257, 271.
8. T.N. Subramanian, 'The Dalavaypuram Copperplate Grant of Parantaka Viranarayana Pandya', in *Transactions of the Archaeological Society of South India: 1962–65*, Madras: Archaeological Society of South India, 1969, pp. 1–32.
9. R.S. Sharma, *Sudras in Ancient India: A Social History of the Lower Order down to circa A.D. 600,* 2nd edn, Delhi: Motilal Banarsidass, 1980, pp. 264–5.
10. Pattattalmangalam CP (793) and Velurpalayam CP (852), in Subramanian, ed., *Thirty Pallava Copper Plates.*
11. *South Indian Inscriptions* (hereafter *SII)*, vol. II, nos. 4–5; Noboru Karashima, *South Indian History and Society: Studies from Inscriptions A.D. 850–1800*, Delhi: Oxford University Press, 1984, pp. 43–7.
12. S. Sankaranarayanan, et al., eds., *Tiruvindalur Copper Plates*, Chennai: State Department of Archaeology, 2011, pp. 85–9, 91–104.
13. Ibid., pp. 134–6.
14. K.V. Ramesh, ed., *Dictionary of Social, Economic, and Administrative Terms in South Indian Inscriptions*, vol. 1, New Delhi: Oxford University Press, 2012, pp. 63–4.

15. Karashima, *South Indian History and Society*, pp. 71–3.
16. *SII*, vol. XIX, no. 357; *Inscriptions of the Pudukkottai State*, no. 427.
17. *SII*, vol. XXXIV, no. 153, line 14; See also Y. Subbarayalu, *South India under the Cholas*, New Delhi: Oxford University Press, 2012, p. 219.
18. *SII*, vol. IV, no. 223.
19. Noboru Karashima and Y. Subbarayalu, 'An Inscription on the Pedestal of the Bronze Buddha Image of the Mr. and Mrs. John D. Rockefeller 3rd Collection: International Character of Nagapattinam Merchants during the Chola Period', *Journal of East-West Maritime Relations*, vol. 3, 1994, pp. 13–18.
20. *SII*, vol. VI, no. 439; *Inscriptions of the Pudukkottai State*, no. 362.
21. *ARE*, 1908, no. 479; 1925, no. 189; *SII*, vol. XVII, no. 603.
22. J. Duncan M. Derrett, 'Two Inscriptions concerning the Status of Kammalas and the Application of Dharmasastra', in *Professor K.A. Nilakanta Sastri 80th Birthday Felicitation Volume*, ed. S. Ganesan et al., Madras: University of Madras, 1971, pp. 32–55.
23. Such supra-local assemblies are met with first among the itinerant merchant groups from the tenth century onwards and a century later among the landholding groups too. See Subbarayalu, *South India under the Cholas*, pp. 132–3.
24. *SII*, vol. VI, no. 439. This inscription is elaborately discussed in K.V. Subrahmanya Aiyer, 'Largest Provincial Organisations in Ancient India', *Quarterly Journal of the Mythic Society*, n.s., vol. 45, no. 4, 1955, pp. 29–47ff.
25. Subbarayalu, *South India under the Cholas*, pp. 96–7.
26. P. Shanmugam, 'Paṭṭaḍai and Industries in the Tamil Country under the Vijayanagar Rule', *Journal of Asian and African Studies*, no. 37, 1989, pp. 31–49; N. Karashima, *Towards a New Formation: South Indian Society under Vijayanagar Rule*, Delhi: Oxford University Press, 1992, pp. 32–3.
27. Vijaya Ramaswamy, *Textiles and Weavers in South India*, 2nd edn, New Delhi: Oxford University Press, 2006, p. 7 (map).
28. Karashima, *Towards a New Formation*, pp. 141–69.
29. The evidence cited in Burton Stein, *Peasant State and Society in Medieval South India*, Delhi: Oxford University Press, 1980, pp. 196–7 to associate the Kammāḷa/Rathakāra with the Left Hand group of castes during the Chola times is a late one taken from the colonial period records of the seventeenth and eighteenth centuries.
30. Y. Subbarayalu and S. Rajavelu, eds., *Inscriptions of the Vijayanagara Rulers*, vol. V, pt. I (Tamil Inscriptions), Bangalore: Indian Council of Historical Research: Southern Regional Centre & Delhi: Primus, 2014, ins. nos. 167, 439.
31. Karashima, *Towards a New Formation*, pp. 159–60.
32. Ibid., pp. 165–7.

11

Community Networking of Panchananamuvaru

The Sculptors and Smiths of Precolonial Andhra

I. LAKSHMI

This essay attempts to show how the community identity of the craftsmen has evolved and consolidated through marked professional skills, and how temple-building has helped all the artisan communities to come together and be identified as one group, despite the difference in professional specialization. This is an interesting case where the specialization in craft did not contribute to the proliferation of caste. Temple-building brought the artisans closer with interdependent craft activities and enabled them to emerge with a unified identity, as the Vishwakarmas.

There is an interesting judgement[1] given in 1814, which the Vishwabrahmins proudly quote to state their ritual superiority over the brahmins. The *thirpu*, i.e. the judgement, was given in the context of a conflict between one Panchangam Gundaiah, a brahmin, and one Margasahaya Achary, a Vishwabrahmin. Panchangam Gundaiah is said to have stopped Margasahaya Achary from performing a marriage as a priest and accused him of belonging to the shudra caste and thus not fit to perform the rituals. Margasahaya Achary had then put a case against the brahmin community in the *adalat* (court) of Chittoor. Margasahaya Achary argued that the fifteen sages whom the brahmins show as their *gotra* ancestors were not pure brahmins.

* I would like to thank Professor Vijaya Ramaswamy Krishnan for giving me the opportunity to present this paper in the seminar. I also thank Dr Emani Siva Nagi Reddy and Ekambarachary for sharing valuable information with me.

Rushya Sringa, Kausika, Jambaka, Goutama, Adya, Agastya, Vyasa, Vasishta, Narada, Koundinya, Matanga, Mandava, etc., were all not pure Brahmanas. The real pure Brahmanas are only the Viswabrahmanas whose birth is not polluted. They made themselves as raja gurus. The administrators should realize this. The work of the sons of 'Panchamukha Brahma' [the five-faced Brahma], i.e. the Viswabrahmanas, is useful to all the living beings, as such according to Yajur Veda they are the real Brahmanas. This is established without doubt. Even if there are any derogatory statements about the silpis in Mahabharata, they are interpolations made later by the corrupt Brahmanas. They are not as authentic as the Vedas. Thus, not to be taken seriously . . . even the Puranas quoted by the Brahmanas were written by the polluted Brahmanas.[2]

Here, we need to note that the point they were making was that the 'administrators should realize this'. This is because the East India Company was offering brahmins the posts of *dubhashis*, to translate the scriptures and the other literary works into English. As the Vishwakarma community was also well versed in traditional knowledge, they started competing with the brahmins for these posts and thus started to claim a higher ritual status. This became necessary for the Vishwakarmas as these craftsmen were thrown into unemployment due to the lack of patronage to their crafts due to British domination in trade and their exploitative rule over India.

The judge presiding over the case, Daker Dora, gave a ruling statement that—

Mr Achary had shown the evidence as only the Vedas prove Viswakarma as the superior of all the gods and of everything. And the Viswabrahmanas worship the Lord of Lords, i.e. the Viswakarma. He is above Brahma, Vishnu, and Siva as he created them. Mr Gundaiah had shown that the evidence of puranas cannot be taken seriously as they were written by Vyasa who was not a pure Brahmana, but a son of a fisherwoman. They say they are pure which is not true because the Vedas are superior to everything. Thus, the Viswabrahmanas are entitled to carry out their Vedic practices. Hereafter the Brahmanas should not create any disturbance to the Viswabrahmanas in performing their rituals.[3]

Apart from contesting in the court of law to assert their ritual status in the colonial period, the Vishwakarmas were also consolidating their community identity through quoting early literary compositions like *Andhra Viswakarma Puranamu* and *Viswakarma Vagmayasuchika*, and by invocations from the Vedas, particularly the *Viswakarma Suktam*. A lot of works, like *Viswakarmabrahmana Vamsagamamu*, *Viswabrahmana Sarvaswamu*, and *Brahmanulu Evaru? (Who are the Brahmanas?)*, to cite a few, were also written to establish their ritual status. The early works mention 'Vishwakarma', while the nineteenth and the twentieth century works use 'Vishwabrahmin' for their community identity as can be noticed in the titles of the works. This is a conscious attempt on their part to establish a higher status.

Even the community organizations established in the twentieth century, like Vishwabrahmana Sangam and Vishwabrahmana Dharma Peetam, are also working towards emphasizing their ritual status, apart from working for modernization of their crafts and creating employment opportunities, while giving importance to women's education. In both ways, i.e. through their writings as well as through community organizations, they emphasize that Vishwakarma is the professional identity, while Vishwabrahmin is their status identity (and not just a caste identity).

The Vishwabrahmana Sangam, established in 1903, was the first community to form an organization of the Vishwakarmas for their upliftment. It is in the later years that the other communities formed their specific caste organizations. The Vishwabrahmana Sangam states that according to the scriptures, there is a *niyamavali*, i.e. a stipulated code of conduct, for the Vishwabrahmins, which is as follows:

1. They should possess the prefix Brahmasri for their names, and Acharya, Sarma, Sastri should be their suffix.
2. They should not say their work/profession as their caste. The caste name is Vishwabrahmin, but not Vishwakarma *kula*.
3. They should have *gotra* and *sakha*.
4. They should perform *upanayana*.
5. They should perform *nityakarmas* every day.
6. They should perform all Vedic rituals.
7. The implements which they use for their professions are to be worshipped.

It also runs a few monthly and weekly magazines like the *Swarnamanjari* and the *Pranavavedi*, which are full of traditional knowledge and spiritual teachings. Largely, the concerns which they present are regarding the preservation of the Sanatan Dharma (the eternal truth of the Vedic religion) and their ritual status. The writings in the magazines are oriented towards regaining their past glory and boosting the confidence of the young members of the community by building faith and skill in their crafts. To emphasize their superiority over the brahmins, the following hymns can be cited:

Viswani Karmani Yaswanah Viswakarma.

(All the *karmas* [actions] are in Vishwakarma. The whole of creation is an act of Vishwakarma [*Viswakarma Suktam*].)

Na bhumi na jalam chaiva na tejo nacha vayavah!
Nacham Brahma nacham Vishnu nacham Nakshatra tarakah!
Sarva sunya niralambo svayambhu Viswakarmanah![4]

(When there was nothing at all, no earth, no water, no light, no air, no Brahma, no Vishnu, and no stars, Vishwakarma emerged on his own and created everything.)

The point we need to note is that the progenitor of the Vishwakarma community here is not the architect among the gods, as mentioned in precolonial sources, but the creator of the whole universe and the lord of lords. So, we find a contrast in situations between the precolonial times, particularly till the sixteenth century, and the colonial times.

Before going into the antiquity of regional references to the Vishwakarmas, I would like to cite four inscriptions which present a spirit that is just a contrast to the aforementioned assertions.

Three inscriptions[5] from Palnad Taluk, Guntur district, acquaint us with a famous line of architects who built some temples in the area. They were first mentioned in an inscription from Aingaripalem, written in the characters of the seventh century, where it has been stated that the temple of Jalpesvara was built by one Kalgarabharanacharya. It states—*Chaturthasyadhikarena Karmajna Kusala Prade Kalgarabharanacharya acharyyo Pravarojini*—which means, in the fourth cadre of power, i.e. fourth in order (of castes) was born the great master Kalgarabharanacharya, who takes care of the welfare of the artisans. We can see here that they (the artisans) had no inhibition to declare themselves as belonging to fourth class/caste, which actually did not matter much, as most of the ruling families too stated themselves as belonging to this fourth caste.

The next inscription from the same place mentions Kamoja, a pupil of the master architect Kalgarabharanacharya, who is described as the ornament of the Vishwakarma *kula* and the acharya of the Jalpesvara temple. Another interesting inscription from Macherla dated 1101 CE gives the pedigree of the Vishwakarma *vamsa* (lineage) of architects Navoju and Tippoju, who built the Adityesvara temple at that place. It has been stated there that Vishwakarma, the progenitor of the architects, was the son of Brahma and father-in-law of the Sun. So, in this version, Vishwakarma was son of Brahma, not his creator. Vishwakarma is also said to have converted the rays of the Sun into divine weapons such as the discus of Vishnu and the like. Some of the famous acharyas are enumerated in the inscription and are stated to have been experts in cutting lingas of Shiva and in preparing images. There is an interesting mention of the Vishwakarma *vamsa*, which shows that an attempt to ascertain a higher ritual status had been made earlier as well.

Till the sixteenth–seventeenth centuries, the artisans' constant focus was on acquiring expertise in their crafts and on learning and writing scientific works related to their craft, like the *Viswambhara Vastusastra*, the *Viswakarmana Silpasara*, the *Nighantu Ratnakaramu*, the *Viswakarma Mahatmyamu*, etc. All these works are quoted in the *Viswakarma Brahmana Vamsagamamu* written in 1934, along with citations from Vedic literature, to establish the antiquity and superiority of the Vishwabrahmins.

We find only one instance of conflict in an undated inscription (we can roughly place it in the precolonial period on the basis of the information available) from Siddhavaram,[6] which provides very interesting information regarding a dispute between the *silpis* and the brahmin priests. According to it, the brahmins denied the right of the *silpis* to be seated on the wooden chariot during the Radhotsava celebration. The offended *silpis* appealed to the ruler Matli Anantabhupala (a chief) to restore their privilege. After a long hearing from both the sides, the chief gave a decision favourable to the *silpis*.

Now we shall shift our focus to the historical past of sculptors and smiths. Though the history of carving can be traced back to the prehistoric period, the inscriptional references to the craftsmen are found only from the second century BCE. Early sculptures are found in Warangal and Khammam districts, while early Brahmi inscriptions mentioning the names of scribes are found in some Amaravati epigraphs.

An Amaravati inscription refers to one *rajalekhaka* named Balaka, who could be the official scribe of a local chief ruling the area around Amaravati or mid-coastal Andhra.[7] Similarly, one Raja Somaka[8] occurs in an inscription discovered in recent times on a hillock in the outskirts of Vaddamanu near Amaravati. Both of these inscriptions are in second century BCE characters. One Culla Gomaka was the scribe of the Guntupalli Brahmi inscription, datable to the first century BCE.[9] As can be observed from these inscriptions, we find references to individual *silpis*, rather than to any organization in the early centuries.

Another Amaravati inscription in Brahmi of the second century BCE refers to one Pashanika. The word *pashanika* denotes the persons involved in quarrying, cutting, and dressing of stones, or in simple terms, workers in stone.

We also get references to architects from the first century CE onwards. Two more epigraphs from Amaravati, datable to first–second centuries CE, mention Navakammika Buddharakshita, Mahanavakammika Aditya, Mahanavakammika Dharmarakshita, and Pradhana Navakammika Chanda, who were incharge of the renovation works of the stupa and vihara at Dhanyakataka.[10] Here the terms *navakammika*, *mahanavakammika*, and *pradhana navakammika* suggest the gradation that took place depending on the individual capabilities and expertise of the architects engaged in the repair work. Likewise, the Buddhist structures at Nagarjunakonda were built and maintained by *navakammikas* Ananda and Chandramukhi. Here the name Chandramukhi suggests that women were also equally engaged in architectural activity. Certain works were also executed by the *silavaddhakis* (again workers in stone), *dhammanandi*, and *vidhika*.[11] The Kondavidu plates mention that Prithvimula Raja appointed a *navakammika* of Aprasaila Vihara, located probably at Nagarjunakonda for the maintenance of the religious structures at Gunapasapura.[12]

An inscription from Jaggayyapeta mentions *avesanis* (the term *avesani* means a foreman of artisans or stonecutters) Siddhartha and Naga Chandra, who donated some slabs and pillars to the *torana dwara* for the local stupa.[13] A label inscription reading *Tuluchu Vanru* (in Telugu) meaning rock carvers, scoopers, engravers, or quarrymen, has come to light from Keesaragutta, a Vishnukundin site near Hyderabad. The inscription is in fourth century CE characters.[14]

The other early references to early craftsmen include those to sculptors working on crystal and diamond, called *manikaras*. The crystal relic caskets recovered from Bhattiprolu and Amaravati stupas testify to the artistic skills of the early Andhra *manikaras*. It is also to be mentioned here, that a fine specimen of a Buddha head carved out of a crystal was recovered from the Maski excavations, which is now on display in the State Museum, Hyderabad. Though early Brahmi inscriptions do not mention the term *lohakara*, the occurrence of a bronze image of a mother and child from Dhulikatta (datable to the second century BCE), a few Buddha images recovered from Amaravati, Nelakondapallu, and Buddham (datable to the third–fourth centuries CE), and a bronze image of a prince holding a bow, reported from Nagarjunakonda (from the same period), attest to the existence of *lohakara silpis* in early Andhra.

Thus, early references to craftsmen in stone consisted of *rajalekhakas* (the scribes), *pashanikas* (stonecutters), *avesanis* (foremen), *silavaddhakis* (stone carvers[?]), *navakammikas* (craftsmen executing repair works), and *manikaras* (workers in precious stones). These references enable us to understand that workers in stone were classified depending upon their skills. However, this did not result in emergence of any kind of status groups as the gradation is based on individual skills, and the identity of the craftsmen was just based on the material they were working with.

There is an interesting instance where a monk himself was an architect, or an architect turned into a monk. Prithvimula's Godavari plates record the gift of a village called Kattacheruvu to a Buddhist monk-architect for building a vihara on the Gunapasapuram hills during the sixth century.

There are also references to expert *silpis* being assigned work in different kingdoms. An inscription found at Badami[15] mentions the names of some sculptors, which are identical to those of the Western Chalukyan inscription of Veleswaram in Andhra and, both the inscriptions are datable to the sixth century CE. Another inscription datable to the sixth century CE at Pattadakal (Karnataka) refers to one Silpi Velanati Gundaya of Venginadu (Andhra).[16] It can thus be seen that *silpis* with expertise were moving between kingdoms. It can also be observed from the given citations that in none of these contexts we find the architects claiming any caste status.

However, we find a gradation among the sculptors depending on their work capabilities. As cited already, the *silpi* responsible for building the Jalapesvara temple at Madugula in seventh century CE bore the title Kalgarabharanacharya, meaning an ornament among the stone sculptors, and a master. The Bhairavakonda inscriptions mention the sculptors Velugunta Acharlu and Kuravadi Acharlu, who excavated the local rock-cut caves.[17] On palaeographical grounds, these inscriptions are datable to the seventh century CE. Another inscription from Palnad states that two years later, the same architects, Navoju and Tippoju, added a *nagastambha* to the same Adityesvara temple (mentioned earlier).[18] All these inscriptions come from Palnad Taluk of the Guntur district. From seventh century CE, Palnad seems to have witnessed a considerable volume of temple-building. This activity gave rise to the famous line of architects (acharyas/masters). An inscription set-up on the Indrakiladri hill in Vijayawada, datable to ninth century CE, was engraved by Silpi Vijayacharya.[19] The stone inscriptions of the Adikesava temple at Chebrolu were engraved by Silpi Chandanacharya and Silpi Gundoju.[20] The Rupala Sangamesvaram inscriptions, datable to ninth century CE, mention one Kasachari Yogoju, who built the Sangamesvaram temple[21] in Kurnool district. This temple was built during the Rastrakuta rule. Thus, it is from seventh century that we find the architects carrying the epithet 'acharya' and 'oju' (both meaning master/teacher). All the aforementioned inscriptions also refer to the individual *silpis* as beneficiaries of grants.

From the eleventh century, we get references to another rank of architects called *sutradharis*. They are superior craftsmen possessing different skills. It is stated that the Nandampudi inscription of the eleventh century of Raja Raja was composed by Nannaya, the great Telugu poet and was engraved by Gundacharya, the royal scribe.[22] An inscription from Vollala in Nalgonda district dated CE 1097 mentions one Sutradhari Juvvapacharya who engraved it.[23] *Sutradharis*, i.e. *silpis* of higher order, were also engaged for engraving stone inscriptions. Inscriptions from Vollala, Macherla, Panugal, Mukkamala, and Jalalpur mention the names of *sutradharis* Juvvapacharya, Nagacharya, Tippoju, Bammoju, Bommalaya, and Malloju. One of the *sutradharis* seems to have supervised the works of some *takshaka* and *vardhaki* as well.[24] An inscription[25] of CE 1124 from Guduru refers to Sutradhari Kommoju as the writer and scribe of the inscription. Thus silpis/architects were working at various levels and were gaining importance.

From eighth century onwards, we get references in inscriptions to craftsmen as an organized body, engaged in the temple-building. Inscriptions found at Alampur, Satanikota, Mahanadi, Prathakota, Vijayawada, and Regonda, belonging to the period between the eighth and tenth centuries CE,[26] refer to the activity of the organizations of sculptors and smiths such as 'Sri Utpatti Pidugu', 'Panchananamuvaru', and 'Saraswatigana'. An inscription from Chalukya Bhimavaram dated 1097 CE mentions *silpis* Viddachari and Mallachari as 'Saraswatigana Padapankaja Bhramaras' and 'Saraswatigana Manoranjakas', meaning that these two sculptors were like bees at the lotus feet of the organization called Saraswatigana (the learned group among the architects) and would delight the learned architects.[27] As the term Saraswatigana was found earlier in the Kalyani Chalukyan inscription of Posavur[28] in Karnataka, in which a *silpi* called Padmoja was similarly mentioned as 'Saraswatigana Padapankaja Bhramara', it can be understood that this particular organization was operating in different kingdoms. Inscriptions from Draksharama, datable to eleventh century CE, refer to *silpis* Virarajendra Chola Chary and Chalukya Sundarachary, who migrated from Chola and Chalukya kingdoms respectively to Vengi

(Andhra).[29] The Saraswatigana seems to have deputed some *silpis* to work at Chalukya Bhimavaram in the eleventh century CE. Regarding Panchananamuvaru, we shall deal separately in the later part of the essay. These references enable us to understand how the craftsmen were getting organized and building a network beyond their localities.

Almost all the inscriptions speaking about the Vishwakarmas are from the temple context. Their presence in inscriptions is next to the rulers and brahmins. The increasing number of references to the Vishwakarma community point to their rise to prominence. Their rise to prominence is directly linked to the large-scale construction of temples from the eleventh century due to the spread of Vaishnava and Saiva cults. Bhakti cults of eleventh–twelfth centuries, by promoting idol worship, led to the large-scale construction of temples. Temple constructions were taken up not only by the ruling sections but also by all those sections who could afford so through collective contributions.

It is from the eleventh century onwards that we get references to *agasalis* (also, *agasalas* or *akkasalas*), i.e. the goldsmiths, in inscriptions as a group associated with temples. The aforementioned Chalukya Bhimavaram[30] inscriptions refer to Akkasala Pochoju and Agasala Pochoju. The Pulimamidi[31] epigraph also mentions Akkasala Pochoju.

It is interesting to note that women participation in carving stone idols and building temples is attested by a few inscriptions dated to the twelfth century CE from Ganapesvaram in Krishna district, which refer to Kasachari Maguturi Mallikarjuna, his wife Veeramma, and their son Akkabattudu, who had participated in building the local Ganapesvara Mahadeva temple.[32] Likewise, the Macherla epigraph[33] dated 1111 CE, mentions that all the family members of Silpi Kacharya Tippoju were experts in carving Shiva lingas and other idols, construction of beautiful temples, and had the knowledge of using different varieties of tools skilfully. The inscription further informs that his sons Nagachary, Banachary, and Potana were not only experts in building four types of temples (*Chatur Vidha Prasada*), but were also engaged in doing research and new experiments in building technology. They possessed the knowledge of selection of suitable sites for various structures (*Vasthu Kshetra Vidah*). It is also stated that the acharyas/architects of the temple were experts in the building of four kinds of mansions (*Prasadeshu Chaturvidheshu*), in grasping geometry involved in the study of *Vastusastra* (architecture), and in gracefully handling the implements of the profession (*Vastu Kshetravidha Prasasta Vachasah*).[34]

These narrations establish the fact that with the rise in temple constructions, the architects and sculptors were continuously occupied and were also improving their skills and knowledge at the family level to meet the demand for varied constructions.

From the twelfth century onwards, we get references to land grants being made, even when a tank was built. In Warangal, we find an inscription dated 1112 CE, from Medapalli on a pillar on the tank bund. It is composed in three languages—Kannada, Sanskrit, and Telugu. The Telugu part records a gift of two *marturs* of land to the *kase* (architect) Parvatoju.[35] The gift here is made in the context of construction of a tank along with the temple of Acheswara and Vishnudeva.

A record of the year 1104 CE from Valiveru, Tenali Taluk, Guntur district, registers the gift of land to a *silpi/kase*, who built the Svayambhudeva temple at Valiveru.[36] The *kase*, as the inscription states, also made repairs to the temple from time to time. This enables us to understand their continued presence in temple maintenance. We hear of another such gift in 1257 CE to the artisans who built a mandapa of the temple of Svayambhudeva at Edavalli, Narasaraopet Taluk, Guntur district.[37]

Apart from the ruling community, we find an instance of a village community making grants to the artisans. An inscription from the same taluk as earlier, the date of which is missing, states that the villagers granted a piece of land to an *akkasala* Kamoju.[38]

It is in the eleventh-century inscriptions from Amaravati,[39] Juttiga,[40] and Nandyalampet[41] that we find mention of the deities of artisans such as Kammatesvara and Kalikadevi or Kammateswaridevi, as the gods of smiths and sculptors, while Agasaleswara was the deity of *agasalis*. References to temples of community gods of various artisan and trading communities with grants of land appear in inscriptions from the twelfth century, attesting their continuous progress. There is a process of steady growth in the status of these craftsmen that can be seen when we notice them becoming donors of land from the position of recipients of grants.

We get a number of references to the continuously rising status of the artisans as they were participating in both state administration and temple functioning. An inscription from Chebrolu dated 1118 CE says that, Surana, titled 'Viswakarmakula Bhushana', son of Kannoju and Prolama, served the chief of Giripaschima country (west of Kondavidu), King Erramanda, who owed allegiance to the Chola King Kulottunga I. Surana, as a general of the army, is stated to have rendered meritorious service to King Erramanda in checking the Western Chalukya depredations of his territory. The grateful king rewarded him by making him his 'Mahapradhani'[42] and conferring on him various insignia of royalty. A Nadindla epigraph dated 1141 CE refers to one Nukandi, who has the title of 'Karmarabharana', i.e. ornament among the blacksmiths,[43] and who, on account of his valour and bravery, was appointed as military general in the court of Kulottunga Gonka, the Velanati king.[44] Blacksmiths were very important functionaries as they were the makers of the armoury. They must have been close to the rulers.

It may be noted here that the architects mention themselves as 'Vishwakarma *kula*' members, but not as 'Vishwabrahmins'. *Silpis* also took part in the village administration as a fourteenth century inscription from Nagulapadu[45] attests. These instances suggest the artisans growing as an influential community.

Another inscription[46] from Matedu of 1120 CE mentions the gift of land to Kesavajiyya, the *sthanapati* of the temple, for offerings (*naivedya*), worship, and for lamps in the temple. This would imply that they were performing either priestly functions or were custodians (as the mention of him as a *sthanapati* attests) of the temple. We also find, with the spread of Saiva cult, many non-Brahmin pundits performing priestly functions in temples. Their participation in temple administration and worshipping as priests are also attested by other inscriptions. An inscription[47] from Vadlapalli refers to one Bhimajiyya (architect), who set-up the *kalasa* over the temple at his own expense and was conferred priesthood in the temple in 1211 CE. Another inscription[48] from Pillalamarri from the thirteenth century refers to priests Pujari Ramajiyya, Pujari Prolajiyya, and Pujari Kommajiyya, along with the people given lodging in the Pillalamarri fort. (The term 'jiyya' is used as suffix by the Vishwakarma community to indicate a respected person.)

A Malkapuram inscription dated 1261–2 CE is the first to refer to the word *sthapati*.[49] According to it, the artisans working in gold, copper, stone, wood, iron, and clay, who were also considered as Karunapita-*silpis*, could be called *sthapatis*. This is one inscription which considers *kumbhakara*, the potter, as a *sthapati* along with the Vishwakarmas. Another inscription from same place and same year (1261 CE) refers to *vadla* and *tvasta*, meaning a worker in wood and a bronze smith respectively, working together in the context of making a chariot. The carpenter is stated to be the expert in making wooden chariots.[50] We need to understand why in particular contexts the artisans were called *sthapatis*. This suggests their rise in rank. A *sthapati* could be a member of the trustee body. These references to individual potters and carpenters as members of a body are dated to the thirteenth century. This may be because their rise to prominence was a little later than the architects in the context of temple construction.

The growing economic status of the artisans is further attested by the epigraphs where we notice them moving from receiving gifts to making grants, as already mentioned in the context of eleventh century. This trend continued in later centuries as well. An epigraph[51] of 1300 CE from Nadigudem states that Agasala Devoju made a gift of a palmyra grove to the temple of Mallikarjuna Mahalinga of Taduvaya. Another inscription[52] of 1316 CE records *agasalis* making a gift along with the *ashtadasa praja* of the village at the rate of one *chinna* per furnace. An inscription from Anantapur district[53] mentions that certain privileges were granted by the Vijayanagar King Harihara I (1336–57 CE) to the Panchalas as a reward for making a throne. Likewise, an epigraph from Tellapur dated 1418 CE refers to two *silpis*, namely Agasala Mailoju and Ailoju, who made a Kantabharana decorated with golden flowers and glass beads, which was presented to the wife of the Bahamani ruler Firozsha.[54] The Kokatam inscription[55] of 1518 CE refers to a gift made by a certain Agasala Malloju.

These indicate that we get early references to the architects, while references to goldsmiths, blacksmiths, carpenters, and potters surface only from the eleventh, twelfth, and thirteenth centuries respectively. The inscriptional presence of these groups of artisans suggests not only their rise to prominence but also indicate their rise in ritual status.

Now we shall move to the study of Panchananamuvaru, a collective organization of five types of craftsmen—architects, blacksmiths, carpenters, bronze smiths, and goldsmiths—becoming one social and economic group connected to each other's work in the context of temple construction. This is where specialization of profession did not lead to the proliferation of caste, in spite of having specific professional identities. These professional identities too were fluid, as we shall see in the later part of the essay.

An inscription from Amaravati[56] describes the Panchananamuvaru as belonging to the Vishwakarma *vamsa*. The legend of the origin of the Vira-Panchalas, who were the same as Panchananamuvaru, is given in a twelfth century inscription,[57] which says that Vishwakarma, the son of Brahma, was the progenitor of the architects and the father-in-law of the Sun. Members of the Vishwakarma *kula* even today trace their ancestry 'to the five sons of Viswakarma of whom the first born Manu worked in iron, the second Maya in wood, the third Tvastram in brass, copper and alloys, the fourth Silpi in stone and the fifth Viswajna was a gold and silver smith and jeweller'.[58] Vishwakarma or Brahma is also known as 'Panchanana' or the five-faced. Thus, the Panchananamuvaru were called so because they traced their descent from Panchanana.

References to Panchananamuvaru come directly from their own grants from the twelfth century onwards. The context of their grants (land grants and tax gifts to temples) would indicate their rise as an organization. An inscription from Udayagiri[59] records a gift by the Panchananamuvaru of Udayagiri, Nellore, Koratur, Gandavaram, and a number of other places in the *rajya* of Udayagiri and the Panchananamuvaru of the 74 *Ahanas* (units of work places) of the world. The Amaravati epigraph referred to earlier registers a gift to a temple by the *padunalugu-tapala*-Panchananamuvaru (artisans from fourteen places) from the region between the hills of Kondapalli and Bezawada. Another inscription from Amaravati records a gift to a temple by the Panchananamuvaru of Srirangarajukonda-sima, Nandigama, and other places in Nantavadi. Nantavadi, a variant of Natavadi, was a territorial division and corresponded roughly to the modern Nandigama Taluq in the Krishna district.[60] An inscription from Palakol[61] registers a gift by the Panchananamuvaru of *akhila-desalu* or all territories. This seems to imply that there was a *desa* unit (*desa* was yet another territorial division of this time) and a federation of all the *desa* units. All these inscriptions imply the territorial organization of the Panchananamuvaru at different levels. It helps us understand how the network of craftsmen was built at local levels and then extended, cutting across regions.

One of the Amaravati records[62] mentioned already states that on behalf of or at the behest of (*Pampuna*) the fourteen *tapala*-Panchananamuvaru from the region between the hills of Kondapalli and Bezawada, a certain Mallaya Mahapatra gifted to Kamathesvara of Dharanikota the *pannu* or tax paid by the Panchananamuvaru of Dharanikota and the *palya-pannu* paid by the Panchananamuvaru of Amaresvaram. A second epigraph[63] from Amaravati states that Mallaya Mahapatra, on behalf of the Panchananamuvaru of Srirangarajukonda-sima and of Natavadi assigned to Kamathesvara of Dharanikota the *palyam-payindi* of Amaravaram. An epigraph[64] from Palakol states that the Panchananamuvaru (of all the *desas* or of the 74 *Ahanas*) exempted one Kasa Surasari from *pannu-kudu* to enable him to work or as a reward for his service in the temple of Ramalinga. The exact nature of the taxes mentioned in the two Amaravati inscriptions and the Palakol epigraph is not clear. An undated inscription from Udayagiri[65] informs us that the Panchananamuvaru of Udayagiri, Nellore, Koratur, Gandavaram, Duvur, Atukur, Jaladanki, Kodavalur, Allur, Kovur, Vavveru, Prabhakarapatnam, Krishnarayapatnam, Sariyapalli, Rapur, Kandukur, Podili, Kanigiri, Kegipa, and other villages in the Udayagiri *rajya* remitted the taxes to the treasury of the god Sri Raghunayakulu at Udayagiri. From this, it is evident that artisans were organized as Panchananamuvaru at village and town levels, and it is also evident that the artisan community of the different places of Udayagiri *rajya* had an assembly. Acting on behalf of the community, the composite body of Panchananamuvaru submitted to the treasury of the deity the taxes they collected from the members.[66]

They were also gradually engaging in land transactions as evidenced in another epigraph. A record[67] from Panchadharala registers the sale of some land by Pamchalulu and Nayilu (barbers) of that place to a certain Buddasani. Their growing strength in society can be understood from the following incident. An inscription from Kanaganapalle dated 1533 CE mentions that the Panchananamuvaru of thirty-two villages had left the place and migrated to distant places like Pakala and Kundrupisima due to imposition of heavy taxes on them.[68] As a united body, the Panchananamuvaru could protest against state authority. After realizing that the villagers suffered a lot in the absence of the Panchananamuvaru, as they could not get various implements useful for agriculture, domestic, and religious purposes, the Panchananamuvaru was approached and informed about a reduction in the taxes. Consequently, the Panchananamuvaru returned to their original villages and resumed their professions.

It looks that a section of the metalworkers were engaged in supplying metals and were called 'Panchalohbeharulu' or 'Panchalohadhipatulu', and were making their crafts separately. An epigraph[69] from Srikakulam states that the Panchalohadhipatulu granted exemption to the . . . from *bogaram-pannu* and all other *pannus*. The Panchalohadhipatulu and Panchalohbeharulu were dealers in five metals, who were supplying metals to the artisans.

The consistent growth of the artisans can be attested till the sixteenth–seventeenth centuries. A sixteenth century inscription from Adoni[70] refers to Panchananamuvaru who were among the members of the *ashtadasa samayas* (eighteen bodies of communities) looking after the local administration.

It may be observed that from eleventh century to fourteenth century, the temple-building activity was taking place in a large scale, and the artisans' position was also elevated. From the twelfth century onwards, they regulated their economic activity and attained power as an organized body to control their funds collected in the form of taxes from the members. Their activities kept expanding with the growth of the organization. Progress in their social organization and economic activity led to the rise in their ritual status as can be witnessed by their long *prasastis*.

Initially, their *prasasti* in their grants from the twelfth century was not too long. Gradually they give a bigger *prasasti*, containing details of their knowledge and skill in the profession. It runs as follows: '*Samasta-devata-nistaraka, Tribhuvananirmitadhara, Sriparvat-alamkara, Anamta-sabda-sastra-purana-paravara, Gambhira-dhira-dhirottarana, Jagaddhita-karana, Sarva-jana-purushardha yuktulu*.'[71] But the *prasasti* found in a record from Vontimetta[72] (of the sixteenth century) is quite elaborate:

Samastaloka Nistaraka Tribhuvana Nirmitadhara
Sri Anantasastra Purana Paravara Gambhiradhara Dhirodharaka
Jagahita Kartaraka Satkara Pratibhuktayuktaraka Atulita Pratapa
Ananta Brahmanda Andaja Pindaja Vitalayukta Vara Pemdota Puraadhisvara
Srimat Mahajyoti Prakasa Kamatesvara Devara Divya Sri Pada Padmaradhakulainatuvanti
Rumjayu, Gavalambunnu, Pulitolutekkyambunnu, Garuda Dhvajambunnu, Kanakahalelu, Pasidi Vimjanaralu, Andalamunnu, Manulakiritamunnu, Panchamahavadyamulugala.

The meaning of this *prasasti* is as follows: They are like the refuge of the whole world and the founders of the three worlds. They are adept in all sciences and Puranas. They are the seekers of the welfare of the world, they know the way to command respect and possess matchless valour. They are the lords of Vara Pemdota, which contained in it all the worlds (Pemdota in Palnad, is considered to be the place of origin of architects[73]). They are the worshippers of the lotus feet of Lord Kamatesvara who shone with eternal brilliance. They are entitled to various royal insignia, like leather musical instrument, a sword, the banner of Garuda, a golden musical instrument, golden fans, golden palanquin and a crown studded with diamonds, and five certain musical instruments.[74] An eulogical inscription of Panchananamuvaru from the same place extols them as the builders of 'Sabda Sastras' and 'Lokahitakarins', whereas the Nandyalmpet inscription mentions them as builders of the 'Saptasagaras', the sculptors of 'Astadikpalas' and 'Astadiggajas', which almost means the creators of the universe.

We should observe here that the community identity as Vishwakarma *kula* and Vishwakarma *vamsa* are used in the context of the Panchananamuvaru and it is in the context of the organization only that we get the *prasasti* with legendary origin.

However, for the individual *silpis*, we get their professional identity and no *prasasti* except the names of their parents and the guru/acharya/master. Two interesting things can be observed here—one is that the artisans had no inhibitions to state themselves as belonging to the *chaturtha* (fourth) class/caste, and the other is that, unlike their modern caste status as Vishwabrahmin, they claimed their social status as being Viswakarma *kula*, which is a collective social group of artisans. Another important thing is that they all took pride in their professional identity.

A record of the fifteenth century from Amaravati[75] extols the Panchananamuvaru, born in the Vishwakarma *vamsa* in the following manner. They are the refuge to all gods and prime architects of the three worlds (*Samasta Devatanistaraka, Tribhuvananirmitadhara*). They are ornaments of Sri Parvata (*Sri Saila*), well-versed in all sastras and Puranas, possessed of courage and prowess, and attainers of the *Purusharthas*, sought after by all people (*Sriparvat-alamkara, Anamta-sabda-sastra-purana-paravara, Gambhira-dhira-dhirottarana, Sarva-jana-purushardha yuktulu*).

The nature of the organization of the artisan community of Andhra becomes clear when we consider the copperplate inscription of the sixteenth century, from Vontimetta[76] in the Cuddapah district. The inscription gives an elaborate *prasasti* of the community cited already and then proceeds to say that Panchananamuvaru of the places like Tirupati, Kalahasti, and Chandragiri met at *mukhamandapa* of the Kalikadevi temple and made a convention. According to this convention, certain dues were to be paid to one Yellayya of Vontimetta, who performed the various assignments of the community meritoriously. It was resolved that a *ruka* on each carpenter's bench, on each forge of the smith, on each chisel of a mason, and on every marriage occasion, should be paid to the said person on the condition that he undertakes to serve the community from time to time.

Apart from regulating economic activity and the finances, the artisans also regulated ritual activity of the temples. An inscription from Udayagiri dating to the sixteenth century[77] states that one Konetayya Deva Maharaja, a chief of Udayagiri, performed a car festival of the deity of Raghunathanayakulu and erected a stone inscription prescribing the ceremonies to be observed in future festivals. According to this inscription, when the deity in the chariot passes through the holy streets, with the dancing girls and servants inside the car, a member of the Panchananamuvaru, wearing a headcloth and another piece of cloth loosely wrapped round the waist, and having only a sandal mark between the eyebrows, and not chewing betel, should go round in front of the chariot, with a chisel, a mallet, a nail, and a sickle in his hands. A sixteenth century inscription from Udayagiri refers to *silpis* holding chisels in their hands, who were given prime importance and were allowed to walk in front of the temple chariot at the time of Radhotsava.[78] All this enables us to understand the continuous upward mobility of the artisans in the precolonial period.

As the work of the Panchananamuvaru, the five crafts, was associated with temple-building, they can also be considered a spiritually oriented group. The blacksmith (*kammari*), the stonemason (*silpi*), the carpenter (*vadrangi*), the metalworker (*kanchera*), and the jeweller/goldsmith (*agasali*) do not have any kind of hierarchy, but consider the blacksmiths as their elder brother as they provide tools to all the craftsmen. Even the legend already cited also testifies that the eldest son (Manu) of Brahma worked in iron.

Like their social organization, the artisans' professions were also flexible, as there were instances of shifts in craft. For instance, carpenters and goldsmiths were also engaged for engraving inscriptions. To cite an example, Mallancharya, the carpenter of the village Chamgadu, inscribed the Changadu plates dated 1504 CE.[79] A Srikurman inscription dated 1763 CE refers to a Rathakara Silpi Sankara, who was proficient in carving both on stone and wood.[80] He was also said to be one of the best composers and engravers of inscriptions. Even at present, interchange of crafts is a common phenomenon. This could be because of the interdependence of the craft activities of the artisans, apart from their common legacy of tradition. An inscription of Pedakakani dated 1518 CE for the first time refers to *kammaris*, i.e. blacksmiths who manufactured and supplied different types of chisels required for splitting and carving stone.[81] It mentions that Kammari Puttabathudu has assisted in sharpening the chisels and supplied them to Silpi Basava Battudu, the builder of the local Vireswara temple. Similarly, Agasala Bairoju, a goldsmith by profession, has engraved the Kokatam inscription dated 1518 CE. In another instance, Vadlakanachikandu (wood carver) Tinnoju[82] and Rathakara Silpi Samlara engraved the inscriptions of Velpucherla and Srikurmam dated 1545 CE and 1763 CE respectively.

These professions were also open to other professional groups, as temple-building created more opportunities for skilled people and was lucrative too. A unique inscription from Varikunta in Cuddapah district dated 1529 CE refers to a *silpi* by the name Tippana Boya, belonging to the Boya (tribal) community, who built the local temple for a lump sum contract of 20 *rukas*.[83] This inscription also reveals that artisans other than those in the Viswakarma *kula* could also participate in temple-building and that temple works were assigned on contract basis. The Boya community was initially a tribe in Andhra. It played a vital role in shaping the fate of the kingdoms, as observed by S. Nagaraju, as they were living in the border areas of the kingdoms on east and west. They were well-equipped fighters and the rulers were engaged in wooing them. This tribal group was getting absorbed into the main society and was thus getting into productive activity as well. We are aware of such processes all through our past. Many inscriptions from the eighth century show the Boyas as being connected to the functioning of temples, as they were to maintain the gifts that were made to the temples.

This kind of competition might also have made the artisans shift to one another's craft and to consolidate their identity as one social group. This case study of a social group would enable us to understand that caste is not a static identity.

The artisans' assertions of high ritual status from the seventeenth century through rishi *gotras* indicate a shift in thinking due to changes that happened in political and professional lives. A Tirupati inscription dated 1606 CE is the earliest record which refers to a *swarnakara silpi* belonging to *Suparna gotra*.[84] A work called *Viswakarma Gotranamavali* was also composed in this period. Next to it, the Nandyalampet inscription[85] dated 1748 CE refers to the *gotras* of the Panchananamuvaru. According to it, the Panchananamuvaru had originated from the five faces of Vishwakarma, and they had their *gotras* named after the five rishis, namely, Saanaga, Sanaatana, Ahabhuuna, Pratna, and Suparna, representing the *silpis*.[86] The Srikurmam inscription dated 1763 CE extolls the *rathakara silpi* called Sankara with a title 'Sarvottama Silpi'.[87] The Nandyalampet inscription also refers to the fact that Panchananamuvaru had a separate *lanchana*, i.e. insignia. According to this inscription, the Panchananamuvaru were even said to have their own flag 'Hanumadwaja Lanchana', a symbol of high status in the society. A contemporary Telugu work, *Yogasaktaparinayam*, gives a detailed account on how the *silpis* got the Hanumadwaja Lanchana.

There was a gradual decline in the condition of the Panchananamuvaru from the eighteenth century due to the exploitative economic policies of the British, mechanization, and so on. Thus, their assertions of higher status from the eighteenth century is the result of the neglect they suffered in the society. Their life in independent India is also pathetic as they are in poverty and are in the list of the backward classes. They might be using this listing for benefits, but they seem to be suffering a conflict, as culturally they feel superior to the other classes, being a historically educated community with traditional knowledge.

Notes

1. *Chittoor Zilla Adalat Thirpu*, 1814, Chaturpudi Village, Chittoor Zilla, Case file no. 78/1885/421–22.
2. Ibid.
3. Ibid.
4. *Viswakarma Suktam*, cited in Vaddapati Niranjan Sastry, ed., *Viswakarma Brahmana Vamsagamamu*, 2nd edn, Vijayawada: Viswakarma Sahitya Prachara Mandali, 1997, pp. 2–4.
5. *Annual Report of Epigraphy* (hereafter *ARE*), 331, 332, 333 of 1937.
6. P.V.P Sastry, ed., *Inscriptions of Andhra Pradesh: Cuddapah District*, vol. III, Hyderabad: Government of Andhra Pradesh, 1981.
7. C. Sivaramamurti, *Amaravati Sculpture in the Madras Government Museum*, Madras: Government Press, 1942, p. 277.
8. Article by I.K. Sarma in *Bharati*, June 1986, p. 8.
9. R. Subrahmanyam, 'The Guntupalli Brahmi Inscriptions of Kharavela', *A.P. Epigraphical Series*, no. 3, 1968, p. 2.
10. Sivaramamurti, *Amaravati Sculpture*, ins. no. 33.
11. *Epigraphia Indica*, vol. XX, p. 17.
12. V.V. Krishna Sastry, *Three Grants of Prithvi Sri Mularaja from Kondavidu*, Hyderabad: Government of Andhra Pradesh, 1992.
13. *Luders' List*, nos. 1202, 1206.
14. V.V. Krishna Sastry, 'Early Saiva Vestiges at Keesaragutte', in *Saivism in Andhradesa*, ed. K.T. Reddy, Hyderabad: Archaeological Department of Andhra Pradesh, 1994, p. 45.
15. E. Sivanagi Reddy, 'Silatamra Sasanallo Andhradesa Silpula Charitra, Samskriti—Konni Visheshalu', *Sahitya Masapatrika*, vol. II, no. 3, July 1996, pp. 1–16.
16. C. Sivaramamurti, *Early Eastern Chalukya Sculpture*, Madras: India Press, 1962, p. 11.
17. *South Indian Inscriptions* (hereafter *SII*), vol. X, nos. 47, 54.
18. Ibid., no. 66.
19. Ibid., no. 33.
20. *SII*, vol. VI, nos. 109, 113.
21. *Annual Report on Epigraphy in Andhra Pradesh, 1966–67*, p. 25.
22. E. Sivanagi Reddy, 'Annexure II', in *Contribution of Viswakarmas to the Science, Technology and Culture of Indian Origin*, ed. V. Ganapati Sthapati, Chennai: Dakshina Publishing House, 2000, p. iii.
23. P.V.P. Sastry, ed., *Inscriptions of Andhra Pradesh: Nalgonda District*, vol. 2, Hyderabad: Government of Andhra Pradesh, 1992, pp. 35–42.
24. *SII*, vol. IV, no. 949.
25. N. Ramesan, *Inscriptions of Andhra Pradesh: Warangal District*, Hyderabad: Government of Andhra Pradesh, 1974, ins. no. 27.
26. Reddy, 'Silatamra Sasanallo Andhradesa Silpula Charitra, Samskriti—Konni Visheshalu'.

27. E. Sivanagi Reddy, 'Guilds of Sculptors and Architects in Andhra', *JAHRS*, vol. XXXIX, 1995, pp. 177–82.
28. *Epigraphia Carnatica*, vol. VII, no. 1080.
29. *SII*, vol. VI, nos. 235, 236.
30. *SII*, vol. V, no. 80.
31. Reddy, 'Silatamra Sasanallo Andhradesa Silpula Charitra, Samskriti—Konni Visheshalu'.
32. Ibid.
33. *SII*, vol. X, no. 66.
34. Ibid., no. 65.
35. *IAP: Warangal District*, no. 21.
36. Ibid., no. 61.
37. Ibid., no. 356.
38. Ibid., no. 122.
39. Ibid., no. 219.
40. *IAP: Warangal District*, no. 749.
41. *IAP: Cuddapah District*, vol. III, no. 161.
42. *SII*, vol. VI, no. 117.
43. *SII*, vol. II, nos. 117, 673.
44. *SII*, vol. VI, no. 673.
45. Ins. no. 48, Department of Archaeology and Museums, Hyderabad, 1991.
46. *IAP: Warangal District*, no. 25.
47. *IAP: Nalgonda District*, vol. 2, no. 33.
48. Ibid., no. 53.
49. *SII*, vol. X, no. 395.
50. Ibid.
51. *IAP: Nalgonda District*, vol. 1, no. 94.
52. Ibid., no. 100.
53. *ARE*, no. 804 of 1917.
54. E. Sivanagi Reddy, 'Silpis Inscriptions of Tellapur', *Aradhana*, June 1996, p. 16.
55. *IAP: Cuddapah District*, vol. II, no. 267.
56. *SII*, vol. VI, no. 219.
57. *ARE*, 1910, pt. II, para. 60.
58. A. Coomaraswamy, *The Indian Craftsmen*, n.d., p. 56.
59. *Nellore District Inscriptions*, vol. III, Udayagiri, no. 21.
60. K. Iswaradutt, *A Historical Geography of Andhradesa*, n.d., p. 186.
61. *SII*, vol. V, no. 158.
62. *SII*, vol. VI, no. 219.
63. Ibid., no. 220.
64. *SII*, vol. V, no. 158.
65. *Nellore District Inscriptions*, vol. III, Udayagiri, no. 21.
66. R. Narasimha Rao, *Corporate Life in Medieval Andhradesa*, Hyderabad: Andhra Pradesh State Archives, 1967.

67. *SII*, vol. VI, no. 666.
68. *SII*, vol. XVI, no. 104.
69. *SII*, vol. IV, no. 972.
70. *ARE*, no. 18 of 1918, Appendix A, paras 84–5.
71. *SII*, vol. VI, no. 219.
72. *Local Records*, vol. 18, p. 404.
73. See the introduction in Srinatha, *Palnativira Charitra*, Madras: Vavilla Ramaswamy Sastry and Sons, p. 70.
74. The title of 'Panchamahavadya' means that the community obtained the permission to use, in public, certain musical instruments which were generally conferred on vassals as a gift of honour by their feudal lords. Many chiefs of various dynasties donned this title and are usually described in epigraphs with the title 'Samadhigata Panchamahasabda'. The five musical instruments were *sringa, tammata, sankha, bheri,* and *jayaghanta.* See *Indian Antiquary*, vol. XIV, p. 202 and *Indian Antiquary*, vol. VII, p. 106.
75. *SII*, vol. VI, no. 209.
76. *Local Records*, vol. 18, p. 404.
77. *Nellore District Inscriptions*, vol. III, Udayagiri, no. 20.
78. *Nellore District Inscriptions*, vol. I, Udayagiri, no. 44.
79. *IAP: Cuddapah District*, vol. II, no. 78.
80. *SII*, vol. V, no. 1079.
81. *SII*, vol. IV, no. 602.
82. *IAP: Cuddapah District*, vol. II, no. 1005.
83. Ibid., no. 107.
84. Sadhu Subrahmanya Sastry, ed., *Report on the Inscriptions of the Devasthanam Collection with Illustrations*, Madras: Tirumala Tirupati Devasthanams, 1930, p. 316.
85. *IAP: Cuddapah District*, vol. III, no. 161.
86. These *silpis* are mentioned as *gotra* rishis in the *Brihadaranyakopanishad.* Hence, they are called 'pancha rishi gotras'. According to the present day *silpis*, there were 125 rishis of the *gotras*, working in iron, wood, copper, stone, and gold. See R. Narasimha Rao, *Corporate Life in Medieval Āndhradēśa*, New Delhi: The University Grants Commission, 1967.
87. *SII*, vol. V, no. 1203.

12

Mobility and Identity

A Study of Vishwakarma Panchalas of Karnataka

NAGENDRA RAO

An important aspect that is observed in case of craftsmen and artisans is their migratory nature, and the resulting changes in their social and economic statuses. Over a period of time, one can note the changes in the social status of the Vishwakarma Panchalas (five communities of craftsmen). For instance, it is seen that in the sixth century BCE, the *rathakaras* enjoyed a relatively superior status as compared to their status later on.[1] The higher status of the *rathakaras* in this period can be attributed to political support that they received. Their decline can be considered as consequence of the feudal economy, which failed to support such craftsmen. The Vishwakarma Panchalas responded to the contemporary political, social, and economic changes by migrating to various regions of Karnataka. Decline of the kingdoms, such as the Rashtrakutas, resulted in the decline of patronage offered to the artisans and craftsmen, compelling them to migrate to other regions that witnessed state formation. Along with this, demand for craft products in particular regions encouraged migration of craftsmen to those zones. In addition, the emergence of temples, brahmin settlements, and commercial centres in a particular region would result in the migration of people from different parts of the macro region to that micro region. This explains the migration of craftsmen from Tamil Nadu, Andhra, Goa, Gujarat, and also north India, to Karnataka. This essay attempts to locate reasons for the changing statuses of artisans in Karnataka from the tenth to sixteenth centuries. In the course of study,

* I would like to thank Professors Vijaya Ramaswamy, R.N. Misra, and Lakshmi Thirumalai for their valuable suggestions.

it will be shown that agrarian developments, formation and expansion of state, and the process of urbanization, with religion and commerce as its base, contributed to the migration of artisans and craftsmen, who moved to various regions of peninsular India.

Migration of craft groups also affected their social status considerably, particularly in the local Puranas of the new territories. The Alupa, Hoysala, and the Vijayanagar inscriptions provide valuable information regarding the social change that was taking place in Karnataka. They inform that there was the migration of the craftsmen such as the stonemasons and weavers from interior parts of Karnataka to the coastal regions.

Region and Setting

The region selected for the present purpose is Karnataka, a place known for its commercial network. The South Kanara district of coastal Karnataka had a social and economic relationship with other parts of Karnataka and the whole of peninsular India as well. Such a relationship was inevitable as the region emerged as a major commercial centre, having contacts not only with Indian commercial towns but also overseas towns in Arabia, Africa, and later, Europe.

Empirical details concerning craft production can be found in the works of scholars such as K.S. Shivanna,[2] K.S. Kumara Swamy,[3] P. Gururaja Bhatt,[4] K.V. Ramesh,[5] B. Vasantha Shetty,[6] and Jagadish Shetty.[7] It is apparent that a considerable number of sources are available to study the changing status of the Vishwakarma Panchalas in Karnataka. However, the theories of these scholars differ to some extent from those of Kenneth R. Hall,[8] R. Champakalakshmi,[9] James Heitzman,[10] and Vijaya Ramaswamy,[11] who take into account contemporary theories concerning political economy.

Hall situated craft production in the context of the patronage that the artisans received from the Cholas. Champakalakshmi showed the importance of identifying craftsmen in temple centres, as they determined their jati status. Heitzman has shown that gifts were used by the artisan communities in order to achieve legitimacy and validation. The study by Ramaswamy is also significant, as she has analysed the complex social set-up of the Vishwakarma Panchalas. This essay will follow the work of Ramaswamy to locate the artisanal communities of Karnataka in proper historical and social context.

One may begin with the following quotation taken from the work of Carla Sinopoli:

> ... the organization of production in any complex society must be viewed as a variable conditioned by a range of factors. These include economic, social, and symbolic dimensions, which determine the importance of the good to the elite classes and to the society as a whole, as well as technological characteristics of the product, including raw material availability and productive requirements.[12]

In this framework, a brief outline of the political history of the region becomes important. Since ancient times, the territories of Karnataka have been ruled by kingdoms such as the Alupa, followed by the Hoysala and the Vijayanagar. From the sixth to the tenth centuries CE, evidence regarding craft activities is found largely in the form of temples constructed by the Chalukyas and the Rashtrakutas. The period between the tenth and the sixteenth centuries become important for the patronage that artisans received from Hoyasala and Vijayanagar kings. For example, the Hoysalas patronized Jaina *basadis*. As such, one can find reference to large numbers of *basadis* that were constructed in South Kanara, which became major Jaina centres, consisting of towns such as Karkala, Venur, Mudabidare, and Dharmasthala. The rise of Vijayanagar led to the construction of Vaishnava temples and *mathas* in coastal Karnataka, on account of the Bhakti movement led by Madhwacharya of Udupi, leading to the emergence of a large number of temples in this region. In the meantime, the region was also emerging as an important commercial zone. This was because, by the end of the tenth century, Arab traders became notable in the sources (historical) of the region, e.g. in the inscriptions. Other foreign traders such as the Jews and Muslims followed them, as can be found from the emergence of the trade guild called the *hanjamana*. Both these traders and craft guilds participated in the construction of religious buildings. The aim of these groups was to achieve legitimacy through grants made to these places of worship.

Around the temples, the social caste status of the Vishwakarma Panchalas was determined. By implication, the craftsmen who were associated with the royal temples as a part of the sacred space obtained a higher social status when compared with those craftsmen who were not associated with the major temples. At the same time, they had their own autonomous caste assemblies, which acted as pressure groups to obtain concessions and grants from kings. The expansion of religious and commercial urban centres might have contributed to the migration of artisans to regions of coastal Karnataka. Their settlements can be found in clusters at different places such as Udupi, Karkala, and Mangalore. In the course of study, an attempt will be made to identify the regions inhabited by Panchalas. In this essay, an attempt will also be made to identify the various waves of migration of artisans to the region. The first wave of migration, for example, can be noticed from the east, while the second wave of migration is discernible from the northern part of western coastal India. The first wave of migration can noted from regions such as the interior parts of Karnataka and the Tamil country. The second wave was from Goa, primarily due to the arrival of the Portuguese, which threatened particular communities of artisans, such as goldsmiths, who established their settlements in regions such as Udupi. In this essay, an attempt has been made to situate the Vishwakarma Panchalas in the society of Karnataka. In the process, the essay will also refer to the changing political, economic, and social conditions of craftsmen in various parts of Karnataka, as it is not possible to limit the study regarding crafts to just one district in coastal Karnataka. This is because, unlike the agrarian populace, the craft groups and traders were considerably affected by the political, social, and economic changes in various parts of Karnataka and south India as a whole.

This study is basically empirical and analytical, and it aims to make a significant historiographical contribution to the study of the Vishwakarma Panchalas of Karnataka. This is because, in other parts of peninsular south India (such as Tamil Nadu and Andhra Pradesh), scholars such as Ramaswamy, Carla M. Sinopoli, and several others have already made significant studies with reference to craft groups. In the context of Karnataka, there is need for analysis of the relationship between political, social, and economic developments that had significant implications for craft groups such as the Panchalas.

Patron-Client Relationship

There is a need to identify the multiple factors responsible for emergence of craft production. In the context of Karnataka, the production of crafts was influenced by the demands of the elite classes, who were the major consumers. At the same time, the artisans also provided service to the rural communities. The two worlds sometimes interacted with each other, while at the same time maintaining a distance from each other. In this respect, the temples, *basadis*, and royal families become the major patrons of craft production, while the masses demanded production of essential goods from the craftsmen. To provide service to the patrons, the craftsmen (the clients), were prepared to relocate to new territories. For example, in the eleventh century, the craftsmen moved to coastal

Karnataka in order to legitimize the position of the newly founded local dynasties, such as the Bairarasa of Karkala and the Ajila of Venur. The clients obtained material as well as social benefits from their patrons in the form of wages and enhanced social status.

Centralized and Non-Centralized Production

Sinopoli categorizes craftsmen into those belonging to the 'centralized' and the 'non-centralized' regions. It is possible to suggest that centralized production that took place in the metropolis and other core regions was large scale and monitored by the state. The Hoysalas for example, could control and monitor the activities of stoneworkers including the sculptors and the engravers in the major administrative and commercial centres such as Belur and Halebid. The craftsmen, on the other hand, in the non-centralized zone, had to deal with reduced demand for craft goods, particularly from the elite classes. Centralized production could be found in the core territories, while non-centralized production was seen in the peripheries, particularly in regions controlled by feudatories. At the same time, there were situations when the craftsmen were compelled to move from the centralized zones to non-centralized zones. For instance, the compulsion of building Jaina *basadis* in coastal Karnataka forced the Hoysala monarchs to encourage craftsmen to move to this region. This led to construction hundreds of Jaina *basadis* and statues of Jaina gurus there.

Vishwakarma Panchalas of Karnataka

As in other parts of peninsular India, in Karnataka too, there is reference to craftsmen who were termed Panchalas, implying that they were of five types. They were—goldsmiths, brass smiths (or braziers), blacksmiths, carpenters, and masons. In the Hoysala period, there was the initiation of contact between the ports and hinterland of Karnataka, and this contributed to the development of trade in this region. This, in turn, resulted in the emergence of trade centres in the interior and the coastal regions. Along with trade, there was also the emergence of craftsmen in the form of Panchalas. In actuality, *hanjamana* in coastal Karnataka and *anjuvannam* in the Tamil country are considered as representing the Panchalas. Nevertheless, differences between *hanjamana* and *anjuvannam* have been noted.[13]

Role of Craft Guilds

A relationship between craft and trade guilds gradually came into being under the Hoysalas. It is possible that there emerged craft groups that formed part of the trade guilds. There is reference to trade guilds such as the *balanju*, the *nanadesis*, the *gavares*, the *nakhara*, and the *hanjamana*, which included the craftsmen such as potters, blacksmiths, and other metalworkers. *Settikaras* were the merchants who lived in the streets called *keris*. They were mainly weavers. *Halaru* refers to an association of various professional groups such as goldsmiths and carpenters had become a part of the guild, which protected their interest. It is also possible that the Panchalas had become an important part of the urban trade network, as found in the regions such as Karkala and Mudabidare, known for the Jaina *basadis*. For example, there is reference to an association (or guild) called *halaru* in Karkala.[14]

The *keris* of Barkur and Basaruru are famous, comprising houses of craft groups. The traders of these regions traded in agricultural and non-agricultural commodities. South Kanara maintained trade relations with the Ghats. The Udyavara inscription belonging to the ninth century CE refers to such an interaction with the up ghat town called Purigere. This commercial relationship appears to have continued in the medieval period as well.[15] It is possible that *keris* comprised of members of the Vishwakarma Panchalas. From the eleventh century onwards, one obtains numerous references to the Panchalas and the traders living in the *keris*, and their associations.

The inscriptions of the Western Gangas, Hoyasalas, and Vijayanagar give clear references to the craftsmen who were responsible for the engravings on stone. They became important members of the craft guilds. However, one needs to differentiate between poets, writers, and engravers. There are inscriptions which are known for their poetic quality. It is apparent that writers and engravers did not possess such ability. The writers were officials who were entrusted with the work of writing official orders, including land grants.[16] Engravers were the least literate people, even though they needed to possess reasonable reading and writing abilities. In this sense, one can give a higher social status to the Vishwakarma Panchalas such as the stone engravers and smiths as compared to other artisans, such as potters and weavers. This is because, before engraving on stone or copperplate inscriptions, the engravers had to read and understand them. It is possible that they obtained preliminary education while learning the art of engraving.

It is suggested that the Western Ganga copperplate grants were engraved by the Vishwakarma craftsmen, who are considered to be goldsmiths. Some of these Vishwakarma craftsmen were eulogized as being skilled in arts and crafts, including painting, and there is reference to the title of 'Visvakarmacharya', which was possibly given to an artist who had achieved considerable expertise in his field.[17]

The social status of the craftsmen was determined around temples and *basadis*—the religious institutions. For example, in the case of *nakhara* guilds, the members patronized Nakhareshwara, a Saiva deity. It appears that the *nakharas* gave munificent donations to Saiva temples, while the *settikaras* supported Jaina faith.[18]

The presence of *settikaras* can be noted in regions such as Barakuru and Karkala, where the practice of Jainism became prominent. In the construction of a large number of Jaina *basadis*, one can note the role of stonemasons and carpenters, who specialized in this art.

Wages

Information regarding the wages paid to artisans and craftsmen is available from different sources. There was a practice of making payment to artisans in kind in coastal Karnataka. For example, one inscription refers to the payment of 5 *muras* of paddy per year to a potter.[19] Another inscription found in Mudukeri refers to the payment of 9 *muras* of paddy per year to a carpenter for the work in a temple.[20] Again, a fourteenth-century Alupa inscription refers to the payment of 5 *mude* paddy to artisans, such as potters, for the period of one year. Thus, it can be understood that artisans and craftsmen worked for payment in kind. The inscription also refers to similar payment to carpenters for their work in a *matha*.[21] Besides being paid in kind, artisans were also allowed to own land. They could, thus, practice both agrarian and non-agrarian professions. As a result of the ownership of land, the artisans usually remained attached to the village, and seldom moved out. Craftsmen, on the other hand, could move out of village seeking new avenues to exhibit their craftsmanship. It is possible that in the agrarian and religious sectors, craftsmen settled for lesser wages as compared to commercial sector. The artisan who provided service to agriculturists could not have demanded a higher wage due to the low level of wages that prevailed in this category of commodity production. One can assume that they charged more for non-agrarian and secular functions, because by providing cheaper service to temples and *basadis*, craftsmen could improve their social prestige and attain religious merit.

It is apparent that craftsmen such as the Panchalas had the temptation of economic gain in their exhibition of craftsmanship. Nevertheless, they had another huge attraction. They could improve their caste status by associating themselves with temple, in the process of the construction of these religious structures and other allied projects. It is possible that similar practices existed in various parts of Karnataka during the period between the eleventh and sixteenth centuries. Craftsmen could also improve their social position by providing similar services in the Jaina *basadis*. To some extent, Jainism was inspired by the social and religious model created by Hinduism.

A Hampapura inscription of the thirteenth century refers to the work and payment of Achari Aliba (in 1221 CE) and Mamcha (in 1242 CE). They were paid 6 *gadyanas* (gold coins) each for carving and repairing a hero stone respectively, and for establishing a roof. Mamcha here is also called Mamchoja,[22] the suffix 'oja' indicating that he was an established craftsman. Another Hoysala inscription of the thirteenth century CE, engraved by Achari Masanoja, mentions that payments were made to craftsmen in *gadyanas*. It appears that the craftsmen mentioned earlier charged premium payment for the work done for carving and repairing the hero stone and for constructing a roof. It is possible that semi-skilled artisans, who provided essential services in the village, did not charge such a large amount, as compared with the wages of major craftsmen. The fact that craftsmen were identified in the inscriptions with their names and surnames indicates the important position that they held in the society. This trend can be seen in various parts of Karnataka, including coastal Karnataka.

Artisans and Craftsmen

There is a need to differentiate between artisans and craftsmen. While artisans were a settled group, providing service to other members of the settlement, craft groups were usually mobile groups that specialized in particular fields. The artisans generally provided service at a small scale in the villages. They were also allowed to own land, as can be understood from the expression *badagiya bayala gadde* (cultivable land belonging to the carpenter).[23] The *badagi* or carpenter had become an important part of the society, providing service in different scales. There are also evidences to suggest that artisans owned land called *bettu*.[24] It would be interesting to note here that the carpenter repairing household implements can be considered as an artisan, while the carpenter providing service at a temple would obtain the status of a craftsman.

It is possible that large numbers of artisans such as carpenters and goldsmiths had become part of the streets called *keris* where merchants also lived.

In this chapter, blacksmiths and metalworkers are mentioned separately, mainly because these two fields of craft production needed different skills. Blacksmiths mostly produced commodities that were needed for the production of craft goods. To give an example, agriculturists needed iron ploughshares for their work. The metalworkers needed a different type of skill. They provided service to the temples by producing bronze statues and other goods. Similarly, they also produced the household utensils. The pertinent treatment of blacksmiths and metalworkers indicate diversification and advancement that emerged in craft production. Besides, they possessed distinct identities as part of the Vishwakarma Panchalas.

Blacksmiths

There is reference to the activities of blacksmiths in the work *Letters of Medieval Jewish Traders*.[25] This work further informs that in the twelfth century, the Jewish traders initiated trade with coastal Karnataka. In this work, there is reference to a trader named Abaham Yiju among others, who participated in the Aden–Mangalore trade network. It is apparent that he obtained resources not only from Mangalore but also from Malabar. In a letter, betel nut merchants and dealers in cotton are mentioned, implying that the Jews carried out trade in betel nut and cotton. In the process, they also maintained contact with traders and artisans. Internal trade centres such as Kanbayat (Cambay), Tana, Malabar, Kayankannur, and Mangalore are also mentioned in the book.[26] However, it is in the context of the Malabar trade that we find reference to trade in refurbished iron. Interestingly, it is mentioned that the Jews took various types of iron from India. It is also stated that iron formed an important part of the shipment from India to Aden. It is possible that like in Malabar, in Mangalore too, artisans created refurbished iron or renewed iron to be shipped to Aden.[27]

A fourteenth-century inscription refers to *kammarasalu* (workshop of the blacksmith).[28] It may indicate that there were workshops of blacksmiths who provided service to the local community. It is also possible that blacksmiths became an important part of the agrarian economy. An inscription belonging to 1542 CE refers to the agrarian activities of a blacksmith. Here, the word used is *kammara*.[29] Again, there is a reference to use of the term *kammara kodage* in an inscription dating to 1449 CE. This implies that the implements for irrigation were built and maintained by blacksmiths and other artisans.

Metalworkers

Apart from engravers and sculptors, there are also references to bronze workers, who were involved in the construction and repair of temples. Jewish documents from the twelfth century throw light on this aspect. There is reference to a brass factory of Abaham Yiju, which was located at Dahbattan. S.D. Goitein locates it in Malabar, where there is a port named Valarpattanam. Metal objects such as basins and ewers are also mentioned, along with covers of bronze vessels. There was a practice of producing vessels and their covers separately, which shows specialization in production. The implication is that there were craftsmen who specialized in the production of a single commodity. It shows an advancement achieved by the craftsmen in their art. However, one needs to note that these references are found in the context of Malabar.[30] In another context, there is reference to the Indian bronze factory of Abraham Yiju, who had established his contacts with traders in Mangalore and Malabar. It is mentioned that from the West, there was shipment of items made of copper, tin, and also old bronze vessels. The Indian artisans refurbished or repaired them, and then they were sent back to the West. Of the goods that were sent to India, one can find references to copper vessels, table bowls, broken ewers, a deep washbasin, a particular quantity of golden yellow copper, and a piece of Egyptian lead. There is also mention of two table bowls for two dishes for a servant. The precise weight and structure of the copper vessels that were ordered are also mentioned. For example, an order refers to a lamp that was to be made from copper, with octagonal columns. Its base had to be in the lampstand form. Gold or currency was sent as payment for the coppersmiths. The document mentions that copper required for building different items was sent in a canvas. There is also a reference to the order of making two bowls for drinking water.[31] Washbasins of different size are also mentioned.

In the fourteenth century CE, there is a reference to the Minister of Viraharihararaya instructing a bronze worker or *kanchigara* for the preparation of a bronze lampstand. The braziers in this case are mentioned as Kaloja and Anakoja, the sons of Marala Nadoja. They are described as belonging to *Patana* or town, thereby showing the presence of craftsmen in the urban context.[32] This inscription shows that like the Hoysalas, the Vijayangar kings also continued to patronize craft production, particularly in the urban centres. It implies that there was a continuity between the Hoysala and Vijayanagar policies concerning craftsmen. Such activities can be considered as a part of centralized production. The suffix 'oja' here indicates that a Panchala community like the *kanchigaras* were also considered belonging to the elite social group.

Urbanization and monetization must have contributed to the rise of the braziers. In the earliest inscriptions, there is reference to a metal called *kanchu* and *kil-ganchu*, meaning a kind of copper or brass or bell metal. One comes to know that *kanchu* and *kil-ganchu* were used as coinage metals.[33] There is also reference to the collection of taxes in the form of coins. Again, the reference to weights and measures indicate the role of blacksmiths, as most of the weights were made of iron or other metals.[34]

The *kanchigaras* might have played an important role in the minting of coins. Since the twelfth century, one can note the emergence of gold coins. For example, the term *pandya gadyana* (gold coin of Pandya, the Alupa ruler) was issued by Kavi Alupendra of the Alupas.[35] There is reference to *Barakura gadyana* (gold coin of Barakuru) and *Mangalura gadyana* (gold coin of Mangaluru), thereby showing regionalization and localization of the task of minting. Based on the evidence that the coins were named after King Pandya and places such as Barakuru and Mangaluru, it might be suggested that mints were established in coastal Karnataka. It is also possible that this implied the establishment of a settlement of metalworkers in Barakuru and Mangalore. *Gadyana* also comprised of other metals, apart from gold. This hints at the fact that goldsmiths and braziers might have worked in the mints in order to mint different kinds of coins. Coins were also brought from outside regions, and were converted into local currencies. An instance of this is found in the case of the Barakuru mint. The metalworkers must have achieved considerable sophistication to provide service to the state by minting various kinds of coins that needed considerable expertise and knowledge on the part of the craftsmen who produced them.[36]

In the thirteenth and the fourteenth centuries, the Panchalas had emerged as important contributors to the economy. They are described as paying taxes called *panchalaterige*, *panchakarukadere*, and *vojavari*. The Panchalas were considered as one category, and were differentiated from other craft producers. Goldsmiths paid taxes called *akkasaliyaya* and *suvarnaya*. It is possible that the goldsmiths, being highly paid for their service, emerged as the major tax payers among the craftsmen. In the sixteenth century, *kammaras* or blacksmiths emerged as major tax payers when compared to other Panchalas. This tax is referred to using terms such as *kammarasunka*, *kabbunadere* (tax on iron), *kulumedere* (tax on the implement called *kulume*), and *kammarikeya dashavanda*. The reference to *dashavanda* implies that blacksmiths paid one-tenth of their income as tax.[37] It is thus apparent that Panchalas were well-paid craftsmen who enjoyed an important position in the society. At the same time, a few changes in the position of a few Panchala categories can be noted. For example, it appears that in the thirteenth century, the stonemasons enjoyed state patronage, while in the sixteenth century, the blacksmiths began to enjoy this privileged position.[38] It is true that the Vijayanagar kings continued to indulge in the practice of constructing temples, but importance was also given to the manufacture iron implements, including weapons. Consequently, blacksmiths had to pay more tax as compared to other craftsmen.

In the sixteenth century, there were instances when the Panchalas competed with other elite groups for social dominance. For example, a sixteenth century inscription refers to such a conflict between Panchalas and the corporate group called *halaru* in the temple of Chennigaraya of Belur. In this case, the Panchalas were asked to limit themselves within the boundaries of a specified locality. Within their territory, they could build houses and perform ceremonies such as marriages and other social functions. However, the Panchalas were also given a few privileges during the festivals at Vidyanagar, the capital city of Vijayanagar.[39] The inscription is significant because it implied that the Panchalas derived confidence enough to challenge the authority of *halaru*.

Artisans in the Agrarian Context

In the rural space, there was emergence of the *ayagara* system, which provided for land grants to artisans who provided their service to members of a village. This system led to self-sufficiency of the members of the village. Several inscriptions refer to *ayagaras* such as *badagi*, *kammara*, and *akasali* (goldsmith). Carpenters and blacksmiths provided services such as the manufacture and repair of ploughs and other agricultural implements. This led to the emergence of a long-term understanding between peasants and artisans. In return for this service, the artisans received *ayam* or shares of the agricultural produce.[40] A few members of the Panchala community also acted as *ayagars*, obtaining a share of the produce and remaining an important part of the village community. It is possible that they obliged by the rules of the village community. At the same time, in the urban centres, their character changed.

Caste Status

It is apparent that *acharis* did not enjoy a higher economic position in coastal Karnataka. Duarte Barbosa, while referring to carpenters, states, 'Another lower lineage amongst these gentiles is called ajare. Their business is that of quarrymen and carpenters, and others are blacksmiths, carvers of metals, and silversmiths.'[41] The word *ajare* here refers to *achari*, which is used in coastal Karnataka. Barbosa rightly pointed out that they were given lower social status. This quotation shows the difference between various craftsmen and artisans. While carpenters were given a lower social status, blacksmiths and other metalworkers were given a higher social status. It shows the emergence of stratification among the craftsmen and artisanal groups.

Mobility

Mobility of Panchalas, particularly in coastal Karnataka, was not only due to political destabilization in the core territories of ruling dynasties (such as the Hoysalas), but also due to the process of urbanization and state formation in coastal Karnataka. As the Hoysalas, who patronized Hinduism and Jainism, established their domination in the coastal parts of Karnataka, there was the need for a large number of craft groups, who organized themselves into guilds around Hindu temples and Jaina *basadis*. The Hoysala style of architecture influenced the construction of temples and *basadis* in coastal Karnataka. The emergence of urban centres such as Barakuru and Mangalore was due to state patronage, increase of commerce, and popularity of Jainism. Karkala, Venur, and Mudabidare also emerged as important urban centres away from the coastal region of Karnataka. There are references to rich merchants giving donations of land to temples and *basadis* in regions such as Karkala and Barakuru. In the administrative centres too, there was the need for large numbers of craft groups, including the Panchalas. Goldsmiths, for example, could provide service to elite sections in the society. At the same time, there was an ongoing commercial relationship between the coastal regions and the Ghats. Along with the growth of commerce, there was the emergence of demand for artisans in coastal Karnataka, leading to their migration to this region from interior Karnataka.

The need for workers in copper grew as the kings and chieftains issued copper grants. For example, there is a reference to a copperplate inscription discovered in Humcha Jain *matha*. The inscription incidentally refers to people with surnames such as Agrawala and Sahu, who belonged to northern India.[42] It is possible that they were also Jainas. Barbosa mentions that in coastal Karnataka there was a practice of using coins called *pardaos*, which were gold coins issued by the Vijayanagar King Krishnadevaraya. Copper was needed for the production of coins, cooking pots, and other utensils as well. One also finds reference to the traders of Malabar, who brought iron to Bhatkal, a port of Karnataka.[43] From these, we can assume the role of blacksmiths and coppersmiths, who must have worked in order to produce the various weights and measures demanded by the traders. Augmented trade in the fifteenth and sixteenth centuries due to the emergence of traders contributed to further expansion of activities of craftsmen such as blacksmiths and smiths of other metals, as there was further demand for the goods produced by these craftsmen.

The kings of dynasties such as the Alupa constructed forts and other large structures, which needed stoneworkers, masons, and carpenters. This is proved by the reference to a *keri* in Barakuru called Kotakeri. *Kota* or *kote* in Kannada means fort. Thus, there was the need for stoneworkers to construct forts. Incidentally, not far away from Barakuru, there is a place called Kota. It is possible that fort-like structures were built in this region, either by the state or by the members of the town. In Barakuru there is also a *kalluchappara* or stone *mandapa* (structure), which is an instance of the work of stonemasons.[44]

The *keris*, too, were undergoing expansion. There is reference to construction of a new street called *hosakeri*.[45] The term *hosa* in Kannada means new. This shows the need for settlement of artisans who would work as carpenters, blacksmiths, and stonemasons in different structures.

It can be seen from different sources that in the Hoysala period, the Panchalas had established themselves as important communities in the social structure of the region. Their position further improved under the Vijayanagar kings. This is observable from the reference to the Virapanchalas under Devaraya II of Vijayanagar. The inscriptions of this period refer to the *akkasale* or goldsmith, and also to craftsmen such as stoneworkers and masons. In the fourteenth-century inscriptions, the Virapanchalas traced their origin to Manu. They claimed to possess the knowledge of Vedas and were trained in different arts and crafts, along with training in reading, writing, prose, poetry, logic, and grammar. Various privileges were granted to the Virapanchalas in Vijayanagar.

They were allowed to construct houses in certain localities, thereby allowing them to work in a group rather than as individual workers. The Virapanchalas established their own corporations that further improved their social position. There is also a reference to the guild of the Virapanchalas, which had the power to punish members for violating guild rules.[46] Urbanization that took place in Karnataka during the period between the fourteenth and sixteenth centuries CE is partially responsible for this development. This is because, the Vijayanagar administrators needed the Panchalas for construction of forts, buildings, and canals. Architects, engineers, masons, and stoneworkers, who specialized in this work, became indispensable for the Vijayanagar monarchs.

It is possible that a large number of craftsmen migrated to coastal Karnataka from south India as well as other parts of Karnataka. This maybe because the local artisans lacked the technical expertise needed to produce colossal statues, temples, and *basadis*. Consequently, they had to be brought in from outside. Most of the craftsmen served elite sections in the society.

A Dharmasthala copperplate inscription belonging to late seventeenth century refers to the connection of service groups such as washermen and musicians with Kanchi. When a dispute arose between the washermen and the musicians, it was taken to the court of the artisans at Kanchi.[47] The dispute was thus settled by taking it to a region which was outside of where these two groups were settled. This shows that artisans remembered their earlier connections with that region. The inscription also mentions a number of persons and places outside coastal Karnataka. There is a reference to *gramapramukhas* such as Doddachilli Raghava Shettaru and others. It is possible that even before the seventeenth century, many artisans and craftsmen had migrated to the region. During this period, craftsmen were outsiders and the inclusion of their names did not matter either to the society or to themselves. It is possible that many craftsmen did not settle down permanently in coastal Karnataka, even though they had temporary settlements at places such as Karkala and Venur.

It is possible that many artisans providing essential services had become a part of the society of coastal Karnataka. In support of this view, one can cite the reference to a colony of *madivalas* or washermen. The colony was called *madivalabettu*.[48]

The temples employed a large number of people who performed different functions. The functionaries were both brahmins and non-brahmins. At the same time, there are references to artisans called *achari* mentioned in a fourteenth-century Vijayanagar inscription. It refers to Virachari's son Nambiyachari.[49] Even though the profession of the *achari* is not mentioned, one may assume that artisanal occupation had become hereditary, and was pursued by particular castes. Here, the craftsmen are referred to as *achari* and not as acharya. This shows that the craftsmen there had not enjoyed the supreme social position that they obtained in other parts of Karnataka. Nevertheless, one cannot underestimate the role of craftsmen in the construction of thousands of temples and *basadis*. It is possible that goldsmiths had established permanent settlements in coastal Karnataka. This can be derived from the fact that many goldsmiths migrated from Goa, particularly after the Portuguese persecution. Goldsmiths had established their own *mathas* in coastal Karnataka and they had emerged as landowners. An inscription belonging to 1562 CE refers to *akkasaleya mathada gadi*,[50] which implies that goldsmiths owned *mathas*. It is also apparent that the services of carpenters, stonecutters, and sculptors were in considerable demand. The carpenters exhibited their skills by preparing huge wooden cars (chariots or raths) and wooden images of gods and goddesses.

In coastal Karnataka, there are not many inscriptions referring to *kallukuttigas* or stonecutters and sculptors. However, it is not possible to undermine their position. The stone inscriptions and beautiful sculptures show the important role that they played. They engraved inscriptions, thus helping the rulers to publicize their activities and maintain records. *Kallukuttiga paddana* (a folklore text) refers to the activities of stoneworkers. It mentions the construction of Jaina monuments at Karkala. This work refers to artisans as *acchava*. There is also a reference to Kanchi.[51]

It was common among artisans to have migrated from Kanchi to Vijayanagar. The Vishwakarmas of Karnataka even today send their contributions to Kanchi. Those who collected these contributions were called *ponos makkalu*.[52] It is possible that different groups of artisans did not migrate to coastal Karnataka simultaneously. Based on the study of the architecture of the region, it can be suggested that some stoneworkers came to the region in the seventh and eight centuries CE. The bronze workers came to the region in the tenth century. During the period between the eleventh and the thirteenth centuries, stoneworkers came from Belur and Hasan. In the fifteenth century, many craftsmen came from Hampi. Carpenters and blacksmiths also migrated from Kerala and Shimoga. The *paddanas* refer to *tacchavaru*, who were blacksmiths, from Malenadu. Goldsmiths are recorded to have migrated from north Karnataka.[53]

Identity

The smiths and stonemasons had surnames such as 'Achari', 'Ovaja' and 'Oja'. At the same time, craftsmen were also identified by their first names, such as Isvarayya, Iruvanna, Perumaledeva, Mahalingayya, Kirtinarayana, and Somanatha. One can note that the term *ayya* refers to persons of prominence. Based on this, it is possible to assume that craftsmen such as smiths were men of prominence, who were respected for their skill.[54]

There is a reference to the *achari* whose first name was Masanoja, and he is described as engraving, looking into a *patrasasana* or palm-leaf inscription. This implies that inscriptions were initially written on palm leaves, and later it was copied into permanent stone inscriptions. In the fifteenth-century inscriptions, there are clear references to names of Panchalas, including stonemasons and workers. There are names such as Bayiroja, Maliyoja, Ketoja, Mandalikachari, Puradachari, Virachari, Ketana, Mallana, Panditoja, and Viranacharya. There is reference to terms such as *ruvari*, the person who designed the plan of a sculpture, and *kallukuttiga*, the person who executed this plan, which shows specialization among these professionals.[55]

As mentioned earlier, it is possible that persons with the surname Oja were prominent in their fields. It is interesting to note that many Sthanika brahmins had the surname Oja. This shows the attempt of Vishwakarma Panchalas to improve their position in the society as they were praised for their knowledge of literature and arts.

It is interesting to note that according to D.C. Sircar, Oja or Ojha is a designation derived from the Sanskrit term *upadhyaya*. In Bengali, *upadhyaya* becomes Ojha, and in Maithili, it becomes Jha.[56] As these terms are used in the context of north India, one can assume that in this region brahmins were addressed as Ojha and Upadhyaya. The designation Oja considerably improved the caste status of the Vishwakarma Panchalas. This also implies an attempt on their part to achieve a status similar to the brahmins. They had several points in their favour as well. They were invariably related to temple construction, and the Ojas, in the case of Karnataka, had emerged as an elite community. Naturally, they attempted to usurp the caste status of the brahmins.

The term acharya is used to refer to the religious leader of Buddhism and Jainism. An acharya is also an architect and master mason. In some cases, an acharya is also considered to be a master goldsmith. A stonemason can be considered as an acharya as well. It is possible that the Oja and Sthanika had higher social and economic statuses. The ordinary artisans were not highly skilled, while acharyas and Ojas were experts, having specialized knowledge in the art of planning their work. Acharyas and Ojas had to work on the minute details as well, and they could train other artisans in achieving perfection in their work.[57]

Like in other parts of Karnataka, a large number of inscriptions were issued in coastal Karnataka as well. However, it is interesting to note that most inscriptions do not mention the name of the craftsmen in coastal Karnataka, unlike in the other parts of Karnataka. What could be the reason for this discrepancy? It is possible that the engravers had not become part of the society of coastal Karnataka, as they were generally outsiders. Nevertheless, some inscriptions recognized differences between the writer and the engraver. For example, an Alupa inscription belonging to the early thirteenth century refers to a writer Channaya Senaboga and an engraver Kaliyachari.[58] It is possible that Channaya Senaboga was an official who was in charge of issuing the inscription, while Kaliyachari was given the task of engraving the text of the inscription.

It is in the context of Jaina *basadis* that there are a few references to the engravers. This is because the Jaina inscriptions were clearly influenced by the inscriptions of other parts of Karnataka. It is also possible that the Hoysalas introduced this practice in coastal Karnataka in a large scale. For example, the Hiriyangadi inscription of Mangalore mentions that Mayoja, the son of Eragoja engraved inscription by looking at the text. The inscription refers to the Jaina religious leader Charukirti Panditadeva.[59] A fourteenth-century inscription mentions that the text was written by one Bammarasa. However, it does not refer to the engraver.[60]

The sources called *kaifiyats* are traditional historical records, collected by administrative historians.[61] For example, *kaifiyats* included in the Mackenzie collection become useful in reconstructing the social history of coastal Karnataka. Another *kaifiyat*, the origin of which can be traced to the Ghats, gives information regarding the history of the kings of Karkala. There are references of local principalities fighting over the issue of construction of Jaina *basadis*. For example, in Karkala, there was the construction of a *basadi* called Chaturmukha *basadi*, a Jaina temple with four faces or sides. It is mentioned that Bairarasas attacked the local chieftain and included it in his kingdom. In this way, one gets reference to the emergence of the dynasty of Bairarasas. They built Jaina *basadis* in the region. There is also reference to the Jaina teacher called

Kirti Guru and King Pandyappa Odeya, who followed the instructions of Kirti Guru. Again, it is said that Chikkannachari created the statue of Gomateshwara, who is venerated by the Jainas. However, it is also mentioned that the king (Bairarasas) got the hands of Chikkannachari amputated, with the view to prevent the installation of similar statues in other regions. This shows that kings attempted to monopolize artisans and craftsmen in order to prevent other kings from imitating their examples. Consequently, Chikkannachari sought the shelter of the local ruling family of Ajilas.

The *kaifiyat* also describes the Ajilas as having erected a statue of Gomateshwara at Venur, another place known for the prevalence of Jainism.[62] When Bairarasas of Karkala achieved the feat of constructing the statue of Gomateshwara, the Ajilas also aimed to achieve this feat. This led to struggle between the two dynasties. It is not clear, however, whether Chikkannachari was actually punished or rewarded for his achievement. Nevertheless, there are Gomateshwara statues both at Karkala and Venur. Besides these, there are hundreds of *basadis* (Jaina temples) in different parts of coastal Karnataka.

An inscription belonging to Malaguru, Mandya district, is significant because it presents a eulogy of the Vishwakarma Panchalas. In it, there is reference to a craftsman called Gavaracharya. He is said to be '… the illustrious Maya, Visvakarma and Totakacharya, skilled in handicrafts like gold work, metalwork, stonework, jewel work, woodwork, painting, calligraphy, iconography and all other skilled handwork, a descendent of Visvakarma . . .'[63] The eulogy is followed by a detailed genealogy of the artist. In the process, there are descriptions of craftsmen such as Hoysalacharya, Suracharyya, Kallabhoja, Manikachari, Suroja, Ketoja, Mahachari, Nakharachari, and Malloja. The inscription also reveals that smiths gave a payment of one *haga* per family for maintenance of the temple of the locality.[64] This inscription is important due to various reasons. The eulogy of the craftsman can be considered as being quite exaggerated, but it is interesting to note that the craftsman in question was an expert in different fields. The family of the craftsman had the tradition of producing different types of items made of gold and other metals, and stone. The attempt to achieve the status of acharya also indicates the process of brahminization, as many brahmins assumed the title acharya. The inscription also attempted to legitimize the position of the craftsmen by linking them with Lord Vishwakarma.

The Bairapura inscription of Mandya district and Krishnarajpet taluk, belonging to the fourteenth century, makes clear reference to the Panchalas who are described as having a respectable position in the society. They are described as sureties. The Panchalas mentioned include Ojayita Lakhoja, goldsmith Sabeyoja, goldsmith Manchi, and Hiriya Kamoja. The document was approved by prominent residents of the locality.[65] This record is important because it highlights the role of the Panchalas, such as goldsmiths. It is possible that they had emerged as affluent members in the society and naturally, they were approached to provide surety to the sale deed. It is clear that people who had names with the suffix oja had emerged as prominent not only in the locality but also other regions of Karnataka. The term *hiriya* means elder and it is possible that other members in the society respected Hiriya Kamoja. It is interesting to note that the Vishwakarma Panchalas could interact with the Sthanika brahmins who occupied a respectable position in the society. The association with brahmins also enabled the Panchalas with surname Oja to improve their caste status.

The inscriptions of the Hoysala period refer to large numbers of sculptors such as Dasoja, Chavana, Malliyanna, Maloja, Echana, Chaloja, Nagoja, Kadoja, and others. There is also reference to titles such as Vidyadara of the Hoysala king and *ruvari*.[66] It is clear that these sculptors and other Panchalas had emerged as an important part of the society, and the state also recognized their importance.

Role and Functions

In the context of Barakuru in coastal Karnataka, it is found that Panchalas such as carpenters, stonecutters, and sculptors played an important role in the contemporary society and economy. The skilled craftsmen, such as the carpenters, participated in the construction of temples like the Panchalingeshwara temple and built (as in case of the carpenters) other items such as wooden cars or chariots (raths), wooden statues, wooden chains and buds. Mudukeri has a few specimens of artworks created by the Vishwakarma Panchalas. In the South Kanara district, there was practice of making huge wooden dolls called *tattirayas*, which were taken out during the festivals.[67] The carpenters also played an important role in the activities such as construction and maintenance of wooden bridges. A fourteenth-century inscription refers to construction of a wooden bridge by the queen Chikkayi Tayi. The inscription also gives information regarding the technology of construction of bridges. The bridge was called *sanka*, and was constructed over a river, which connected the western part of Barakuru and an island called Bennekudru.

The bridge had a wooden framework and was constructed using stone poles and wooden planks. The size of the bridge was 4 ft. and it was made of three planks. The administrator called Tirumaleshwara Nayaka was made responsible for the maintenance of the bridge. The income from a village called Harady was kept aside for the maintenance of the bridge.[68] The inscription reveals that many workers were involved in the construction and installation of the wooden bridge. One may assume that similar works in other parts of Karnataka also demanded large numbers of carpenters. Again, the role of carpenters was indispensable in maintenance of boats that arrived at the ports. Even though coastal Karnataka was not a major shipbuilding centre, the craftsmen had the knowledge of building ships. The Portuguese also hired the service of carpenters in repairing ships. This allowed carpenters to enhance their economic position in society. For example, Barbosa[69] refers to transportation of commodities in boats called *zambuquos*. Obviously, carpenters were needed for their construction and maintenance. One can suggest that local craftsmen had achieved the technical skills needed to maintain and repair these boats and ships. There was initiation of inter-regional trade in the form of interaction between coastal zones and up-ghat regions. Bullock carts were used for the purpose of transportation in the plain regions. This again implies the need for the service of carpenters and blacksmiths, who needed to build and maintain wooden carts and metal implements. It is clear that there was much demand for carpenters due to the development of agriculture. Plough-based cultivation led to the demand for the production of large numbers of wooden ploughs. Apart from these, there was the use of implements such as ploughshares, hoes, and sickles. This implies the need for blacksmiths, who could make and repair various iron implements. One can assume that this category of workers can be termed as artisans, who stayed in their village and provided service to the peasants.

The goldsmiths and jewel merchants also played an important role in the society of coastal Karnataka. This is revealed by the reference to *manigarakeri*, or a street of dealers in gems and precious stones. This implies the existence of goldsmiths and similar craftsmen who had achieved excellence in their profession. It is possible that the *manigaras* maintained contact with inter-regional as well as international traders. This is because, there is reference to associations called *halaru* and *elame*, which included different professional groups.[70]

The craftsmen called *kallukuttigas* or stoneworkers too played an important role in the society in Karnataka. Their role in temple construction and creation of statues is notable. In the regions such as Barakuru, Mangalore, and Karkala, large numbers of inscriptions were issued. Stoneworkers played an important role in the work of engraving these stone inscriptions. This also enhanced their prestige in the eyes of the authorities, as they assisted the state in publicly announcing its policies.[71] In one inscription, there is reference to *kallukuttiga* Kannappa.[72] It is evident that the stoneworkers were given an important position in the society, as they are mentioned in the inscription.

Conclusion

The Vishwakarma Panchalas of Karnataka, like their counterparts in other parts of peninsular India, participated in social and economic processes. Nevertheless, their caste or social status depended mainly on the patron-client relationship. The state patronage to a particular Panchala community was not permanent, as different kingdoms could patronize different communities. This is found in the case of Hoysala and Vijayanagar. In the twelfth and thirteenth centuries, sculptors, who were termed 'ojas' and 'acharyas', obtained a dominant position in the society, and their association with religious structures considerably enhanced their position. This is because, the Hoysalas were known for the construction of a large number of temples and *basadis*. However, under the Vijayanagar kings, blacksmiths emerged as a more important group, as compared to the stoneworkers.

In a place where there was centralized production, craftsmen enjoyed a relatively superior position, as compared to regions that had non-centralized production. For example, in coastal Karnataka, which was non-centralized production zone, craftsmen such as the sculptors did not enjoy a significantly high position in the society. In the centralized production regions however, the craftsmen could considerably improve their economic positions. The identities of the craftsmen were more visible in these regions as well, because one finds references to the Panchalas with their names, titles, family history, and achievements. On the other hand, in non-centralized zones, the identities of the craftsmen were not prominently visible. Nevertheless, in both regions, the Panchalas provided service to the elite class, which became the major consumers of their products.

Mobility is another important development over time which can be noted from various sources. Craftsmen did not necessarily migrate due to oppression or economic problems. The expansion of political boundaries was responsible for migration of artisans. For example, when the Hoysalas expanded their territories to Tulunadu, it attracted craftsmen who were asked to construct hundreds of *basadis* and temples. The process of urbanization and related activities was another development, which led to the widespread mobility of craftsmen. For example, rise of towns such as Belur, Halebid, Karkala, and Venur contributed to this development. In the Vijayanagar period, there is reference to Virapanchalas, who were even involved in clashes with local inhabitants regarding construction processes and territorial ownership.

Artisans and craftsmen worked at two different spaces. At the village level, artisans obtained agricultural produces and provided service to members of the village. The attempt was to supply essential commodities to the village people, in exchange for payment mainly in kind. In the urban space, craftsmen such as engravers, writers, stonemasons, goldsmiths, carpenters, and bronze workers become dominant, as they were associated with the construction of religious structures. With the view to enhance their legitimacy, a few craftsmen also constructed their own *mathas* or religious institutions.

Notes

1. Frits Staal, *Discovering the Vedas: Origins, Mantras, Rituals, Insights*, New Delhi: Penguin Books, 2008, p. 67.
2. K.S. Shivanna, *The Agrarian System of Karnataka (1336–1761)*, Mysore: University of Mysore, 1983.
3. K.S. Kumara Swamy, *Prachina Karnatakadalli Shilpachariyaru* (in Kannada), Bangalore: Kannada Sahitya Parishat, 1996.
4. P. Gururaja Bhatt, *Studies in Tuluva History and Culture*, Kallianpur: Self-published, 1975.
5. K.V. Ramesh, *A History of South Kanara: From the Earliest Times to the Fall of Vijayanagara*, Dharwar: Karnatak University, 1970.
6. B. Vasantha Shetty, 'Barakuru—A Metropolitan City of Antiquity', unpublished Ph.D. thesis, Mysore University, 1985.
7. B. Jagadish Shetty, 'The Agro-Economic Relations and Social Structure in Dakshina Kannada (A.D. 1000–1600)', unpublished Ph.D. thesis, Mangalore University, 1992.
8. Kenneth R. Hall, *Trade and Statecraft in the Age of the Cōḷas*, New Delhi: Abhinav Publications, 1980.
9. R. Champakalakshmi, *Trade, Ideology, and Urbanization: South India, 300 BC to AD 1300*, New Delhi: Oxford University Press, 1996.
10. James Heitzman, *The Gifts of Power Lordship in an Early Indian State*, New Delhi: Oxford University Press, 1997.

11. Vijaya Ramaswamy, 'Vishwakarma Craftsmen in early Peninsular India', *Journal of Economic and Social History of the Orient*, vol. 47, no. 4, 2004, pp. 548–82.
12. Carla M. Sinopoli, 'The Organization of Craft Production at Vijayanagara, South India', *American Anthropologist*, n.s., vol. 90, no. 3, 1988, p. 580.
13. Ramesh, *A History of South Kanara*, p. 252.
14. Ibid., p. 255.
15. Bhatt, *Studies in Tuluva History and Culture*, p. 201.
16. *Epigraphia Carnatica* (hereafter *EC*), n.s., vol. VII, 1979, p. cxix.
17. Ibid.
18. Ramesh, *A History of South Kanara*, p. 261.
19. *South Indian Inscriptions* (hereafter *SII*), vol. VII, no. 330, 1986.
20. Ibid.
21. Ibid.
22. *EC*, vol. VII, n.s., 1977, p. 206.
23. *SII*, vol. VII, no. 324.
24. *Mysore Archaeological Report*, 1923, nos. 104, 107.
25. S.D. Goitein, *Letters of Medieval Jewish Traders*, Princeton, NJ: Princeton University Press, 1973.
26. Ibid., pp. 62–4.
27. Ibid., pp. 186–7.
28. *SII*, vol. XXVII, no. 341, 2001.
29. Ibid., no. 185.
30. Goitein, *Letters of Medieval Jewish Traders*, p. 188.
31. Ibid., pp. 192–6.
32. *EC*, vol. IX, n.s., 1990, p. 19.
33. Ramesh, *A History of South Kanara*, p. 273.
34. Ibid., p. 272.
35. *SII*, vol. VII, no. 381.
36. Ramesh, *A History of South Kanara*, p. 277.
37. Swamy, *Prachina Karnatakadalli Shilpachariyaru*, p. 110.
38. Swamy, *Prachina Karnatakadalli Shilpachariyaru*.
39. *EC*, vol. IX, n.s., p. 26.
40. Shivanna, *Agrarian System of Karnataka*, pp. 124–6.
41. Duarte Barbosa, *A Description of the Coasts of East Africa and Malabar: In the Beginning of the Sixteenth Century*, London: Elibron Classics, 2005, p. 140.
42. Vasantha Shetty, 'Barakuru', p. 319.
43. Barbosa, *A Description of the Coasts of East Africa and Malabar*, pp. 189–90.
44. Vasantha Shetty, 'Barakuru', p. 273.
45. Ibid., p. 268.
46. H.M. Nagaraju, *Devaraya II and His Times: History of Vijayanagara*, Mysore: Prasaranga, University of Mysore, 1991, p. 136.

47. Keladi Gunda Jois, 'Dharmasthaladalliruva Tamrashasana' (in Kannada), *Lochana*, n.d.
48. *Annual Report of South Indian Epigraphy*, 1931–2, no. 282.
49. *SII*, vol. VII, no. 267.
50. *SII*, vol. IX, part 2, 1986, no. 673.
51. Paltadi Ramakrishna Achar, *Kalkuda Kallurti Samskriti Shodha* (in Kannada), Puttur: Paltadi Ramakrishna Achar, 1998, pp. 17–25.
52. Ibid., p. 51.
53. Ibid., pp. 55–6.
54. *EC*, vol. VII, n.s., p. cxx.
55. Ibid.
56. D.C. Sircar, *Indian Epigraphical Glossary*, Delhi: Motilal Banarsidass, 1966, p. 222.
57. *EC*, vol. VI, n.s., 1977, p. 461.
58. K.V. Ramesh and M.J. Sharma, *Tulunadina Shasanagalu* (in Kannada), vol. I, Mysore: Geeta Book House, 1978, p. 72.
59. Ibid., p. 97.
60. Ibid., p. 108.
61. *Kaifiyats* narrate the traditional history of coastal Karnataka. They are important because they offer alternative views concerning the region. In actuality, a few details such as erection of Bahubali statues in Karkala and Venur are established facts. One obtains information regarding the process of construction of Jaina statues and *basadis* from the *kaifiyats*. In this sense, it becomes significant to study these *kaifiyats*. Myths apart, they also narrate local history.
62. K. Kushalappa Gowda and K. Chinnappa Gowda, *Dakshina Kannada Jilleya Kaifiyattugalu*, Ujire: Dharmasthala Manjunatheshwara Pustaka Prakashana Male, 1983, pp. 10–12.
63. *EC*, vol. VI, n.s., p. 461.
64. Ibid.
65. Ibid., p. 478.
66. *EC*, vol. XI, 1911–12, pp. 44–6.
67. Vasantha Shetty, 'Barakuru', p. 401.
68. Ibid., pp. 138–9.
69. Mansel Longworth Dames, ed., *The Book of Duarte Barbosa: An Account of the Countries bordering the Indian Ocean and their Inhabitants*, New Delhi: Asian Educational Services, 1989, p. 184.
70. Vasantha Shetty, 'Barakuru', p. 275.
71. Ibid., p. 403.
72. *SII*, vol. VII, no. 382.

13

Aiṅkuḍi Kammāḷar

Reflections on the Temple Craftsmen and Beyond from Medieval Kēraḷam

ANNA VARGHESE

Introduction

The history of medieval Kēraḷam is intertwined with the growth and proliferation of structural temples and the subsequent emergence of occupational groups in association with these temples. Among these occupational groups, craftsmen and artisans were prominent and indispensable for the construction and maintenance of the temples. K.V. Krishna Aiyyar writes that artisans and craftsmen claimed their descent from Vishwakarma.[1] In this essay, I would like to look at the history of artisans and craftsmen from the region of Kēraḷam between the ninth and seventeenth centuries CE. These are the communities associated with temple crafts, like the five groups called the Aiṅkuḍi Kammāḷar, which includes *āśāri*, *mūśāri*, *taṭṭān*, *kallan*, and *kollan*. Going beyond the Aiṅkuḍi Kammāḷar within the temple, this essay also looks at the craftsmen outside the temple, associated with the larger society. It traces a transition of craftsmen from an occupational group to a caste in the journey from medieval to contemporary periods.

The background of this essay is inclusive of the debates regarding the presence of the rule of the Cēra Perumāls and the second Kulaśēkhara Empire of Makōtai.[2] In the Kēraḷam region, along with political stability and revival of Hinduism against the stronghold of heterodox sects in southern India, there was also the proliferation of temples, temple related occupational groups, and temple centered village communities,[3] in tune with the larger Bhakti movement.[4] In other regions of southern India there are arguments regarding temple centred urban settlements,[5] but such arguments are not too prevalent in the context of Kēraḷam. Another argument is about the large scale changes in the agrarian system and relation between the means of production and mode of production in the agrarian sector in the region. Agriculture received a new boost due to the increase in land gifts to the brahmins and the temples. The *brahmadēyams*, *dēvaswom* lands, and *virutti* lands (those given to individuals in return for their services) changed the idea of land ownership and consequently, the socio-economic structure of the land. The agrarian routines by the thirteenth–fourteenth centuries are said to have been subsistence-oriented. The self-sufficiency of these villages is another debatable point. The crafts communities fitted well into this paradigm; be it in expansion with the temples or in support to the agrarian villages. The various sources used to develop this paper are: inscriptional evidence from early medieval and medieval periods (ninth to seventeenth centuries CE), ethnographic accounts of colonial historians, ethnographic surveys undertaken by me, oral traditions, and secondary literature.

Historiography

We find colonial writings on the history of Kēraḷam, which deals with the craftsmen in the region. Francis Day (1863), who was the Civil Surgeon of British Cochin and medical officer to the government of the Raja of Cochin, wrote *The Land of the Perumals, or Cochin: Its Past and its Present.*[6] Here he has described the class of artificers as the 'four-joined-in-one' race, consisting of four distinct classes—*arjaree* (carpenters), *moojaree* (braziers), *perincolum* (smiths), and the *taṭṭān* (silversmiths).

K.P. Padmanabha Menon, whose works were a turning point in the historiography of Kēraḷam, also looks at the craft groups as castes. He looks at the divisions in the Kammāḷar caste, mentioning them as *ajari*, *moojari*, *thattan*, *kollan*, and *kallan.*[7] Elamkulam Kunjan Pillai (1957), one of the pioneers in writing the history of Kēraḷam, in *Keralacharithrathile Iruladanja Edukal*[8] mentions that the Kammāḷar were among the jatis that were present in Kēraḷam before the seventh century CE. Here, he also mentions that the *āśāris* practiced fraternal polyandry.

Komattil Achyutha Menon talks of the division of the artisans into five leading classes or divisions called 'Ainkudi Kammalar' or 'Anjuvarnakkars' including carpenters, braziers, goldsmiths and coppersmiths, masons, and leatherworkers.[9] The Anjuvarnakkar are said to have occupied separate villages outside the fortified walls of the main towns and their villages were called *maṇigrāmams* or villages of trading artisans or classes. These artisan groups took community names from their occupation; it was essentially domestic and largely hereditary. George W. Spencer wrote about the feature of south Indian temples[10] whereby they distributed the property of the wealthy to others by employing artisans, peasants, and shepherds, and by lending money to agriculturists. P.S. Velayudhan has given detailed accounts of the various artisan groups, treating them as different castes.[11]

Nalamkel Krishna Pillai has provided a brief account of the different temples in Kēraḷam. His work *Mahakshetrangalude Munnil*[12] (*Great temples*) gives us glimpses on the activities of the *mūśāri* of Vaikom temple, the community of Mundappuzha *acāris*, who built *cuṇḍan-vaḷloms* for a boat race in association with the Aranmula Parthasarathy Temple, and Uḷiyannūr Perumtaccan of Parayi Peṭṭa Panthirukulam clan, who built the Chengannur Mahādēva Temple. P.K. Balakrishnan in his book *Jativyavasthithiyum Keralacharithravum* opines that the *śilpa*jāti or artisanal caste had six groups comprising it—*marayāśari, kallāśari, kollan, mūśāri, taṭṭān*, and *tōlkollan.*[13]

James Heitzman wrote about a developmental pattern connecting temples with the expansion of urbanism and the agrarian economy in south India. He gave an account of the lands allotted to temple personnel like *taccar* (carpenters), *taṭṭān* (goldsmith), temple donations, dues, and growing social stratification and conflict within the commercial and artisan communities of the temple cities.[14] His work concentrated on Tamil regions which have a remarkable difference with the Kēraḷam region of my study. The presentation of temple cities in their richness and pomp is debatable in case of Kēraḷam, considering its limited economic resources. The commercial and artisan communities in Kēraḷam do not seem to be as influential and prosperous as their counterparts in Tamil Nadu. The much discussed *Idaṅgai-Valaṅgai* caste struggles within these communities[15] are absent in Kēraḷam. These readings significantly brought out the differences between the regions under consideration.

Dr S. Sundararajan's book, *Ancient Tamil Country: Its Social and Economic Structure*, discusses *Purananuru*, a Tamil literary text which mentions castes like *karumiyar* (metalworkers), *kuyavan* (potter), *kollan* (ironsmith), *tachchan* (carpenter), etc., and it indicates a society based on professional hierarchy or differences. For example, *tachchan* was a community based on profession: 'They were a community distinguished by skilled labor.'[16]

Rajan Gurukkal discusses the professional brahmin caste groups, non-brahmin functional caste groups, non-specialized worker's group, warrior cum *karalar* groups, artisans and craftsmen, and tillers of the soil.[17] In his essay, 'From Clan and Lineage to Hereditary Occupations and Caste in Early South India',[18] Gurukkal refers to the occupational groups of *kollan* and *kuyavan*. The *kuyavan* were potters, a domestic group who took to pot-making as their full-time occupation, and *kollan* referred to the blacksmiths. These full-time craftsmen groups (*kollan* and *kuyavan*) became separate domestic segments that branched off from their primary clans in the process of hereditary specialization, by the turn of the Christian era. There are also archaeological evidences of metalwork, glass industry, brick constructions, weaving industry, pearl fisheries, stonecutting, and pottery. Gurukkal talks about the presence of *kolavan*, a domestic group who specialized in metalwork, as early as *c*.200 BCE in south India.[19]

Kuttikattu Purushothaman Choan, in *Nayarude Aadimathavu Pulayi Cherumi Ezhavarudeyum*,[20] has written a not so usual history of Kēraḷam's different caste groups. This book discusses about the argument on whether the ancestors of the craftsmen belonged to Azerbaijan and migrated to south India following a row with the Armenians. But due to lack of valid evidence, it is difficult to take this book into confidence.

Professor M.G.S. Narayanan, mentions that *taccan, taṭṭān*, and *ācāri* are terms employed in Kēraḷam for the Kammāḷar or artisan classes.[21] With reference to the titles like 'perumtaccan' and 'perumtaṭṭān', Narayanan observes that though these artisan classes were not admitted into the temples, they were given special privileges in view of their services to the temple and the right to use the king's name was one of that.[22] 'The rulers nominated some of them as the royal architects with the title of "perumtaccan" or "perumtaṭṭān", meaning "the great architect with the right to use the king's name"'.[23] He draws epigraphical evidences to prove that *vāniyar* (oil pressers), *taccar* (carpenters or smiths), and *vellālar* and *vellainātar* (agriculturists) had taken to hereditary occupations.

A. Sreedhara Menon, in *Cultural Heritage of Kerala*, has attributed a distinct chapter named 'Handicrafts of Kerala'.[24] But while giving a fair idea of the distinct craft items, he does not mention much about the artisans, and only classifies them into communities—even Muslim and Syrian Christian. He talks about many people employed in the manufacture of handicrafts on a hereditary basis. He mentions castes like *cembōṭṭi* (coppersmith), *taṭṭān* (goldsmith), *kaṇṇan* (brazier or bell metal worker), *taccan* (carpenter), *kollan* or *kaṛuvan* (blacksmith), etc. He traces the origin of the bell metal industry to the eighth century CE.

The community of *kaṇṇans* produced a variety of images of gods and goddesses, large *varpus* (shallow basin of hemispherical shape), and lamps of different patterns for religious and non-religious purposes. The *pañcalōhā* (an alloy of five metals) was used to manufacture images of deities or life-size statues of popular persons. The images of Hindu deities were designed on the basis of the norms prescribed in the *Tantra Samuccaya* or *Śilparatna*, and approved by the *tantris* (priests). Carving and art work in granite also had its origin in the seventh or eighth century CE. The main centre of this was Chengannur in Pathanamthitta district. Granite was available from nearby places like Thittamel and *kriṣnaśila*, a special rock for manufacturing idols for consecration in temples, was obtained from Omallur.

K.N. Ganesh has written about the evidences obtained from megaliths and pointed to the role played by different craft communities in the region.[25] The number of brass plates and statues, and bell metal and brass articles obtained suggests the presence of *mūśāris*. The clay deposits found in Kollam and Kasargod districts explains the abundant presence of earthen pots from the megaliths. *Uṇṇuneeli Sandēśam*, a fourteenth century CE literary work, while describing the market in Kollam, refers to the sale of large number of earthen bowls (*maṇcaṭṭi*).[26] This would strengthen the point on the presence of *cāliyan* or *vēlar*. Many of the megalithic artifacts were iron wares and there was the presence of iron ore deposits in Malabar region. The *kollan* would have specialized in purification of the iron ore to make these wares.[27] The *taṭṭān* would have been a necessary presence as the members of the affluent families were fond of gold ornaments, ranging from the *tōḍa* (earring), *kaḍukkan* (earring usually worn by men), *arañjāṇam* (girdle), bangles and *ratna mōtiram* (stone rings). The *āśāri* made houses and other buildings, boats, *pallakku* (palanquin), and *cangāḍams* (large wooden planks joined together for transportation in waterways).

Kaviyoor Murali has made a study on the *Purananūru*.[28] He has attempted to list out the various jati groups illustrated in *Cilappatikāram* and *Maṇimēkhalai*. *Kaṇṇan* and *chembukoṭṭi*, who worked in copper and tiles, and *taṭṭān*, who worked in gold, were *jatis* of the period of *Cilappatikāram*. Though there are debates about the age of this work, the author takes it to be the fifth century CE.[29] *Pulayar, kollar, taccan, veḷḷālan, parayan, kūttar, kuśavar,* was some of the jatis in the time of Maṇimēkhalai.

Nicholas B. Dirks has argued that caste in fact is neither an unchanged survivor of ancient India nor a single system that reflects a core cultural value.[30] He opines that 'the occupational groups specific to village life such as washers, blacksmiths, barbers and carpenters have been seen by others to express the quintessential character of caste as being defined by the division of labor and the provision of a complete array of social services for an agricultural economy.'[31]

There are historians from the south who have worked intensively on crafts production and craftsmen. Vijaya Ramaswamy in her essay, 'The Kudi in Early Tamilaham and the Tamil Women from Tribe to Caste'[32] refers to *kuyavar* (potters), *kollar* (blacksmiths), and *tachchan* (carpenter), as types of craftsmen and social groups in Sangam society. In the article titled 'Through History',[33] Ramaswamy pictures the history of craftsmen in south India from the pre-Christian era, down to the seventeenth century of colonial intervention. She points to the loss of freedom and decline of indigenous crafts due to the colonial methods like the 'putting out system'.

Ramaswamy in her article *Vishwakarma Craftsmen in Early Medieval Peninsular India*,[34] analyses the dynamics of social change among craft groups with particular reference to smiths, masons, and carpenters by focusing on the processes of temple building and urbanism in the Cōla-Pallava period. She states that the five craft groups—*taṭṭān* (goldsmith), *kaṇṇan* (brazier), *karuman* or *kollan* (blacksmith), *tachchan* (carpenter), and or *kal-tachchan* (mason) were known in the Tamil country as Kammāḷar, in Karnataka as Panchāḷar and in the Andhra as the Panchananamvaru. She writes that the social mobility of craft groups depended, among other things, on their importance to the economy and the changing nature of technology. She also writes that 'the terms *perum tachchan* and *perum kollan*, meaning the "great craftsman" also appear in many inscriptions from Tamil Nadu, and in some cases also indicate the employment of subordinate carpenters or goldsmiths working under the master-craftsman.'[35]

Kesavan Veluthat sees the emergence of prosperous trade and artisan guilds as part of the process by which the stratified society underwent standardization.[36] However none of these works have tried to look into the history of craftsmen from medieval Kēraḷam in particular.

Defining the Craft Communities in Kēraḷam

Medieval Kēraḷam must have possessed skilled workers of high craftsmanship, as is evident by the production of swords, shields, umbrellas, gold and silver ornaments, vessels, bows, arrows, and woodworks of exquisite patterns. The *āśāri*, *mūśāri*, *taṭṭān*, *kallan*, and *kollan* conventionally came under the title of Aiṅkuḍi Kammāḷar. 'The Jātinirṇaya would add a sixth also, viz., *tacan* or *ircakollan*, i.e. those whose work is to fell trees and saw timber.'[37] 'In the Cochin State instead of the *tacan*, the *tōlkollan*, the worker in leather forms the sixth subdivision, the *tacan* coming under the head of *mara-āśāri* or carpenter.'[38] However, this essay would limit itself to the five-fold division of the Aiṅkuḍi Kammāḷar.

The Aiṅkuḍi Kammāḷar can be defined as follows:

1. *Āśāri*: *marapaṇikkan/taccan/īrcakollan*. He is a worker in wood. *Taccan* refers to hewer of wood and *īrcakollan* to sewer of wood.
2. *Mūśāri*: *cemboṭṭi/kaṇṇan*. He is a brazier or coppersmith. He works in roofing tiles, or is a brass/bell metal worker.
3. *Taṭṭān*: He is a goldsmith or coppersmith.
4. *Kallan/kallāśāri*: He is worker in stone, or a stonemason.
5. *Kollan/karuvan*: He is worker in iron, or a blacksmith.

The ethnographic studies have come up with the following divisions among them.

Marayāśāri or *āśāri* group included five subcastes:

1. *taccan*: a generic term which denotes one who cut trees.
2. *īrtaccan*: one who is engaged in sawing or splitting of wood.
3. *koḷḷiveṭṭikaḷ*: one who took to cutting of firewood (*koḷḷi* means firewood, *veṭṭuka* means to cut), or one who examined the trees before felling (*parikṣa* means to examine).
4. *eṭṭilapariṣa*: who would have been a group of merchants (*eṭṭiyan* in Malayalam means *ceṭṭiyan* or merchant, *pariṣa* refers to any set or class of people).
5. *pūḷiyāśāri/pūḷitaccan*: sand carpenters (*pūḷi* is the earth put to roots of trees).

Ironsmith or *kollan* had three subdivisions:

1. *pariṣakollan*: the class or set of *kollans*.
2. *kadaccikollan*: the cutler, may be the labourer blacksmiths of lower rank (*kadaiṣiyar* means lowest/last).
3. *tīporikollan*: one who did soldering and handled the furnace (*tīpori* means spark).

Kallan had two subdivisions:

1. *śilpiyāśāri*: who made sculptures out of stones.
2. *kallāśāri*: who worked in stone.

The members of these subdivisions differed in the kind of work they did and also their position in the society. Most of these were endogamous groups, who refused inter-dining and some even observed untouchability among themselves. Thus, they created division of labour within the different groups of labour.

Stories from the Past

From the oral traditions, one would quickly identify the artisans in Kēraḷam as migrants from Tamil Nadu, belonging to the Tamil Vishwakarma caste or Aiṅkuḍi Kammāḷar from Tamil Nadu. In another section of this essay, an attempt has been made to probe into the issue of how the Kammāḷar groups of Kēraḷam were different from the migrant groups.

My fieldwork, undertaken in 2009, brought me in direct association with many people who could tell me the oral traditions. Vishwakarma, the divine architect, is said to have had five sons, namely, Manu, Māya, Śilpa, Tvaṣṭa and Daivagna. The *āśāris* are said to be the descendants of Māya, the *mūśāris* the descendants of Tvaṣṭa, and the *kollan*, the descendants of Manu.

Professor Sivam of the Vasthuvidya Gurukulam, an institution under the Department of Culture, Government of Kēraḷam, for the promotion and preservation of traditional architecture and mural painting, Aranmula, Pathanamthitta district, traced the origin of craftsmen to *aiṅkudi-manu* (*kollan*), *mayan* (*acāri*—wood), *tvasta* (*taṭṭān*), *śilpi* (stone statues, temple construction), and *visvajnan* (*mūśāri*). He said that *vāstuvidya* had its traces even in the Indus Valley Civilization and Dravidian cultures.

There are published legends regarding Vishwakarma. The sister of the great sage Brhaspati was an intellectual and a wise lady. She married the eighth Vasu, Prabhāsa. Their son is Vishwakarma, father of the *āśāri* group. They lived by doing manual labour.[39] Another tradition goes that the Vishwakarmas were brought to Kēraḷam by Paraśu Rāma, but they left for Ceylon on being pressed by one of the early Perumāḷ *satraps* of Cranganūr to marry into the community of washermen, after they had, by a special arrangement of a marriage shed, trapped and put a large number of that community to death.

Edgar Thurston has given an account of a similar legend, pertaining to the Kammāḷas, from the writings of Canter Visscher.[40] During the reign of Cēra Perumāḷ, a washerwoman, whose house was adjoined to that of an *āśāri* (carpenter), while occupied in washing a cloth in water, accidentally got ashes on the cloth and having no one to hold the other end of it, sought the help of the *āśāri's* young daughter who was alone at home. The girl, unaware of the social restrictions of untouchability, helped the woman. The washerwoman, emboldened by this act, entered the *āśāri's* house a few days later. On being questioned, the washerwoman replied that he (the *āśāri*) belonged to her caste now as his daughter had helped her with the cloth. The *āśāri*, learning of the disgrace that had befallen him, killed the washerwoman. Upon this, the woman's friends complained to the Perumāḷ king, who, in turn, threatened the carpenters. Consequently, the latter took refuge in Ceylon. The Perumāḷ king, now embarrassed at the unavailability of artisans to make necessary items for his kingdom, begged the king of Kandy to send them back. At the request of the carpenters, the king (of Kandy) also sent two *chegos* (cōgans) and their wives to accompany them (the carpenters) to witness the Perumāḷ king's conduct towards them and to protect them. The cōgans were entitled to receive (from the Perumāl king) three measures of rice at the occasions of death, marriage, and other ceremonies of the artisans.

The Epigraphical and Literary Past

Studies on the evidences from stone and copperplate inscriptions give an idea of the lives of the craftsmen in association to the growing temple corporations of medieval Kēraḷam. Elements of patronage were clearly recorded, with land grants and payments in cash and kind to the craftsmen from the rulers of the country, as well as the authorities of the temple. The history of medieval craftsmen is closely knit with the history of the sacred temples. Likewise, the status of master craftsmen can be seen as one in close association with the patronizing agents, as we see evidences of their high sounding titles. The practice of naming artisans after the title of the king was common. 'Perum' was a generic title used to refer to master craftsmen, like *perumtaṭṭān* and *perum kollan. Perumtaṭṭān* was also called *taṭṭāraparangōḍan* or *taṭṭārakaṇāran.* The name of the *nāḍu* was used as part of the artisan's title in the case of districts.

Another point is that a reading of the artisan groups from the inscriptions, from an understanding of them as caste groups from the later ethnographic and colonial records, can be problematic because in the earlier inscriptions they are referred to as occupational groups, mostly in association with the temples. Later, with characteristics of jati endogamy and hereditary, they turned into exogamous caste divisions.

Āśāri or *Taccan*

An *āśāri* or *taccan* is a person who works on wood, i.e. a carpenter. They are also called *marāśāri/marayāśāri* or *marapaṇikkan* (*maram* in Malayalam denotes tree), *tacan*, or *taccar*. Claiming to be descendants of Māya, they are the occupational group who took to carpentry. *Āśāricci* denotes the woman of the group. The traditional *nālukeṭṭu* (mansions) of Kēraḷam were designed and fabricated by these artisans according to the principles of *vāstu*. They were experts in the art of wood carving.

The *āśāri*, *mūśāri*, *taṭṭān*, *kollan*, and *kallan* conventionally came under the name of Kammāḷars. *Paṇikkan* is the generic name of these groups, meaning worker. 'Mūttāśāri' is the honorific title of the learned among them, proficient in *tacu śāstram* (science of architecture), architectural lore, in calculating formulae, and so on. 'In the Cochin state instead of the *tacan*, the *tōlkollan*, the worker in leather forms the sixth subdivision, the *tacan* coming under the head of *mara-āśāri* or carpenter.'[41]

A stone inscription from Cōkkūr, in Puthūr village, belonging to King Kōta Ravi of 898 CE,[42] mentions a *perumtaccan* (unnamed), Ciṟṟaṟaiyil Nankaiyar, and Cēravannāṭṭu Ceṭṭiyār. A stone inscription from Tiruvancikkulam dated *c.*1036 CE of King Rājasimha records a royal order. Amaicculḷurutti Kōyil Adhikāriaḷ stated that he was pleased to grant a *puraiyiḍam* to the chief architect of Rājasimha.[43] The revenue payment was fixed and a fine was prescribed for violation of rules. The *perumtaccan* (chief architect) is mentioned as 'Irayingapperuntaccan', i.e. the chief architect of Rājasimha. It was the custom for the royal architects, goldsmiths, carpenters, and merchants, etc., to be known by the king's name.

A stone inscription from Chēḷannūr has a reference to the *perumtaccan*. The name of king and regnal year are not clear. The palaeographic and linguistic features date the inscription to the late eleventh century. The scribe's name is stated as Kāri alias Perumtaccan.[44]

A mention of the term *taccācāriyan*, denoting the master carpenter of the temple of Uḍaiyār Karaikkoṇḍēśvaramuḍaiya-Nāyinār from 1228 CE has been recorded.[45] The *taccācāriyan*, named Sūryan Poṟkoḍi alias Iravivarma-āchāryan, at the instance of the Kaḍigaipaṭṭiṇam village assembly, engraved on stone an order regarding the assignment of land and income for expenses of *śrībali*.[46]

An increase in the knowledge of mathematical calculations in the medieval period was the consequence of the increasing need for developing *tacuśāstram* (architecture). A new division of *taccanmār* developed with the widespread construction of temples and *kōvilakams* (royal palace or mansion). Ganesh cites Uḷiyannūr Perumtaccan as an example of this group.[47]

The *taccar* are mentioned in the Tamil poems also. 'The poems mention *ūrtaccan* suggesting carpentry a full time hereditary occupation just as in the case of *kollan*.'[48] It is said that the services of artisans like the *taccar* were sought forth very much in the *marutam tiṇai*, it being an ecosystem of plough agriculture. From the evidences gathered from different types of boats and from specialists in sea fishing, it can be speculated that there existed a specialized group of boat-building *taccar* in ancient Tamilaham.

Mūppan was generally the leader of the community of *āśāris*, whom the Zamorins used to appoint. 'They were granted special privileges and control over their fellow community men.'[49] The same practice prevailed in medieval Cochin also. *Pūḻiyāśāri* was considered lower in status and even an untouchable among the other subcastes. This may be due to the legend that they returned long after the others from their exile in Ceylon and thus were not allowed to rejoin the caste.

Mūśāri

A *mūśāri* is a bell metal worker or a coppersmith. The common Malayalam term for a coppersmith is *cembōṭṭi*.[50] However, we do not find the use of this term in inscriptions or literary works till the fourteenth century CE. This term may have come into use later. *Mūśāri*, the descendants of Tvaṣṭa, are braziers. They manufacture household utensils as well as bell metal images. They make the household articles like *kiṇḍi* (goblet), *caṭṭi* (frying pan), *montha* (glass tumbler), *viḷakku* (lamp), etc.

One does not hear much about the availability of copper in the region. Ganesh states that there are pointers that copper came to Kēraḷam from outside.[51] In the case of bell metal used for making lamps, we find many references in inscriptions to substantiate its widespread use in the region. Instituting perpetual bell metal lamps was a very common practice in temples in medieval Kēraḷam. References to the number of donations made for the bell metal lamps, the measure of ghee set apart for lighting them, the lands donated for their establishment, or for provision of animals, are ample from the region. This proves that bell metal was in abundant use and was important in the temple economy of medieval Kēraḷam.

Perpetual lamps were instituted in the temples of Agamic deities. This came in as a strong, indispensable part of daily worship and installation of deities within the temple. The increased significance of the lamps in the temples of the Kēraḷam region further amplifies the role of *mūśāris* in the social scenario. There was the practice of gifting lamps as 'perpetual lamps' (*kedāviḷakku/anthaviḷakku-keda/antha*, meaning that which never extinguishes) to temples by 10 CE.

The Huzur office plates of Ko Karunandaḍakkan (864–5 CE) refer to a donation made for burning perpetual lamps in the Viṣṇubhaṭṭāraka temple in the village of Pārthivaśēkharapuram. Śaḍaiyan Tanichchege alias Teṇṇāttukōṇ, who perpetually took up the enjoyment of the *kārāṇmai* (right of cultivation, office of a *kārāḷan*, a freehold), and *kīḻpādi* of the garden (the *kārāḷan's* share from the land) named Neḍuma . n in Kīḻūr situated on the west of Medugu, granted its *kārāṇmai* and *mē. rpādi* (owner's share on those lands) for burning the perpetual lamps.[52] This installation of perpetual lamps invariably points to the presence of *mūśāris* and the role they played during the proliferation of temples by the ninth century CE.

A rock inscription of 9 CE in the south *prākāra* of the Shiva temple at Tiruviḍaikkōḍu of the King Ko Karunandaḍakkan records the gift of twenty-five cows by Seḻiyanda for maintaining a perpetual lamp. The donation, made in an assembly of townsmen and others (the inscription is fragmented), by the order of Saḍaiyaṉ, of twenty-five full-grown cows, which neither die nor become old, was for the purpose of burning, at the rate of one *uḻakku* of ghee per day, a perpetual lamp before the Mahadēva at Tiruviḍaikkōḍu.[53] It is mentioned that the cows do not die or grow old because they multiply and hence their number shall remain not less than twenty-five. Even if some die, the number and quality remain the same. Another rock inscription in the south *prākāra* of the Shiva temple at Tiruviḍaikkōḍu[54] records the gift of a perpetual lamp to the Mahādēva. This is dated to 9 CE, in the month of *Piraṭṭāśi*, and it will also burn at the rate of an *uḻakku* of ghee a day. The details of the gift have been worn out from the inscription.

The Parthivapuram stone inscription of *Kollam* 98 (923 CE)[55] mentions one Kumaran Nārāyanan alias Panchavan Brahmādhirajan of Idaikulattur, who set-up two perpetual lamps in the temple of Vishnu at Pārthivaśēkharapuram. This is suggestive of the fact that there were makers of lamps either associated with the temple or in close vicinity of the temple. The Kaviyūr stone inscription of year 4052 of the Kali era (950–1 CE)[56] mentions that from 15 *kalams* (pots of paddy) got from the field called Eṭṭikari, two perpetual lamps must be burnt before the god of Kaviyūr. This piece of land was offered by two private individuals, one of whom was Narayanan Keyavan. Here, the reference to perpetual lamps, usually bell metal lamps, indicate the presence of bell metal workers (*mūśāris*). These lamps might also have been huge stone lamps with a provision to light them with oil.

The Kollur Madom plates of Udaya Mārttāṇḍa Varman also record terms like *ākkal vāṇiyar*, which are believed to have been used to refer to smiths. It mentions twenty *parai* of paddy being set apart for the *ākkal vāṇiyar* from the land grants.[57] Another inscription on the south base of the Viṣṇu temple at Parthivapuram village in Vilavankōṭu of the Cōla-Pāndya dynasty, belonging to King Sundara Cōḷa Pāṇḍya in Tamil Vaṭṭeḷuttu, refers to the stone steps and a gift of a perpetual lamp to the temple.[58] This indicates the presence of *mūśāris* and *kallans* in association with the temple.

A stone inscription from the Mahādēva temple at Kuricci in Caṅganāccēri, dated *Kollam* 595 (1420 CE) states that one Kumaran covered the roof with copper and had the purification ceremony performed in Mēdam.[59] Kumaran could be the person who made donations for the work, or he might have been the supervisor of the work. It could hardly be the name of the worker. The reference implies that copper was an easily available material for construction and that coppersmiths were also readily available.

The Nāvāykkuḷam stone inscription of *Kollam* 614 (1439 CE)[60] states that the King Vīra Mārttāṇḍa Varman of Kīlappērūr, the head of the Jayatuṅganāḍu branch of the Vadaśēri Illam, began the repairs to the temple of Śankaranārāyaṇa Mūrti of Nāvāykkuḷam and built the temple out of stone, built the central shrine and the mandap, and covered the *paḍippurai* with copper. It might be that stone and copper were considered as privileged media of construction in 15 CE. It is seen that society at large had the concept of assigning mud as the popular medium of construction of houses for the common people. 'The local convention required that houses of wood and stone be built only for kings and Gods.'[61]

In *Uṇṇiyaccicaritam*, in one of the starting verses there is a reference to a temple at Triccaḷari, which was constructed using copper by the Purakiḷār king out of his bhakti.[62] This reveals the presence of coppersmiths who were employed in the construction of temples. In the verses which describe Uṇṇiyacci, we find references to different types of lamps like hand lamps and *nanmaṇi* lamps.[63] There is the mention of a lamp in which spices were burnt.[64] This shows that among the various bell metal workers, there were people with high levels of expertise who could make different kinds of lamps, and these lamps were a part and parcel of the social life of people at that time. Hence, when the poet uses these symbols of lamps to describe the beauty of Uṇṇiyacci, the readers can easily relate to this.

In *Uṇṇiyaccicaritam*, in the portion about the description of the market, there is a mention of threads made by melting metals. It is stated that fifty of these metal threads will be enough to impart copper colour to a dress material.[65] This again points to the expertise in metalwork and garment-making.

Taṭṭān

They are goldsmiths, also called *swarṇapaṇikkan* or *swarṇāśāri. Taṭṭāti* is the word for the women of the group and *taṭṭakuḍi* is their dwelling place. They follow the occupation of manufacturing jewellery, which also includes setting of precious stones in ornaments, manufacture of silverware, plating of metal articles, and metal engraving. Gold and silver ornaments in various designs are made by them. The Tamil Vishwakarma is an artisan community seen in Kēraḷam. They migrated from Tamil Nadu and are addressed as *pāṇḍitaṭṭān* or *kammada* by the Keralites. They are a community of goldsmiths. These artisans do modelling and engraving on gold and silver and sometimes on stone and wood also.

The references to *taṭṭān* groups associated with temples are evident in literary sources of the time period between the eight and sixteenth centuries CE. The *Uṇṇuneeli Sandēśam*,[66] which Elamkulam P.N. Kunjan Pillai has dated between 1350 and 1365 CE, has evidences of place names which are closely associated with the goldsmiths. There are references to a *Taṭṭānkāvu* or *Tiṭṭayil purayiḍam* (land belonging to a *taṭṭān*), which had a Gaṇapati temple earlier.[67] This might have been the place allotted to the *taṭṭanmar* (goldsmiths) by the temple authorities. This place was near the Umayanallūr temple (near Kollam, which was the capital of Vēṇāḍ till 1525 CE) and an old pathway of Kollaperuvaḷi.

Another place, whose name is associated with the *taṭṭān* is Taṭṭārambalam, between Kāyamkuḷam and Kanḍiyūr.[68] This place is near two Viṣṇu temples. From this, we can infer that this must have been a settlement of goldsmiths, who lived near the two temples.

References to the individual names of *taṭṭāns* are found from the period of the Pallavas also. 'A *thattan* called Nripatunga of the period of Pallava King Nripatunga was the son of Madevi Perum Thattan and the grandson of Uditodaya Perum Thattan. A *mahakashtakari* (great architect) named Parameswara is mentioned in the period of Pallava King Parameswara alias Nandivarman Pallava Malla.'[69]

The inscription of the Shiva temple at Kaṇḍiyūr, dated 946 CE,[70] mentions two men—Iravi Kumaran of Kōdikkulam and Tirukkuṇrappolan Rāman-Taṭṭān—as holding the *pandāravāriyam*. This suggests that Tirukkuṇrappolan Rāman-Taṭṭān was considered worthy of holding the coveted post of *pandāravāriyam*, which denoted a position of power in the temple.

The inscription of the ninth year of the reign of Parantaka Pāṇḍya records that the king had set up ten beautiful golden lamps of rare workmanship for the god at Anantapuram.[71] He granted the village of Tayanattu for the upkeep of these golden lamps in the temple at Anantaśayanam (Trivandrum). This inscription proves the significance and prestige attached to gold in the region. Moreover, if the inscription records of having rare workmanship, there must have been *taṭṭāns* of exemplary expertise, who were appointed to manufacture these lamps.

This instance reminds one of the Ēḷaraponnāna in Ēṭṭumanūr Mahādēva temple. On the eighth day of *Valiya Viḷakku* festival, the image of the deity is taken in a procession to a specially decorated site called *āstāna maṇḍapa* in the north-west corner of the temple. It is only in this day that the unique treasure of the temple, Ēḷaraponnāna—the seven and a half elephants representing the *aṣṭadikpālakas* (guardians of the eight cardinal directions)—are also displayed. Seven of these golden elephants are two feet in height while the eighth is a foot high. It is also said that the Ēḷaraponnāna represents the *aṣṭadiggajams*, which are Airāvatam, Pundarīkam, Kanmudam, Añjana, Puṣpadantam, Supradīkam, Sarvabhauman, and Vamana. These precious figures of seven big elephants and one baby elephant in solid gold, along with a *paḷukka kula* (a bunch of areca nuts) made of gold, were gifted by Maharaja Kārthika Thirunal in ME 964 (Malayalam Era), i.e. 1789 CE. Each of the seven elephants weighs about 90 kg. and the smaller one, half of that. This is another example of how gold continued (something that it still does) to be held in very high esteem as a metal to be used to make gifts to god.

The name of a *taṭṭān* is seen in the Tirunelli copperplate inscription of Śrī Bhāskara Varman. This inscription mentions of the person who wrote it—Bāluśśēri Gaṇapati Nīlakaṇḍan alias Kurumbranāṭṭu

Perumtaṭṭān.[72] It read as 'Kaṇapati Nīlakaṇḍanāyina Kuṟumburai Perumtaṭṭan'.[73] This *taṭṭān* might have been an important person in his field, who was attached to the king's palace, and when an order was issued regarding the Tirunelli temple, it was written by him. This association to the king may have been the reason for his being named the *perumtaṭṭān* of the *nāḍu* as well.

The Kottayam copperplate inscription of Vīra Rāghava Cakravartin, who claims to be a lineal descendant of Vīra Kērala Cakravartin, dated to the fourteenth century CE, ends with the signature of the goldsmith who engraved it. He boasts of the title 'Śēraman-lōka-pperundaṭṭān',[74] i.e. 'the great goldsmith of the world [which belongs to] the Cēra king'. This shows the custom of the kings conferring titles on royal artisans. The copperplate has a mention of 'maṇigrāmam' as a title conferred upon a person by the name of Iravikoṟṟan.[75] The king conferred the title of 'maṇigrāmam', and certain honours and rights connected therewith, on Iravikoṟṟan of Magōdaiyarpaṭṭiṇam who was also called Śēramān-lōka-pperuñjeṭṭi. It is clear that Iravikoṟṟan was a merchant. The epithet *ceṭṭi* (merchant), the trade rights, the sources of revenue thrown open to him, who was a head of *maṇigrāmam*, gives the view that *maṇigrāmam* was a trading corporation as well. Line 11 of the inscription is translated thus, 'We [also] gave the oil-mongers and the five [classes of] artisans as [his] slaves.'[76] The grant was not personal, but hereditary and perpetual. Line 22 of the inscription can be translated in this way—'The handwriting of Śēraman-lōka-pperun-daṭṭān Nambi Śaḍeyan̲, who wrote [this] copperplate with the knowledge of these [witnesses].' There is also the reference to Aiṅkuḍi Kammāḷar, the five classes of artisans, who were the *āśāri*, *mūśāri*, *taṭṭān*, *kallan/kallāśāri*, and *kollan*. Here, we need to note the fact that these five classes of artisans were transferred as slaves. This low position of the artisans is in dire contradiction with the high status of the great *taṭṭan*—Śēraman-lōka-pperundaṭṭān Nambi Śaḍeyan̲, who was given the right to be called after the king's name, and whose name was engraved as part of the inscription. This rightly points to the feature of hierarchy that existed within these artisan groups, and how, when one person rose to a privileged position, the others were in such a low state that they were sold as slaves.

An inscription on a stone lying in the north side of the yard of the Vishnu temple at Parthivapuram village during the Cōḷa Dynasty, in Tamil language, is by the King Vira Cōḷaperumāḷ. It states that Sankaran Ranasingan set-up a silver idol in the temple.[77] Consequently, it can be agreed upon that there were *taṭṭāns* working on the silver entrusted for this.

A Kanyakumari plate[78] has records that King Bālarāma Varma Kulaśēkhara Perumāl had ordered and provided 3,000 *paṇam* for the expenses of making a silver idol for *śrībali* and *tiruvaṇḍippākkaṭṭai* (beam to be put at the entrance) to the accountant of the temple of Kannimākumarippagavati-Amman. The inscription mentions the measures of gold and silver utilized in making the image for *śrībali*, indicating specialized work undertaken by craftsmen for the purpose. This indicates that as part of the practice of patronage, extended by the kings, the activities of the craftsmen were monitored by the kings. The kings were well aware of the works done by craftsmen who worked in silver and other metals. Interestingly, we find mention of *ceṭṭis* (merchants) of Kōṭṭār, who, along with *śāntikkar* (priests), *piḷḷaimār* and *taḷattār* (managers), temple ryots, *nāṭṭār* (influential citizens), and *nagarattār* (citizens), are recorded to have given *vaḻipāḍu* in the estimate of income of the temple. This suggests that the temple definitely would have been an active centre or associated with trade with the presence of *ceṭṭis* among the devotees, as well as other influential sections of the societal setup. The craftsmen and the mode of production would have been affected by their presence, and it is possible that these rich sections made donations for buildings and craftworks outside the direct mention of this inscription.

Uṇṇiyaccicaritam has descriptions regarding the appearance of the heroine, Uṇṇiyacci. It is stated that she wore a gold ornament on her waistline.[79] This points to the importance of gold as a material for making ornaments among the affluent class and the presence of *taṭṭāns* who made them. In the description about Śrīparvatam market in *Uṅṅiyāḍicaritam*, one finds mention of the *ceṭṭis* who were gold merchants, and *pāṇḍi taṭṭāns* and *āśāris*, who were merchants.[80] These groups of people thus were very much a part of the daily lives of the common people in the latter half of the fourteenth century CE.

Kallan

They are also called *kallāśāri/mūppar*. They are traditional stonemasons or sculptors. They make stone statues for temples and make steps for the temple ponds (*kuḷam*). They are also proficient in the art of stone carving. Images of gods and goddesses are sculptured by them. *Kallāśāris* and *śilpiyāśāris* may have been increasingly active in the eighth and ninth centuries CE, when the Kēraḷam region saw influences of heterodox sects like Buddhists and Jainas in art and architecture. The rock-cut Jaina images of Chitaral Hill of the ninth century CE and the stone image of Buddha in sitting posture at Mavelikara (around the same time) are indications of this. The cave temple at Kaviyūr dated to the eighth century CE has a stone sculpture of the *dvārapāla* (chieftain). This figure of the chieftain or the donor bear resemblances to Pallava *dvārapālas* and other figures of the Drāviḍa country. Stella Kramrisch opines that 'the stone sculptures in Travancore although few in number are representative of South Indian sculpture from the eighth to sixteenth century.'[81] These evidences points to a healthy exchange of ideas and concepts between artisan communities in south India. This may also be indicative of the influence of migration of artisans from the Tamil country.

A stone inscription from Tiruvangūr of King Bhaskara Ravi, the date of which is thought of to be as 997 CE or 1013 CE, records that Makalur Nārāyanan Kēcavan built a *balikkal* and instituted regular expense of *nāḻi* rice.[82] This refers to the active presence of stonemasons—*kallan* or *kallāśāris*.

A stone inscription from Rāmantaḷi at the foot of Ēḻimala, at base of the central shrine of Narayankaṇṇur temple, dated 1075 CE, belonging to King Kunda Āḷupar,[83] records that Hiranyagarbhan constructed the image of the deity (not specified). The *śrīkōyil* (the sanctum sanctorum of the temple) was built in granite with the help of Kunda Āḷuparaiyar, and Chandraśēkharan constructed the shrine. This was done in the time of Kunran Bhaṭṭan and Bhaṭṭa Nāraṇan. This shows the time of renovation of the temple. Here the king was the donor for the image and the *śrīkōyil.*

A stone inscription in the Shiva temple at Mannancēri, dated *Kollam* 878 (1703 CE),[84] shows that stonework in the temple was given significance and Ceruvelli Iṭṭiṇṇan is mentioned to have contributed to some portion of the stonework in the temple. On the other side of the same pillar, it is recorded that the southern block was built by the same individual. This is dated *Kollam* 872 (1697 CE) and is in Tamil Vaṭṭeḷuttu script.[85] On another pillar in the same temple, dated, *Kollam* 878 (1703 CE), *Karkaṭakam* 18, the completion of some stoneworks is recorded in Tamil Vaṭṭeḷuttu.[86] This may suggest that individuals also would have considered it a privilege and status symbol to take part in temple construction and that stonework constituted a significant portion of the temples to attract sponsors. This also suggests that even individuals may have employed the *kallans*, besides the temple authorities or rulers.

Kollan

A *kollan* is also called a *kaṛuvan*. The term *perumkollan* is often used to indicate a great *kollan* or a renowned *kollan*. *Kollakurupu* is the headman of the smiths, *kollathi* is the women folk, and *kollapura kollakudi* refers to their house. They work as blacksmiths for the different communities. They also work as agricultural labourers. They manufacture locks and keys, cutlery, knives, small-scale weapons, agricultural implements like ploughshares, mattocks, weeding spuds, and weaving instruments like thread wheel, *koduvāḷ*, and *adi irumbu*. A *tīkollan* is an ironsmith who makes wheels for carts. Kathikkarans form a small community of blacksmiths found in Marungur in Agasthiswaram taluk, Travancore. 'They were engaged in the manufacture of steel and in the smelting of iron ore obtained from a mine at Vannathumkulam near Suchindram.'[87]

There is the reference in *Uṇṇuneeli Sandēśam* to *kōṭṭayil kollans*' house near the Iravipuram palace.[88] These *kollans* or blacksmiths may have been associated with the palace, and so the king had given them the land to settle there.

Women

Women among the artisan classes generally had a secondary status. They were confined to household duties and mainly assisted in traditional occupations. They were regarded as being 'impure' during menstruation periods and childbirth. During these periods, they were not allowed to take part in any ritual or religious functions, which otherwise they would have been a part of. Also, women at large did not have the right to inherit family property.

Women had roles in agricultural practices, collection of fuel (like dry wood), and fetching water in pots. Women among *kollan* also made mats out of palmyra leaves (*ōlapai*) and sold them. Though they contributed to the family income and sometimes controlled the family expenditure, they did not have much say in the major decisions of the family.

The Cruise over Centuries

With a shift from the sacred to the profane, the craftsmen claim a fall in their status. One cannot possibly disentangle the history of crafts from the history of jati and caste system. Even though the craft groups of the region belonged to various castes, they came under the larger classification of 'Kammāḷars'. Moreover, the economic status and social position of the groups were liable to change.[89] The upward and downward social mobility of the craft groups largely depended on their economic status, which kept altering over different time periods.

The artisan classes were often not placed high in the society. In course of time, they merged into the social system of the region (Kēraḷam) as a natural process. 'Those who were engaged in the artisanal activities, such as the different varieties of smiths, carpenters, washermen, etc., were lower on the scale.'[90] The artisan groups have expanded in the society over time in proportion to the expansion of wetland agriculture. There were 'further refinements in the graded hierarchy of caste society to which more and more professional groups came into being as so many endogamous kinship groups.'[91] Groups like *taccar* and *tattar* are mentioned as parts of the vast Dravidian society. They may have gradually sunk further into the bottom of the social organization with the influx of the Aryan brahmins. These divisions were based on hereditary professions and were sometimes reinforced by their place of origin.[92]

The Parthivapuram stone inscription of *Kollam* 98 (923 CE)[93] mentions the potter Śeṅgōdan, who, with his brothers and nephews, were entitled to the repair and maintenance of the Vishnu temple, the *vādli-māḍam* (hall over the gateway and the gateway), and the *śurḷu-maṇḍapam* (space where devotees made a procession or circle around the central shrine). This reference brings out the hereditary nature of those who were involved with the repairs and maintenance of the temple. The craftsmen involved in the repair work might have been contacted by generations of the potter's family.

By the fifteenth century CE, the notions of 'purity' and 'pollution' became so strong in Kēraḷam that the craft communities were denied close intermingling with the other social groups and castes. An evidence of this can be seen from a stone inscription from the Parthivapuram village during the Cōla-Pāṇḍya dynasty, dated *Kollam* 616 (1441 CE).[94] It refers to an order issued by the king (unnamed) while staying at the house of Kṛṣṇan-Acyutan of Kalcirai, that the *taccar*, *kollar*, *kolaccar*, etc., living between Poykai and Tōvāḷai, shall not enjoy the privileges of throwing stones[95] or even knocking at doors. This may also be suggestive of the fact that these groups might have taken to these activities, and that there might have been complaints to the king about it. Consequently, he put an end to these practices through a royal order.

The Mitrānandapuram inscription of 1486 CE[96] records that an individual *nambi* by the name of Oliññanambi Pavitrankāli

Piladiśuvaran was among the prominent people who were instrumental in carrying out repairs to the Vishnu temple of Mitrānandapuram. He was also responsible for consecrating the idol and covering the pinnacle of the temple with copper.

In this context, a reference from *Uṇṇicirutēvicaritam* becomes relevant. Scholars have dated this literary work to the latter half of the fourteenth century CE. In the *caritam*, where a description of the Ciṭṭaṅgāḍi market is given, we come across a conversation between the slave women of Uṇṇicirutēvi's house. In that portion, there is a dialogue which says that a slave woman was born among the *jonakar* (a low caste) and *taccar*. In other words, the poet is suggesting that *taccar* had a low social status and that the slave woman was rightfully born in that group.[97]

The occupational group of *āśāris* claimed a higher status in the social hierarchy, which may be because wood was a plentifully available raw material in the Kēraḷam region. The constructions with exquisite wooden roofing and elaborate wooden carvings became popular with the rise in significance of Nair *taravāḍ*. 'The nālukeṭṭu and eṭṭukeṭṭu nair houses having four or eight roofs and a corresponding number of wings, sets of apartments of rooms, appear to have been built in conformity with *vāstu-śāstra* from the days of Viśvakarma prakasha and the Bṛhat Samhita.'[98] We have inscriptional reference to a brahmin architect named Bālakāntāra from a lithic record[99] engraved on the *oṟṟakkal* mandap of the Padmanābhasvamīn temple. It says that King Bālamārttanda Varman, with the assent of a certain Padmanābhēndra-Yōgi, rebuilt from *vimāna* to *dīpaśāla* through a brahmin architect Bālakāntāra, set up the *oṟṟakkal*, the images of the gods Padmanābha, Lakshmī, Bhūmi, the *parivāradēvatās*, the serpent couch, and also performed the *kumbhābhiṣēkha* ceremony.[100] This is a clear inscriptional evidence denoting the caste of the architect. Since it was engraved on the *oṟṟakkal* mandap, it was a record of public display, suggesting the motive behind the engraver, here the king.

The economic activity of the artisan communities was very much related to the social set-up. It is seen that these communities actively took part in paying taxes or contributed to the welfare of the temples, sometimes even forcibly. There is a palm leaf document in Tamil Malayalam script,[101] in possession of Kombi Achchan, the head of one of the branches of the Palghāt royal family residing at Koṇikkal-edam, dated Saka 1693, *Kali* 4722, *Khara*, *Kārttigai* 8, i.e. 1771 CE. It states that the members of the four divisions of the artisan class (*taṭṭān*) living in four villages, resolved to agree for the levying of a poll tax on the members of their community living in these villages, in order to meet the expenses of the daily worship of God Viśvanāthasvāmin, Goddess Viśālākshi Amman, and God Sabhāpati at Kalpātti.

One however, does not come to know which group of the artisans was exempted in this case. Since it was a poll tax and not a donation, there is some amount of power and force involved from the authorities, here, the temple authorities, in imposing the tax on the four groups of artisans. This shows that even in the eighteenth century, the status of certain groups of artisans remained low and they faced exploitation at the hands of the higher authorities.

Even though the notion of purity and pollution was there in early Kēraḷam, the settlement pattern in the society reveals the mixture of the entire population living together. 'Availability of water in every field made it possible for every household to have their own sources of water and therefore the so called polluting sections could live in the neighborhood of "pure" sections without polluting the most important sources of water.'[102] Yet another cause for the interspersed settlement pattern is the fact that individual villages in Kēraḷam were not marked and a place 'outside a village' could scarcely be identified.

A list of the distance of pollution each community had to maintain with others is given in Table 13.1.[103] This denotes the distance that these communities had to maintain with others in order to keep up the 'purity quotient' in the society. This distance of untouchability is *tīṇḍāpāḍu-dūram*.

The economic life of the artisan community is often associated with the proliferation of temples. 'All arts and crafts were integrated with the agrarian society as localized customary services.'[104] It is seen that the temples at times acted as an institutional force in regulating and monitoring the artisan groups, who were often made to settle in temple lands, in order to ensure their services to the temples. The right to occupation of land was thus given to ensure service to the temples. Very soon this led to the localization of services of artisans and their receding to the servile position of mere bondsmen of the temple.

The artisan communities were mainly involved in agricultural activities by indirectly supporting cultivation through the manufacture and supply of necessary tools and implements. 'Services of the blacksmiths and the carpenters were essential for the ruling sections, their retainers, other owning groups and ordinary members of the society including agricultural as well as non-agricultural sections and this seems to explain their presence in every *dēśam* units.'[105]

TABLE 13.1: *Tīṇḍāpāḍudūram* for different communities

Communities	*Tīṇḍāpāḍudūram (in ft.)*
Kshatriya to Brahmin	2
Vaishya to Kshatriya	2
Shudra to Vaishya	2
Vaishya to Brahmin	6
Āśāri to Nāyar	24
Kammāḷar, Tiyyar, and Mukkuvar to others	24
Kammāḷa to Nāyar	24
Āśāri to Brahmin	36
Kammāḷa to Brahmin	36
Kollan to others	24
Pulayan, Parayan, Vaḷḷuvan, and Kāṭṭāḷan to others	64
Nāyāḍi to others	72

There was also the understandable recognition of political power and submission to the authorities. 'There was a custom of blacksmiths, carpenters, basketmakers and umbrella makers supplying tools, implements and articles of daily use made by them to the aristocratic families on festive occasions.'[106] Remuneration in cash or kind, in addition to a meal, was given in return to them.

Issues of Migration

The history of crafts communities in Kēraḷam would not be complete without a mention of the migration of many of these groups from the neighbouring regions. The migrant communities have very much formed a part of the local, social, and cultural milieu of the land. These communities had regional variations in cultural practices.

Pāṇḍi taṭṭān, or the Tamil Vishwakarmas, migrated to Kēraḷam at the invitation of different rulers. It is pointed out that as carpenters (*āśāri*) were available in the region, only four subgroups—*kollan, kallāśāri, taṭṭān*, and *mūśāri*—came from Tamil Nadu. Within Kēraḷam were artisans with similar professions, who called themselves Vishwakarmas. They were divided in five groups—*āśāri, mūśāri, taṭṭān, kollan*, and *kallāśāri*, who were carpenters, braziers, goldsmiths, blacksmiths, and stonemasons respectively. Though the professions were the same, they differed in culture, traditions, and customs. The *pāṇḍi taṭṭāns* had specific *gōtras* and practiced exogamous marriage. 'Many Tamil *kammāḷans* have naturalized themselves on the west coast and speak Malayalam.'[107] They refused to intermarry or inter-dine with the Malayalam Kammāḷas.

This essay raises a question as to how far we can read the history of artisan and craft groups of Kēraḷam out of the old edifice of migrant 'Aiṅkuḍi Kammāḷas' as an indigenous group with characteristics which makes them known to the region. Their social practices, nature of work and finished products, and economic activities—all prove that they had an indigenous character. Kramrisch, who studied about the art and architecture of Travancore, has opined that the artisans' works in Kēraḷam is considered as the Kēraḷam school of architecture pertaining to Malabar/west coast of south India.[108]

Makers of *Āranmuḷa Kaṇṇāḍi*

The Tamil Vishwakarmas are renowned in Kēraḷam for the production of a type of metal mirror called *āranmuḷa kaṇṇāḍi*. The mirror is made of a combination of tin, copper, and bronze, and is said to have had an incidental origin while the artisans were making a crown for the Pandalam Raja.[109] Sreedhara Menon attributes the secret behind the *āranmuḷa kaṇṇāḍḍi* to the Tamil Kammāḷa and draws evidence from an eighteenth century CE mural in the Padmanābhasvāmi temple, Thiruvananthapuram.[110]

P. Gopakumar, the master craftsman of Aditi Handicrafts Centre at Āranmuḷa in Ceṅgannūr, Pathanamthitta district of Kēraḷam, traced his ancestry to the Tamil Vishwakarma community from Śankarankōvil in Tamil Nadu. His ancestors were invited and offered settlements in Āranmuḷa by the then Travancore Raja, in connection with the work in eight temples in central Travancore. The Ceṅgannūr temple was one of them. The Kaviyūr temple, which is noted for the stonework and the stone figure of *dvārapāla* is one among these eight temples.

Conclusion

An analysis of the evidences from various sources regarding the Aiṅkuḍi Kammāḷar from Kēraḷam in medieval times points to certain facts. One of them is that there definitely were indigenous craftsmen in the region, irrespective of the migrations from other regions of the southern part of the country. These craftsmen contributed their own skills and efforts towards the production of a variety of items, some of them for rituals with sacred significance, and the others for utility in daily lives. The royal patronage towards these craftsmen and artisans is clear from the inscriptional evidences. From the *caritam* sources, we find their presence in market areas, and hence their role and importance in providing products for daily use for common men, as different from the craftsmen we see in inscriptions who made idols to be consecrated in the sacred space of the temples. Hence, we find a rich presence of the Aiṅkuḍi Kammāḷar in medieval Kēraḷam, both within and outside the sacred space of the temple. They thus were an indispensable presence in the larger society.

Notes

1. Krishna K.V. Aiyar, *A Short History of Kerala*, Ernakulam: Devi and Company, 1966.
2. M.G.S. Narayanan, *Perumals of Kerala: Political and Social Conditions of Kerala under the Cera Perumals of Makotai (c. 800 A.D.-1124 A.D.)*, Calicut: Xavier Press, 1996.
3. Rajan Gurukkal, *The Kerala Temple and the Early Medieval Agrarian System*, Sukapuram: Vallathol Vidyapeetham, 1992; Narayanan, *Perumals of Kerala*.
4. Kesavan Veluthat, 'Religious Symbols in Political Legitimation: The Case of Early Medieval South India', *Social Scientist*, vol. 21, no. 1/2, 1993, pp. 23–33, see http://www.jstor.org/stable/3517836, accessed on 26 April 2010.
5. Devangana Desai wrote about the time period between 900 and 1300 CE in south India as being one of the third phases of urbanization. She opined that this was the period of social transformation in south India, as it showed the development of huge agrarian corporations presided over by temple-centred brahminical settlements, *dāna* to temples and brahmins by the rulers who sought their support in legitimization of their authority, etc. Devangana Desai, 'Social Dimensions of Art in Early India', *Social Scientist*, vol. 18, no. 3, 1990, pp. 3–32, see http://www.jstor.org/stable/3517423, accessed on 20 April 2010. Also, see Noburu Karashima, *History and the Society in South India: The Cholas to Vijayanagar*, New Delhi: Oxford University Press, 2001.
6. Francis Day, *The Land of the Perumals, or Cochin: Its Past and its Present*, New Delhi: Asian Educational Services, 2006.
7. K.P. Padmanabha Menon, *History of Kerala*, vol. 3, Ernakulam: Cochin Government Press, 1933.
8. Elamkulam Kunjan Pillai, *Keralacharithrathile Iruladanja Edukal*, Kottayam: National Book Stall, 1957.

9. Komattil Achyutha Menon, *Ancient Kerala: Studies in its History and Culture*, Thrissur: National Book Stall, 1961, p. 195.
10. George W. Spencer, ed., *Temples, Kings and Peasants: Perceptions of South India's Past*, Madras: New Era Publications, 1987.
11. P.S. Velayudhan, ed., *Kerala Charithram*, vol. 1, Ernakulam: Kerala History Association, 1973. T.K. Gangadharan also refers to castes and subcastes, taking evidences from inscriptions. However, he shares the idea that 'each new caste or subcaste was formed from the various professional groups of hereditary nature.' T.K. Gangadharan, *Evolution of Kerala History and Culture*, Calicut: Calicut University Publication, 1999, p. 187.
12. Nalumkel Krishna Pillai, *Mahakshetrangalude Munnil*, Kottayam: Sahitya Pravarthaka Cooperative Society Ltd, Kerala, 1980.
13. *Marayāśari* included five subcastes—*thachan* (who cut trees), *iirthachan* (who cut the felled trees), *kollivettikal*, *ettilaparisha*, and *poozhiyashari*. Again, *kollan* had three subdivisions—*palishakollan*, *kadachikollan*, and *theeporikollan*. *Kallāśari* also had two subdivisions—*shilpiyashari*, who made sculptures out of stones, and kallashari who worked in stone. Balakrishnan further mentions that *moosharis*, who worked in roofing tiles, also had two subcastes. P.K. Balakrishnan, *Jativyavasthithiyum Keralacharithravum* [1983], Kottayam: D.C. Books, 2008, p. 362.
14. James Heitzman, 'Temple Urbanism in Medieval South India', *The Journal of Asian Studies*, vol. 46, no. 4, 1987, pp. 791–826, see http://www.jstor.org/stable/2057102, accessed on 20 April 2010.
15. Karashima, *History and the Society in South India*, p. 162; Vijaya Ramaswamy, *Textiles and Weavers in Medieval South India*, New Delhi: Oxford University Press, 2006, p. 58.
16. S. Sundararajan, *Ancient Tamil Country: Its Social and Economic Structure*, New Delhi: Navrang, 1991, p. 79.
17. Gurukkal, *Kerala Temple and the Early Medieval Agrarian System.*
18. Rajan Gurukkal, 'From Clan and Lineage to Hereditary Occupations and Caste in Early South India', *Indian Historical Review*, vol. 20, 1993–4, pp. 22–33.
19. Ibid.
20. Kuttikattu Purushothaman Choan, *Nayarude Aadimathavu Pulayi Cherumi Ezhavarudeyum*, Thrissur: Akshara Publications, 1993.
21. Narayanan, *Perumals of Kerala.*
22. Ibid., p. 153.
23. Ibid.
24. A. Sreedhara Menon, *Cultural Heritage of Kerala*, Madras: S. Viswanathan Printers and Publishers, 1996.
25. K.N. Ganesh, *Keralathinte Innalekal*, Thiruvananthapuram: Department of Cultural Publications, Government of Kēraḷam, 1997.
26. Ibid., p. 28.

27. For an account of the megalithic evidences and relation to the occupation groups, see the first and second chapters *Keralathinte Innalekal.*
28. Kaviyoor Murali, *Purananooru-Oru Paddanam*, Kottayam: D.C. Books, 1999.
29. Ibid., p. 44.
30. Nicholas B. Dirks, *Castes of Mind: Colonialism and Making of Modern India,* New Jersey: Princeton University Press, 2001.
31. Ibid., p. 75.
32. Vijaya Ramaswamy, 'The Kudi in early Tamilaham and the Tamil Women from Tribe to Caste', in *From Tribe to Caste*, ed. Dev Nathan, Shimla: Indian Institute of Advanced Study, Rashtrapathi Nivas, 2011.
33. Vijaya Ramaswamy, 'Through History', *Seminar*, vol. 523, 2003, pp. 48–53.
34. Vijaya Ramaswamy, 'Vishwakarma Craftsmen in Early Medieval Peninsular India', *Journal of the Economic and Social History of the Orient*, vol. 47, no. 4, 2004, pp. 548–82, see http://www.jstor.org/stable/25165073, accessed on 1 January 2014.
35. Ibid., p. 560.
36. Kesavan Veluthat, *The Political Structure of Early Medieval South India*, New Delhi: Orient Longman Ltd., 1993.
37. Padmanabha Menon, *History of Kerala*, p. 370.
38. Ibid., p. 372.
39. Purushothaman Choan, *Nayarude Aadimathavu Pulayi Cherumi Ezhavarudeyum*, p. 264.
40. Edgar Thurston and T.K. Rangachari, *Castes and Tribes of Southern India*, vol. 3, New Delhi: Asian Educational Services, 1993, p. 136.
41. Padmanabha Menon, *History of Kerala*, p. 372.
42. M.G.S. Narayanan, 'Index to Cera Inscriptions: A Companion Volume to Thesis on "Political and Social Conditions of Kerala under the Kulasekhara Empire"', unpublished Ph.D. diss., University of Kerala, Thiruvananthapuram, 1972, ins. no. A.8, p. 8. Also, see no. 13 of 1901 in *South Indian Inscriptions* (hereafter *SII*), vol. 7, no. 172, p. 72.
43. Narayanan, 'Index to Cera Inscriptions', no. A.58, p. 65. See no. 225 of 1895 in *SII*, vol. 5, no. 789, p. 340. Also, see T.A. Gopinatha Rao, ed., *Travancore Archaeological Series* (hereafter *TAS*), vol. 6, pt. 2, 2003, no. 138, p. 191.
44. Narayanan, 'Index to Cera Inscriptions', ins. no. A.76, p. 83.
45. Tirunayinarkurichchi inscription dated *Kollam* year 403 from Kadigaipattinam in the Eraniel taluk of Padmanabhapuram division, K.V. Subrahmanya Aiyar, ed., *TAS*, vol. 4, pt. 1, 1999, no. 14, p. 86.
46. *Śrībali* refers to the ceremonial procession with the image of the deity around the *nalambalam* of the temple.
47. Ganesh, *Keralathinte Innalekal*, p. 275.
48. Rajan Gurukkal and M.R. Raghava Varier, *Cultural History of Kerala*, vol. 1, Thiruvananthapuram: Department of Cultural Publications, Government of Kēraḷam, 1999, p. 167.

49. Narayanan, 'Index to Cera Inscriptions', p. xcvii, ins. no. 120.
50. Hermann Gundert, *A Malayalam and English Dictionary*, Trivandrum: Nava Sahithya Publications, 1982, p. 395.
51. Ganesh, *Keralathinte Innalekal*, p. 276.
52. T.A. Gopinatha Rao, ed., *TAS*, vol. 1, 1988, ins. no. 1, p. 31.
53. Rao, *TAS*, vol. 1, ins. no. 1, part 2, p. 34.
54. Rao, *TAS*, vol. 1, ins. no. 1, part 3, p. 37.
55. The inscription is from a Vishnu temple at Parthivapuram, a village 5 mi. south-east of Kulitturai, the headquarters of Vilavangodu taluk of the South Travancore division; Rao, *TAS*, vol.1, ins. no. 16.A, p. 403.
56. The inscription is from a Shiva temple at Kaviyūr; Rao, *TAS*, vol. 1, ins. no. 16, p. 407.
57. These plates are from Kilimanur in Chirayinkil taluk, Trivandrum; Aiyar, *TAS*, vol. 4, pt. 1, no. 7, p. 37.
58. R. Vasudeva Poduval, *Travancore Inscriptions: A Topographical List*, New Delhi: Asian Educational Services, 1990, ins. no. 5, p. 168.
59. Ibid., p. 124; also, see A.S. Ramanatha Ayyar, ed., *TAS*, vol. 7, 2004, p. 137.
60. Rao, *TAS*, vol. 1, ins. no. 16, p. 423.
61. Stella Kramrisch, *Dravida and Kerala in the Art of Travancore*, Switzerland: Artibus Asia Publishers, 1953, p. 24.
62. Mughathala Gopalakrishnan Nair, ed., *Uṇṇiyaccicaritam*, Thiruvananthapuram: The State Institute of Languages, 2011, p. 3. Also, see P.K. Narayana Pillai, ed., *Uṇṇiyaccicaritam*, Thiruvananthapuram: Department of Publications, University of Kerala, 2009, pp. 10, 11.
63. Nair, *Uṇṇiyaccicaritam*, p. 20.
64. Ibid., p. 22.
65. Ibid., p. 35.
66. Elamkulam P.N. Kunjan Pillai, *Uṇṇuneeli Sandēśam—From the Historical Perspective*, Trivandrum: Sahityaniketan, 1969.
67. Ibid., p. 95.
68. Ibid., p. 112.
69. See notes to the tenth chapter in Narayanan, *Perumals of Kerala*, p. xciii.
70. This inscription is from the 123rd year of the God at Kaṇḍiyūr, Mavelikkara; Rao, *TAS*, vol. 1, ins. no. 16, p. 416.
71. The inscription is from the Kanyakumari temple at Cape Comorin in present Tamil Nadu, dated twelfth or thirteenth century CE; Rao, *TAS*, vol. 1, ins. no. 3, p. 56.
72. Puthusseri Ramachandran, *Kerala Charithrathinte Adisthana Rekhakal (Kerala Inscriptions)*, Thiruvananthapuram: Kerala Bhasa Institute, 2007, p. 77.
73. Ganesh, *Keralathinte Innalekal*, p. 183.
74. V. Venkayya, 'Kottayam Plate of Vira-Raghava', *Epigraphia Indica*, vol. 4, ed. E. Hultzsch, New Delhi: Archaeological Survey of India and Government of India, 1979, no. 41, pp. 290–7.

75. Ibid., p. 290.
76. Ibid., p. 296.
77. Poduval, *Travancore Inscriptions*, ins. no. 4, p. 167. Also see Rao, *TAS*, vol. 1, pp. 295–6.
78. The plate is dated to *Kollam* year 935–6 (1760–1 CE), from Kanyakumari; Aiyar, *TAS*, vol. 4, pt. 1, no. 23, p. 114.
79. Nair, *Uṇṇiyaccicaritam*, p. 20.
80. Sundaram Dhanuvachapuram, *Unniyadicaritam*, Thiruvananthapuram: The State Institute of Languages, 2007, p. 107.
81. Kramrisch, *Dravida and Kerala in the Art of Travancore*, p. 26.
82. Narayanan, 'Index to Cera Inscriptions', ins. no. A.50, p. 57. Also, see no. 16 of 1901 in *SII*, vol. 7, no. 176, p. 75.
83. Narayanan, 'Index to Cera Inscriptions', ins. no. B.21, p. 111.
84. Poduval, *Travancore Inscriptions*, p. 127.
85. Poduval, *Travancore Inscriptions*, ins. no. 2, p. 127.
86. Poduval, *Travancore Inscriptions*, ins. no. 3, p. 127.
87. T.K. Velu Pillai, *The Travancore State Manual*, vol. 1, Thiruvananthapuram: Gazetteers Department, Government of Kēraḷam, 1996, p. 849.
88. Kunjan Pillai, *Uṇṇuneeli Sandēśam*, p. 97.
89. 'The social status of professional caste groups has kept changing over historical space and time.' See Vijaya Ramaswamy, *Craft and Artisans in South Indian History*, Indian History Congress Presidential Address, Medieval Section, Mysore, 2003.
90. Kesavan Veluthat, *The Early Medieval in South India*, New Delhi: Oxford University Press, 2009, p. 257.
91. Ibid., p. 264.
92. Narayanan, 'Index to Cera Inscriptions', p. 154.
93. Inscription from Vishnu temple at Parthivapuram; Rao, *TAS*, vol. 1, ins. no. 16.A, p. 403.
94. Poduval, *Travancore Inscriptions*, ins. no. 6, p. 168.
95. The practice of throwing stones might have been done as a means of protest against the higher classes of the society. This could also have been a way of getting attention, which annoyed the higher castes. Though the artisan groups had to observe the distance laid out in the notion of purity and pollution, they were a group which did have the privilege to be considered as not untouchables. They could have initially had the right to come in proximity of the higher castes.
96. The inscription is from Mitrānandapuram, Trivandrum, dated *Kollam* 660; see T.A. Gopinatha Rao, ed., *TAS*, vol. 3, 1992, ins. no. 5, p. 27.
97. Sundaram Dhanuvachapuram, *Uṇṇicirutēvicaritam*, Thiruvananthapuram: The State Institute of Languages, 2005, pp. 92–3.
98. Kramrisch, *Dravida and Kerala in the Art of Travancore*, p. 88.
99. The Kanyakumari plate of the time of Bālarāma Varman, Aiyar, *TAS*, vol. 4, no. 23, p. 114.

100. These works are said to have been done between 1729 and 1733 CE (*Kollam* year 904–8).
101. T.N. Subramaniam, *South Indian Temple Inscriptions*, vol. 2, Madras: Government Oriental Manuscript Library, 1954, no. 981 D.2949-44, p. 916. Also, see *Epigraphia Indica*, vol. 15, pp. 145–50.
102. M.R. Raghava Varier, *Village Communities in Pre-Colonial Kerala*, New Delhi: Place Names Society of India, Mysore and Asian Educational Services, 1994, p. 11.
103. Information taken from C.A. Menon, ed., *Keralolpathi*, Madras: University of Madras, 1953; Thurston & Rangachari, *Castes and Tribes of Southern India*.
104. Gurukkal, *Kerala Temple and the Early Medieval Agrarian System*, p. 84.
105. Varier, *Village Communities in Pre-Colonial Kerala*, p. 17.
106. Ibid., p. 15.
107. Thurston & Rangachari, *Castes and Tribes of Southern India*, p. 135.
108. Kramrisch, *Dravida and Kerala in the Art of Travancore*.
109. King of Pandalam, a place now in the Pathanamthitta district of Kēraḷam.
110. Sreedhara Menon, *Cultural Heritage of Kerala*, p. 173.

Editor and Contributors

VIJAYA RAMASWAMY is former Professor at the Centre for Historical Studies at Jawaharlal Nehru University. She won the British Council Award in 1981, and in 1988 was awarded the Fulbright Senior Fellowship for Berkeley, California. In 1998, she received the Indo-Shastri fellowship award. In 2017, she was co-recipient of the prestigious Discovery International Award, which was awarded by the Australian Research Council (ARC), for 2017–20. She is the Partner Investigator, along with Professor Mahesh Sharma, on the ARC Discovery Project Award 'Building India: Religion, Craft, and Infrastructure in Contemporary Asia', of which Professors Kirin Narayan and Ken George of the Australian National University are the Co-Chief Investigators. Her major publications include *The Song of the Loom: Weaver Folk Traditions in South India* (2013), *Historical Dictionary of the Tamils* (2007), and *Textiles and Weavers in South India* (revsd edn., 2006). The book *Walking Naked: Women, Society, Spirituality in South India* (1997) has won her the Best Woman Historian Award in 2000. She is currently a Tagore Fellow at the Indian Institute of Advanced Study, Shimla.

JAN BROUWER is former Project Coordinator at IGNCA and ANSI and Professor of Anthropology at NEHU (Shillong) and USD (Mysore). He was also Director of the Centre for Advanced Studies on Indigenous Knowledge Systems in Mysore. He has authored *The Makers of the World* (1995) and *Coping with Dependence* (1988) and a number of articles in different books and journals. His forthcoming books are 'The King's Game' (with co-author Mark Avery) and 'Insight into Northeast India: Annotated Indigenous Narratives'. He travels in south India with his themed talk entitled 'Me and My Shadow—Anthropology as a Tool' originally presented at SIETAR India Conference 2018, Pune. He also applies anthropological tools for capacity building at MNCs and academia through his company Anthropology Business Consultancy (R), Mysore.

JAYA JAITLY has worked with crafts people for four decades, and serves in many advisory bodies related to crafts and livelihoods, Social Science studies, and other public causes. She has an intimate knowledge of the craft traditions of the country. In 1986, she founded an association of crafts people called the 'Dastkari Haat Samiti'. She has also conceptualized and established 'Dilli Haat', a crafts marketplace in Delhi in 1994. She has authored *Life among the Scorpions: A Memoir of a Woman in Indian Politics* (2017), *The Artistry of Handwork* (2014), and the seminal work *Crafts Atlas of India* (2012). She has also edited *Crafts of Jammu, Kashmir and Ladakh* (1990) and published case studies of the economic and social conditions of crafts people, called *Vishwakarma's Children* (2001), among other books. She has created twenty-four artistic craft maps documenting locations of production of different crafts in India, and has also been working on combining crafts skills with calligraphy in regional scripts.

GEORGE VARGHESE K. is former faculty at MCPH, Manipal Academy of Higher Education (MAHE), and currently affiliate researcher to the 'Egalitarianism Project' in the Department of Anthropology, University of Bergen, Norway. He is also the President of the Deleuze and Guattari Studies in India Collective (DGSIC). He has published on the anthropology of both the Syrian Christians and the Vishwakarma community in Kerala. He has authored *Swarna Keralam: Jathi Prathisandhiyum Agolavatkaranavum* (2006). He has co-edited (with Paul Patton) 'Deleuze in India' (2018), a special issue of *Deleuze and Guattrai Studies*. His forthcoming books are *Deleuze and Anthropology*, and *Deleuze, Guattari and India: Transdisciplinary Vectors and Interconnections* (co-editor with Ian Buchanan).

I. LAKSHMI is former Professor of History at Osmania University. Her areas of interest include agriculture, irrigation, urbanization, emergence of regional polity, and women in Telugu literature. She has co-edited (with A. Satyanarayana) *Privileging Women Agency in History: Work, Worship, Leisure and Pleasure* (2010). She is a course writer and editor for B.R. Ambedkar Open University and also the editor of the state textbooks of Telangana.

R.N. MISRA is former Professor of Ancient Indian History at the Universities of Gwalior and Allahabad. He has authored *Ascetics, Piety and Power: Saiva Siddhanta Monastic Art in the Woodlands of Central*

India (2018); *Śilpa in Indian Tradition: Concept and Instrumentalities* (2009); *Prachina Bharatiya Samaj, Artha-vyavastha evam Dharma* (1992); *Sculptures of Dahala and Daksina Kosala* (1987); *Yaksha Cult and Iconography* (1981); *Bharatiya Murtikala ka Itihasa* (1978); and *Bharhut* (1971). He has also edited *Outlines of Indian Arts* (2014) and has co-edited (with Chirapat Prapandvidya, Devendra Handa, and Bettina Baumer) *Sahrdaya: Studies in Indian and South East Asian Art* (2006). Apart from these, he has also published 114 papers.

KIRIN NARAYAN is Professor of Anthropology and South Asian Studies at the Australian National University. She is the author of six books, most recently an ethnography, *Everyday Creativity: Singing Goddesses in the Himalayan Foothills* (2016), a writing manual, *Alive in the Writing: Crafting Ethnography in the Company of Chekhov* (2012), and a family memoir, *My Family and Other Saints* (2007). With her colleague Ken George of ANU, she is the Chief Investigator for an Australian Research Council Discovery Award entitled 'Building India: Religion, Craft, and Infrastructure in Contemporary Asia' for research on Vishwakarma traditions in collaboration with Professor Vijaya Ramaswamy and Professor Mahesh Sharma. She was also awarded an American Institute of Indian Studies Senior Fellowship for fieldwork on the project 'Rethinking Creativity with Vishwakarma's Family'.

PUSHPA PRASAD is former Professor of History at the Aligarh Muslim University. Her primary area of interest is Sanskrit and Sanskritic epigraphy. She is the author of *Lekhapaddhati: Documents of State and Everyday Life from Ancient and Early Medieval Gujarat, 9th to 15th Centuries* (2007) and *Sanskrit Inscriptions of Delhi Sultanate, 1191-1526* (1990). She has also published a number of research journals. She has served as the President of the Indian History Congress (Medieval India), Patiala, 2011 and the General President, LXII Annual Congress of the Epigraphical Society of India, Tirupati, 2017.

NAGENDRA RAO is Professor and Head of the Department of History at the Goa University. His areas of interest is the social and economic history of western India, focusing on themes such as state and social formations, the role of brahmins and temples, agrarian relations, and history of trade. He is the author of *Craft Production and Trade in South Kanara: A.D. 1000–1763* (2006) and *Brahmanas of South India* (2005). He is the editor of *Globalization: Pre-Modern India* (2005). He has also authored a number of articles in different journals.

SYED ALI NADEEM REZAVI is Chairman and Coordinator in the Centre of Advanced Study in History at the Aligarh Muslim University. He has around 48 research papers, articles, and reviews published in various journals. He is the author of *Fathpur Sikri Revisited* (2013). He is the co-editor (along with Shireen Moosvi) of the forthcoming *Comprehensive History of India*, vol. IV. He has been a Charles Wallace Fellow at SOAS, University of England (2007) and Fellow at Maison d l'Homme, Paris (2008). He is at present a Fellow at the Shiah Institute, London (since 2014).

Y. SUBBARAYALU was Professor in the Department of Epigraphy and Archaeology at the Tamil University. He has co-ordinated Digital Historical Atlas of South India (2005–8) in French Institute of Pondicherry. He is presently affiliated as a researcher in the same institute. He is the author of *South India under the Cholas* (2011), *A Glossary of Tamil Inscriptions* (2002–3), and *Studies in Cola History* (2001).

ANNA VARGHESE is Assistant Professor at the Department of History and Indian Culture at Banasthali Vidyapith. Her areas of interest include social history of Kerala focusing on the medieval temple social groups, gender in medieval Kerala, and the history of craftsmen in medieval Kerala. She has published several papers including 'Performers of the sacred realm: Ritual Performers in Temples of Medieval Kēraḷam' (2018), 'Temple Women and Work in Medieval Keralam' (2016), and has penned two prize-winning articles (for the best paper) in the *Proceedings of Indian History Congress*. She has also presented more than thirteen research papers at national and international conferences.

Index

www.ingramcontent.com/pod-product-compliance
Lightning Source LLC
Chambersburg PA
CBHW020340100426
42812CB00029B/3200/J
* 9 7 8 9 3 5 2 9 0 8 4 0 0 *